CHILD SOLDIERS AND TRANSITIONAL JUSTICE

SERIES ON TRANSITIONAL JUSTICE

The Series on *Transitional Justice* offers a platform for high-quality research within the rapidly growing field of transitional justice. The research is, of necessity inter-disciplinary in nature, drawing from disciplines such as law, political science, history, sociology, criminology, anthropology and psychology, as well as from various specialised fields of study such as human rights, victimology and peace studies. Furthermore, the research is international in outlook, drawing on the knowledge and experience of academics and other specialists in many different regions of the world.

The series is aimed at a variety of audiences who are either working or interested in fields such as crime and justice; human rights; humanitarian law and human security; conflict resolution and peace building. These audiences include academics, researchers, students, policy makers, practitioners, non-governmental organisations and the media.

All books published within the series are subject to a double-blind peer review by recognised authorities in the field.

Published titles within this Series:

8. Nicola Palmer, Phil Clark and Danielle Granville (chief editors), *Critical Perspectives in Transitional Justice* (2011), 978-1-78068-035-4
9. Edda Kristjánsdóttir, André Nollkaemper and Cedric Ryngaert (eds.), *International Law in Domestic Courts: Rule of Law Reform in Post-conflict States* (2012), 978-1-78068-041-5
10. Bas van Stokkom, Neelke Doorn and Paul van Tongeren (eds.), *Public Forgiveness in Post-Conflict Contexts* (2012), 978-1-78068-044-6
11. Ilse Derluyn, Cindy Mels, Stephan Parmentier and Wouter Vandenhole (eds.), *Re-Member. Rehabilitation, Reintegration and Reconciliation of War-Affected Children* (2012), 978-94-000-0027-4
12. Anne-Marie de Brouwer, Charlotte Ku, Renée Römkens and Larissa van den Herik (eds.), *Sexual Violence as an International Crime: Interdisciplinary Approaches* (2012), 978-1-78068-002-6
13. Estelle Zinsstag and Martha Albertson Fineman (eds.), *Feminist Perspectives on Transitional Justice: From International and Criminal to Alternative Forms of Justice* (2013), 978-1-78068-142-9
14. Josep M. Tamarit Sumalla, *Historical Memory and Criminal Justice in Spain. A Case of Late Transitional Justice* (2013), 978-1-78068-143-6
15. Catherine Jenkins (ed.), Max du Plessis (ed.), *Law, Nation building and Transformation The South African experience in perspective* (2014), 978-1-78068-184-9
16. Susanne Buckley-Zistel and Stefanie Schäfer (eds.), *Memorials in Times of Transition* (2014), 978-1-78068-211-2
17. Nico Wouters (ed.), *Transitional Justice and Memory in Europe (1945–2013)*, 978-1-78068-214-3
18. Agata Fijalkowski and Raluca Grosescu (eds.), *Transitional Criminal Justice in Post-Dictatorial and Post-Conflict Societies*, 978-1-78068-260-0
19. Agata Fijalkowski and Raluca Grosescu (eds.), *Transitional Criminal Justice in Post-Dictatorial and Post-Conflict Societies*, 978-1-78068-260-0

For previous volume in the series, please visit http://tj.intersentia.com

Series on Transitional Justice, Volume 20

CHILD SOLDIERS AND TRANSITIONAL JUSTICE

Protecting the Rights of Children Involved in Armed Conflicts

Bo Viktor Nylund

intersentia
Cambridge – Antwerp – Portland

Intersentia Ltd
Sheraton House | Castle Park
Cambridge | CB3 0AX | United Kingdom
Tel.: +44 1223 370 170 | Fax: +44 1223 370 169
Email: mail@intersentia.co.uk
www.intersentia.com | www.intersentia.co.uk

Distribution for the UK and Ireland:
NBN International
Airport Business Centre, 10 Thornbury Road
Plymouth, PL6 7 PP
United Kingdom
Tel.: +44 1752 202 301 | Fax: +44 1752 202 331
Email: orders@nbninternational.com

Distribution for Europe and all other countries:
Intersentia Publishing nv
Groenstraat 31
2640 Mortsel
Belgium
Tel.: +32 3 680 15 50 | Fax: +32 3 658 71 21
Email: mail@intersentia.be

Distribution for the USA and Canada:
International Specialized Book Services
920 NE 58th Ave. Suite 300
Portland, OR 97213
USA
Tel.: +1 800 944 6190 (toll free) | Fax: +1 503 280 8832
Email: info@isbs.com

Artwork on cover: Author Jan Jordaan, title 'Hurt', medium Linocut, 1999. From the *Universal Declaration of Human Rights – International Print Portfolio*, Article 5, published by Art for Humanity, South Africa, 1999.

ISBN 978-1-78068-394-2
D/2016/7849/65
NUR 828

GPRC
Guaranteed
Peer Reviewed
Content

British Library Cataloguing in Publication Data. A catalogue record for this book is available from the British Library.

ACKNOWLEDGEMENTS

This book is based on my PhD thesis, which was accepted by the Graduate Institute of International and Development Studies, Geneva, in 2014. My sincere thanks go to Professor Andrew Clapham as the thesis supervisor and to Professor Vincent Chetail as second reader. Thank you for your guidance and support throughout the process of study and writing, in particular, the constructive comments and suggestions during the preparation of the *mémoire préliminaire de thèse*, which spurred me to make a greater effort and dig deeper into the law. Thank you also to Professor Matthew Happold for having agreed to be the third panel member to review this thesis.

I am grateful to colleagues and friends providing comments, inputs, and entertaining discussions about law and practice relevant to the thesis: Camille Gervaix, Cecile Aptel, Christine Watkins, Emilia Richard, Evelyne Schmid, Gabor Rona, Ghada Kachachi, Ida Hyllested, Insaf Nizam, Jelena Pejic, Lara Scott, Monika Sandvik, Osman AbuFatima, Pernille Ironside, Rachel Brett, Saudamini Siegrist, Takhmina Karimova, and Subajini Jayasekaran. Some of you have been colleagues in the field addressing the issue of child recruitment, and from these situations, there are records of engagement with children that have guided the work. I want to especially thank those of you who contributed the quotes that have been included in the beginning of each chapter, and which are left as anonymous as possible in order not to expose those children, their families, or those of you who worked with them.

My appreciation goes to my supervisors at UNICEF (from Khartoum to New York Headquarters to Geneva Headquarters to Bujumbura), who over the past several years have signed and approved of requests for special leave and study leave: Ted Chaiban, Susan Bissell, Leila Pakkala, and Andres Franco. More importantly, you were incredible people to work with and I learned so much from you – thank you!

In finalizing the manuscript for publication, I have also greatly benefited from the comments of two reviewers in a double-blind review process, as well as the three general editors of the Intersentia Series on Transitional Justice.

And for first-class editing: Catherine Rutgers, thank you so much! It was a true pleasure working with you, and thanks for being based in a different time zone so that we were able to do the editing and back-and-forths during odd hours.

I want to express gratitude to Shelby Cullom and Kathryn Davis. Thanks to the scholarship provided through your generous donation to the Graduate Institute, I was able to spend significant time on study and writing during periods when I was not working.

And, to complete these acknowledgements with a very important expression of gratitude, I am thankful for the support and understanding and encouragement from my wife, Monika, and our children, Emma, Lisa, and Elias.

ABOUT THE AUTHOR

Bo Viktor Nylund is a protection and legal practitioner who throughout his career has focused on advocacy and engagement with state and non-state actors with a view to driving accountability in the implementation of human rights. Bo Viktor has a Ph.D. in International Law, as well as Master's degrees in law and political science from Columbia University Law School and Abo Akademi University.

Bo Viktor has served as a protection officer with the Office of the High Commissioner for Refugees (UNHCR) in Geneva and Kenya/Somalia from 1994 to 1996. Since 1998 he has worked with the United Nations Children's Fund (UNICEF) in the areas of development and humanitarian programming, corporate social responsibility, child protection, humanitarian policy and planning, and children's rights based in Bangkok, Colombo, Khartoum, New York, Geneva and Bujumbura. In 2010, he also supported the Office of the High Commissioner for Human Rights (OHCHR) in the development of an Office-wide strategy for engagement in humanitarian action. Currently, Bo Viktor is the UNICEF Representative in Burundi.

The views expressed in this book are those of the author and are not necessarily shared by UNICEF or the UN.

CONTENTS

LIST OF ABBREVIATIONS

AP	Additional Protocol
CPA	Comprehensive Peace Agreement
CRBP	Children's Rights and Business Principles
CRC	Convention on the Rights of the Child
DDR	disarmament, demobilization, and rehabilitation
FPLC	Forces Patriotiques pour la Libération du Congo (Patriotic Forces for the Liberation of Congo)
GC IV	Geneva Convention Relative to the Protection of Civilian Persons in Time of War
ICC	International Criminal Court
ICRC	International Conference of the Red Cross
ILO	International Labour Organization
JEM	Justice and Equality Movement
LTTE	Liberation Tigers of Tamil Eelam
MONUC	United Nations Organization Mission in the Democratic Republic of the Congo
MRM	monitoring and reporting mechanism
OPAC	Optional Protocol on the Involvement of Children in Armed Conflict
PMSC	private military security company
RCD-ML	Rassemblement congolais pour la démocratie – Mouvement de libération (Rally for Congolese Democracy-Liberation Movement)
SCSL	Special Court for Sierra Leone
SCWG	Security Council Working Group
SLM/A	Sudan Liberation Movement/Army
SPLA	Sudan People's Liberation Army
SRSG-CAAC	Special Representative of the Secretary-General for Children and Armed Conflict
TMVP	Tamil Makkal Viduthalai Pulikal
UK	United Kingdom
UN	United Nations
UNHCR	Office of the United Nations High Commissioner for Refugees
UNICEF	United Nations Children's Fund
UPC	Union des patriotes congolais (Union of Congolese Patriots)

UPC-RP	Union des patriotes congolais pour la reconciliation et la paix (Union of Congolese Patriots for Reconciliation and Peace)
USA	United States of America

CHAPTER 1

OBJECTIVE, SCOPE, AND TRANSITIONAL JUSTICE AS AN ANALYTICAL FRAMEWORK

"I am opposed to the recruitment of any person under 18. I think it is dangerous for children like myself to join a movement or even government forces if you end up taking part in military operations. I believe that school is the natural place for any child, and when I get back home, I will pursue my education once again."[1]

INTRODUCTION

Following the first codification of the prohibition against child recruitment in international law in the late 1970s, the global debate about the recruitment and use of children in armed conflicts took on a new level of importance two decades later. The 1990s marked the first decade of implementation of programmes to "rehabilitate" children who had been involved in armed conflicts.

The use of child soldiers is not a new phenomenon. Children have historically suffered disproportionately during war, and armed groups and forces have recruited children to serve in armed conflicts. But as international responses to providing for the recovery and reintegration needs of former child soldiers increased, the flow of information and awareness of this issue as a child rights violation led to a great deal of attention. As the focus intensified, approaches to ending the use of child soldiers evolved and diverged into separate actions by varying actors, not always consistently pulling in the same direction, yet all with the same aim in mind.

This book offers an approach to establishing a coherent synthesis that will contribute to further protection of the rights of children in armed conflicts, building on developments through the spring of 2015. Chapter 1 outlines the overall objectives and scope, and the framework of analysis, and provides an

---

1 The quotations at the beginning of each chapter are authentic statements from conflict situations in various locations and were contributed by colleagues who have worked on these issues in the field. The quotes are presented anonymously to avoid exposing those children, their families, or the people who worked with them.

introduction to the issue of child recruitment and how it entered the international legal and political debates.

1. OBJECTIVE AND SCOPE

Transitional justice is the organizing framework for this work on child soldiers, and an overall objective is to identify ways to enhance the response to address child recruitment.[2]

Since the 1980s, judicial and non-judicial approaches associated with a society's efforts to come to terms with a legacy of abuses – the transitional justice mechanisms – have sought to address accountability, truth-seeking, institution building, and reconciliation and recovery among war-affected populations.

The issue of child recruitment is being examined here through the transitional justice lens, recognizing, however, that transitional justice is not tightly defined for all uses and purposes. The transitional justice approach has been designed so that it could be adapted and contextualized for different settings, themes, and circumstances.

Transitional justice and the issue of child recruitment do not provide for an immediate fit. The origin of transitional justice theory was focused on the notion of political change and a move towards democracy, and its development was based primarily on experiences in South Africa, Latin America, and Eastern Europe after the end of the Cold War. One key characteristic of transitional justice is this aspect of political change, moving a society and its government towards greater adherence in applying the tenets of democracy and abiding more closely to human rights, or replacing the current regime with a new one that has a stronger commitment to democracy and human rights. While this is the ultimate aim of transitional justice, it is not a journey that always looks the same.[3]

Tackling child recruitment does not aspire to change entire regimes, but placing the issue squarely in a transitional justice framework aims to support action to end this grave violation against children's rights. As such, in addressing

---

2 For purposes of this book, the terms "child soldier" or "child recruitment" are used when referring to the phenomena in general terms. It is important to note that "child soldier" does not have any legal significance as it is not used in any legal instruments. Legal terminology is used throughout as relevant in discussing the specific instruments that deal with child soldiers and the specific meaning of the language in question. A "child" is defined as any person under the age of 18, as per the Convention on the Rights of the Child.

3 For example, Teitel grounds her work in experiences coming out of the Cold War and as such the orientation around "democracy" as the ultimate goal comes out strongly. Ruti G. Teitel, *Transitional Justice* (Oxford: Oxford University Press, 2000), 3. Arthur highlights that while all societies grapple with similar questions as they go through the transitional justice phase, they look to balance moral imperatives and claims for justice with the need for a more just political order in the future. Paige Arthur, "How Transitions Reshaped Human Rights: a Conceptual History of Transitional Justice," *Human Rights Quarterly* 31, no. 2 (2009): 321–367.

the situation of child recruitment various alternatives to punishment can express the normative message of political transformation and the strengthened rule of law, with the goal of furthering democracy as a tool for a more human rights abiding society in the long run.

Why base this analysis on transitional justice, and how is it different from considering the issue of child recruitment in the context of protecting human rights? One prominent scholar and practitioner has identified useful criteria for the field that highlight why considering transitional justice adds value in and of itself. According to Paige, transitional justice is clearly distinguishable from human rights, the field out of which it emerged; implies a set of actors who have common aims and who are thus oriented towards one another in their practice; has developed institutions that advance those aims; and advances distinctive criteria of judgement and self-legitimization.[4]

Transitional justice as used here is more of an organizing framework of different legal fields and actors, rather than an end in itself. It is used in an effort to assemble the relevant elements of law and justice that can illuminate the question of how child recruitment can be addressed. As stated by Teitel, "*Transitional Justice* adopts a largely inductive method, and exploring an array of legal responses, it describes a distinctive conception of law and justice in the context of political transformation."[5] (emphasis in the original)

It is the push for new approaches and perspectives that makes the framework useful for the study of child recruitment. When analysed through the transitional justice lens, child recruitment and action to address this violation against children's rights takes on many modes and appearances. Likewise, practitioners in the various transitional justice areas come from different walks of life. As such, there is much to learn between different professions and areas of expertise, so as to maximize action in a joint effort.

1.1. OVERARCHING GOALS

Much of the recent work by academics in this field has effectively brought together some pieces of the puzzle, but no contribution takes the holistic perspective with respect to child soldiers. As a result, action to end the recruitment and use of children by armed forces and groups remains compartmentalized in different approaches by different actors and stakeholders and is not taken to its fullest potential. Building on this realization, there are three overarching goals:

- Use the transitional justice framework as a tool to analyse the question of how law and justice have been applied to promote a transition towards a

4 Arthur, "How Transitions Reshaped Human Rights," 324.
5 Teitel, *Transitional Justice*, 4.

society where children's rights are protected with a view to end child recruitment. This goal further takes into account that the transitional justice framework also allows for the development of aspirations, that is, the approach recognizes the importance of actions undertaken to apply the law and justice even with no transition in sight.
- Uncover and show some of the areas of common interest among different actors involved in addressing child recruitment, along with an analysis of how the interlinkages between different areas of transitional justice can be integrated more forcefully to bring about greater results than if the areas operate independently. The assumption is that a holistic approach will enhance the ultimate goal of transitional justice as it relates to child recruitment.
- Thereby, suggest ways and means through which action to stop the recruitment and use of children could be made more effective.

1.2. ORGANIZATION AND KEY AREAS OF RESEARCH

Elements that make up the transitional justice theory allow for an organizing framework, and while there is no single theory of transitional justice – and it is not a term with a fixed meaning – there are elements and sets of issues that are considered to be legitimate responses in a transitional justice approach.[6]

The framework is divided into six substantive sections, covering the areas of rule of law, criminal justice, historical justice, reparatory justice, institutional justice, and participatory justice. Each element is necessary in order to reach the overarching goals as identified above; each chapter begins with more detailed research questions. The chapters are outlined here to provide an overview of the key areas considered and the overarching legal considerations as related to child recruitment:

- Chapter 2 on the rule of law assumes that there is a coherent international and national legal framework relevant to the recruitment and use of children; that the law is predictable; and that limits have been established through the law.

6 Arthur, "How Transitions Reshaped Human Rights," 359. Why not post-conflict justice? Transition to peace is rather different, and not all situations where child recruitment is rampant are situations of armed conflict, so the approach can fit into a non-conflict context as well. Also, it will not be sufficient to bring about peace: there also needs to be the transition to a regime that is more likely to bring about change and ensure the protection of human rights. Writing focused on post-conflict justice tends to focus on bringing about accountability through criminal procedures and bringing about accountability through force or "humanitarian intervention." It does not necessarily consider the role of the affected population and the balancing between peace and justice. For an example of approaches to post-conflict justice, see M. Cherif Bassiouni, ed. *Post-Conflict Justice* (Ardsley, NY: Transnational Publishers, Inc., 2002).

The chapter analyses the law to consider what is prohibited under international law and where the limits should be drawn for what is acceptable behaviour.
- Chapter 3 on criminal justice establishes that violators of human rights must be punished for crimes committed. The chapter focuses on a review of the application of the law through the *Lubanga* case.
- Chapter 4 on historical justice considers that the facts of past violations must be established. The chapter considers the aspect of historical justice from the perspective of the United Nations (UN) Security Council mechanism on monitoring and reporting and the extent to which this mechanism can promote justice in situations of transition.
- Chapter 5 on reparatory justice focuses on the rights of victims to rehabilitation or compensation for harm. The chapter analyses how the notion of repair has developed from the perspective of child recruitment and how it fits with other components of transitional justice.
- Chapter 6 on institutional justice considers the ways that institutions change when there is political change in support of the implementation of justice. The chapter focuses on how institutional change can address the situation of child soldiers, and how judicial and non-judicial mechanisms and institutional reform processes can protect the rights of child soldiers.
- Chapter 7 on participatory justice balances the rights and responsibilities of former child soldiers in transitional justice processes. The chapter puts forward an analysis of how children as victims or survivors, as well as witnesses or alleged perpetrators of crimes, have engaged in transitional justice processes and how their rights are protected in these contexts. The discussion in this chapter is limited to children's participation in criminal justice processes because other processes, such as participation in truth commissions, have already been written about extensively.
- Chapter 8 provides overall conclusions on the law related to child recruitment and to moving forward with a transitional justice approach.

The assumption throughout this study is that there is added value in approaching the issue of child recruitment from the perspective of transitional justice. This approach looks not only at the transition element, it is also aimed to systematize knowledge and practice and to understand the relationships between justice measures and transition.

2. TRANSITIONAL JUSTICE AS AN ANALYTICAL FRAMEWORK

Transitional justice as an analytical framework is advantageous in that it allows for comprehensively considering the various angles of how to tackle a particular issue. The distinct areas of work and expertise that form part of transitional justice, as noted above, include the rule of law, criminal justice, historical justice, reparatory justice, institutional justice, and participatory justice. As a result, transitional justice allows consideration of the issue of child soldiers from the perspective of human rights lawyers, judges, child protection practitioners, historians, social workers, case workers, humanitarian aid practitioners, and psychologists, among others. In addition, even from within the same area of expertise, it allows people who are working in different occupations to relate to each other.

The following example illustrates how transitional justice could allow diverse actors to conduct their work in the context of a common game plan, learning and benefiting from their respective areas of expertise. In defining life-saving criteria for humanitarian response, the UN system has recognized in the area of child protection the need to provide "identification, registration, family tracing and reunification or interim care arrangements for separated children, orphans and children leaving armed groups/forces." However, there is no activity included for the monitoring and reporting of grave violations of child rights as part of humanitarian activities.[7] For broader protection and human rights work there has been an activity included for 'protection by presence', but it does not specify the monitoring and recording of human rights or child rights violations. By considering more proactively their actions within a framework of transitional justice, humanitarian actors and human rights monitors could see how their efforts are linked and contribute towards long-term change in a more effective joint undertaking.

The issue is also one of balance, giving each of the elements of transitional justice sufficient consideration. This was also critically considered in the Secretary-General's Report on the Rule of Law and Transitional Justice in 2004:[8]

> The international community has rushed to prescribe a particular formula for transitional justice, emphasizing either criminal prosecutions or truth-telling, without first affording victims and national constituencies the opportunity to consider and decide on the proper balance. The international community must see transitional justice in a way that extends well beyond courts and tribunals. The challenges of post-conflict environments necessitate an approach that balances a variety of goals, including the pursuit of accountability, truth and reparation, the preservation of peace and the building of democracy and the rule of law. A comprehensive strategy should also pay special attention to abuses committed against groups most affected by conflict, such as minorities, the elderly, children, women, prisoners, displaced persons and refugees, and establish particular measures

7 Office for the Coordination of Humanitarian Affairs, Central Emergency Response Fund: Life-Saving Criteria, (26 January 2010).

8 *Report of the Secretary-General on the Rule of Law and Transitional Justice in Conflict and Post-Conflict Societies*, UN Doc. S/2004/616 (23 August 2004), para 25.

> for their protection and redress in judicial and reconciliation processes. For example, protection measures for children can include provisions for hearings in camera, pre-recorded testimonies, videoconferencing and the use of pseudonyms to protect the identity of child witnesses.

More than a decade later, it is still timely to consider children's rights in the context of transitional justice in a holistic manner.

The remainder of this section provides the background on the analytical framework and explicates the focus of transitional justice as an area of research and study to date.

2.1. TRANSITIONAL JUSTICE AS APPLIED TO THIS RESEARCH

The analytical framework relies on several recognized scholars in the area of transitional justice along with the theory and practice of various institutions involved in this area of work. However, the framework adopted here goes beyond their work and adapts what they have identified as elements of transitional justice. There are certain gaps in the theories that had been developed for more general and high-level transitional justice processes, but bringing several of them together allows for a suitable approach to the study of child recruitment. Adapting existing theoretical frameworks makes it possible to apply transitional justice to the issue of child recruitment and ensure that all aspects relevant to addressing child recruitment are being considered.[9]

Efforts to move beyond the theoretical frameworks developed by others do not necessarily signify shortcomings in their work. The transitional justice theory grew out of a global political era characterized by many political changes of worldwide significance. In using the transitional justice framework it is important to ask, transition to what? In the context of the 1980s, for example, it is helpful to remember that there was a shift towards "democracy"[10] as the preferred option for a society to protect and respect human rights.[11] This was a

9 This includes the work of such scholars as Neil Kritz and Steven Ratner, as well as Teitel and Arthur, but also the frameworks developed by the United Nations, the International Center for Transitional Justice, and various other actors.

10 Although "democracy" in this context is used to indicate leadership that seeks to protect and promote human rights, use of the word also has a political history. During the 1980s, there were substantial debates over whether the Western style of democracy was, in fact, a good model, because in some contexts it tended not to have very strong social protection and services, which in communist countries were considered to be essential. However, democracy on its own is not sufficient to bring about accountability for the wrongdoings of past regimes. See Steven R. Ratner, "New Democracies, Old Atrocities: An Inquiry in International Law," *The Georgetown Law Journal* 87 (1999): 707–748.

11 Arthur, "How Transitions Reshaped Human Rights," 336.

very important shift for human rights activists and those seeking to achieve change on the ground in post-conflict situations.

Ruti Teitel, who claims to have coined the phrase "transitional justice," is one of the key authors on the background and theory around the approach and has contributed a great deal towards its current acceptance and appreciation among practitioners from different areas of work.[12] Teitel uses the concept of transitional justice as a tool for change in leadership and moving on, and much of her early work builds on processes that were followed in the former Soviet Union and Eastern Europe, and in Latin America. She looks at how totalitarian regimes and military dictatorships are turned into regimes that support freedom and democracy, and how the law plays a role in the context of political transition. In these contexts, she states, "law is a mere product of political change."[13] In other words, the legal responses in situations of transition play an important and constructive role.

Much of the momentum for developing this new focus on transitional justice was due to the end of the Cold War and the fact that human rights gained a great deal of focus and priority on the international development and humanitarian agenda.[14] The foundations for transitional justice and the type of situations that inspired this area of work were somewhat different contexts compared to the prolonged conflicts that had been raging in other parts of the world. "Dealing with the past" in those "traditional" settings and drawing on justice processes in the process of transition was at the basis of what became the transitional justice

12 Ruti G. Teitel, "Editorial Note-Transitional Justice Globalized," *International Journal of Transitional Justice* 2, no. 1 (2008): 1–4. As pointed out by Arthur, there were others who were using the same terminology at the time and who contributed to the debate. See Arthur, "How Transitions Reshaped Human Rights," 329. Also see Kritz's perspective, which in a very similar way outlines different options. Neil J. Kritz, "Coming to Terms with Atrocities: A Review of Accountability Mechanisms for Mass Violations of Human Rights," *Law of Contemporary Problems* 59: no. 4 (1996): 127–152. The approach adopted also builds on *Report of the Secretary-General on the Rule of Law and Transitional Justice in Conflict and Post-Conflict Societies*, UN Doc. S/2004/616 (23 August 2004). The elements around participatory justice are strongly featured in this report. The report taking stock of progress in 2011 also emphasized the child protection and participation aspects as an important element of transitional justice to be followed up by the UN system. *Report of the Secretary-General on the Rule of Law and Transitional Justice in Conflict and Post-Conflict Societies*, UN Doc. S/2011/634 (12 October 2011, para 78).

13 Teitel, *Transitional Justice*, 3.

14 These were also the times of debates about neutrality of aid and the humanitarian imperative, and the importance of not taking sides in the political context. See *Code of conduct for the International Red Cross and Red Crescent Movement and non-governmental organisations in Disaster Relief*, (1994). The development of the Code of Conduct was sponsored by Caritas Internationalis, Catholic Relief Services, the International Federation of Red Cross and Red Crescent Societies, International Save the Children Alliance, Lutheran World Federation, Oxfam, and the World Council of Churches (members of the Steering Committee for Humanitarian Response), together with the International Committee of the Red Cross.

theory and the process for protecting human rights in transitions to democracy beginning in the late 1980s.[15]

Despite this focus on moving towards democracy, there is a broader concept of transitional justice looking at the aspect of "overcoming the past" and moving forward after human rights violations. The translations between different contexts and cultures also put different meanings to the words.[16] This type of thinking typically combined three areas of interest to someone who wants to focus on transitional justice: the morals of a society and human rights; the law; and the politics of the situation.[17]

It is also important to note that the field of transitional justice has identified a range of measures as the legitimate justice measures, including prosecutions, truth telling, restitution, and reform of abusive state institutions. This is the reason for making use of a framework that is based on some of those measures but goes beyond what might traditionally have been included.[18] As Arthur recognizes, the boundaries for what is considered to be part of transitional justice have consistently been pushed, often in response to practical difficulties encountered in new political contexts. No situation is the same as the other, and no single solution will fit in all contexts.[19]

In fact, "transition" has meant very different things in different societies, from revolution or transfer of power to regime change, independence, or political reform. Teitel also recognizes that not all regimes move at the same speed or with the same force, but transitional justice nonetheless builds on the premise of "what is deemed just is contingent and informed by prior injustice."[20]

Transitional justice in this study is not necessarily used as a concept that demonstrates an overhaul in political change; while there is a push for change, it may not necessarily be happening at the time. Children should not be in the armed groups and forces in the first place, and as a result, much of the advocacy work for the release of children and the study on the practice of recruitment and use by armed forces and groups takes place in the midst of armed conflict.

---

15 Arthur, "How Transitions Reshaped Human Rights," 324.

16 David A. Crocker, "Reckoning with Past Wrongs: A Normative Framework," *Ethics and International Affairs* 13: 1 (1999): 43–64.

17 John H. Herz, *From Dictatorship to Democracy: Coping with the Legacies of Authoritarianism and Totalitarianism* (Westport: Greenwood Press, 1982).

18 For instance, the UN analysis of rule of law and transitional justice brings in current issues that can be considered as part of a pragmatic framework. See *Report of the Secretary-General on the Rule of Law and Transitional Justice in Conflict and Post-Conflict Societies*, UN Doc. S/2011/634 (12 October 2011).

19 Arthur, "How Transitions Reshaped Human Rights: a Conceptual History of Transitional Justice," 326. See also Alison Smith, "Basic Assumptions of Transitional Justice and Children," in *Children and Transitional Justice*, ed. Mindy Jane Roseman Sharanjeet Parmar, Saudamini Siegrist, Theo Sowa (eds.) (Cambridge: Human Rights Program at Harvard Law School, 2010), 33. Smith views the beginning of the exercise as a consideration of which models would be best suited for a particular context.

20 Teitel, *Transitional Justice*, 6.

The situation in Sudan may serve as an example, with a long-standing conflict between the North and the South but also in the East, as well as in Darfur in the West – all situations where child recruitment has taken place. While the arrest warrant for President El Bashir has been issued by the International Criminal Court, there are few signs of "transition."[21] There could be an expectation of change for strengthened respect of the standards relevant to child recruitment in such contexts, at least in certain parts of the country and during certain periods of time, but that does not necessarily mean there is a move towards democracy, which is a much larger concept. Nonetheless, there is an expectation for a guarantee of non-repetition and a move from less to more respect for the rule of law and human rights for a situation to be in transition.

Common to all of the existing frameworks described above are the areas of rule of law; criminal justice; historical justice; and reparations.[22] In developing a framework for this study it is clear that these areas are all of great relevance to the issue of child recruitment, albeit sometimes from a slightly different perspective because of the issue at hand.

Rule of law is considered a relevant part of the organizing framework as child recruitment is a well-developed area of law, with international legal frameworks defining the prohibition of child recruitment, and many countries have put in place domestic legislation. An international body through the Committee on the Rights of the Child also exists to monitor the implementation of the law. For the purposes of the overview developed through this study, it is important to clarify how the law has developed at the international level, due to the fact that it is somewhat complex in that the prohibition of child recruitment is covered in several parts of international law.

Criminal justice is certainly the next step in moving beyond the prohibition of the act of recruitment and use of children to making it a criminal act. Given that the *Lubanga* case was recently concluded this area is considered of great importance in this study.

Establishing the facts relevant to the situation of child recruitment in a given situation is also of great significance to the organizing framework as these facts are needed in order to advocate for children's release and develop programmes for their reintegration. Historical justice as considered in this study focuses on the monitoring and reporting mechanism established by the UN Security

21 *The Prosecutor v. Omar Hassan Ahmad Al Bashir*, Warrant of Arrest for Omar Hassan Ahmad Al Bashir, ICC-02/05-01/09-1 ICC (4 March 2009).

22 See Teitel, *Transitional Justice* and Arthur, "How Transitions Reshaped Human Rights: a Conceptual History of Transitional Justice," 355–357, where all of these four elements are featured, but also for instance how practice has evolved in that the search engine on the site of the International Centre for Transitional Centre categorizes publications into the areas of criminal justice; national prosecutions; children and youth; institutional reform; gender justice; truth and memory; and reparations. See https://www.ictj.org/publications, accessed on 22 August 2015.

Council as it is the main vehicle globally for collecting information relevant to grave violations against children, including child recruitment. This mechanism is inherently political, and at the same time connects to the area of institutions building to respond to the issue of child recruitment. Nevertheless, the focus on the monitoring and reporting mechanism is warranted as it is not extensively written about, and its main purpose is to establish the facts on the ground. Truth and reconciliation commissions and similar institutions that have been set up to establish the facts in situations of transition have been studied elsewhere and are not considered part of this work.[23]

Similarly, the area of reparations is very relevant for the study as there is significant practice related to the recovery and reintegration of child soldiers which requires long-term commitment and sustained efforts. Reparations have also been considered in the context of the *Lubanga* case, and as such it is useful to consider how these different approaches complement each other.

In designing the framework for this study, some areas can be considered to have less relevance. For example, the area of constitutional justice that has been considered by some of the main scholars in this field is of limited relevance in relation to the situation of child soldiers. Constitutional justice may be of relevance in a given country, however, in this study where relevant it has been incorporated under the chapter on the rule of law. Also, while the issue of gender is an important focus and the separate consideration of the impact on boys and girls of great relevance in understanding the situation of child soldiers, gender has been mainstreamed throughout rather than pulling it out as a separate stream in the organizing framework, thereby allowing gender to be reflected upon in each of the chapters.

In carrying out the research for this study it soon became clear that there are some significant legal considerations that do not fit nicely within any of the streams in the existing frameworks. Experience has shown that there is a need to engage young people in decision-making processes and to allow for their participation, while at the same time considering not just the right to participation, but also the responsibilities such participation might bring into the picture.[24] The Secretary-General's report taking stock of progress in the area of transitional justice in 2011 also emphasized the child protection and participation aspects as an important element of transitional justice to be followed up by the UN system. While the report did not make participation aspects into a stream of transitional justice, it did provide the impetus for purposes of this study to consider participatory justice as an important part of

---

23 See further section I.2.2. below.

24 Article 12(1) of the Convention on the Rights of the Child emphasizes: "States Parties shall assure to the child who is capable of forming his or her own views the right to express those views freely in all matters affecting the child, the views of the child being given due weight in accordance with the age and maturity of the child."

the organizing framework.[25] Elements of restorative justice have been included in the chapter on participatory justice.

Finally, some scholars have considered administrative justice broadly speaking as an important overall area of focus, which area in may situations may consider issues such as power-sharing or giving attention to how access to services is equitable in a transition period. While this is of relevance to the issue of child recruitment, this stream has been considered mainly from the point of view of how peace processes have considered the issue and how institutions have been set up to respond to the situation of child soldiers, hence the inclusion of institutional justice in the organizing framework.[26]

As mentioned above, child recruitment is a very well-developed area of legal work at the international level and thus presents an opportunity to analyse the issue through the transitional justice lens. The chapters that follow will demonstrate how the law is predictable and so it is not difficult to foresee the consequences of violating the law.

Law is a crucial component of political transition, independent and critical for transforming societies coming out of conflict/totalitarian regimes. The cases are many and different, but the concept of transitional justice allows for an analytical framework within which the very different and distinct processes of each situation can be analysed. The structure of the society, the experience that society has gone through, the legal culture, the political traditions – all determine the type of transitional justice response that is appropriate and politically feasible. The law becomes an organizing framework for political transition.[27] While the way transitional justice is shaped varies from situation to situation, the process is not arbitrary, it is constructed in accordance with some major themes. The law in these situations is transitional, not foundational, in that it allows construction of the key political changes in both individual rights and responsibilities but also considers the shifting powers of state structures.

At the same time, there is a fine line between settling accounts for past human rights violations and not upsetting the prospect of transition towards democracy. For a society to "move on" it is not possible to pay attention only to elements of justice: it is equally important to consider what will allow peace to prevail, and at what stage peace comes at the cost of justice.[28] In the area of child recruitment, the study of how peace agreements have been adopted and

---

25 *Report of the Secretary-General on the Rule of Law and Transitional Justice in Conflict and Post-Conflict Societies*, UN Doc. S/2011/634 (12 October 2011, para 78.

26 Arthur considers this area in great detail, but also recognizes that legal-institutional reform by no means is sufficient on its own, but needs to be complemented by progress in other areas of transitional justice. Arthur, "How Transitions Reshaped Human Rights: a Conceptual History of Transitional Justice," 359.

27 Teitel, *Transitional Justice*, 214, and Crocker, "Reckoning with Past Wrongs: A Normative Framework," 47.

28 Guillermo A. O'Donnell and Philippe C. Schmitter, *Transitions from Authoritarian Rule: Tentative Conclusions about Uncertain Democracies* (Johns Hopkins University Press, 1986).

implemented offers interesting lessons on whether justice is truly achieved in the way child recruitment issues are dealt with. It also raises the concept of furthering peace and justice together in a balanced way:

> The notion of "transitional justice"... comprises the full range of processes and mechanisms associated with a society's attempts to come to terms with a legacy of large-scale past abuses, in order to ensure accountability, serve justice and achieve reconciliation.[29]

Transitional justice comes at a cost because it is implemented at a time when there can be many dividing forces in a country and many competing interests. Therefore, it also entails give and take more than other areas of justice. Nonetheless, the transitional justice framework is used to demonstrate how a society can best move towards considering the issue of child recruitment as a grave violation against children's rights and begin to address it in a holistic way as outlined above, cutting across the rule of law, criminal justice, historical justice, reparatory justice, institutional justice, and participatory justice.

2.2. TRANSITIONAL JUSTICE AND CHILDREN: AN EVOLVING AREA OF STUDY AND RESEARCH

While progress was made in transitional justice as an area of study and practice during the 1990s, an evolving area of study and research concerning the connection between transitional justice and children took much longer to appear. It was not until a decade later that questions focused on children became part of the transitional justice debate.

Comprehensive research on children and transitional justice began with a consideration of international criminal justice and children and the publication of the No Peace Without Justice and United Nations Children's Fund (UNICEF) book in 2002.[30] The focus of research at the time was on the new area of criminal justice and how the provisions of the International Criminal Court and other interim tribunals might be applied. There was also significant interest in the question of children as perpetrators, which had been debated during the establishment of the Special Court for Sierra Leone and subsequent procedures established to exclude children from prosecution.[31]

---

29 *Report of the Secretary-General on the Rule of Law and Transitional Justice in Conflict and Post-Conflict Societies*, UN Doc. S/2004/616 (23 August 2004), para 8.

30 No Peace Without Justice and UNICEF Innocenti Research Centre, *International Criminal Justice and Children* (Rome: NPWJ/UNICEF, September 2002).

31 This discussion began even before the Court was actually established. See, for example, *Report of the Secretary-General on the Establishment of a Special Court for Sierra Leone*, UN Doc. S/2000/915 (4 October 2000).

Later research focused on practical case studies from country situations, continued research on international criminal law and children, and the participation of children in truth commissions. In addition, there was an important debate over general standards to be applied in order to protect the rights of children in transitional justice mechanisms. In dealing with issues related to children, child soldiers had not been viewed as rights holders whose rights are protected throughout the transition period in a holistic way as envisioned in the Convention on the Rights of the Child (CRC).[32] Transitional justice forums have tended to deal with child soldiers as victims rather than stakeholders, placing them at risk of further victimization through these processes.

Towards addressing this issue, a series of conferences was organized by the UNICEF Innocenti Research Centre, beginning in 2005, with follow-up conferences in 2007 and 2008. These events focused on practical experiences and UNICEF activities at the country level, but they also promoted attention to and understanding of children's roles in transitional justice mechanisms. This work culminated in a conference on children and transitional justice co-convened by the Innocenti Research Centre and the Human Rights Program of Harvard Law School, in April 2009, to consolidate ongoing research and further the debate on emerging issues. During the conference, the Key Principles for Children and Transitional Justice were developed, with the aim of protecting the rights of children who are involved in transitional justice mechanisms and processes. The Principles are intended to better inform the participation of children in truth, justice, and reconciliation processes and serve as groundwork for further elaboration and consensus-building on the role of children in transitional justice.[33]

Child recruitment, meanwhile, has been the topic of a great deal of writing, much of which is relevant to analysing the situation of child soldiers from a transitional justice perspective. However, few authors cover more than one or two elements of the transitional justice approach: there is research and writing that bridges the rule of law and criminal justice areas of work, or criminal justice and participatory justice, but linking several areas in the transitional justice sphere is uncommon.

This work is the outcome of original, in-depth research and analysis of primary sources on child recruitment and transitional justice, including the

---

32 The CRC covers the full spectrum of child rights, including civil and political rights, as well as economic, social, and cultural rights. Convention on the Rights of the Child, 28 I. L. M. 1448 (1989).

33 *Key Principles for Children and Transitional Justice: Involvement of Children and Considerations of Children's Rights in Truth, Justice and Reconciliation Processes*, (2009). Outcome of Children and Transitional Justice Conference, Harvard Law School, Cambridge, Massachusetts, USA, 27–29 April 2009. The Principles include key aspects of child protection and participation in transitional justice.

travaux préparatoires for fundamental legal instruments and court documents for the *Lubanga* case. It aims to bring the relevant areas of transitional justice together in a new and comprehensive approach that spans all the relevant points from a child rights perspective.

The goal is to take the analysis of the law to its next level by thoroughly considering the intentions of the drafters. It also connects the body of law with how it is implemented at the domestic level, and through that examination, seeks to find the most appropriate entry points for solutions to the legal issues at stake. In analysing the successes and failures of the UN Security Council monitoring and reporting mechanism, as well as the mechanism's relationship to other aspects of transitional justice, it examines the country-level reporting and advocacy efforts that have followed from the improved data gathering and knowledge base regarding the situation of children on the ground. In addition, this work and the analysis of existing literature on child soldiers in a context of transitional justice illustrate the need to not just complement but move beyond existing studies to address the important question of how the rights of child soldiers can be better protected.

Rule of law: Scholars concentrating on the prohibition of child recruitment under international and domestic law have considered existing legal standards in international humanitarian law and human rights law, along with more recent writing that adds the element of international criminal law.[34] Most writers, however, have not considered the law beyond the international legal framework and how it applies to the domestic context.[35] Another common gap in this literature is the lack of analysis as to what action can be taken for the law to be implemented or accountabilities addressed, rather than leaving the standards in a vacuum as open-ended advocacy with no analysis of what the successes and failures have been to date.[36]

---

34 Coomaraswamy's analysis of the OP-CAAC and its connectivity with other instruments provides a good argument as to why universal ratification of the OP-CAAC will be of use. See Radhika Coomaraswamy, "The Optional Protocol to the Convention on the Rights of the Child on the Involvement of Children in Armed Conflict Towards Universal Ratification." *The International Journal of Children's Rights* 18, no. 4 (2010): 535–549. See also Steven Freeland, "Child Soldiers and International Crimes – How Should International Law Be Applied?" *New Zealand Journal of Public International Law* 3, (2005): 303–328.

35 For an exception, see Matthew Happold, *Child Soldiers in International Law*, (Manchester: Manchester University Press, 2005).

36 By way of example, Timothy Webster does go beyond just looking at the law and begins to consider that the Security Council has some role to play, but could then further consider the full potential of the implementation mechanisms. See Timothy Webster, "Babes with Arms: International Law and Child Soldiers" *George Washington International Law Review* 39, (2007): 227. Jennifer Silva provides a good legal overview of the issues, but concludes with open-ended advocacy. Jennifer R. Silva, "Child Soldiers: A Call to the International Community to Protect Children from War." *Suffolk Transnational Law Review* 31, (2007): 681. Alison Renteln and Amy Abbot provide examples of what the standards are with a rather descriptive perspective. Alison Dundes Renteln, "Child Soldier: The Challenge of Enforcing International Standards" *Whittier Law Review* 21, (1999): 191 and Amy Beth Abbott, "Child

In addition, few writers analyse the law from the perspective of what was intended by the drafters. For instance, Tiny Vandewiele in her overview of the Optional Protocol on the Involvement of Children in Armed Conflicts fails to consider how the *travaux préparatoires* may inform the interpretation of key provisions.[37] While the *travaux préparatoires* are meant to be complementing analysis derived from the text itself, rather than authoritative legal language, they do provide important contextual information on the reasoning behind certain wording at the time when the treaty was drafted.[38]

Although there has been some analysis of the question of age, surprisingly few authors have gone beyond what is stated in the legal instruments.[39] Mary-Jane Fox provides an interesting analysis of the age dilemma in light of cultural relativism, which is not much different from any other complex human rights issue: she puts the issue of age on the table by framing it as universal, though it is sometimes perceived as a Western perspective and a more local understanding of the law may also be applied.[40] But Fox's writing does not consider what to do in distinct situations or how much room should be left for interpretation while maintaining authority around the law.

Criminal justice: Child recruitment and criminal justice has received a great deal of attention. Several writers have focused on the question of whether or not child recruitment as a crime under customary international law had gained the force of law at the time of adoption of the Statute of the Special Court for Sierra Leone, while later writing analyses the subsequent judgements of the Court.[41] Some authors have focused on the language found in the Rome Statute; more recently, some have begun to analyse the *Lubanga* case, although they discuss very specific aspects of the judgement rather than a full analysis of the case from a child rights or practitioners' perspective.[42] For instance, Peter Singer's

---

soldiers: The use of Children as Instruments of War." *Suffolk Transnational Law Review* 23, (1999): 499.

37 Tiny Vandewiele, *A Commentary on the United Nations Convention on the Rights of the Child: Optional Protocol on the Involvement of Children in Armed Conflicts*, (Leiden: Martinus Nijhoff Publishers, 2006).

38 See Vienna Convention on the Law of the Treaties, article 31(3)(c).

39 Ann Sheppard, "Child Soldiers: Is the Optional Protocol Evidence of an Emerging "Straight-18" Consensus." *International Journal of Children's Rights* 8, (2000): 37–70.

40 Mary-Jane Fox, "Child soldiers and international law: patchwork gains and conceptual debates." *Human Rights Review* 7, no. 1 (2005): 42–44.

41 See for instance Noah B. Novogrodsky, "Litigating Child Recruitment Before the Special Court for Sierra Leone." *San Diego International Law Journal* 7, (2005–2006): 421–426. Mark Iacono, "The Child Soldiers of Sierra Leone: Are they Accountable for Their Actions in War?" *Suffolk Transnational Law Review* 26, (2002–2003): 445–468. John R. Morss "The Status of Child Offenders under International Criminal Justice: Lessons from Sierra Leone." *Deakin Law Review* 9, (2004): 213–226.

42 See for instance Roman Graf, "The International Criminal Court and Child Soldiers." *Journal of International Criminal Justice* 10, (2012): 945–969; Rosalyn C. E. Roberts, "The Lubanga Trial Chamber's Assessment of Evidence in Light of the Accused's Right to the Presumption of Innocence." *Journal of International Criminal Justice* 10, (2012): 923–943; and Anja

comprehensive work on child recruitment looks at criminalization as one of the elements of deterrence, and has not considered the indirect impacts of criminalization, such as the possibility that military commanders in other situations may react by hiding the fact that they have children in their ranks.[43]

Following the early writing on seeking to better understand the crime of child recruitment as defined in the Special Court for Sierra Leone and the International Criminal Court, authors seem to have pushed away from a legalistic approach. There is a significant amount of study in the area of children's participation in truth and reconciliation commissions,[44] but it reflects a tendency to discuss children's issues in non-judicial mechanisms, perhaps because children's issues are more easily reconcilable with this type of forum.

Historical justice: There is very limited coverage in academia on aspects of historical justice as related to child recruitment, including elements of the monitoring and reporting mechanism established by the UN Security Council. However, some of the early writing on child recruitment that looked to establish evidence of the widespread recruitment and use of children in armed conflict can be considered as part of historical justice.[45] Importantly, a focus on children in the context of transitional justice has helped bring attention to gender issues.[46] While the monitoring and reporting mechanism has begun to influence other UN reporting initiatives, such as fact-finding missions and inquiries, it is not yet appearing in academic writing on the Security Council mechanism and has not been considered by writers in the transitional justice sphere or elsewhere.[47]

Wiersing, "Lubanga and its Implications for Victims Seeking Reparations at the International Criminal Court" *Amsterdam Law Forum* 4: 39, (2012): 21–39.

43 Peter W. Singer "Talk is Cheap: Getting Serious About Preventing Child Soldiers." *Cornell International Law Journal* 37, (2004): 561–586.

44 Michael A. Corriero, "The Involvement and Protection of Children in Truth and Justice-Seeking Processes: The Special Court for Sierra Leone," *New York Law School Journal of Human Rights* 18 (2001–2002): 337–360.

45 See, for instance, Rachel Brett and Irma Specht, *Young soldiers: Why they choose to fight*: International Labour Organization, (2004) and Ilene Cohn and Guy S. Goodwin-Gill, and Institut Henry-Dunant, *Child Soldiers: The Role of Children in Armed Conflict* (Oxford University Press, 1994). Goodwin-Gill and Cohn provide an overview of critical legal interpretations and elements of rule of law, but also consider historical justice and issues around why children join, how this can be prevented, and the impact on children who join the ranks.

46 Gender has been a focus in many of the standards that have been developed for practitioners and which are studied in subsequent chapters of this book. For academic work, see, e.g., Yvonne E. Keairns, *The Voices of Girl Child Soldiers* (Geneva: Quaker United Nations Office, 2003), and Abigail Leibig, "Girl Child Soldiers in Northern Uganda: Do Current Legal Frameworks Offer Sufficient Protection?," *Northwestern University Journal on International Human Rights* 3 (2005): i.

47 Katy Barnett and Anna Jefferys, *Full of promise: How the UN's Monitoring and Reporting Mechanism can better protect children*, Network Paper, Number 62 (September 2008) and Sophie Hodgson, "Whose Action Plan? An Analysis of the UN Security Council Resolution 1612 Action Plan and Monitoring and Reporting Mechanisms in Nepal." *Journal of Human Rights Practice* 4, no. 2 (2012): 164–186.

Within the community of non-governmental organizations, however, it has received some attention, especially in the context of considerations around how to engage with the mechanism and what the implications are for the organizations.[48]

Recovery and reintegration: Writing on the area of recovery and reintegration of child soldiers is mainly the contribution of practitioners in the field, and most of it is very analytical.[49] Although it has contributed greatly to the way programmes are shaped and delivered, such writing is rarely linked to broader justice for children or transitional justice processes. An exception is Mark Drumbl's book *Reimagining Child Soldiers*, which maintains that the policy guidance at hand, especially the Paris Principles, separates recovery and reintegration from justice and insufficiently addresses the accountability of former child soldiers.[50] There is also field research on the reasons children join military groups or forces, which provides interesting insights, including for recovery and reintegration purposes.[51]

Participatory justice: One area that has been widely covered in academic writing is whether or not child soldiers should be held criminally responsible for crimes carried out during armed conflicts.[52] Recent critics of practice in the child soldiers domain focus on the failure to address the responsibilities of these children for having committed international crimes and seek to dispute the concept that these children are helpless victims who know no better than to follow the leaders of their armed group or force.[53] Their positions traverse two extremes: contending that children should not have been recruited in the first place and, therefore, should not be held accountable; and putting children on the stand as perpetrators, including in international criminal justice forums. Much

48 Watchlist on Children and Armed, *The 1612 Monitoring and Reporting Mechanism: A Resource Pack for NGOs, Second Edition*, (2015).

49 Andrew Brooks, *The Disarmament, Demobilisation and Reintegration of Children Associated with Fighting Forces*. Dakar: UNICEF, (2005); Neil Boothby, Jennifer Crawford, and Jason Halperin. "Mozambique child soldier life outcome study: Lessons learned in rehabilitation and reintegration efforts." *Global Public Health* 1, no. 1 (2006): 87–107; and Alcinda Honwana, "Negotiating Post-war Identities: Child Soldiers in Mozambique and Angola." *Codesria Bulletin* (1999): 4–13.

50 Mark A. Drumbl, *Reimagining Child Soldiers in International Law and Policy*. (New York: Oxford University Press, 2012).

51 Brett, Rachel, and Irma Specht, *Young soldiers: Why they choose to fight*. (International Labour Organization, 2004).

52 See Paola Konge for a good analysis of the issue, arguing for the need to establish a minimum age of criminal responsibility. The article is a good analysis of what happens to children in this process. Paola Konge, "International Crimes & Child Soldiers." *Southwestern Journal of International Law* 16, (2010): 41. See also, David M. Rosen "Who Is a Child-The Legal Conundrum of Child Soldiers." *Connecticut Journal of International Law* 25, (2009): 81; Matthew Happold, *Child Soldiers in International Law*: Manchester University Press (2005) and Farkhanda Zia-Mansoor, "The Dilemma of Child Soldiers: Who is Responsible?" *The King's College Law Journal* 16, (2005): 388–399.

53 See Drumbl, Reimagining Child Soldiers, 60.

of the writing in this area considers the legal issues carefully; however, regardless of whether the authors are for or against holding children to account, the writing generally fails to take the arguments to a full conclusion.[54]

Although most writers do not consider the link between criminal justice and the need for recovery and reintegration, one proponent of holding children accountable is Ilene Cohn, who makes the direct link between holding children to account as a prerequisite for successful reintegration. Nonetheless, Cohn does not consider what the elements of this theory will be in practice and what the pros and cons are with the different approaches.[55] Megan Nobert goes so far as to say that we should prosecute these children, but not convict them, without considering what happens in the interim and the importance of the process.[56]

Some writers focus on the fact that there is no international law on the topic and argue for the necessity of a new international law, or the formation of international customary law standards, without analysing what is already in place that could inform decisions about how children should be held to account.[57] Also, there is some limited coverage of child soldiers as witnesses that focuses on experiences in the Special Court for Sierra Leone or the International Criminal Court.[58] The use of truth and reconciliation processes for the purposes

---

54 There are some exceptions, however, and Musila provides a good perspective on how the guidance in the law is sufficient, and argues for the need to focus on implementation with a view to finding innovative solutions to use restorative justice approaches. Godfrey M. Musila. "Challenges in Establishing the Accountability of Child Soldiers for Human Rights Violations: Restorative Justice as an Option." *African Human Rights Law Journal* 5, (2005): 321–334.

55 JA Robinson is among those who advocate for responsibility to be placed on adults who recruited the children rather than holding former child soldiers accountable. JA Robinson. "The right of child victims of armed conflict to reintegration and recovery." *Potchefstroom Electronic Law Journal/Potchefstroomse Elektroniese Regsblad* 15, no. 1 (2012). Luz Nagle provides an excellent analysis of the issues to consider in the context of holding child soldiers responsible for crimes; however, the context of their recovery and reintegration is not considered. Luz Estella Nagle. "Child Soldiers and the Duty of Nations to Protect Children from Participation in Armed Conflict." *Available at: http://works.bepress.com/luz_nagle/3* (2010). Ilene Cohn takes a very categorical approach and advocates for holding children accountable because they need it in order to successfully rehabilitate and reintegrate. See Ilene Cohn. "Progress and Hurdles on the Road to Preventing the Use of Children as Soldiers and Ensuring their Rehabilitation and Reintegration." *Cornell International Law Journal* 37, (2004): 538–539.

56 Nobert, Megan. "Children at War: The Criminal Responsibility of Child Soldiers." *3 Pace International Law Review Online Companion* 1, (2011).

57 Sara A. Ward, "Criminalizing the Victim: Why the Legal Community Must Fight to Ensure that Child Soldier Victims are Not Prosecuted as War Criminals." *Georgetown Journal of Legal Ethics* 25, (2012): 821–857. Ward Suggests using truth and reconciliation commissions which is a good alternative, while suggesting to rewrite the OP to guide states on when and if to prosecute children. See also Crystal E. Lara, "Child Soldier Testimony Used in Prosecuting War Crimes in the International Criminal Court: Preventing Further Victimization." *Southwestern Journal of International Law* 17, (2011): 309.

58 No Peace Without Justice and UNICEF Innocenti Research Centre, *International Criminal Justice and Children* (Rome: NPWJ/UNICEF, September 2002).

of addressing issues relevant to children has been elaborated upon by several writers, and their analysis is rather comprehensive, which is why this manuscript does not seek to add further to existing literature on the topic.[59]

Transitional justice: Specifically linking transitional justice and child recruitment in a comprehensive way is a new approach. The Aptel-Ladisch publication on "child-friendly" transitional justice begins to bring together child rights and transitional justice more broadly, but refers to the broader set of children's rights and does not consider, for example, the relevance of historical justice in the context of child-sensitive approaches.[60] Matthew Happold's book *Child Soldiers in International Law* is one of the more comprehensive overviews with respect to the legal aspects of child recruitment, and it includes the involvement of the UN.[61]

Drumbl's recent work on child soldiers considers recruitment from a transitional justice perspective, although more strongly challenging policy aspects than those of law, and some of the arguments it presents do not fully consider the many contexts within which issues of child recruitment have been addressed, often in very complex legal environments. Although it is comprehensive and usefully critical of contemporary approaches, the work fails to recognize some of the on-the-ground realities.[62] Child soldiers cannot be categorized as a homogenous group, rather, they live in a wide range of individual situations. Nonetheless, Drumbl's work is a significant contribution to the discussion, including his proposition that former child soldiers can be supported through a restorative and local justice approach in support of reintegration.[63]

The issues noted above will be examined in detail in other chapters of this book, while bringing the various elements together in a transitional justice approach. The goal is to take the analysis of the law to its next level by thoroughly considering the intentions of the drafters. The aim is also to connect the body of law with how it is implemented at the domestic level, and through that examination, find the most appropriate entry points for solutions to the legal issues at stake. In analysing the successes and failures of the UN Security Council monitoring and reporting mechanism, as well as the mechanism's relationship to other aspects of transitional justice, this work examines the country-level reporting and advocacy efforts that have followed from the improved data gathering and knowledge base regarding the situation of children on the ground.

---

59 See, for instance, Drumbl, *Reimagining Child Soldiers*, 181.

60 Ladisch, Cecile Aptel and Virginie, Through a New Lens: A Child-Sensitive Approach to Transitional Justice, (2011).

61 Happold, Child Soldiers in International Law.

62 Drumbl, Reimagining Child Soldiers in International Law and Policy, 27.

63 Ibid., 207–209.

The detailed analysis of the *Lubanga* case below considers how the gathering of evidence impacts on activities taking place with armed groups and forces, as well as the implications of the overall focus on child recruitment beyond criminal justice to the sphere of transitional justice. What is new in this area is the aspect of linking recovery and reintegration with the right to reparations, and considering how recovery and reintegration can provide an increased focus on accountability. This element is brought in and builds on the *Lubanga* case experience, while drawing more generic conclusions on the evolving trends in how recovery and reintegration efforts can be linked to the broader justice and reparations discussions. The analysis of the responsibilities of former child soldiers focuses on the end goal, both in terms of addressing the accountability of these children and for purposes of supporting their recovery and reintegration.

The *Lubanga* case provides important entry points for the organizing framework, as the points of connection between the case and children's rights provide for good analysis of the different areas that must be considered. Not only are there questions around the criminal justice process of the *Lubanga* case itself bringing to life the provisions of the Rome Statute for the International Criminal Court, but also questions of reparations, the recovery and reintegration of children who have been released, and the impact of the participation of children in the process itself.

3. CHILD RECRUITMENT: AN OVERVIEW OF THE HISTORY

Globalization and the shifts in world politics have changed the way that wars unfold and, therefore, the ways that children are affected by armed conflicts; there is a distinct increase, for example, in the reports of incidences of armed groups and forces deliberately targeting schools, teachers, and humanitarian aid workers.[64] Attention to the situation of children associated with armed groups or forces has also increased, including growing awareness of the exploitation of children for sexual purposes and rape of children while serving with armed groups and forces.

64 Office of the Special Representative of the Secretary-General for Children and Armed Conflict and UNICEF, *Machel Study 10-Year Strategic Review: Children and Conflict in a Changing World* (New York: OSRSG-CAAC and UNICEF, 2009). The Machel 10-year review grappled with the notion of changing warfare in that there was very little data available to say that the impact on children changed. Nonetheless, the review identified three contexts that were particularly complex and that had an impact on children in particular: the proliferation of armed groups, the emergence of resource wars, and the internationalization of terrorism. See also Saudamini Siegrist, "Child Rights and Transitional Justice," in *Children and Transitional Justice*, ed. Mindy Jane Roseman Sharanjeet Parmar, Saudamini Siegrist, Theo Sowa (eds.) (Cambridge: Human Rights Program at Harvard Law School, 2010), 9–14.

In the ranks of armed groups and forces, children are involved in such activities as cooking and cleaning, as well as direct military activities: fighting, guarding checkpoints or commanders, or undertaking espionage on behalf of the commanders.

This section offers an introduction to the history of child recruitment and the international legal developments leading to recognition of child recruitment as a human rights violation.

3.1. HISTORICAL EXAMPLES

Children in the ranks of armed forces have been reported from all major conflicts in history, albeit not in any systematic manner because their involvement has only recently become prohibited under international or domestic law. There were also no systems to gather information and consider specific issues related to children who were in the ranks of the armed groups or forces, and because it was not a crime, it would not surface prominently in the discussions following armed conflicts.[65]

There are accounts from the Napoleonic era, in the late 18th century and early 19th century, that children of French soldiers were trained by the Government and often accompanied their fathers into the army. With the exception of a couple of years, France experienced some 20 years of warfare during this time. Nonetheless, it seems that Napoleon was somehow in line with international legal obligations of today, as he stated that 18-year-old boys are too young to wage war and that none should be sent to the take direct part in hostilities. "Instead, they should remain in France, where they would be clothed, armed, and drilled."[66] The law of 1796 also imposed a requirement throughout the country to recruit young men between the ages of 20 and 25, but boys went to military school and wore uniforms in order to be ready for warfare at age 20.[67]

There are also some examples from the Second World War. The most prominent relates to the Hitler Jugend troops, which fought very visibly during the final stages of the conflict.

Hitler Jugend began in 1926 as the youth arm of the Nazi party, for boys aged 14–18, and by 1936 membership was mandatory for Aryans. Even in the early

---

65 There are also writers who claim that children were not directly involved in the past, but there is actually some evidence to the contrary; the main issue is the lack of extensive information. Drumbl, for example, states: "Historically, their [children's] involvement in war was not usual. Nor was it encouraged in the case of front-line participation. But neither was it repudiated as a matter of law. Responsibility for child soldiering did not trigger criminal punishment." Drumbl, *Reimagining Child Soldiers in International Law and Policy*, 27.

66 Gates, Scott, and Simon Reich, Child Soldiers in the Age of Fractured States (Pittsburgh: University of Pittsburgh Press, 2010), 129.

67 See further Alain Pigeard, *L'armée de Napoléon: Organisation et vie quotidienne* (Paris: Tallandier, 2000).

days, these children wore uniforms and had ranks just like in the army. During the early stages of the war, however, they did not appear much in the fighting ranks until they became adults; by 1940 they were active in auxiliary roles, such as helping out after air raids. By 1943 these children were a military reserve due to the large military losses, and this is when the 12th SS-Panzer-Division Hitler Jugend was formed.[68] One of the well-known situations where these children, mostly aged 16–18, actively participated in the conflict was in June 1944 as part of the German defence in the Normandy campaign. By 1945 Volkssturm recruited children as young as 12 who were actively involved in the defence during the Battle of Berlin. Many adult leaders of the Hitler Jugend were put on trial by Allied authorities, but none was convicted for the leadership of the Hitler Jugend.[69]

An example that was linked to the political and national turmoil in Europe following the First World War is from the Finnish Civil War, which was fought in 1918 shortly after Finland had become independent in 1917. The fighting took place between what were commonly called the "whites" and the "reds" over who would have leadership of the Grand Duchy of Finland. Both the whites and the reds recruited children between 15 and 17 years old, including girls. On the reds' side, female troops, both girls and women, were recruited from the industrial parts of the country.[70]

The whites were from the more affluent families, while the reds were mostly poor people from the countryside. The children participated actively in what was a very bloody war with widespread summary executions. But regarding any specific considerations for children during the war or after it, historical accounts have very little to say other than that children were in the ranks of the parties to the conflict.[71]

Decolonization and the period following the Cold War brought about many new civil wars and internal conflicts rather than armed conflict between

---

68 Hubert Meyer, *The 12th SS Volume One: The History of the Hitler Youth Panzer Division* (Winnipeg: Stackpole Books, 2005).

69 For instance, Baldur von Schirach was one of the leaders of Hitler Youth and stood on trial in Nuremberg. However, there were no charges relevant to having involved children in the conflict. The judgement recognized that "while Gauleiter of Vienna Von Schirach continued to function as Reichsleiter for Youth Education and in this capacity he was informed of the Hitler Jugend's participation in the plan put into effect in the fall of 1944 under which 50,000 young people between the ages of 10 to 20 were evacuated into Germany from areas recaptured by the Soviet forces and used as apprentices in German industry and as auxiliaries in units of the German Armed Forces." Nonetheless, he was held guilty under Count IV related to anti-Jewish measures leading to crimes against humanity. See *The Trial of German Major War Criminals. Proceedings of the International Military Tribunal sitting at Nuremberg, Germany* Part 22 International Military Tribunal (Nuremberg) (1 October 1946).

70 Marko Tikka, *Terrorin Aika. Suomen Levottomat Vuodet 1917-1921* (Jyväskylä: Gummerus, 2006).

71 Anthony F. Upton, *The Finnish Revolution 1917–1918* (Minneapolis: University of Minnesota Press, 1980).

state-organized armed forces. The wide array of armed groups meant that armed activities became significantly less organized and disciplined than could have been expected to be the case in wars fought between states' armed forces. This presented, to some extent, new realities that led to a more widespread practice of children being recruited and used by both armed groups and armed forces.

Prominent among the causes behind child recruitment – and some of the worst crimes facing children while fighting in the ranks of armed groups and forces – is the flow of small arms that make it feasible for children to have the capacity to fight on the front line; the divide between ethnic, political, and religious groups, leading to children being recruited by groups that are not from their own background and then ending up killing their own families and community members; the proliferation of armed groups and widespread inclusion of children in different roles, many of which cause severe psychosocial consequences for children; indiscriminate use of weapons leading to children's loss of life and limb; the availability and use of drugs as part of the war strategy, leading to horrific crimes and reintegration difficulties; and the use of children as suicide bombers.[72]

However, children are not just victims or targets of warfare: if they have become soldiers fighting in the ranks of armed groups or forces, they most likely must kill to survive and are sometimes perpetrators of crimes. This is the reason they may be targeted for direct participation in the conflict and why they are also active agents and have responsibilities due to their participation in the conflict.

It is important to recognize that child soldiers are not easily categorized to fit within a single definition.[73] Each situation and each conflict has its own dynamics that play out differently in terms of how children are impacted by becoming part of an armed group, and each child has an individual experience while attached to an armed group or force.[74]

---

72 OSRSG-CAAC and UNICEF, *Machel Study Strategic Review*, 9.

73 Wessells emphasizes that "numerous misguided, oversimplified images have been constructed of child soldiers." See Michael Wessells, "Psychosocial Issues in Reintegrating Child Soldiers," *Cornell International Law Journal* 37, no. 524 (2004): 513–525, 515.

74 Drumbl also introduces an interesting concept of the aid agencies being the ones who portray child soldiers as innocent victims to the extreme, and hence have distorted the picture of what is the real situation. While this is certainly known to have been the case in some situations, the aim here is to establish a balance between the different perspectives. Drumbl writes: "This first image, therefore, typifies the child soldier as a faultless passive victim. A second image, which harmonizes with the victim narrative, is that of child soldiers as irreparable damaged goods." But he also suggests that there are many different categories of child soldiers due to the varied roles and contexts: "Although it would determine all children associated with armed forces or armed groups to be a generally protected class, a more fine-grained approach would encourage internal segmentation. One outcome of such segmentation would be to tailor policies toward the specific needs of subgroups and, within those subgroups." Drumbl, *Reimagining Child Soldiers*, 7 and 43.

3.2. INTERNATIONAL LEGAL DEVELOPMENTS

The recognition of child recruitment as a grave violation of international law and as an advocacy issue among human rights activists has evolved over time, especially during the past 20 years. While it is impossible to determine the true number of child soldiers, the global figure is currently estimated at 250,000.[75]

It is difficult to generalize about the age of these children, or how they have been recruited by armed forces and groups, but one can safely say that these practices exist; children are recruited by force and through voluntary recruitment and play a wide variety of roles during armed conflicts; and their ages range from being born into armed forces and groups up to the age of 18 years.[76]

Children have suffered disproportionately in armed conflicts: they are caught in the crossfire, unable to defend themselves, separated from their families, and have insufficient access to services and humanitarian assistance. Historically, including during the World Wars and other major conflicts, the "children and women first approach" prevailed, whereby humanitarian aid activities and support provided should first serve women and children. There was little recognition of children as agents in armed conflicts, with distinct rights and responsibilities. As such, the early instruments that were part of international humanitarian law considered special protection measures for children in situations of armed conflict in very general terms.[77]

Legal developments specific to child recruitment also show the recognition of the issue as part of a global debate and human rights issue. With the drafting of the Additional Protocols to the Geneva Conventions, the first negotiations on the issue of the recruitment and use of children took place at the international level. The Additional Protocols were being developed in recognition of the need for more detailed protection in situations of international armed conflict and to ensure sufficient protection measures were available in situations of non-international armed conflict. The Additional Protocols recognized the varying roles that children played in the ranks of armed groups and forces, although

---

75 The first estimates of child soldiers put the figure at 300,000. In recent years there have been many more or less successful reintegration programmes, and the estimate is now at 250,000, indicating a slight improvement. It is not possible to know for certain, however, that the number of child soldiers is decreasing. The early estimates were made in Rachel Brett and Margaret McCallin, *Children: The Invisible Soldiers* (Stockholm: Rädda Barnen, 1998).

76 Some writers make general statements such as this: "Readers may find it surprising, but most child soldiers are neither abducted nor forcibly recruited. The international legal imagination, nevertheless, heavily emphasizes this path to militarization." Drumbl, *Reimagining Child Soldiers*, 13. For an analysis of some of the root causes, see Farkhanda Zia-Mansoor, "The Dilemma of Child Soldiers: Who is Responsible?," *The King's College Law Journal* 16 (2005): 388–399.

77 See further in chapter 2 below.

even then, very little was known about the practice and the impact it had on children.[78]

The development of the Convention on the Rights of the Child was the first effort to bring the issue of child recruitment outside the sphere of international humanitarian law. The initiative for the CRC came from the Government of Poland, which submitted a draft convention to the Commission on Human Rights in 1978. This was prior to celebration of the 20th anniversary of the Declaration on the Rights of the Child during the International Year of the Child in 1979, and it would take another 10 years for the Convention to be adopted in 1989.[79] Not surprisingly, the provisions related to child recruitment were particularly difficult to agree upon – partly, because it was outside the scope of what was considered human rights law and also because it was a complex issue and not easy to agree upon by consensus as was otherwise the norm in the process for the development of the CRC. Importantly, the Convention also recognized the right of children affected by armed conflict to recovery and reintegration support.[80]

The Optional Protocol on the Involvement of Children in Armed Conflict was initiated at the Day of General Discussion on children in armed conflict, organized by the Committee on the Rights of the Child in 1992. This discussion resulted in the establishment of a working group that held six sessions for drafting the Optional Protocol between 1995 and 2000 and led to its adoption in 2000.[81]

In the late 1990s, the development and adoption of the Rome Statute of the International Criminal Court was another important step with a focus on the criminalization of the recruitment of children under international law.[82]

---

78 International Committee of the Red Cross, "Conference of Government Experts on the Reaffirmation and Development of International Humanitarian Law Applicable in Armed Conflicts," Geneva, 24 May – 12 June 1971: Committee III on "Protection of Civilian Population against Dangers of Hostilities" (January 1971), 46. Protocol Additional to the Geneva Conventions of 12 August 1949, and Relating to the Protection of Victims of International Armed Conflicts (Protocol I), adopted 12 August 1949, entered into force 7 December 1978, reprinted in 1125 UNTS 3. Protocol Additional to the Geneva Conventions of 12 August 1949, and Relating to the Protection of Victims of Non-International Armed Conflicts (Protocol II), adopted 12 August 1949, entered into force 7 December 1978, reprinted in 1125 UNTS 609.

79 The Declaration of 1959 only dealt very generally with children affected by armed conflict in stating that "The child shall in all circumstances be among the first to receive protection and relief." It had made no reference to child recruitment. Declaration of the Rights of the Child, UNGA Resolution 1386 (XIV) of 10 December 1959, enter from Endnotes, article 8.

80 Article 39 of the CRC, on recovery and reintegration, is further considered in chapter 5.

81 See *Committee on the Rights of the Child, Day of General Discussion on Children in Armed Conflict*, UN Doc. CRC/C/10 (1992). The Optional Protocol on the Involvement of Children in Armed Conflict was adopted by UN resolution A/RES/54/263 of 25 May 2000 at the fifty-fourth session of the General Assembly, entered into force 12 February 2002, reprinted in 39 ILM 1286 (2000).

82 The Rome Statute of the International Criminal Court, adopted 17 July 1998, entered into force 1 July 2002, reprinted in 2187 UNTS 90.

3.3. THE CONCEPT OF "CHILD SOLDIERS"

While the following chapters will offer interpretations of the different aspects of the concept of "child soldiers" and will further delve into the legal considerations alluded to above, it is important to reiterate that the term "child soldier" is only used for colloquial purposes, while the language in the law has referred more to the act of recruitment and use of children, as well as their involvement in armed conflict.

Given the history of children's involvement in armed conflict, the intention of the ICRC's interventions during the drafting of the 1977 Additional Protocols was to show the need to regulate recruitment and participation in hostilities. At the time, children's direct involvement was the main concern.[83] In the legal arena, this continued to be the case in the development of the 2000 Optional Protocol, which focuses on the involvement of children, e.g., no direct participation, but also prohibits forced recruitment of anyone under age 18. The Optional Protocol in itself did not make much progress on the question of voluntary recruitment of children.

In parallel, more programmatically oriented standards were developed to ensure that children needing support for release, recovery, and reintegration would not fall between the cracks due to the limitations of legal definitions. As such, the 1997 Cape Town Principles aimed to prevent the recruitment of children and to inform the process of demobilization and social reintegration of child soldiers – defining a "child soldier" as "any person under 18 years of age who is part of any kind of regular or irregular armed force or armed group in any capacity, including but not limited to cooks, porters, messengers and anyone accompanying such groups, other than family members. The definition includes girls recruited for sexual purposes and for forced marriage. It does not, therefore, only refer to a child who is carrying or has carried arms."[84]

Ten years later, through the adoption of the 2007 Paris Commitments and Principles, decision makers made it very clear that the approach was "to end the unlawful recruitment or use of children by armed forces or groups."[85] In other words, developing these pragmatic standards to help children who had become involved in armed conflicts was not about rewriting the law or filling gaps in the law, rather these initiatives were to apply the law through a number of useful programmatic guidelines. The Paris Principles build on the definition developed in the Cape Town Principles, and provide further clarity in that "a child associated with an armed force or armed group" is the terminology used to

83 See further section II.1.2 below.

84 *Cape Town Principles and Best Practices, adopted at a symposium on the prevention of the recruitment of children into armed conflicts and on demobilization and on social reintegration of child soldiers in Africa*, (Cape Town, 30 April 1997).

85 *Paris Commitments, The Paris Commitments to Protect Children from Unlawful Recruitment or Use by Armed Forces or Armed Groups*, (2007), principle 1.

describe "any person below 18 years of age who is or who has been recruited or used by an armed force or armed group in any capacity, including but not limited to children, boys and girls, used as fighters, cooks, porters, messengers, spies or for sexual purposes. It does not only refer to a child who is taking or has taken a direct part in hostilities".[86]

These definitions and others are incorporated in the text below, and the relevant terms are used as appropriate for the specific context, including the "recruitment and use of children", their "involvement in armed conflict", and "children associated with armed groups and forces", as well as references to the colloquial term "child soldiers".

3.4. THE BEGINNINGS OF THE END TO CHILD RECRUITMENT

The response to the situation of war-affected children in Mozambique provided some of the first consolidated lessons as to what it means to respond to the recovery and reintegration needs of former child soldiers.[87] Since then, many lessons have been learned and programmes for the recovery and reintegration of child soldiers are systematically implemented.[88]

In 1994, in adopting a resolution on the impact of armed conflict on children, the General Assembly requested the Secretary-General to appoint an expert, working in collaboration with the Centre for Human Rights (currently the Office of the High Commissioner for Human Rights) and UNICEF to undertake a comprehensive study on the situation of children affected by armed conflict.[89] Graça Machel, of Mozambique, was appointed to this position, marking a first effort to gather information relevant to the impact of armed conflict on children and leading to a compilation of the key areas of concern, which resulted in what came to be called the Machel study.

The Machel study was ground-breaking research as far as the focus on children and armed conflict is concerned. It dealt with several significant areas, including the participation of children in armed conflict; the relevance and adequacy of existing standards; the question of improved protection of children during armed conflicts, including from indiscriminate use of all weapons of war,

---

86 *The Paris Principles and Guidelines on Children Associated with Armed Forces or Armed Groups*, (February 2007), section 2.1.

87 The first review of a programme that had focused on recovery and reintegration, including of former child soldiers, was the review of the Children and War project in Mozambique from 1995, which covered the implementation of the programme between 1988 and 1995. Alcinda Honwana and Enny Panizzo, *Final Evaluation of the Children & War Project: A Program of Save the Children Federation – USA* (Maputo: Save the Children, 1995).

88 See chapter 5 for further details.

89 *Resolution on Protection of Children Affected by Armed Conflicts*, UN Doc. A/RES/48/157 (20 December 1993).

especially anti-personnel mines; and the promotion of children's physical and psychological recovery and social reintegration.[90]

The study stimulated increased action and political commitment to protect children from the negative consequences of armed conflicts. There was a call for system-wide enhanced engagement on the part of the United Nations (UN) on behalf of conflict-affected children, focusing on an appeal to address the widespread recruitment and use of children and to address issues facing conflict-affected children in peace agreements, as well as a call for an enhanced response across the board.[91]

Also in response to the Machel study, the position of a Special Representative of the Secretary-General on Children and Armed Conflict was created. The first Special Representative was appointed in September 1999.[92] In addition, the study prompted the formation of a global advocacy movement to stop the use of child soldiers and to improve accountability for violations against the rights of children during armed conflicts.[93]

In March 2014, the Special Representative and UNICEF initiated the campaign Children, Not Soldiers, which seeks to end by 2016 the recruitment and use of children by government armed forces in conflict. The goal is to work with eight governments that engage in the recruitment and use of children to end such practices. This is done through intensified advocacy with the concerned governments, and also through the signing and implementation of action plans that allow for concerted efforts to release and reintegrate former child soldiers. While progress has been made during the course of the campaign so far, and six of the eight governments signed action plans with the UN, some of the situations that witnessed progress in terms of signs for the release of children have since gone back into conflict. At the same time, it may be important to link these new advocacy initiatives to existing ones, such as the promotion of endorsements and ratification of the Paris Principles and the Optional Protocol, respectively.[94]

---

90 *United Nations General Assembly Resolution on the Rights of the Child*, UN Doc. A/RES/51/77 (20 February 1997).

91 The 1996 State of the World's Children focused on children in war and also included specific references to child recruitment. UNICEF, *The State of the World's Children 1996 (Children in War)* (New York: Oxford University Press, 1996).

92 The first person to hold this position was Olara Otunnu, followed by Radhika Coomaraswamy. The position is currently held by Leila Zerrougui.

93 The Coalition to Stop the Use of Child Soldiers, now known as Child Soldiers International, is one of the most significant signs of this movement; for further information see www.child-soldiers.org.

94 The eight governments in the campaign are Afghanistan, Chad, the Democratic Republic of the Congo, Myanmar, Somalia, South Sudan, the Sudan, and Yemen. The Sudan has not signed an action plan, and Yemen joined in the process of signing an action plan later than the other governments. Since the signing of the plan in Yemen, the situation has deteriorated significantly. Among these states, Myanmar and South Sudan have not endorsed the Paris Principles, while Myanmar, Somalia, and South Sudan have not ratified the Optional Protocol. For the states that have endorsed and/or ratified, it would be important to then use this in follow-up advocacy discussions, for instance, at the level of the Committee on the

Following this increased political attention given to the issue, the Security Council began debates on children and armed conflict in 1998. The Security Council process took a new direction towards understanding the impact on children: it continued to highlight the issue of recruitment and use of children, but it also highlighted children as targets of warfare – through intentional attacks on schools and hospitals; denial of humanitarian access; and the killing and maiming, abduction, and sexual exploitation of children.[95]

A serious effort to include children's issues specifically in peace agreements was also initiated during the late 1990s. This effort, however, has never been systematic nor comprehensive, and the main focus in peace agreements relevant to children has remained on the issue of child recruitment.

Overall, the information gathered and the level of awareness about child recruitment has increased dramatically over the past 25 years. Modern communications technology has also heightened global awareness regarding issues affecting children in armed conflict, and has significantly enhanced the capacity and ability to record and provide factual evidence of the situation of children. Today's commanders of armed forces and groups seek recognition for their political agendas (if they have one) and do not want to hide in their bunkers. Rebel groups fighting in Syria, for example, are using Skype to communicate with the outside world.[96] On the other hand, the ever-increasing availability and speed of communications technology make it much more difficult to hide from human rights obligations, including those related to child recruitment.

CONCLUSION

The issue of child recruitment has received a great deal of attention in terms of establishing legal clarity, and a global movement to stop child recruitment has evolved during the past almost 40 years. However, there is little research that deals with the full cycle of events from the act of recruitment itself and reasons behind why children join, to collection of information about the involvement of children in armed conflicts and, finally, children's release and reintegration.

Rights of the Child. See further *Annual Report of the Special Representative of the Secretary-General for Children and Armed Conflict*, Leila Zerrougui, UN Doc. A/HRC/28/54 (29 December 2014).

95 These factors were the foundation of the "six grave violations" established in the Secretary-General's report of 2005, which proposed an action plan for the establishment of a Security Council monitoring, reporting, and compliance mechanism. See chapter 4 for further details on the Security Council mechanism. [See Report of the Secretary-General on Children and Armed Conflict, UN Doc. A/59/695-S/2005/72 (9 February 2005).

96 Amy Chozick. "For Syria's Rebel Movement, Skype IS a Useful and Increasingly Dangerous Tool." *New York Times*, 30 November 2012.

Likewise, little legal scholarship has considered the foundation of the law relevant to child recruitment beginning with the *travaux préparatoires* for the various legal instruments, nor has anyone linked research on child soldiers to the broader political arena in the negotiation of peace agreements and in the Security Council. As per article 32 of the Vienna Convention on the Law of Treaties the preparatory work of a treaty and the circumstances of its conclusion may be used as supplementary means of interpretation. No doubt, understanding the context within which a treaty provision has been adopted allows for a sense of direction when the meaning of a provision is unclear or can be interpreted in different ways.

The aim has been to complement existing research and study on the topic. This work is also an attempt to bring theory and practice closer together so as to provide a useful tool for both academics and practitioners. In addition, it aims to bring the perspective of protection practitioners into the core of the legal debate by analysing the interface between the different aspects of transitional justice in an academic context and transitional justice in a context of taking action to end the recruitment and use of children to participate in armed conflicts.

The actions that can lead to change and transition in the area of child recruitment are the actions that need to be pursued. It is not just transition or justice: it is the interrelationship between the two and the interrelationship between all the different aspects of justice. The question is whether transitional justice is justice only when it is successful. If the transition fails, as is the situation in many countries with child soldiers, can the justice platform still provide a useful forum for analysis and spur further coherence in action?

While the overview in chapter 1 introduces the issue of child soldiers and how it became a key focus on the international political and advocacy agendas, subsequent chapters cover these developments in more detail and discuss how they apply in practice. Chapter 2 describes in greater depth the relevant law on child soldiers and investigates how humanitarian and human rights law is manifest in different international instruments and areas that affect child recruitment.

CHAPTER 2

CHILD RECRUITMENT AND THE RULE OF LAW

International Law and the Prohibition against Recruiting and Using Children to Take Direct Part in Hostilities

I asked: "What were your duties as a child soldier in the movement?"
He said: "I led some of the boys in the armed group who prepared tea and food, washed the cars, and carried our belongings."
I asked him: "What happened if those boys did not do what you told them to?"
He replied: "You hit him with the Kalashnikov."
I asked him: "Would the commander do the same to you if he found out?"
He replied: "Nobody asks and nobody would report on you. You hit him so hard that the others will not be impolite again."
I asked him: "If somebody older than you, like a commander, ordered you to do something you do not like, what do you do?"
He replied: "If he is a senior commander, I will obey him; but if he is an ordinary person, I hold a Kalashnikov and he holds a Kalashnikov and the one who fires first will defeat the other."

INTRODUCTION

The rule of law implies that there is a high predictability as to how known rules will be applied, as opposed to arbitrary action by government or non-state actors.[97] The situations where child recruitment and use take place are inherently unstable, however, underscoring the considerable need to promote the overall elements of the rule of law in order to strengthen this aspect of transitional justice. This can present both challenges and opportunities, as there is scope to introduce new ways of looking at the issues.

One great challenge is to determine what law prevails in a situation where there could be several options. In this regard, both *ex post facto* legislation and

---

97 Crocker, "Reckoning with Past Wrongs: A Normative Framework," 55–57.

differences in application of the law due to the nature of the conflict or the actor involved in carrying out the violation must be taken into consideration – recognizing that the law of a previous regime may have shortcomings or there may be no law in place on the issue of concern.

Chapter 2 considers the circumstances of the child's participation during a conflict and extends the focus to encompass the end result for the child, as well as the aim of prohibiting and redressing the act itself – regardless of the situation on the ground.[98] The chapter includes a description of the elements of international law that provide measures for the protection of children's rights and establish guidelines for the prevention and prohibition of child recruitment, with a focus on the traditional sources: international humanitarian law and international human rights law. Three broad questions are considered:

- What are the primary issues in the legal debate relevant to child recruitment and use, as reflected in the drafting history of the fundamental documents of international humanitarian law and the child rights domain?
- What is the current status of the prohibitions against recruitment and use of children by armed groups and forces in international law, particularly as reflected in their implementation in domestic jurisdictions?
- To what extent has the law been applied and, therefore, the recruitment and use of children criminalized and perpetrators convicted for such crimes?

This analysis of the evolution of the law is divided into three parts: (1) review of the legal developments in international humanitarian law, beginning with the drafting history and interpretation of the relevant provisions in the Geneva Convention IV and in the Additional Protocols; (2) analysis of child rights as part of the international human rights framework based on the Convention on the Rights of the Child and the Optional Protocol on the Involvement of Children in Armed Conflict; and (3) examination of how the prohibitions against recruitment and use of children have been materialized in national jurisdictions, including the consideration of child recruitment as a crime. Each of the three sections seeks to establish the pertinent details regarding key legal issues around the questions of age; forced versus voluntary recruitment; applicability of the law to state versus non-state actors (armed forces as opposed to armed groups); and the application of the notion of "direct participation in hostilities."

---

98 This chapter does not consider the element of predictability in terms of what law is applied, which is an important consideration in the context of rule of law as applied to transitional justice. This is discussed further in chapter 7 on participatory justice in the context of children as alleged perpetrators, and children being charged under terrorist and emergency laws. See also *Report of the Secretary-General on the Rule of Law and Transitional Justice in Conflict and Post-Conflict Societies*, UN Doc. S/2004/616 (23 August 2004), para 10.

1. INTERNATIONAL HUMANITARIAN LAW

This section presents an analysis of the legal developments within relevant international humanitarian law and builds on three major instruments: the Geneva Convention Relative to the Protection of Civilian Persons in Time of War (GC IV), of 1949, and the two Additional Protocols, of 1977.[99]

1.1. PROVIDING AN INITIAL FOCUS ON PROTECTION OF CHILDREN IN ARMED CONFLICT THROUGH THE FOURTH GENEVA CONVENTION

The humanitarian implications of civil war were part of a continuing discussion at the International Conference of the Red Cross (ICRC) since the beginning of the 20th century, including at the Xth Conference in 1912, where there had been a specific focus on the impact of civil war on children.[100]

The XVIth International Red Cross Conference, held in London in 1938, passed a resolution asking the International Committee and the National Red Cross Societies to apply the humanitarian principles established in the Geneva Conventions and the Tenth Hague Convention of 1907. The foundational concerns were set on obtaining medical treatment for those who are wounded or sick, including prisoners of war, and the safety of medical personnel and supplies; humane treatment for all political prisoners, including exchange and release when possible; respect for the life and liberty of non-combatants; facilities for the transmission of personal news and the reunion of families; and effective measures for the protection of children.[101]

In 1945, the Bolivian Red Cross prepared an initiative to develop a Draft Convention for the Protection of Children in the Event of International Conflict

99 The Geneva Convention Relative to the Protection of Civilian Persons in Time of War, adopted 12 August 1949, entered into force 21 October 1950, reprinted in 75 UNTS 287, articles 14, 24, and 51. Protocol Additional to the Geneva Conventions of 12 August 1949, and Relating to the Protection of Victims of International Armed Conflicts (Protocol I), adopted 12 August 1949, entered into force 7 December 1978, reprinted in 1125 UNTS 3. Protocol Additional to the Geneva Conventions of 12 August 1949, and Relating to the Protection of Victims of Non-International Armed Conflicts (Protocol II), adopted 12 August 1949, entered into force 7 December 1978, reprinted in 1125 UNTS 609.

100 See Xth International Red Cross Conference, *Resolution XIV: Civil War* (Geneva 1921). This resolution in paragraph 5 made reference to children in passing by stating that the Conference condemns the political hostage system, and emphasizes the non-responsibility of relatives (especially children) for the acts of the head of other members of the family, which could lead to the ICRC making a public statement about the situation.

101 XVIth International Red Cross Conference, *Resolution XIV: Role and Activity of the Red Cross in time of Civil War* (London, 1938), a-e.

or Civil War.[102] Discussing this within the realm of the preliminary conference, the delegations decided to integrate provisions regarding children in the new "Civilian Convention" instead of developing a separate instrument for children; they considered that it is "difficult to disjoin two questions which are in practice so closely related, since children in wartime share the fate of the civilian population, particularly of their mothers."[103]

Following this decision, children's issues were integrated in the development of GC IV, which was based on pre-existing provisions that were revised and supplemented and new ones drawn up by the Diplomatic Conference held in Geneva, 22 April–12 August 1949.

The age used to define a child in the Geneva Conventions is 15, with the exceptions of 18 as the minimum age for carrying out labour when under occupation, for the death penalty, and the age for evacuation to be decided on a case-by-case basis.[104]

Dealing with children as a protected category in fairly general terms, the universally ratified GC IV does not mention the issue of child recruitment specifically. However, there is more in this Convention that is applicable to child recruitment than first meets the eye. Although the bulk of its provisions apply to armed conflict between states,[105] the bedrock provision of article 3 (which is common to all Geneva Conventions) provides for a set of minimum standards that must be respected by all parties to conflict and are applicable to both international and national situations of conflict.[106] In addition, article 14 of GC IV establishes safety zones, including those according special protection measures in times of war for children below age 15.[107]

Article 24 includes general measures relating to child welfare, with a focus on those who are under age 15 and have been orphaned or separated from their

---

102 International Committee of the Red Cross, *Report on the Work of the Preliminary Conference of National Red Cross Societies for the study on the Conventions and of various Problems relative to the Red Cross, Geneva, July 26 – August 3, 1946*, (Geneva, 1947), 101.

103 Ibid., 102.

104 Jean S. Pictet (ed.), *Commentary: IV Geneva Convention Relative to the Protection of Civilian Persons in Time of War* (Geneva: International Committee of the Red Cross, 1958), 139. According to the Commentary, it was meant to be flexible in the context of evacuation so as to allow for the parties to the conflict to reach agreement depending on the context.

105 The GC IV is applicable "to all cases of declared war or of any other armed conflict which may arise between two or more of the High Contracting Parties, even if the state of war is not recognized by one of them." It also applies to situations of occupation.

106 On some of the debates around how such standards can be applied, see Jean-Daniel Vigny and Cecilia Thompson, "Standards fondamentaux d'humanite: quel avenir?," *Revue Internationale de la Croix/Rouge/International Review of the Red Cross* 82 (2000): 917–940.

107 The early submission to Government Experts by the ICRC put the age at 16, see International Committee of the Red Cross, *Report of the Work of the Conference of Government Experts for the Study of the Conventions for the Protection of War Victims, Geneva, April 14–26, 1947*, Series 1, no 5b (1947), 300. See also reference to several such camps having been set up during the Second World War by the ICRC, in Pictet, *Commentary: IV Geneva Convention*, 185.

families due to war. This provision includes a clause whereby education for these children should be delegated to "persons of a similar cultural tradition" whenever possible. The parties are also charged with the responsibility to "facilitate the reception of such children in a neutral country for the duration of the conflict with the consent of the Protecting Power, *if any*, and under due safeguards for the observance of the principles." (emphasis added)

During discussion of this provision at the diplomatic conference that developed the Geneva Conventions, Committee III made an important interpretative point with respect to the use of "if any" in article 24:

> When the children in question are nationals of the country in which they are, they have no Protecting Power; but if the children are of enemy nationality, they have one; and it is for this reason that the expression "if any" is employed. It is designed to ensure the supervision of the Protecting Power, so that protected children shall not be compulsorily transferred in order to be subjected to ideological training.[108]

Article 50 of GC IV elaborates the protection of children through provisions whereby an occupying power may not change the child's personal status under any circumstances or enlist a child in "formations or organizations subordinate to it." Article 51 on enlistment and labour further specifies that the occupying power may not require "protected persons" to serve in armed or auxiliary forces or compel anyone under the age of 18 to work, specifically excluding work of any kind that would necessitate taking part in military operations.[109]

During the diplomatic conference for the Geneva Conventions, there was only limited discussion of the death penalty for crimes committed during armed conflict, although the International Union for Child Welfare submitted a letter to Committee III that included the following statement:

> We are well aware that it is possible for young people to commit acts which in the case of adults would incur the death penalty, but we believe that in the great majority of cases these minors do not realize the full implication and the consequences of the acts which they commit. It would therefore be unhuman to inflict a sentence on them which is absolutely irrevocable.[110]

It is not clear, however, that the reference to young people who commit such acts carrying the death penalty denotes that those children could have been child soldiers.

Despite the fact that child recruitment had been a feature of Hitler's warfare during the Second World War, for example, through mobilization of

108 International Committee of the Red Cross, "Final Record of the Diplomatic Conference of Geneva of 1949" (1949), 820. See also, Pictet, *Commentary: IV Geneva Convention*, 187.

109 Ibid., 293.

110 "Final Record of the Diplomatic Conference of Geneva of 1949," 131.

Hitlerjugend and the use of children towards the end of the war,[111] the *travaux préparatoires* make no further reference to discussions about recruitment or use of children by armed forces.

In the GC IV as it was finally adopted, the main elements that can be applied to prohibiting child recruitment and use relate to an occupying power being prohibited from placing children *en masse* into politically oriented educational institutions and the restrictions on labour for children under the age of 18. These provisions continue to have relevance in international armed conflicts today.

1.2. THE ADDITIONAL PROTOCOLS AND THE SHIFT TOWARDS SPECIFIC PROVISIONS RELEVANT TO CHILD RECRUITMENT

After several decades of implementation of the Geneva Conventions, debates within the UN on the impact of armed conflicts on children led to the Declaration on the Protection of Women and Children in Emergency and Armed Conflict in 1974,[112] which focused on children and women as civilians and did not yet consider child recruitment as an issue. The first effort to recognize child recruitment as a stand-alone issue in international law accompanied the adoption of the Additional Protocols to the Geneva Conventions in 1977.

The provisions found in Additional Protocol I (AP I) are applicable to states or the "parties to the conflict" in situations where there is an international armed conflict[113] and to states in the context of an occupation. Protection for children is articulated in article 77, paragraphs 1–3:

1. Children shall be the object of special respect and shall be protected against any form of indecent assault. The Parties to the conflict shall provide them with the care and aid they require, whether because of their age or for any other reason.
2. The Parties to the conflict shall take all feasible measures in order that children who have not attained the age of fifteen years do not take a direct part in hostilities and, in particular, they shall refrain from recruiting them into their armed forces. In recruiting among those persons who have attained the age of fifteen years but who have not attained the age of eighteen years, the Parties to the conflict shall endeavour to give priority to those who are oldest.
3. If, in exceptional cases, despite the provisions of paragraph 2, children who have not attained the age of fifteen years take a direct part in hostilities and fall into

---

111 Hans-Dietrich Nicolaisen, *Die Flakhelfer: Luftwaffenhelfer und Marinehelfer im Zweiten Weltkrieg* (Berlin: Ullstein, 1981).

112 *Declaration on the Protection of Women and Children in Emergencies and Armed Conflicts*, UN Doc. 3318(XXIX) (1974).

113 The application is the same as for the Geneva Conventions, namely, the AP I applies "to all cases of declared war or of any other armed conflict which may arise between two or more of the High Contracting Parties, even if the state of war is not recognized by one of them."

> the power of an adverse Party, they shall continue to benefit from the special protection accorded by this Article, whether or not they are prisoners of war.

Additional Protocol II (AP II) applies to non-international armed conflicts[114] and to armed forces and armed groups with the same standards. The provision related to child recruitment is found in article 4(3):

> (c) children who have not attained the age of fifteen years shall neither be recruited in the armed forces or groups nor allowed to take part in hostilities;
> (d) the special protection provided by this Article to children who have not attained the age of fifteen years shall remain applicable to them if they take a direct part in hostilities despite the provisions of subparagraph (c) and are captured.

However, "situations of internal disturbances and tensions, such as riots, isolated and sporadic acts of violence and other acts of a similar nature"[115] are excluded from the scope of the Protocol. This is a significant limitation, given that child recruitment often takes place during low-intensity conflicts.

During the negotiations that led to the Additional Protocols, the ICRC introduced child recruitment as an issue at the Government Experts Conference in 1971, when it was highlighted as one of three key issues related to children that the new protocols needed to address. At the time, the ICRC stated that child recruitment "has not even been studied up to now, yet it is the most important one [of the three issues] since children are becoming increasingly involved in war, being either used to assist irregular forces, or made the subject of military operations."[116] The following language was proposed:

> Children of less than 15 years of age (or: children, or: young children) shall be the object of special protection;
> The Parties to the conflict shall make every effort to keep them away and safe from military operations.

The first paragraph was introduced as a broad provision to complement the protections generally extended to civilians under the Geneva Conventions and

114 AP II applies "to all armed conflicts which are not covered by article 1 of the Protocol Additional to the Geneva Conventions of 12 August 1949, and relating to the Protection of Victims of International Armed Conflicts (Protocol I) and which take place in the territory of a High Contracting Party between its armed forces and dissident armed forces or other organized armed groups which, under responsible command, exercise such control over a part of its territory as to enable them to carry out sustained and concerted military operations and to implement this Protocol." See article 1 of the Protocol.

115 See article 1(2) of AP II.

116 International Committee of the Red Cross, "Conference of Government Experts on the Reaffirmation and Development of International Humanitarian Law Applicable in Armed Conflicts," Geneva, 24 May–12 June 1971: Committee III on "Protection of Civilian Population against Dangers of Hostilities" (January 1971), 46.

the new Additional Protocols. The second was intended to protect children against the effects of military operations, which means that children should not be the object of an attack or be used as auxiliary military personnel – two obligations incumbent on all parties to a conflict. The idea of keeping children away from military operations was also intended to mean that the parties would take "passive" precautions.[117] In preparation for the diplomatic conference, these provisions were further elaborated, and the draft Additional Protocols submitted for consideration included the following in article 68(1–3) on the protection of children:

1. Children shall be the object of privileged treatment. The Parties to the conflict shall provide them with the care and aid their age and situation require. Children shall be protected against any form of indecent assault.
2. The Parties to the conflict shall take all necessary measures in order that children aged under fifteen years shall not take any part in hostilities and, in particular, they shall refrain from recruiting them in their armed forces or accepting their voluntary enrolment.
3. The death penalty for an offence related to a situation referred to in Article 2 common to the Conventions shall not be pronounced on persons who were under eighteen years at the time the offence was committed.[118]

1.3. KEY LEGAL CONSIDERATIONS RELEVANT TO SPECIFIC PROVISIONS OF THE ADDITIONAL PROTOCOLS

During the diplomatic conference, delegations introduced a number of changes relating to age. The Brazilian delegation introduced a proposal to raise the age from under 15 to under 18.[119] This proposal was supported by Czechoslovakia, Nigeria, Venezuela, Uruguay, and Yugoslavia, but it was rejected by such powerful states as Canada, Japan, Germany, and the United Kingdom – which cited practical issues hinting at the fact that they did not want to change their customary stance. Japan, for example, argued that "in many countries… youths over the age of fifteen either could or had to undergo military or similar service

117 Ibid., 49.

118 International Committee of the Red Cross, "Draft Additional Protocols to the Geneva Conventions of August 12, 1949" (Geneva, October 1973), 86.

119 "Official Records of the Diplomatic Conference on the Reaffirmation and Development of International Humanitarian Law Applicable in Armed Conflicts, Geneva (1974–1977): Volume XV" (Bern: Federal Political Department, 1978), 65–66. See also "Official Records of the Diplomatic Conference on the Reaffirmation and Development of International Humanitarian Law Applicable in Armed Conflicts, Geneva (1974–1977): Volume III" (Bern: Federal Political Department, 1978), 301.

and should an armed conflict break out would almost inevitably be engaged in hostilities."[120]

Debate around how to define a child continued to be contentious because there were many different standards already being applied in domestic jurisdictions.[121] Delegations did not reach consensus easily on the issue, and the agreed-upon language was a compromise between the desire of some delegations for a lower age limit and of others hoping to broaden the scope for involvement of children who "voluntarily" enlisted.[122] In addition, although there had been a discussion during the development of the Additional Protocols on the issue of forced versus voluntary recruitment, it does not specifically appear in the final text as adopted. It could be argued that recruitment covers both forced and voluntary forms for joining armed groups and forces, however, in the *travaux préparatoires* there is no evidence to this effect.

The question of direct participation in hostilities was also the subject of debate during the diplomatic conference. There were at least three main proposals on the table: one referring to children not taking "part" in hostilities; another referring to children not taking "any part" in hostilities; and the third referring to a prohibition against taking "direct part" in hostilities.[123] Apparently,

---

120 Statement by the Government of Japan, "Official Records of the Diplomatic Conference on the Reaffirmation and Development of International Humanitarian Law Applicable in Armed Conflicts, Geneva (1974–1977): Volume XV," 67.

121 As stated in the Report to the Committee III on the work of the Working Group submitted by the Rapporteur: "It should also be noted that the Working Group decided not to place specific age limits in paragraphs 1 and 4 and that there is no precise definition of the term 'children'. Whether persons of 16, 17 or 18 years of age would, thus, have to be detained separately from adults is left to national law, traditions, and the decision of the Parties to a conflict who, it is expected, will act in light of the purposes of this article." According to the ICRC Commentary, the Conference intentionally did not give a precise definition of the term "child." The moment at which a person ceases to be a child and becomes an adult is not judged in the same way everywhere in the world. Depending on the culture, the age may vary between about 15 and 18 years. See, e.g., Claude Pilloud et al., *Commentary on the Additional Protocols: Of 8 June 1977 to the Geneva Conventions of 12 August 1949* (Dordrecht: Martinus Nijhoff Publishers, 1987), 4549.

122 The Rapporteur providing feedback from the working group for this provision during the Diplomatic Conference reported that: "Paragraph 2 reflects a compromise in which a flat ban on recruiting children under 15 is coupled with a more flexible restriction, on the acceptance of voluntary services, i.e., to 'take all feasible measures' to prevent them taking a direct part in hostilities. The Working Group recognized that sometimes, particularly in occupied territories and in wars of national liberation, a total prohibition on the voluntary participation of children under 15 would be unrealistic. The final sentence of paragraph 2 was also part of the compromise with those who wished a higher age limit on recruitment." Official Records Volume XV, 522.

123 The language introduced by the Pakistani delegation quite late into the negotiations was: "Children below the age of fifteen years shall neither be recruited in the armed forces or groups nor allowed to take part in hostilities." See "Official Records of the Diplomatic Conference on the Reaffirmation and Development of International Humanitarian Law Applicable in Armed Conflicts, Geneva (1974–1977): Volume IV" (Bern: Federal Political Department, 1978), 20.

the understanding of some delegations was that involvement of children in roles other than playing a direct part would be permissible: in introducing the amendment to increase the age to 18, the Brazilian delegation argued that without the amendment the language allowed for children to be involved in auxiliary roles.[124]

Few spoke against including auxiliary duties as part of the definition for prohibiting direct participation, and the Greek delegation said that "a Government could not be denied the right to accept children as volunteers for the performance of auxiliary duties." It also argued that children under age 15 could not remain passive if the country was confronted by aggression. The ICRC prepared a preliminary explanatory note to resolving this question:

> The Parties to the conflict shall neither encourage nor tolerate any participation whatsoever by children in the hostilities; not only shall direct participation in the hostilities be prohibited, but also any other act in relation with the latter: transmission of military information, transport of arms, ammunition and war material, sabotage, etc.[125]

This definition of "any part in hostilities" was further emphasized by the ICRC during the diplomatic conference, but its approach was explicitly supported only by the Swiss delegation.[126]

---

124 The Brazilian delegation emphasized that "in the first place, special circumstances might make it difficult to establish the exact age of an adolescent, and then there were special situations that might arise, for example, where persons under eighteen wished to take part in order to defend still younger persons or to assist them when no adults were present. However, it should be noted that the ICRC text did not categorically prohibit the possible presence of minors in military activities, so that it could be said to allow for such cases. That being so; the age limit might be set at eighteen as a general condemnation of the policy of using minors for military purposes." "Official Records of the Diplomatic Conference on the Reaffirmation and Development of International Humanitarian Law Applicable in Armed Conflicts, Geneva (1974–1977): Volume XV," 65.

125 "Draft Additional Protocols to the Geneva Conventions of August 12, 1949," 87. The Swiss delegation suggested that specific language should be added for a provision stating that children should also not participate in auxiliary activities, such as collecting information, transmitting orders, and carrying munitions and foodstuffs. "Official Records of the Diplomatic Conference on the Reaffirmation and Development of International Humanitarian Law Applicable in Armed Conflicts, Geneva (1974–1977): Volume XV," 67.

126 The ICRC commentary concludes that auxiliary duties would be covered: "Examples would include, in particular, gathering and transmission of military information, transportation of arms and munitions, provision of supplies etc. The intention of the drafters of the article was clearly to keep children under fifteen outside armed conflict, and consequently they should not be required to perform such services; if it does happen that children under fifteen spontaneously or on request perform such acts, precautions should at least be taken; for example, in the case of capture by the enemy, they should not be considered as spies, saboteurs or illegal combatants and treated as such." Pilloud et al., "Commentary on the Additional Protocols", 901.

It is interesting to note that AP II has a different standard than AP I, which states that children under 15 shall "neither be recruited" nor "allowed to take part." AP II does not include the notion of "direct" participation, thus providing broader protection than in international armed conflicts.[127] The language adopted quite late at the diplomatic conference included "direct" for both Additional Protocols, and it is not clear what happened following the conference and the actual presentation of the instruments for ratification or why the word "direct" does not appear in AP II.[128]

One justification to leave out the notion of direct participation in AP II could be that there is need for a more strict application of prohibiting armed groups in non-international conflicts from using children in conflict under any circumstances; hence, it was important to cover children's participation in general and omit reference to "direct participation" only.[129] On the other hand, an argument could be made that children in armed groups who participate in any form in the hostilities are also legitimate targets, making the context of non-international armed conflicts even more precarious for protection of children in situations where they are in fact fighting in the ranks of armed groups.[130]

The answers to the question of direct participation could be seen as contradictory: on the one hand, to ensure that as few children as possible are to be considered enemy combatants and hence legitimate targets, it is important that the provision is narrowly interpreted for the duration that children are

---

127 Article 4(3)(c) was adopted late in the negotiations and was introduced by Judge Hussain of Pakistan as an initiative to facilitate adoption of the Protocol without objections. It was adopted by consensus at the 6 July 1997 session, but due to the lack of debate it is not clear that the different standard introduced were fully understood by delegations. See Matthew Happold, Child Soldiers in International Law (Manchester: Manchester University Press, 2005). Happold refers to the experiences of George Aldrich, who was present at the negotiations: Aldrich, George H., "Comments on Ternerier's 'Combatants and Non-Combatants'", in Dekker, Iger F. and Harry H.G. Post, *The Gulf War of 1980–1988: The Iran-Iraq War in International Legal Perspective* (Dordrecht: Martinus Nijhoff Publishers, 1992). See also Daniel Helle, "Optional Protocol on the Involvement of Children in Armed Conflicts to the Convention on the Rights of the Child," *International Review of the Red Cross* 839 (2000).

128 The relevant paragraphs as adopted by consensus at the fifty-ninth meeting on 10 May 1977 read as follows: "(f) take all feasible measures in order that children who have not reached fifteen years of age do not take a direct part in hostilities, and, in particular, to refrain from recruiting them in their armed forces; and (g) continue to accord the special protection provided by this article to children who have not reached fifteen years of age and who, despite the provisions of sub-paragraph (e), have taken a direct part in hostilities and have fallen into the power of an adverse party." "Official Records of the Diplomatic Conference on the Reaffirmation and Development of International Humanitarian Law Applicable in Armed Conflicts, Geneva (1974–1977): Volume XV," 508.

129 This also relates to the way that armed groups have a stricter obligation in the Optional Protocol on the Involvement of Children in Armed Conflict, dealt with further below.

130 See Pilloud et al., "Commentary on the Additional Protocols," 25, on the notion that civilians taking direct part in hostilities lose their protection against attack. See also Sylvain Vité, "Protecting Children during Armed Conflict: international Humanitarian Law," *Human Rights & International Legal Discourse* 5: No. 1 (2011): 14–39.

directly involved in hostilities. On the other, a broad application would be advocated for purposes of providing special protection to children who are captured or who otherwise benefit from transitional justice initiatives, such as recovery and reintegration programmes. Furthermore, children associated with armed groups and forces, especially girls, would fall outside a narrow definition.[131]

The notion of including direct participation in hostilities has been designed to enhance the protection of civilians during armed conflict, and children benefit from the narrowest interpretation. The distinction between civilians and combatants in armed conflict is one of the foundations of international humanitarian law, and the narrower an interpretation of what is considered direct participation provides civilians with protection against direct attack "unless and for such time as they take a direct part in hostilities."[132]

The special protection accorded to children under these provisions is an important consideration. It does not speak to the difficult question of whether it would be a crime to kill a child who is directly participating under AP I or is recruited or taking part under AP II. It would appear that the special protection accorded by these provisions apply when the child has been captured/ surrendered and is in the hands of the adversary, not during combat. In other instances of direct participation a child can be killed just like any other warrior. Once the child has joined an armed group or force, he or she does not maintain the status of a civilian, and under international humanitarian law there appears to be little "special protection" accorded to such a child. This is also the approach taken in recent interpretive guidance on direct participation by the ICRC, where it is considered that "children below the lawful recruitment age may lose protection against direct attack."[133]

Principles of military necessity continue to apply, and warring parties need to take precautions "in determining whether a person is a civilian and, if so, whether that civilian is directly participating in hostilities. In case of doubt, the person must be presumed to be protected against direct attack."[134]

---

131 See, e.g., Keairns, *The Voices of Girl Child Soldiers*. This was also the key point raised by the Special Representative of the Secretary-General for Children and Armed Conflict in her amicus brief to the International Criminal Court. This will be further discussed below. *The Prosecutor V. Thomas Lubanga Dyilo, Written Submission of the United Nations Special Representative of the Secretary-General on Children and Armed Conflict, Submitted in Application of Rule 103 of the Rules of Procedure and Evidence* (18 March 2008).

132 AP II article 13(3). This came up on several occasions during the drafting process, as those who do not take direct part in combat benefit from protections accorded to civilians. See, e.g., discussions at the diplomatic conference in Committee III and the related working groups. "Official Records of the Diplomatic Conference on the Reaffirmation and Development of International Humanitarian Law Applicable in Armed Conflicts, Geneva (1974–1977): Volume XV," 240 and 274. See also Nils Melzer, *Interpretive Guidance on the Notion of Direct Participation in Hostilities* (Geneva: International Committee of the Red Cross, 2009), 20.

133 Ibid., 64.

134 Ibid., 74 (interpretive guidance section VIII).

Finally, it is important to note that the ICRC Study on Customary International Law found evidence of two rules applicable to child recruitment. The first established that children "must not be recruited into armed forces or armed groups", while the second established that children "must not be allowed to take part in hostilities." The ICRC avoided the inclusion of an age into these two provisions, most likely to allow the age to be flexible over time as it has increased and is slowly moving towards 18. The study also separately considered crimes giving rise to individual criminal responsibility, however, in this regard the study only referred to "serious violations of international humanitarian law" without specifying the crime of recruitment and use of children.[135]

2. THE CHILD RIGHTS DOMAIN

The Convention on the Rights of the Child (CRC) and its Optional Protocol on the Involvement of Children in Armed Conflict (OPAC) are innovative instruments. Unlike many other human rights instruments that allow for derogations to be made in situations of public emergency and war, both the CRC and OPAC go beyond: not only do they allow for no derogations be made in times of emergency, they also specifically address the situation of children in armed conflicts.[136]

It can generally be said that the area of protecting children in armed conflicts is a front-runner in spanning the various areas of law.[137] The fact that the CRC continues to apply to armed conflict and emergencies and does not allow for derogations to be made[138] – and that it refers specifically to international humanitarian law in article 38 – serves as a bridge between humanitarian law and international law, maximizing the protection of children in armed conflicts.

---

135 See Rules 136, 137, and 156. Reproduced in Jean-Marie Henckaerts, "The ICRC Study on Customary International Humanitarian Law: Characteristics, Conclusions and Practical Relevance," *The Slovenian Law Revivew* 6 (2009): 225–273, 257–273.

136 See e.g., article 4 of the Covenant on Civil and Political Rights.

137 While discussing the protection of children in armed conflicts, the 25th International Conference of the Red Cross, also recognized in its resolution 9 the development of the CRC and its implications for child recruitment: "[The Conference] expresses its support for the work of the UN Commission on Human Rights regarding the drafting of a Convention on the Rights of the Child and stresses that the protection accorded by the new Convention should be at least the same as that accorded by the Geneva Conventions and the two Additional Protocols." "Protection of Children in Armed Conflicts, Resolution 9," Geneva 23–31 October 1986 25th International Conference of the Red Cross.

138 In the Day of General Discussion on children and armed conflict in 1992, the Committee on the Rights of the Child noted that none of the general provisions in articles 2, 3, and 4 "admit a derogation in time of war or emergency." See *Day of General Discussion on Children in Armed Conflict*, UN Doc. CRC/C/10 (1992), 67. For further details on application of the CRC in armed conflict situations, see Rachel Hodgkin and Peter Newell, *Implementation Handbook for the Convention on the Rights of the Child*, Third Edition (UNICEF, 2008), 660.

Nonetheless, regulating state behaviour towards its own nationals fits well within the international human rights law regime albeit the issue of child recruitment having a strong link to armed conflict situations, whereas in international humanitarian law traditionally issues of state behaviour towards its own nationals would not have been regulated.

Although the OPAC is inherently focused on children involved in armed conflict, it also contains articles that apply to non-conflict situations. The provisions found in these two child rights instruments, and their relevance to child recruitment, are reviewed in the following sections, going through both the drafting history of those provisions and the current practice around their implementation.

2.1. FOCUSING ON CHILD RECRUITMENT THROUGH THE CONVENTION ON THE RIGHTS OF THE CHILD

Article 38 of the Convention on the Rights of the Child, in paragraphs 2–4, provides that:

> 2. States Parties shall take all feasible measures to ensure that persons who have not attained the age of fifteen years do not take a direct part in hostilities.
> 3. States Parties shall refrain from recruiting any person who has not attained the age of fifteen years into their armed forces. In recruiting among those persons who have attained the age of fifteen years but who have not attained the age of eighteen years, States Parties shall endeavour to give priority to those who are oldest.
> 4. In accordance with their obligations under international humanitarian law to protect the civilian population in armed conflicts, States Parties shall take all feasible measures to ensure protection and care of children who are affected by an armed conflict.

The phrasing of article 38 was the most difficult and time-consuming in the drafting of the Convention,[139] at some stages of drafting there were even suggestions that a lack of consensus suggested article 38 should not be included. It is noteworthy that the Convention was drafted on a purely consensual basis, and no provisions of the CRC were taken to a vote at any stage during the drafting. As such, had there not been agreement on the provision in the end, it would have been logical to leave it out. The fact that provisions of the CRC were all agreed to through consensus has important implications in reflecting on

---

139 The drafting of the CRC was carried out by a working group created by the Commission on Human Rights, which crafted the Convention during the 1980s. For more on the drafting history, see United Nations, *Legislative History of the Convention on the Rights of the Child, Volume 1 and 2* (New York and Geneva, 2007).

whether some provisions of the CRC may have risen to the level of international customary law; the drafting of the CRC helped drive the momentum for a number of articles to be considered as international customary law.[140]

Article 1 in the Convention on the Rights of the Child states that 18 is the age of majority, "unless, under the law applicable to the child, majority is attained earlier." The Convention does not define who is a minor, nor does it indicate the age at which a child *should* attain majority. During the drafting, some states argued that age 18 was high, considering that the International Year of the Child had established 15 as the upper age of a child; other delegations preferred the age of 18 to guarantee as broad a protection framework as possible.[141] In light of the need apply the most protective standard, age 18 was agreed upon – offering room for states to develop their own standards within that age limit and giving due regard to other principles of the Convention, including the best interests of the child and non-discrimination.

Until the adoption of the Convention, few legal systems had even considered the question of how to define a child. The Convention itself relies on the general definition of a child as a person under age 18, and it does not specify age limits for any violation other than that in article 38 relevant to child recruitment; minimum ages for employment (article 32); age of criminal responsibility (article 40); and the requirement to make primary education compulsory by implication (article 28).

Although these provisions allow for the age to be set below 18, the Convention's overall protective framework for children up until the age of 18 applies in all cases.[142] In addition, the Committee on the Rights of the Child has consistently requested states to raise the age of majority to 18 in cases when domestic legislation has set a lower age and has reviewed other age limits such as age of criminal responsibility, seeking to increase the age limits.[143]

140 For instance, the Special Court for Sierra Leone included the CRC in its consideration of whether the crime of recruitment and use of children existed in customary international law for purposes of addressing the defence preliminary motion that the Court had no jurisdiction over the case. See *Prosecutor v. Samuel Hinga Norman* no. SCSL-2004-14-AR72(E), 12 (31 May 2004). See also Happold, Matthew, *Child Soldiers in International Law*: Manchester University Press, (2005), 62 and 95.

141 For further background on drafting history for article 1, see United Nations, *Legislative History of the Convention on the Rights of the Child, Volume 1 and 2*, 301–313 (New York and Geneva, 2007).

142 There are other provisions, however, where no age is noted, such as in relation to the minimum age of criminal responsibility in article 40.

143 Hodgkin and Newell, *Implementation Handbook*, 3. See also Human Rights Committee, General Comment 17, the Rights of the Child, article 24 (Thirty-Fifth Session, 1989), UN Doc. HRI/GEN/Rev.1 (1994), 23 and a comprehensive study Don Cipriani, *Children's Rights and the Minimum Age of Criminal Responsibility* *Surrey: Ashgate Publishing, 2009).

2.2. KEY LEGAL CONSIDERATIONS RELEVANT TO SPECIFIC PROVISIONS OF THE CONVENTION ON THE RIGHTS OF THE CHILD

In the drafting deliberations on article 38, which includes child recruitment, the working group engaged in heated discussion around the issue of age, with several attempts by various governments, the ICRC, the Office of the United Nations High Commissioner for Refugees (UNHCR), and international non-governmental organizations to raise the age to 18 for direct participation in hostilities. The states advocating for the age to be increased explicitly to 18, as reflected in the *travaux préparatoires*, included several European countries (Austria, Belgium, Finland, France, Italy, Sweden, Switzerland) a number of Latin American countries (Colombia and Venezuela) and one African country (Algeria).[144] But there was strong opposition to raising the age above 15, including from such states as the Union of Soviet Socialist Republics and the United States of America (USA).

The reservations or declarations filed by states in ratifying the CRC in line with article 51 reflect some of these debates, and while some of them have been titled reservations they are really all declarations that seek to expand the focus of the provision. Several states declared that they would have liked to see a higher age standard or even a categorical prohibition of the use of children in armed conflicts.[145] While such statements may inform the *opinio juris* component of establishing international customary law, the number of states reaching out to make such declarations is relatively small and, as result, they bring no significant legal meaning.[146]

It is important to note in this context, that the African counterpart of the Convention, the African Charter on the Rights and Welfare of the Child, included a broad provision for children under the age of 18 and also broadened to protection against "recruiting any child" in all other provisions: "States Parties to the present Charter shall take all necessary measures to ensure that no child shall take a direct part in hostilities and refrain in particular, from recruiting any child."[147]

---

144 Sharon Detrick et al., *The United Nations Convention on the Rights of the Child: A Guide to the "Travaux Préparatoires"* (Dordrecht: Martinus Nijhoff Publishers, 1992), 502–517.

145 This includes Andorra; Argentina (would have liked the CRC to categorically prohibit the use of children in armed conflict); Austria (will give priority to those who are oldest); Colombia (it would have been preferred to set the age at 18); Ecuador (the minimum age set forth is too low); Germany (the age limit of 15 is incompatible with the provision for the child's best interests in article 3, paragraph 1); Spain (the age limit appears to be insufficient); and Uruguay (domestic law is set at 18).

146 William Schabas. "Reservations to the Convention on the Rights of the Child." *Human Rights Quarterly* 18, no. 2 (1996): 472–491, 480.

147 African Charter on the Rights and Welfare of the Child, adopted in 1990, entered into force 29 November 1999, reprinted in OAU Doc. CAB/LEG/24.9/49 (1990), art. 22(2). See also

There was also some discussion on the issue of direct participation in hostilities, and at one point during the drafting, the Swedish delegation suggested "direct" be deleted in the text to broaden the protection. The proposal was seconded by several delegations who saw it as an improvement over current international humanitarian law,[148] but it was not approved in the end, leaving the Convention to reiterate basically what was already in Additional Protocol I.

The CRC makes reference only to state obligations and does not consider the responsibilities of non-state actors explicitly. Each paragraph of article 38, similar to other provisions of the CRC, refers clearly to the obligations of States parties. Raised in passing by one delegation in the working group, who said that the real problem was "the militarization of children in official, private or informal armies," discussions about non-state parties went no further.[149] States parties could obviously take measures to ensure that children under 15 years old would not be recruited by non-state actors, but the Convention itself places the responsibility, in no uncertain terms, upon states only.

Having said that, the Security Council framework for a monitoring and reporting mechanism aimed at addressing grave violations against children's rights refers to the CRC (as well as the Optional Protocol) and has been used as a point of reference in dealing with non-state actors. Similarly, the CRC has been referred to by the Special Court for Sierra Leone in determining the nature of the customary law obligation, the majority of the Court outlining the need to make reference to international human rights law in addition to international humanitarian law. The majority stated that:[150]

> The widespread recognition and acceptance of the norm prohibiting child recruitment in Additional Protocol II and the CRC provides compelling evidence that the conventional norm entered customary international law well before 1996. The fact that there was not a single reservation to lower the legal obligation under Article 38 of the CRC underlines this, especially if one takes into consideration the fact that Article 38 is one of the very few conventional provisions which can claim universal acceptance.

Steven Freeland, "Child Soldiers and International Crimes – How Should International Law Be Applied?," *New Zealand Journal of Public International Law* 3 (2005): 303–328, 311.

148 Detrick et al., *A Guide to the "Travaux Préparatoires"*, 509.

149 Ibid., 510.

150 See *Prosecutor v. Samuel Hinga Norman: Fourth Defence Preliminary Motion Based on Lack of Jurisdiction (Child Recruitment), para 20 of the decision, see also Amicus Curiae Brief of the United Nations Children's Fund*, Special Court for Sierra Leone, Case No. SCSL-2003-08 SCSL (21 January 2004). See further details in chapter 4 on historical justice. It is noteworthy that the Security Council framework on children and armed conflict and the monitoring and reporting mechanism also lists situations where the state has not ratified the relevant legal instruments, e.g. Somalia, and as a result the standards must at least in part be customary international law.

However, in his dissenting opinion Justice Robertson concluded that the CRC is focused at the negative obligation on governments to avoid recruitment in their national armies. As such, he found the provisions in the CRC were seen to be "a far cry from imposing an international law obligation to prosecute and punish those who enlist child indictees into civil defense forces or militias."[151]

The CRC drafting progression included little substantive discussion on the issue of "forced" or "voluntary" recruitment. On one occasion, the observer for Egypt asked to include a differentiation between "voluntary recruitment" by military schools and obligatory recruitment. However, the topic was never followed up or taken on by other participants. The representative of Algeria introduced an amendment to paragraph 2, which suggested adding the words "against his or her will" in relation to taking direct part in hostilities, but many governments objected to this as against the spirit of the Convention.[152]

2.3. THE OPTIONAL PROTOCOL ON THE INVOLVEMENT OF CHILDREN IN ARMED CONFLICT

The Optional Protocol on the Involvement of Children in Armed Conflict is the most detailed of the instruments dealing with the issue of child recruitment and was negotiated in six working-group sessions between 1995 and 2000. Its main provisions, as stated in articles 1–3, are:

> Article 1
> States Parties shall take all feasible measures to ensure that members of their armed forces who have not attained the age of 18 years do not take a direct part in hostilities.
> Article 2
> States Parties shall ensure that persons who have not attained the age of 18 years are not compulsorily recruited into their armed forces. …
> Article 3, paragraph 2
> Each State Party shall deposit a binding declaration upon ratification of or accession to the present Protocol that sets forth the minimum age at which it will permit voluntary recruitment into its national armed forces and a description of the safeguards it has adopted to ensure that such recruitment is not forced or coerced.[153]

151 *Prosecutor v. Samuel Hinga Norman: Fourth Defence Preliminary Motion Based on Lack of Jurisdiction (Child Recruitment), para 28.*

152 Detrick et al., *A Guide to the "Travaux Préparatoires"*, 506.

153 Optional Protocol to the Convention on the Rights of the Child on the Involvement of Children in Armed Conflict, (2000), articles 1–3. Interestingly, OPAC was developed with a clause that allows states to ratify it as a stand-alone treaty, which allowed ratification by the USA even though not a State party to the CRC. Normally, optional protocols would only be open for signature and ratification by states that have ratified the main treaty. One could also have seen the adoption of the Optional Protocol as an amendment to the CRC itself, as provided for in article 50 of the CRC, in which case it would have been possible to make OPAC truly optional, i.e., there would be no need for consensus to be there but to adopt a

While the first three articles cover the responsibilities of states as outlined above, the next part deals with non-state actors. During the first session of the working group, many expressed hesitation about including provisions for non-state actors as they were "non-parties to the Convention and the Protocol"; at the same time, there were a few proposals to include the responsibilities of non-state actors.[154] Some states did not want to include such provisions because "non-State parties could not be bound by an inter-State treaty"; they maintained that issues related to non-state actors should be dealt with in domestic law.

When the idea was floated that non-state actors should abide by a straight 18 standard (an 18-year age limit for both voluntary and forced recruitment, as well as direct and indirect participation), serious concerns were also raised that this would cause confusion.[155] At the fourth session of the working group, the ICRC provided very important contributions on the question of extending different standards to states and non-state actors. The organization argued that international humanitarian law is based on the principle that parties to conflict must be dealt with on equal footing and therefore obligations should not be imposed on armed groups that are greater than those imposed on states. The ICRC also pointed out that, in international humanitarian law, the fact that one party does not abide by existing standards does not mean that the other party can refuse to apply it.[156]

It was eventually decided that non-state actors should be addressed directly in the Protocol (and not in the preambular paragraph of the Protocol as suggested by one delegation) to provide for criminalization of their actions with a higher standard than that applied to states, as noted in articles 4(1–3) and 5 of the Optional Protocol:

---

standard that provided the maximum protection to children. This was also proposed by the Committee on the Rights of the Child through its vice-chairman at the 5th session of the Working Group. United Nations, *Report of the Working Group on a Draft Optional Protocol to the Convention on the Rights of the Child on Involvement of Children in Armed Conflicts on Its Fifth Session*, UN Doc. E/CN.4/1999/73 (24 March 1999), para 21. Mr. Y Kolosov, vice-chairman of the Committee made the point that the original draft prepared by the Committee had been very simple with a view that it would only change the provision found in article 38. As noted by Mr. Kolosov, "He considered it abnormal that a different degree of protection was provided in the Convention for persons who had attained the age of 15 years and for those of 18 years of age."

154 Such proposals came from the Governments of France, Mexico, and Poland. United Nations, *Report of the Working Group on a Draft Optional Protocol to the Convention on the Rights of the Child on Involvement of Children in Armed Conflicts*, E/CN.4/1995/96s (10 February 1995), para 25.

155 United Nations, *Report of the Working Group on a Draft Optional Protocol to the Convention on the Rights of the Child on Involvement of Children in Armed Conflicts on Its Third Session*, UN Doc. E/CN.4/1997/96 (13 March 1997), 35.

156 ICRC, *Optional Protocol to the Convention on the Rights o the Child on Involvement of Children in Armed Conflicts: Position of the International Committee of the Red Cross*, Fourth session of the working group (1998).

> Article 4
> 1. Armed groups that are distinct from the armed forces of a State should not, under any circumstances, recruit or use in hostilities persons under the age of 18 years.
> 2. States Parties shall take all feasible measures to prevent such recruitment and use, including the adoption of legal measures necessary to prohibit and criminalize such practices.
> 3. The application of the present article shall not affect the legal status of any party to an armed conflict.
>
> Article 5
> Nothing in the present Protocol shall be construed as precluding provisions in the law of a State Party or in international instruments and international humanitarian law that are more conducive to the realization of the rights of the child.

It is important to note the nuanced language of the Protocol referring to the obligation between states and non-state actors, which designates that states "shall" and non-state actors "should." Interestingly, while the shall/should discussion points towards a lower legal standard for non-state actors, the "under any circumstances" as opposed to "all feasible measures" for state actors strengthens the provision. Moreover, the age limit is stricter for non-state actors.

Commentators have claimed that this language weakens the legal obligation for non-state actors by providing only a moral obligation.[157] During the drafting, there was also concern such as that of the Government of Japan's representative, who said the language was unclear, particularly since governments were expected to criminalize certain acts. Subsequently, he stated it was up to signatory states to decide on what measures would be needed in order to implement this provision in the most effective way.[158]

This statement by the Japanese Government reveals a measure of the utility of the provision in that it brings out the fact that even if the legal obligation was weakened regarding by including "should" as part of an international legal obligation, it is still a stronger prohibition. The clear 18-year standard related to age, *vis-à-vis* how children should be treated in the context of activities undertaken by armed groups, allows for recognition of the provision and the issue at the domestic level. As such, when a state prepares implementation legislation for this provision, the Optional Protocol provides the necessary framework to include the prohibition against recruitment of children for both armed forces and armed groups. The provision related to non-state actors in

157 Tiny Vandewiele, *A Commentary on the United Nations Convention on the Rights of the Child: Optional Protocol on the Involvement of Children in Armed Conflicts* (Martinus Nijhoff Publishers, 2006), 42.

158 United Nations, *Report of the Working Group on a Draft Optional Protocol to the Convention on the Rights of the Child on Involvement of Children in Armed Conflicts on Its Sixth Session*, UN Doc. E/CN.4/2000/74 (27 March 2000), para 112.

article 4 on its own for direct application to non-state actors has less legal strength than the remaining provisions aimed at states. The provision nevertheless opens the door for better awareness at the domestic level, both in terms of developing implementing legislation and undertaking advocacy with armed groups in the absence of applicable domestic law.

Some delegations proposed that the Protocol should use the expression "armed conflicts" exclusively and not the word "hostilities," making the point that the word was too vague and did not clearly express the purpose of the Protocol, while the notion of "armed conflict" had a clear definition in international humanitarian law. Other participants preferred the use of "hostilities" for the sake of consistency with the terminology used in article 38(2) of the Convention on the Rights of the Child.[159] The Committee on the Rights of the Child supported the use of "hostilities" as found in the CRC, which is also what was used in the Optional Protocol's final version.[160]

2.4. KEY LEGAL CONSIDERATIONS RELEVANT TO SPECIFIC PROVISIONS OF THE OPTIONAL PROTOCOL

The first difficult question that the working group had to deal with was the issue of age. The very first draft developed during the Committee on the Rights of the Child's Day of General Discussion in 1992 contained very straightforward language. The Committee's draft included two simple articles that stated: "States Parties shall take all feasible measures to ensure that persons who have not attained the age of eighteen years do not take part in hostilities", and "States Parties shall refrain from recruiting any person who has not attained the age of eighteen years into their armed forces."[161]

During the fourth session, the majority of states participating in the working group had accepted the "straight 18" standard.[162] Some states appealed for setting a standard of greater protection since the protocol is optional, but there remained

159 United Nations, *Report of the Working Group on a Draft Optional Protocol to the Convention on the Rights of the Child on Involvement of Children in Armed Conflicts on Its Second Session*, UN Doc. E/CN.4/1996/102 (21 March 1996), para 30.

160 Marta Santos Pais, Rapporteur of the Committee on the Rights of the Child, 17 January 1996.

161 *Committee on the Rights of the Child, Day of General Discussion on Children in Armed Conflict*, (1992).

162 The straight 18 standard refers to the campaign that evolved around the time when the Optional Protocol was being negotiated, under the leadership of the Coalition to Stop the Use of Child Soldiers. It indicated an 18-year age limit, not only for forced recruitment but also for voluntary recruitment, not only for armed forces but also for armed groups, and for both direct and indirect participation. It was the component of the campaign that focused more on the age limit rather than the questions of the type of armed conflict and armed group/force. See Ann Sheppard, "Child Soldiers: Is the Optional Protocol Evidence of an Emerging "Straight-18" Consensus," *International Journal of Children's Rights* 8 (2000): 37–70. For examples and further discussion on the advocacy see Coalition to Stop the Use of Child

several governments that thought the standard for (direct) participation in hostilities should be set at 17 since the real problem was the participation of children under the age of 15. They argued that more emphasis should be put on implementation.[163] Throughout the working group deliberations, statements by the Office of the High Commissioner for Human Rights, UNICEF, the Special Representative on Children and Armed Conflict, and the International Committee of the Red Cross all supported the inclusion of indirect and direct participation and a straight 18 approach.[164]

The age ranges that were finally adopted strengthened the standards. It is important to recognize that the Optional Protocol clearly outlaws the direct participation of children under the age of 18. The language used in the Optional Protocol provides stronger legal force related to forced recruitment under age 18 in using the word "ensure" rather than "shall take all feasible measures," which is the language used for direct participation. OPAC's article 2 is also reinforced by article 2 of the International Labour Organization (ILO) Convention 182 of 1999, which provides that the ILO Convention applies to any child under the age of 18. The substantive provision states that governments will seek to eliminate the worst forms of child labour, including "all forms of slavery or practices similar to slavery, such as the sale and trafficking of children, debt bondage and serfdom and forced or compulsory labour, including forced or compulsory recruitment of children for use in armed conflict."[165]

The next thorny issue was that of direct and indirect participation. There had been several statements made to the effect that in "the field" there is very little distinction between the two, and so the Optional Protocol should "not qualify the participation of children in hostilities." Several governments wanted to include both direct and indirect participation. Yet in the end, the vote went in favour of the smallest common denominator, which determined that only "direct" had to be included.[166]

Soldiers and UNICEF, Guide to the Optional Protocol on the Involvement of Children in Armed Conflict (December 2003).

163 *United Nations, Report of the Working Group on a Draft Optional Protocol to the Convention on the Rights of the Child on Involvement of Children in Armed Conflicts on Its Fourth Session, UN Doc. E/CN.4/1998/102 (23 March 1998), para 22.*

164 *Report of the Working Group on a Draft Optional Protocol to the Convention on the Rights of the Child on Involvement of Children in Armed Conflicts on Its Sixth Session*, UN Doc. E/CN.4/2000/74 (27 March 2000). See also Coalition to Stop the Use of Child Soldiers and UNICEF, Guide to the Optional Protocol on the Involvement of Children in Armed Conflict (December 2003).

165 *ILO Convention No. 182: Worst Forms of Child Labour Convention* (1999). As of 22 February 2013, this instrument has been ratified by 174 states. Holly Cullen, "Does the ILO have a Distinctive Role in the International Legal Protection of Child Soldiers?," *Human Rights & International Legal Discourse* 5: No. 1 (2011): 63–81.

166 See *Report of the Working Group on a Draft Optional Protocol to the Convention on the Rights of the Child on Involvement of Children in Armed Conflicts on Its Sixth Session*, UN Doc. E/CN.4/2000/74 (27 March 2000).

The Optional Protocol was the first instrument to distinguish between compulsory recruitment (in article 2) and voluntary recruitment (article 3). The element of voluntariness firmly integrated in the Optional Protocol by requesting information on safeguards put in place to ensure voluntary recruitment, to be submitted at the same time as a state submits its declaration of age to be applied.

One of the biggest loopholes in the Optional Protocol is that found in article 3(5) where "the requirement to raise the age in paragraph 1 ... does not apply to schools operated by or under the control of the armed forces of the States Parties." At the first session of the working group, various governments made a range of proposals that military schools or training should be allowed for children between ages 15 and 18.[167] These early suggestions, which were not in the end followed, considered that only training would have a sliding scale in age, while the main provisions stood by the age of 18 in recruiting into the armed forces. Had those early suggestions been followed, then the provision for military education would have been the only one allowing for recruitment of children between ages 15 and 18.

Although the discussions on voluntary recruitment and training continued throughout the first several working group sessions, as the bottom line, it is clear that even if the provision on military education does not have an age clause, the *travaux préparatoires* show that states did not intend that training could take place for children below age 15. The general sense was that voluntary recruitment was needed in the age range from 16 and above for school leavers because they looked to the armed forces as an important next step in their career development, and because leaving young adults at that age idle after leaving secondary or high school would not be a beneficial situation. There were also views expressed that in order for 18-year-olds to be able to participate in hostilities they would need to receive training, which would need to take place before they turned 18.[168]

Several lengthy debates followed, and at the sixth and final session several delegations argued that the article on age would not be acceptable unless the language excluded pupils in military schools. These delegations maintained that referring to them in the Protocol or in the article on voluntary recruitment was unnecessary because the purpose of those schools was educational and did not denote recruitment into the armed forces.[169]

---

167 *Report of the Working Group on a Draft Optional Protocol to the Convention on the Rights of the Child on Involvement of Children in Armed Conflicts*, E/CN.4/1995/96s (10 February 1995), paras 27 and 121.

168 See proposals that indicated the necessity of allowing for voluntary recruitment under 18 so as to allow children who have left school to join the military before beginning work, e.g., *Report of the Working Group on a Draft Optional Protocol to the Convention on the Rights of the Child on Involvement of Children in Armed Conflicts on Its Third Session*, UN Doc. E/CN.4/1997/96 (13 March 1997), 31.

169 *Report of the Working Group on a Draft Optional Protocol to the Convention on the Rights of the Child on Involvement of Children in Armed Conflicts on Its Sixth Session*, UN Doc. E/CN.4/2000/74 (27 March 2000). See section H on military schools.

Following the consideration of various proposals in the informal drafting groups, the text of a paragraph on military schools was approved by the working group as a new sub-paragraph 5, followed by the text that was finally adopted:

> The requirement to raise the age in paragraph 1 of the present article does not apply to schools operated by or under the control of the armed forces of the States Parties, in keeping with articles 28 and 29 of the Convention on the Rights of the Child.[170]

3. THE IMPLEMENTATION OF INTERNATIONAL OBLIGATIONS

International standards relevant to the recruitment and use of children need to be followed by legal, administrative, and other measures to ensure the effective implementation and enforcement of the provisions within the national jurisdiction.[171] This section considers how states have integrated the provisions of international law considered above at the national level.

3.1. COMMITTEE ON THE RIGHTS OF CHILD REVIEWS OF OPTIONAL PROTOCOL IMPLEMENTATION MEASURES

To date, efforts to prepare implementing legislation have been ad hoc, and few have covered all the angles necessary to deal with the wide variety of issues. Different legal systems in different countries have resulted in different ways of developing implementing legislation. In some contexts the penal or criminal code has been adjusted, in others it may be a piece of military legislation, and in still others specific pieces of law relevant to the protection of children have incorporated the prohibition of child recruitment.

Reviewing the overall implementation as reported to the Committee on the Rights of the Child through the Optional Protocol provides some insights into how the overall prohibition and criminalization of child recruitment has been handled at the domestic level. While 159 states have ratified the Optional Protocol, as of April 2015 the Committee has reviewed some 90 initial reports relevant to implementing OPAC, followed by concluding observations.[172] In those reviews, the Committee has focused on implementing legislation as an important component. The Committee's guidelines state that "reports should contain information on the legal status of the Optional Protocol in the internal law of the

170 Optional Protocol on Involvement of Children in Armed Conflict, article 3(5).

171 See, e.g., the Optional Protocol, article 6.

172 Status of ratification as of 30 April 2015.

State party, including whether its provisions can be directly invoked before the courts and applied by the national authorities. If internal legislation is required for the application of the Optional Protocol, the State party should indicate the legal amendments adopted."[173]

In addition to the legislative considerations, the Committee has considered issues relevant to data collection, child soldiers seeking asylum, killing and maiming of children, reparations, extraterritorial application of the Optional Protocol including the requirement for double criminality, and implementation of action for the release and reintegration of child soldiers, along with mechanisms in place to ensure intra-ministerial coordination.[174]

Crucially, the Committee has also noted the importance of birth registration as a primary preventive measure for child recruitment.[175]

The rule of law is very dependent on a judiciary that can deal with the transition. Depending on the context, there may be an existing judiciary that needs to interpret new pieces of legislation and/or political processes and approaches and integrate all of that into judicial proceedings. But it may also involve the creation of new judiciary institutions, some of which are temporary in nature (transitional), such as in the case of Timor-Leste.[176] Some have more

---

173 Committee on the Rights of the Child, *Revised Guidelines Regarding Initial Reports to Be Submitted by States Parties under Article 8, Paragraph 1, of the Optional Protocol to the Convention on the Rights of the Child on Involvement of Children in Armed Conflict*, UN Doc. CRC/C/OPAC/2 (19 October 2007).

174 See concluding observation for Australia, paragraph 31, or Sudan concluding observations paragraph 8, where the Committee also recommended that the State party allocate additional funds to the National Committee for Child Welfare. *Report of the Working Group on a Draft Optional Protocol to the Convention on the Rights of the Child on Involvement of Children in Armed Conflicts on Its Sixth Session*, UN Doc. E/CN.4/2000/74 (27 March 2000).and Committee on the Rights of the Child, *Consideration of Reports Submitted by States Parties under Article 8 of the Optional Protocol to the Convention on the Rights of the Child on the Involvement of Children in Armed Conflict, Concluding Observations: Australia* UN Doc. CRC/OPAC/AUS/CO/1 (11 July 2012).

175 The issue of birth registration has been noted in contexts where it has been particularly important for strategies to prevent child recruitment, such as in the contexts of Sierra Leone and the Sudan. See, e.g., Committee on the Rights of the Child, *Consideration of Reports Submitted by States Parties under Article 8 of the Optional Protocol to the Convention on the Rights of the Child on the Involvement of Children in Armed Conflict, Concluding Observations: Sudan* CRC/C/OPAC/SDN/CO/1 (8 October 2010).

176 The Special Representative of the UN Transitional Administration in East Timor established the Special Panels in the District Court in Dili, which held exclusive jurisdiction over murder and sexual offences committed, and universal jurisdiction over genocide, war crimes, crimes against humanity, and torture. (Section 2 on Jurisdiction). A Serious Crimes Unit was established under the Office of the Prosecutor of Timor-Leste to investigate and prosecute these six categories of crimes. The Special Panel for Serious Crimes was made up of three judges: two international judges and one East Timorese judge. United Nations Transitional Administration in East Timor, *On the Establishment of Panels with Exclusive Jurisdiction over Serious Criminal Offences* UN Doc. UNTAET/REG/200/15 (6 June 2000). For further analysis, see M. Cherif Bassiouni, *Crimes Against Humanity: Historical Evolution and Cotemporary Application* (New York: Cambridge University Press, 2011).

capacity than others, but considering the countries that are most seriously implicated by child recruitment, it would be fair to generalize that not only is there a fairly low capacity among judiciary, there is also a lack of child-sensitive procedures and expertise in the judiciary.

The status of the judiciary's capacities is not the only factor that has an impact, especially in the domains of child rights and child protection. Law enforcement officials, armed forces and groups, national child protection authorities, and, particularly in the case of children's issues, social workers – all of these actors play an important role in upholding the rule of law and predictability of provisions related to child rights at the domestic level. For child protection practitioners, the systems approach plays a vital role in linking and building up a system to uphold the rules related to recruitment and use of children by armed forces and groups. For these purposes, it is very common for states to develop plans of action and national implementation models that allow for consistent follow-up.

The Committee rarely makes reference to any framework other than the Optional Protocol in support of putting an end to child recruitment. In the past couple of years, however, some references can be found to the Paris Principles and the monitoring and reporting mechanism of the Security Council. However, these references remain infrequent and inconsistent.[177]

3.2. KEY LEGAL CONSIDERATIONS RELEVANT TO EFFORTS BY STATES TO IMPLEMENT PROVISIONS REGARDING CHILD RECRUITMENT

As noted above, there are many shortcomings in implementing legislation relevant to child recruitment.

---

177 The reference to the Paris Principles is not systematic but appears, for instance, in the concluding observations relevant to Morocco. In the concluding observations relevant to Yemen, there is extensive reference to the non-compliance of both the government and non-state actors in Yemen, with strong links to the monitoring and reporting mechanism. Such links are completely lacking in the review of the situation in Jordan, however, showing lack of understanding of how these different mechanisms can benefit each other. See Committee on the Rights of the Child, *Concluding observations on the report submitted by Morocco under article 8, paragraph 1, of the Optional Protocol to the Convention on the Rights of the Child on the involvement of children in armed conflict*, UN Doc. CRC/C/OPAC/MAR/CO/1 (13 November 2014), *Concluding observations on the report submitted by Yemen under article 8, paragraph 1, of the Optional Protocol to the Convention on the Rights of the Child on the involvement of children in armed conflict.* UN Doc. CRC/C/OPAC/YEM/CO/1 (26 February 2014), and Committee on the Rights of the Child, *Concluding observations on the report submitted by Jordan under article 8, paragraph 1, of the Optional Protocol to the Convention on the Rights of the Child on the involvement of children in armed conflict*, UN Doc. CRC/C/OPAC/JOR/CO/1 (7 July 2014).

One area of concern is related to the distinction between armed groups and forces, and making the law applicable not just to recruitment by armed forces. This is the case with the Sudan Armed Forces Act (2007), which was the first law in the Sudan to recognize the issue of child recruitment,[178] although Sudan's Child Act (2010) provides that "there shall be prohibited the recruitment of children in the armed forces, or in armed groups, or employment thereof to participate in war actions."[179] Likewise, in the context of Sierra Leone, while relevant legislation prohibits both forced and voluntary recruitment, it only applies to recruitment into armed forces.[180]

Some states have simply introduced legislation reflecting their own intake into military services. The Chinese Military Service Law, for instance, provides for voluntary recruitment from the age of 17: "To meet the needs of the armed forces and on the principle of voluntary participation, male and female citizens who have not yet reached 18 years of age by December 31 of a certain year may be enlisted for active service."[181] These pieces of legislation do not necessarily deal with the question of whether there may be armed groups or individuals that recruit children, nor the question of moving beyond the prohibition of child recruitment to making sure the law recognizes it as a crime.[182] In some situations

---

178 The Concluding Observations of the Committee noted that "while the Armed Forces Act (2007) criminalizes the recruitment of persons who do not meet the conditions of recruitment, including the minimum age of 18 years, the State party's penal legislation does not provide for a sanction in the case of the recruitment of children and their use in hostilities by armed groups who are not part of the State party's military." Committee on the Rights of the Child, *Consideration of Reports Submitted by States Parties under Article 8 of the Optional Protocol to the Convention on the Rights of the Child on the Involvement of Children in Armed Conflict, Concluding Observations: Sudan*, (8 October 2010).

179 The Child Act, Sudan (2010), para 43(1). Similar provisions exist in the Philippines, e.g., the Philippines: Republic Act No. 9231: Act Providing for the Elimination of the Worst Forms of Child Labor and Affording Stronger Protection for the Working Child, amending for this purpose republic Act No. 7610, as amended, otherwise known as the "special Protection of Children against Child Abuse, Exploitation and Discrimination Act, The Philippines (December 19, 2003).

180 See Committee on the Rights of the Child, *Consideration of Reports Submitted by States Parties under Article 8 of the Optional Protocol to the Convention on the Rights of the Child on the Involvement of Children in Armed Conflict, Concluding Observations: Sierra Leone* CRC/C/OPAC/SLE/CO/1 (14 October 2010). The Republic of Sierra Leone Recruitment Act (2006) and the Child Rights Act (2007) prohibit the voluntary and compulsory recruitment of children into the State party's armed forces.

181 Military Service Law of the People's Republic of China, China (Adopted in 1984 and amended in 1998), article 12. The Pakistan legislation also states age of recruitment at 17 with no compulsory conscription. See Pakistan: The Pakistan National Service Ordinance. Another example is the Israeli law, which provides for conscription from 18 but registration/call-up begins at 17, and voluntary recruitment is allowed from 17 (Israel Defence Service Law 5746. Age 18 in the Canadian law (National Defence Act).

182 The Committee consistently comments on these issues; see, for instance Committee on the Rights of the Child, *Concluding observations on the initial report of China submitted under article 8, paragraph 1, of the Optional Protocol to the Convention on the Rights of the Child on the involvement of children in armed conflict, adopted by the Committee at its sixty-fourth session*, (29 October 2013) and Committee on the Rights of the Child, *Concluding observations*

that issue has been addressed in laws that are part of implementing the Rome Statute provisions at the national level.

Despite legislation criminalizing child recruitment, states have not made efforts to prosecute offenders based on this crime. In principle, the legislation itself should have a preventive effect, but even in countries where child recruitment has been widespread and the laws are in place, no efforts have been made by states to prosecute offenders.[183] In terms of considering the age in the legislation addressing child recruitment as a crime, some countries have followed the standard of 15 years old[184] provided for in international criminal law, while others have enhanced the standards, for example, by increasing the age to 18 though limiting the applicability of the legislation to situations of armed conflict.[185] Other countries have also included age ranges, but added the age range of 18 years for non-state actors as per the Optional Protocol.[186]

While the vast majority of states that have ratified OPAC have put voluntary recruitment at the age of 18, some states still allow for recruitment at age 17. The

on the initial report of Uzbekistan submitted under article 8, paragraph 1, of the Optional Protocol to the Convention on the Rights of the Child on the involvement of children in armed conflict, adopted by the Committee at its sixty-third session, (8 July 2013).

183 For instance, in Sri Lanka, where Penal Code penalizes the engagement and use of children in armed conflicts in a comprehensive way, no efforts have been made to make use of these provisions through prosecution. Penal Code (Amendment) Act, No. 16 of 2006, Sri Lanka (24 April 2006).

184 See, e.g., United Kingdom, International Criminal Court Act of 2001: "conscripting or enlisting children under the age of fifteen years into armed forces or groups or using them to participate actively in hostilities." Jurisdiction applies only to British nationals, UK residents, or UK residents subject to UK jurisdiction. See also comments made by the Committee on the Rights of the Child in considering the second report of the United States of America, in which the Committee recommends that the US amend the 2008 Child Soldiers Accountability Act in order to criminalize the recruitment and use of children in armed conflict up to the age of 18 years as currently the law criminalizes the recruitment of children under the age of 15 years. Committee on the Rights of the Child, *Concluding observations on the second report of United States of America submitted under article 8, paragraph 1, of the Optional Protocol to the Convention on the Rights of the Child on the involvement of children in armed conflict, adopted by the Committee at its sixty-second session*, (26 June 2013), paras 28–29.

185 General Civil Penal Code No 54, Norway (28 June 2002). The Committee has also consistently pushed states to increase the age to 18 in legislation addressing individual criminal responsibility, going beyond the provisions of the Rome Statute, and for the age of 18 not only to apply to armed groups, but also armed forces. See, e.g., Concluding Observations relevant to Australia 2012, para 21, where the Committee noted with concern that national legislation only criminalizes the recruitment of children under the age of 15 into the armed forces. Furthermore, the Committee is concerned that the criminalization of the acts prohibited therein is limited to recruitment in the context of an armed conflict and does not apply in peace time. Committee on the Rights of the Child, *Consideration of Reports Submitted by States Parties under Article 8 of the Optional Protocol to the Convention on the Rights of the Child on the Involvement of Children in Armed Conflict, Concluding Observations: Australia*, (11 July 2012).

186 The Australian Criminal Code Act of 1995 and as amended in 2007 provides a series of criminal penalties for individuals who used, conscripted, or enlisted children under 15 into national armed forces or children under 18 into other forces.

Committee on the Rights of the Child has encouraged these states to follow the majority of signatories and increase the age of voluntary recruitment to 18.[187]

The lack of universal jurisdiction is a shortcoming, and very few laws allow for prosecution of offenders who carry out the crime of recruitment and use of children outside the jurisdiction of the country where the law was developed. This means that if a national of country X carries out child recruitment in country Y, that person might go free if arrested in country X because it was not a crime that reached beyond the borders of the country. This is a debate that is currently taking place in the context of the conflict in Syria, where there are reports of adult recruitment taking place by various actors, possibly including private military companies, for people from other countries (including European countries) to join the fighting within Syria. Because child recruitment is widespread among the armed groups within the country, unless the country were to have universal jurisdiction over the crime of child recruitment these adults could not be charged for these crimes under domestic law after they return home.

The Committee on the Rights of the Child has consistently requested the States parties to ensure extraterritorial jurisdiction for "these crimes when they are committed by or against a person who is a citizen of or has other links with the State Party, including by entering into multilateral and bilateral agreements for extradition."[188] There are some exceptions, and some countries have developed legislation with an extraterritorial reach, such as the United Kingdom (UK) and the USA. The age of voluntary recruitment in the United States is 17, while the country's Child Soldiers Accountability Act criminalizes the recruitment and use of children under the age of 15. It is a strong piece of legislation in that it provides for universal jurisdiction over any person who has committed the crime of recruiting or using child soldiers.[189] The USA has also been progressive in adopting a Child Soldier Prevention Act, which allows for restrictions on

[187] See, e.g., Concluding Observations on Australia and India: Committee on the Rights of the Child, *Consideration of Reports Submitted by States Parties under Article 8 of the Optional Protocol to the Convention on the Rights of the Child on the Involvement of Children in Armed Conflict, Concluding Observations: Australia*, UN Doc. CRC/OPAC/AUS/CO/1 (11 July 2012), para 18 and Committee on the Rights of the Child, *Concluding observations on the report submitted by India under article 8, paragraph 1, of the Optional Protocol to the Convention on the Rights of the Child on the involvement of children in armed conflict*, (7 July 2014), para 9.

[188] See, e.g., concluding observations on the Philippines, UK, Korea, USA, Chile, Kuwait, Bulgaria, Qatar, Spain, Syria, France, Guatemala, Costa Rica, Kazakhstan, Vietnam, El Salvador, and Switzerland. Two specific examples are: *Committee on the Rights of the Child, Consideration of Reports Submitted by States Parties under Article 8 of the Optional Protocol to the Convention on the Rights of the Child on the Involvement of Children in Armed Conflict, Concluding Observations: The Philippines*, UN Doc. CRC/C/OPAC/PHL/CO/1 (15 July 2008) and *Committee on the Rights of the Child, Consideration of Reports Submitted by States Parties under Article 8 of the Optional Protocol to the Convention on the Rights of the Child on the Involvement of Children in Armed Conflict, Concluding Observations: Spain*, UN Doc. CRC/C/OPAC/ESP/CO/1 (17 October 2007).

[189] Child Soldier Accountability Act of 2008 (United States, Public Law 110–340), para 2442(c(1)).

military assistance to governmental or government-supported armed groups that recruit and use child soldiers.[190] The UK legislation applies to acts committed "outside the United Kingdom by a United Kingdom national or a United Kingdom resident."[191] One important shortcoming in situations of extraterritorial application of the provisions is that of double or dual criminality. Most states require not only that the suspect can be considered to have broken the law of the country where the person is being extradited to, but also that there is a similar law in the extraditing country.[192]

Few pieces of implementing legislation pay any attention to the issue of direct participation, although countries that face child recruitment tend to have some provisions in this regard. In Portugal, language regarding "active use" of children has been introduced without defining what it means.[193] The Colombian Penal Code, for example, was amended to criminalize recruitment and use of children that includes both "direct and indirect" hostilities or armed actions.[194] A particular strength of this law is its great detail regarding reintegration of former child soldiers. The issue of reintegration is also dealt with in the Sudan Child Act.[195]

The Australian legislation has a shortcoming with respect to the "direct participation" of children who have voluntarily enlisted at the age of 17, in that the Defence Instructions 2008 only prevent children under age 18 from involvement in hostilities to the extent that the prohibition does not adversely impact on the conduct of operations.[196]

---

190 Child Soldier Prevention Act of 2008 (United States, Title IV of Public Law 110–457).

191 International Criminal Court Act, United Kingdom (2001), section 51(2).

192 This was considered by the Committee in its review of the situation in the Russian Federation. Not only was the Committee concerned with respect to double criminality as a requirement for extradition, it was also concerned that the offences under the Optional Protocol do not explicitly provide for extraterritorial jurisdiction and that a more general provision "against the interests of the State party" is considered to cover such situations. Committee on the Rights of the Child, *Concluding observations on the report submitted by the Russian Federation under article 8, paragraph 1, of the Optional Protocol to the Convention on the Rights of the Child on the involvement of children in armed conflict*, UN Doc. CRC/C/OPAC/RUS/CO/1 (25 February 2014), paras 18–19.

193 See Committee on the Rights of the Child, *Concluding observations on the report submitted by Portugal under article 8, paragraph 1, of the Optional Protocol to the Convention on the Rights of the Child on the involvement of children in armed conflict*, (24 February 2014), paras 14 and 15.

194 Colombian Penal Code, article 162.

195 The Sudan Child Act 2010 provides in article 44(1): "The competent body of demobilization and re-accommodation shall guarantee the design of special programmes for the demobilization of Child soldiers, and that in co-ordination with the bodies concerned (military, security institutions and the armed groups) for social and economical re-accommodation, and shall take a special care of the demobilized Child soldiers specially those having special needs, during their presence at demobilization centres. (2) The competent body shall rehabilitate the child, who is the victim of armed conflicts, psychologically and mentally and re-accommodate him socially and economically."

196 See Australia concluding observations 2012, para 13, and Sierra Leone concluding observations 2010.

UK legislation excludes deployment of children to take part in hostilities.[197] Nonetheless, the country "inadvertently" sent children age 17 to the front lines in Iraq and Afghanistan, indicating that there were insufficient measures in place to manage this aspect in a context where children are allowed to join the armed forces at age 16.[198] Another contradictory situation prevails in the UK context, whereby 16-year-olds may commit to staying in the armed forces until they are 22, placing them in a situation where they might end up taking direct part in hostilities, based on circumstances in which they were not adults when they made that decision and may not have been sufficiently informed about the consequences of their decision.

3.3. FROM PROHIBITION TO CRIME: CONSIDERATIONS OF CHILD RECRUITMENT AS A CRIME UNDER INTERNATIONAL CUSTOMARY LAW

During the drafting of the Statute of the Special Court for Sierra Leone, in 2000, the UN Secretary-General expressed his view that characterization of the provision related to child recruitment in the Rome Statute as customary law was doubtful, and that he wanted to focus on the crimes of abduction and forced recruitment for purposes of addressing the crime in the context of Sierra Leone.[199] He argued that "while the prohibition on child recruitment has by now acquired a customary international law status, it is far less clear whether it is customarily recognized as a war crime entailing the individual criminal responsibility of the accused." He further elaborated that "owing to the doubtful customary nature of the ICC Statutory crime which criminalizes the conscription or enlistment of children under the age of 15, whether forced or 'voluntary', the crime which is included in article 4 (c) of the Statute of the Special Court is not the equivalent of the ICC provision."[200]

The Special Court provision related to raising individual criminal responsibility for child recruitment reads as follows: "abduction and forced recruitment of children under the age of 15 years into armed forces or groups for the purpose of using them to participate actively in hostilities." This language emphasizes abduction and forced recruitment. Voluntary recruitment was not

197 The Armed Forces Act (United Kingdom, 2006).

198 BBC News, "Under-18s Were Deployed to Iraq," 4 February 2007, http://news.bbc.co.uk/2/hi/6328771.stm.

199 *Report of the Secretary-General on the Establishment of a Special Court for Sierra Leone*, UN Doc. S/2000/915 (4 October 2000), 17–18. See also Wells for a background on addressing crimes against child soldiers at the SCSL. Sarah L. Wells, "Crimes Against Child Soldiers in Armed Conflict Situations: Applications and Limits of International Humanitarian Law," *Tulane Journal of International and Comparative Law* 12 (2004): 287–306.

200 *Report of the Secretary-General on the Establishment of a Special Court for Sierra Leone*, UN Doc. S/2000/915 (4 October 2000), para 21.

considered to be a crime, and the question remained if, in fact, such recruitment would rise to the level of triggering individual criminal responsibility. It is also important to keep in mind that this provision requires a direct link between the act of recruitment "for purposes" of using children. In other words, there is only one crime in question, and the act of abduction or forced recruitment alone would not be considered a crime.

However, the perspective of the Secretary-General doubting the customary law value of the provision was overturned by the Security Council, which requested that the draft agreement between the UN and the Government of Sierra Leone, along with the Statute of the Court, be adjusted "as expeditiously as possible ... as indicated in the attached annex."[201] By this, the Security Council meant that the abduction and forced recruitment of children had to be included as one of the crimes in the Statute of the Special Court.

This issue was further considered by the Special Court, and the Appeals Chamber of the Special Court for Sierra Leone (SCSL) ruled that "prior to November 1996, the prohibition on child recruitment had crystallized as customary international law, as demonstrated by the widespread recognition and acceptance of the norm prohibiting child recruitment in these international instruments, reiterated in the 1990 African Charter on the Rights and Welfare of the Child."[202] It was important for the Court to establish that the crime had been part of international customary law prior to 1996, as it would otherwise have been considered an ex post facto law and the prosecution would request a human rights violation of the *nullum crimen sine lege* rule.[203]

This ruling was in response to the argument by the defence that recruitment of children was prohibited but not criminalized at the time of the crimes alleged in the indictment.[204] The majority of the Chamber focused on how customary law had formed through the widespread ratification and implementation of the Convention on the Rights of the Child and the Optional Protocol on the Involvement of Children in Armed Conflict. The fact that these instruments asked States parties to take measures to implement the instruments, and in the case of the Optional Protocol asked for the behaviour to be criminalized, demonstrated the fact that customary law had emerged. Also, a wide range of countries having introduced legislation for a long period of time demonstrated that the practice among states to criminalize the recruitment and use of children

201 United Nations Security Council, *Letter Dated 22 December 2000 from the President of the Security Council Addressed to the Secretary-General* S/2000/1234 (22 December 2000).

202 Prosecutor V. Samuel Hinga Norman, Moinina Fofana and Allieu Kondewa, Special Court for Sierra Leone, Case No. SCSL-2004-14-AR72(E)(31 May 2004). The judgement relied heavily upon customary international law, drawing on the Amicus Brief of UNICEF.

203 Ibid., see, in particular,the Appeals Chamber considerations in the judgement paras 25–53.

204 For an in-depth analysis of this case, see Matthew Happold, "International Humanitarian Law, War Criminality and Child Recruitment: The Special Court for Sierra Leone's Decision in Prosecutor v. Samuel Hinga Norman," *Leiden Journal of International Law* 18, no. 02 (2005): 283–297.

was seen as an important element to consider when determining whether customary law had emerged.

Justice Robertson, in his dissenting opinion, focuses on the fact that while child recruitment has been criminalized, no case has ever been prosecuted under an international or a domestic jurisdiction. He further concludes that in terms of customary law an obligation on states and armed groups to avoid recruitment and use of children had emerged at the time, but that it was not a criminal offence, either in Sierra Leone or under international criminal law. One of his main arguments focuses on the fact that it was not predictable that child recruitment would be an offence and that there was a lack of actual practice to develop domestic legislation that criminalized child recruitment prior to 1996.

The majority of the Chamber nonetheless concluded that child recruitment was a crime leading to individual criminal responsibility, but as we see from the above, the fact that the Chamber was not united shows that it was not immediately clear and that the decision could have gone in either direction.

CONCLUSION

Child recruitment went from being a non-issue in post-World War II legal developments to a highly sophisticated area of law over the past 30–40 years and continues to advance, with a focus on application and implementation. Interestingly, it is an issue that has spanned across several legal domains, including international humanitarian law, international human rights law and international labour law.

While human rights law generally holds the option to be derogated from in the context of armed conflict, there is no such provision with respect to children's rights under the CRC and its Optional Protocols. These bodies of law provide complementary approaches, and the different bodies of law have their own avenues for addressing accountability.[205] This in itself is an unusual development in the international legal arena, providing for complex legal considerations around the application of the law in armed conflict, in peacetime, and in situations that are low-intensity conflicts in between peace and conflict. Importantly, the CRC and the OPAC continue to apply throughout these

205 Human rights law provides for avenues of address through the treaty bodies that have been established to monitor implementation, such as the Committee on the Rights of the Child, while international humanitarian law generally relies on implementation through criminal law. There has also been an increase in approaches that combine these two bodies of law in seeking to address the situation, such as through commissions of inquiry. For broader consideration around the concurrent application of human rights and humanitarian law, see Jean-Marie Henckaerts, "Concurrent Application of International Human Rights Law and International Humanitarian Law: Victims in Search of a Forum," *Human Rights and International Legal Discourse* 1 (2007): 95–124.

situations, providing for a clear minimum of applicable standards even in situations that are not covered by international humanitarian law.[206]

While states have wanted to be careful in providing for a standard that "should" be applicable to non-state actors, at the same time they have made that standard more strict than what is applicable to states themselves – clearly indicating that it is prohibited behaviour under international law. Even if there is significant practice behind these provisions as far as non-state actors are concerned, traditionally, non-state actors strictly speaking do not contribute to the formation of international customary law.[207] However, considering that states apply the law in negotiations with non-state actors does make a stronger argument for some type of involvement of non-state actors in the development of customary law. Nevertheless, the fact that the standards are different for states and non-state actors does present a problem, including at the level of considering how implementing legislation is prepared to accurately capture the differences. Potentially, the differences could also present a problem in negotiating the release of children in situations where both armed forces and armed groups recruit children, yet different standards may apply.

Although implementing legislation still has many shortcomings in most contexts, many states are making efforts to fill the gaps, and with the monitoring efforts being conducted through the Committee on the Rights of the Child, there is focused advocacy highlighting to states those deficiencies and making recommendations for how to address them.

The Committee has a very important role to play in making the basic prohibition of child recruitment a reality. But the fact that the Committee has little capacity and is severely under-resourced comes through in its concluding observations. Issues are not systematically addressed, and although there have been improvements in the past couple of years with some early signs of recognition of other initiatives, links are rarely made to broader legal and policy debates and other elements of transitional justice.

The law is alive and developing, strengthening the prohibition of child recruitment and becoming more detailed through practice and national developments in domestic legislation focused on the ultimate goal of eliminating all use of children by armed forces and groups. It is also encouraging that there has been a steady increase of state ratifications of the Optional Protocol.

Overall, the age for voluntary recruitment by armed forces appears to settle at 16. Among the total OPAC constituency, some 90 states (60 per cent of those

---

206 See also the standard applied through the Security Council framework on monitoring and reporting in the chapter 4 on historical justice.

207 In addition to evolving practice on this issue, there are some authors who have developed new ways of considering the contribution of non-state actors in the form of quasi-custom. See further Anthea Roberts and Sandesh Sivakumaran, "Lawmaking by Nonstate Actors: Engaging Armed Groups in the Creation of International Humanitarian Law," *Yale Journal of International Law* 37, no. 107–152 (2012) 149.

that have ratified) have placed voluntary recruitment at age 18, while some 35 states have put it at 17, many of them mentioning 17 as an exception with parental consent. This means that some 125 states have adopted a higher standard than legally necessary, indicating that the standard is constantly being pushed towards 18 for both forced and voluntary recruitment out of a total of 150 states that have ratified OPAC.

Due to the "persistent objectors," and the fact that the training provisions in OPAC leave the door wide open to allow children in military schools, it will take considerable effort to raise the age of voluntary recruitment to 18 around the globe as an absolute standard, particularly as related to recruitment into the armed forces of a state.

At the national level, the recruitment and use of children continues to be a sensitive issue, often fraught with political considerations. Children might be in the ranks of certain armed groups, but not with the government, and can therefore be used as part of political leverage to show the relatively stronger adherence with international law of the government as opposed to the armed group(s). Apart from those that deal with individual criminality, few laws pay attention to the fact that non-state actors may also be recruiting children, and that this should be criminalized. While today's conflicts rage mostly within countries, the recruitment trends and movement of people to fight the wars travel across borders, which is why the extraterritoriality of the legislation related to child recruitment is important. At the domestic level, due to the sensitivity of the issue, there are few prosecutions of alleged offenders, leaving legislation ineffective or the potential of the impact of the legislation not taken to its fullest.

With respect to the notion of "direct participation," the law leaves open some considerable questions. Not only is it a complex concept, the drafters of the various conventions have decided to use it – or not to use it, as is the case in AP II – in different ways. There is also little application of this concept because states have not prosecuted individuals based on their legislation, and the main debate on its meaning has been between lawyers at the international level seeking to promote their various interests.

However, it is important that for purposes of law there is a clear distinction between those children who are directly participating, and thereby become legitimate targets in the way that has been defined above, and children who are in different roles associated with armed groups and forces. Both groups of children have been wrongfully recruited, but the two groups of children deserve different forms of protection.

International law has been more clearly defined and designed to create legal obligations for states relevant to child recruitment and the direct participation of children in armed conflict, and these bodies of law have also been careful in providing legal obligations for non-state actors, indicating that they are bound by these provisions. When it comes to forced recruitment, a tougher standard is evident than for voluntary recruitment and direct participation. The trend, beginning with OPAC setting a standard of 18 years along with the ILO Convention 182, has continued to gain strength over the past decade.

How children have been recruited does not feature very strongly in international human rights and humanitarian law. It is nonetheless very clearly distinguished in activities undertaken by armed forces, as distinct from those undertaken by armed groups. States have made sure to include provisions that allow for voluntary recruitment for purposes of their armed forces, and also through other forms of military education. However, for purposes of distinguishing between forced and voluntary recruitment by non-state actors, the law is not very informative and only becomes clearly distinguished in international criminal law and the practice of the International Criminal Court.

In moving from child recruitment being prohibited under international law towards child recruitment being recognized as a crime under international law, the test provided through the considerations of the Special Court for Sierra Leone leaves the question unanswered as to whether the crime of child recruitment at the time was covered by international customary law. Some years have passed since then, and it could more likely be considered the case now since the adoption of the Rome Statute. However, governments have failed to consistently develop implementing legislation that criminalizes the recruitment and use of children.

Chapter 3 proceeds to discuss the detailed aspects related to how these provisions have been adapted and interpreted in the context of international criminal justice.

CHAPTER 3

CHILD RECRUITMENT AND CRIMINAL JUSTICE: THE *LUBANGA* CASE

"I want to take my baby home. I want my parents to help me with him, but am not sure what will happen when I get home."

INTRODUCTION

The criminal justice element of transitional justice is a call to punish leaders of previous regimes and individuals for their wrongdoing. Criminal justice is often what people immediately relate to when speaking of transitional justice. Prosecutions aim to ensure that those responsible for committing crimes are tried in accordance with international standards of fair trial and, where appropriate, punished for crimes carried out.[208]

Key legal questions that are considered in chapter 3 include:

- Considering the current state of the art in turning the conscriptions ("forced") and enlistment ("voluntary") of children for use to participate actively in hostilities into an international crime, what are some of the implications of the recent *Lubanga* judgement?
- What is the role of criminal justice more broadly in bringing about change in the situation of children who are being conscripted and enlisted?

This chapter focuses on international criminal justice because it is the arena where the most detailed developments have taken place with respect to case law. International criminal justice from a post-conflict perspective has its roots in the Nuremberg trials, which brought about a substantial change in considerations of accountability, moving from collective to individual justice and from national to international processes.[209] This was not to prioritize one method over another, but it was a new phenomenon at the time.

208 See Teitel, Transitional Justice, 7.

209 Telford Taylor, *The Anatomy of the Nuremberg Trials – A Personal Memoir* (New York: Alfred A. Knopf, Inc., 1992), 100.

A critical aspect of criminal justice is the concept of the presumption of innocence and a crime having been committed "beyond reasonable doubt."[210] Criminal justice in any jurisdiction is not just about the rights of the victim, but also about the rights of the alleged perpetrator; hence, this chapter aims to carefully consider the different perspectives and prudently weigh the arguments. This is also why it is so important that criminal law is predictable and specific, and that those who are in place to implement that law are well prepared to do so.[211]

In 2006, the first arrest warrant was issued by the International Criminal Court, following determination that there were reasonable grounds for believing that Lubanga was responsible for the war crime of conscripting, enlisting, and using children under the age of 15 to participate actively in hostilities.[212] The decision on the confirmation of the charges was issued in January 2007, and the trial began in January 2009.[213] In the two years and four months that followed, the Court heard 67 witnesses in 204 days of hearings. The verdict was rendered in March 2012, finding Lubanga guilty of the crimes he had been charged with, followed by a sentence for 14 years in July 2012.[214] In August 2012, the Court issued its decision on the principles and procedures to be applied to reparations.[215] The verdict and the sentence were confirmed by the Appeals Chamber on 1 December 2014.[216]

The study of the *Lubanga* case offered in this chapter aims to reveal whether the law has been applied in the way that it appears to have been designed, as

---

210 Article 66 of the Rome Statute on the presumption of innocence states that: "1. Everyone shall be presumed innocent until proved guilty before the Court in accordance with the applicable law; 2. The onus is on the Prosecutor to prove the guilt of the accused; and 3. In order to convict the accused, the Court must be convinced of the guilt of the accused beyond reasonable doubt." See also Rosalyn C. E. Roberts, "The Lubanga Trial Chamber's Assessment of Evidence in Light of the Accused's Right to the Presumption of Innocence," *Journal of International Criminal Justice* 10 (2012): 923–943.

211 Matthew Happold, "Children Participating in Armed Conflict and International Criminal Law," *Human Rights & International Legal Discourse* 5: No. 1 (2011): 82–100.

212 *The Prosecutor v. Thomas Lubanga Dyilo*, Warrant of arrest, ICC-01/04-01/06-37 ICC (10 February 2006).

213 *The Prosecutor v. Thomas Lubanga Dyilo: Decision on the Confirmation of Charges*, International Criminal Court, Case No. ICC-01/04-01/06 (29 January 2007), and *The Prosecutor v. Thomas Lubanga Dyilo: Document Containing the Charges, Article 61(3)(a)*, International Criminal Court, Case No. ICC-01/04-01/06, Reference ICC-01/04-01/06-356-Anx2 ICC (28 August 2006).

214 *The Prosecutor v. Thomas Lubanga Dyilo*, International Criminal Court, Case No: ICC-01/04-01/06, Trial Chamber 1, Judgement Pursuant to Article 74 of the Statute, ICC-01/04-01/06-2842 (14 March 2012). (hereinafter the Lubanga Judgement).

215 *The Prosecutor v. Thomas Lubanga Dyilo*, International Criminal Court, Case No: ICC-01/04-01/06, Trial Chamber 1, Decision establishing the principles and procedures to be applied to reparations, ICC-01/04-01/06-2904 (7 August 2012). The issue of reparations will be further considered in chapter 5.

216 *The Prosecutor v. Thomas Lubanga Dyilo: Appeals Hearing for the Delivery of a Judgment*, International Criminal Court, Case No. ICC-01/04/01/06 (1 December 2014).

described in chapter 2. Criminal law and its procedures also need to be considered from a children's rights perspective, and it is important to consider whether the ICC is well placed to deal with issues related to children, both in terms of crimes against children and in regard to engaging with children as victims and witnesses in the proceedings.

Pursuing criminal justice in post-conflict settings is about advancing the reconstruction of the rule of law in transition. It is important to note that while criminal law and punishment of crimes is generally considered to be retributive, in transition situations it is corrective, pointing in a broader direction towards society as a whole and the issue at hand.[217] Criminal justice relates strongly to other parts of transitional justice and interrelates with the other areas, such as that of determining what reparations are made available to former child soldiers.

This chapter provides an analysis of how criminal justice procedures inform the overall transitional justice approach relevant to conscripting or enlisting children in two parts: (1) an analysis of the case against Thomas Lubanga Dyilo and how the objective elements of the charges were considered by the ICC; and (2) an analysis of the *Lubanga* case and how the subjective elements of the charges were considered by the ICC.

1. THE *LUBANGA* CASE: THE OBJECTIVE CRITERIA

Child recruitment as a war crime was codified through the adoption of the Rome Statute for an International Criminal Court in 1998, which recognized it under international law, leading to individual criminal responsibility.[218]

The debate during the drafting of the Rome Statute of the ICC focused heavily on what level of protection is accorded to children under prevailing international humanitarian and human rights law, and what parts of that law could give rise to individual criminal responsibility. There was strong support for criminalizing child recruitment through codification of what was already

217 See *Report of the Secretary-General on Children and Armed Conflict*, UN Doc. A/58/546-S/2003/1053 (10 November 2003), para 100. As stated in the Secretary-General's report, "Concrete steps should be taken to ensure the earliest possible prosecution of persons responsible for war crimes against children."

218 The Rome Statute of the International Criminal Court, adopted 17 July 1998, entered into force 1 July 2002, reprinted in 2187 UNTS 90. Child recruitment and the circumstances under which it takes place can also be considered a crime against humanity. See the analysis in Matthew Happold, *Child Soldiers in International Law* (Manchester: Manchester University Press, 2005), 135–140.

considered crystallizing as customary international law through the Rome Statute.[219]

At the 1998 Preparatory Committee, delegations considered four options relevant to the crime of recruitment and use of children:[220] Generally, there was overwhelming support for the option that recognized both the recruitment and use of children (option 2). The article recognizing child recruitment as a war crime as finally adopted in article 8(b)(xxvi) and applicable to situations of international armed conflict reads:

> Conscripting or enlisting children under the age of fifteen years into the national armed forces or using them to participate actively in hostilities.

Article 8 paragraph 2(e)(vii) essentially reads the same but is applicable to situations of armed conflict not of an international character. The main difference relates to replacing "national armed forces" with "armed forces and groups." Omitted in the provision related to armed conflicts not of an international character, national was included as a qualifier to "armed forces" in the provision for international armed conflict.[221] Paragraph 2(3)(vii) reads:

> Conscripting or enlisting children under the age of fifteen years into armed forces or groups or using them to participate actively in hostilities.

This section analyses the application of the objective criteria of the crime as included in the Rome Statute. The objective criteria essentially provide the clear assessment of what the law prescribes as a criminal act. The first two parts outline how the Court interpreted the law, while the third and fourth parts analyse how the Court applied the law.

---

219 The Rome Statute in article 8(2(b)) identifies the crimes listed as "serious violations of the laws and customs applicable ... within the established framework of international law."

220 *Report of the Preparatory Committee on the Establishment of an International Criminal Court*, (14 April 1998), 21. The four options were: Option 1: Forcing children under the age of fifteen years to take direct part in hostilities; Option 2: Recruiting children under the age of fifteen years into armed forces or using them to participate actively in hostilities; Option 3: (i) Recruiting children under the age of fifteen years into armed forces or groups; or (ii) Allowing them to take part in hostilities; Option 4: No paragraph (t).

221 Without this addition, the provision may have been applied to the Palestinian situation. The purpose was to limit the armed forces to those of states. As noted in the summary record of the 35th meeting (13 July 1998), the Israeli delegation stated: "The insertion of the word 'national' before the words 'armed forces' did not reflect the object and purpose of the Convention on the Rights of the Child. He noted that the adjective 'national' was not used to qualify the words 'armed forces' in paragraph (f) of section D, which likewise dealt with conscription of children." *Committee of the Whole: Summary Record of the 35th Meeting*, UN Doc. A/CONF.183/C.1/SR.35 (20 November 1998), para 26.

1.1. THE COURT'S INTERPRETATION OF THE LAW: FORCED OR VOLUNTARY RECRUITMENT

In reviewing how the Court considered the question of forced versus voluntary recruitment, and before coming to the conclusion of the Chamber, it is worthwhile to first consider the various points made by both the prosecution and the defence.

The prosecution defined conscription as forcible recruitment and enlistment as voluntary recruitment. It considered that there was a well-established prohibition against both forms of recruitment in international law and that the child's consent does not in any case constitute a valid defence.[222]

The defence relied on a dissenting opinion of the SCSL that "forcible recruitment is always wrong, but enlistment of child volunteers might be excused if they are accepted into the force only for non-combatant tasks, behind the front lines."[223] During the pre-trial phase, the defence also argued that children are seeking recruitment and hence the situation would not rise to a violation of these provisions in the Rome Statute.[224]

In the dissenting opinion in the *Samuel Hinga Norman* case, Justice Robertson divided the crime of child recruitment into three different areas: (1) conscripting children (through compulsion); (2) enlisting children (volunteering); (3) and using children to participate actively in hostilities. He then went on to argue that the second option of enlisting children, especially, "extends liability in a considerable and unprecedented way."[225] Justice Robertson used the Tadić test to highlight the distinctions:[226]

> Requirement iv) begs the very question that we have to decide in this case. It may be accepted that the alleged offence of child enlistment infringes a rule of international humanitarian law (i) and that the violation would be "serious" (iii). Let us assume that by 1996 it had accreted sufficient state practice to be regarded as "customary in nature" (iii). The final question reflected in iv), namely how do we tell whether the rule violation entails individual criminal responsibility, becomes the crucial question – and the passage from Tadić provides in my opinion no assistance in answering it.

---

222 Lubanga Judgement, para 573.

223 Ibid, para 582. See further dissent Justice Robertson ICC-01/04–01/06–2773-Red-tENG, para 36 and footnote 32; SCSL, *The Prosecutor v. Norman*, Case No. SCSL-2004–14-AR72(E), Appeals Chamber, Decision on Preliminary Motion Based on Lack of Jurisdiction (Child Recruitment), Dissenting Opinion of Justice Robertson, 31 May 2004 ("Dissenting Opinion of Justice Robertson"), para 9.

224 *The Prosecutor v. Thomas Lubanga Dyilo*, International Criminal Court, Case No: ICC-01/04–01/06, Transcription No: ICC-01/04–01/06-T-39-EN, 114 (21 November 2006).

225 *Prosecutor v. Samuel Hinga Norman*, Special Court for Sierra Leone (31 May 2004). Dissenting Option of Justice Robertson, para 5.

226 See *Prosecutor v. Dusko Tadić*, Decision on the Defence Motion for Interlocutory Appeal on Jurisdiction, para 94 (2 October 1995).

As a result, he found that in relation to the prohibition on child enlistment, the criteria were not fulfilled as of 1996.

The ICC Chamber confirmed that the approach by the Pre-Trial Chamber – outlining conscription as forced recruitment and enlistment as voluntary recruitment – was suitable.[227] It further concluded that what had been defined as recruitment in international humanitarian law was replaced by conscription and enlistment in the Rome Statute, but that there was no need to consider whether recruitment as defined in the Additional Protocols cover both forced and voluntary recruitment.[228]

The Chamber then went on to clarify that due to the word "or" in the language of the Rome Statute there are three different offences: conscription, enlistment, and use. It further considered that though the purpose behind conscription and enlistment may often be to use children in hostilities, the distinction is not required by the Rome Statute.[229] The Chamber thus decided that the offences of "conscripting and enlisting are committed at the moment a child under the age of 15 is enrolled into or joins an armed force or group, with or without compulsion." In this case, conscripting and enlistment are dealt with together.[230]

As a result of considering conscription and enlistment together, what transpired is that the Court considered only two crimes, even if the pre-trial Chamber stated that there were three crimes involved. Voluntary and forced recruitment were considered as one. In practice, it would also be almost impossible to distinguish between forced and voluntary recruitment, especially among armed groups, because there is usually a mix of reasons why children join.[231] The conclusion reached by the Chamber on this took the legal analysis in a different direction from what had been discussed in the SCSL, whereby the dissenting opinion considered that voluntary recruitment would be more difficult to consider as an international crime.

The question then becomes, why it was necessary to put both types of recruitment into the Statute, if it can be that easily dismissed by the Chamber?

---

227 *The Prosecutor V. Thomas Lubanga Dyilo*, Decision on the Confirmation of Charges, 246. The Pre-Trial Chamber in the Lubanga case viewed the provision "conscripting or enlisting" as an intention to differ between voluntary and forced recruitment, while noting that "'conscripting' is forcible recruitment and 'enlisting' more resembles voluntary recruitment."

228 Lubanga Judgement, para 607.

229 Ibid., para 609.

230 Ibid., para 618. The Pre-Trial Chamber concluded that "the child's consent is not a valid defence." It also stated that the crime is a continuous crime and doesn't stop until such time that it will only cease to be committed when the children leave the armed group or force, or once they turn 15.

231 For a number of examples of the wide variety of reasons that children join, see UNICEF, *Adult Wars, Child Soldiers: Voices of Children Involved in Armed Conflict in the East Asia and the Pacific Region* (Bangkok: UNICEF Regional Office for East Asia and the Pacific, 2002).

This critical legal question goes back to some of the considerations in the dissenting opinion in the SCSL, where there was a discussion as to whether both types of recruitment would be considered and where, at one stage, forced recruitment and abductions were considered to provide for a higher level of responsibility. What the ICC concluded is that it is not necessary to distinguish between the two because the language in the Statute was intended to make sure that all types of recruitment were considered, given that recruitment is never truly voluntary when it comes to children.

As noted in chapter 1, international law, through international humanitarian law and human rights law, did not differentiate between forced and voluntary recruitment: both were labelled simply as "recruitment." Based on the drafting history or otherwise, there was little justification to say that recruitment entails only one or both of these types of recruitment. Considering this history, and the Chamber deciding not to interpret this aspect, gives insights as to why the drafters of the Rome Statute decided to mention both types of recruitment. While the difference between the two types does not need to be considered in the analysis, it is an important feature of the Rome Statute to codify that both types of recruitment are included in order to make sure that the Court was not provided the opportunity to interpret a provision that had only referred to recruitment more generally, which then could have led to a consideration of only forced recruitment – as had been the case in the Special Court for Sierra Leone. Through its purposive interpretation of this provision in the Rome Statute, the Chamber has made clear that there is no need to determine the different ways in which children have been recruited for purposes of one form being less of a crime than another: all forms of child recruitment are illegal.

1.2. THE COURT'S INTERPRETATION OF THE LAW: THE QUESTION OF ACTIVE PARTICIPATION

The next issue dealt with by the Court was defining active participation – effectively establishing who will be considered a child soldier for the purposes of criminal law.

While the provisions for child recruitment in article 8 of the Rome Statute resemble those found in other bodies of international law, the Statute introduced the words "using" children to "participate actively" instead of direct participation in hostilities. Before the diplomatic conference that adopted the Rome Statute, an explanatory note was included to explain the meaning:[232]

232 *Report of the Preparatory Committee on the Establishment of an International Criminal Court*, 21.

> This option seeks to incorporate the essential principles contained under accepted international law while using language suitable for individual criminal responsibility as opposed to State responsibility. The words "using" and "participate" have been adopted in order to cover both direct participation in combat and also active participation in military activities linked to combat such as scouting, spying, sabotage and the use of children as decoys, couriers or at military checkpoints. It would not cover activities clearly unrelated to the hostilities such as food deliveries to an airbase of the use of domestic staff in an officer's married accommodation. However, use of children in a direct support function such as acting as bearers to take supplies to the front line, or activities at the front line itself, would be included within the terminology.

According to some commentators on this provision, "active," as found in international criminal law, is broader than "direct."[233] However, while the *travaux préparatoires* for the Rome Statute are clear in providing a guiding interpretation, indicating that the terms are very similar, the interpretation of the *Lubanga* case reveals some small but important differences. The differences could be considered to flow from the last sentence of the explanatory note above, as it opens the door for some level of creative thinking.

In considering this issue, the prosecution highlighted that child soldiers are those under 18 who participate in any circumstances in an armed group or force. Noteworthy is that the prosecution is using the age of 18 to make a point, even if it is a difficult point to make for criminal law purposes when the Statute clearly refers to age 15, which in itself is not open to interpretation as many other words in the provision might be.

The prosecution argued that protection is not restricted to those who fight but includes all who carry out activities that are essential to the functions of the armed group.[234] The prosecution accepted the Pre-Trial Chamber's approach that activities that are clearly unrelated to the hostilities are excluded (such as domestic staff in army officers' quarters). In the prosecution's perspective, "use to participate actively" refers to situations where children's lives are put at risk in combat, irrespective of their duties. The prosecution also supported the submission of UN Special Representative of the Secretary-General for Children and Armed Conflict (SRSG-CAAC) Radhika Coomaraswamy and her recommendation that those who are sexually exploited or in supportive roles should not be excluded.[235]

233 Otto Triffterer, ed., *Commentary on the Rome Statute of the International Criminal Court (Second Edition)* (Nomos: Baden-Baden, 2008), 470.

234 Lubanga Judgement, para 574. While the prosecution here is making reference to the inclusive approach and the notion of children associated with armed forces and armed groups, there is no reference to the Paris Commitments. See *The Paris Commitments to Protect Children from Unlawful Recruitment or Use by Armed Forces or Armed Groups*, (2007).

235 *The Prosecutor v. Thomas Lubanga Dyilo, Written Submission of the United Nations Special Representative of the Secretary-General on Children and Armed Conflict, Submitted in application of Rule 103 of the Rules of Procedure and Evidence* (18 March 2008).

The defence was well informed in its analysis of the law and activities related to child recruitment and provided a very solid legal analysis submitting that the "broad approach taken in various international instruments, which were designed to afford children the widest possible protection, should not be imported into criminal proceedings before the ICC because tightly-defined criteria are to be applied." Referring to the Paris Principles, the defence argued that the concept of "children associated with armed forces and groups" is too broad and that those children could not be treated as soldiers for purposes of criminal law.[236]

The defence also drew a parallel to the European Convention on Human Rights and the case of *Veeber v. Estonia*, in which it had been decided that a criminal offence must be clearly defined in the relevant laws and that the criminal law should not be broadly interpreted to an accused's detriment.[237] Hence, the defence suggested a narrow application: that a soldier in an armed conflict is one for the purposes of participating actively in hostilities on behalf of the group. The defence here relied on the interpretative guidance of the International Conference of the Red Cross on direct participation.[238]

The defence considered that "actively participating in hostilities" should exclude more than that which is "clearly unrelated to hostilities," which is too broad to include guards and couriers. In line with jurisprudence from the International Criminal Tribunal for the former Yugoslavia, the defence suggested that "actively participating" should be synonymous with direct participation and defined as "acts of war which by their nature or purpose are likely to cause actual harm to the personnel and equipment of the enemy armed forces."[239]

The defence took the approach of drawing a link between direct participation and the law aiming to provide protection to child soldiers who are not fighting on the front line and, therefore, should not be considered legitimate targets. It argued further that only the use of children to participate in military operations within fighting units is addressed in international criminal law.[240]

The victims' representation, on the other hand, wanted a broad interpretation.[241] They argued that "those who drafted the Statute deliberately

---

236 Lubanga Judgement, para 580.

237 The case concerns retroactivity and predictability of the law in reference to the European Convention on Human Rights. *Veeber v. Estonia*, 45771/99 European Court of Human Rights (21 January 2003).

238 *The Prosecutor v. Thomas Lubanga Dyilo*, Closing Submission of the Defence, ICC-01/04/01/06-2773-Red-tENG International Criminal Court (15 July 2011), 34, and Melzer, *Interpretive Guidance on the Notion of Direct Participation in Hostilities*.

239 *Prosecutor v. Dusko Tadić, Decision on the Defence Motion for Interlocutory Appeal on Jurisdiction* ICTY, Case No. IT-94-1-AR72 (2 October 1995), para 40.

240 Lubanga Judgement, para 587.

241 Note the *The Prosecutor v. Thomas Lubanga Dyilo*, Judgement on the Appeals of the Prosecutor and the Defence against Trial Chamber I's Decision on Victims' Participation of

chose the latter formulation so as to encompass a wider range of activities," and if the drafters had meant taking direct part, they would have called it as such.[242] The victims' representatives also considered that the language should be used to protect girls who have been recruited into armed forces and groups.[243]

In its analysis and conclusions on this issue, the Chamber used other parts of international law to get a better understanding. It found what is called an "absolute prohibition" against the recruitment and use of children under age 15 in hostilities in international humanitarian and human rights law through the Additional Protocol II and the Convention on the Rights of the Child. The broad concept of "children associated with armed conflict" was referred to throughout the trial and designed to afford children with the greatest possible protection. The Chamber, however, applied the provisions of the Statute as opposed to this more general concept.[244]

Referring back to the expectation of criminal law being clear and predictable, it is critical that there is a defined line between what is considered criminal behaviour and what is not.

In dealing with the question of the nature of the use of the child, the Chamber concluded that the Elements of Crimes require that "the conduct took place in the context of and was associated with an armed conflict."[245] The *travaux préparatoires* suggest that although direct participation is not necessary, a link with combat is necessary.[246] The words "using" and "participate" have been adopted in order to cover both direct participation in combat and active participation in military activities linked to combat, such as scouting, spying, sabotage, and the use of children as decoys, couriers, or at military checkpoints. It would not cover activities clearly unrelated to the hostilities, such as food deliveries to an airbase or the use of domestic staff in an officer's personal accommodations, but the use of children in a direct support function such as acting as bearers to take supplies to the front line or activities at the front line itself would be included within the terminology.[247]

---

18 January 2008, ICC-01/04-01/06-1432 International Criminal Court (11 July 2008). In this decision the Chamber issued general guidelines concerning the participation by victims during the trial. It was appealed, then partially confirmed and partially reversed. The judgement introduces 11 overall criteria.

242 Lubanga Judgement, para 590. See also *The International Criminal Court: Elements of Crimes and Rules Of Procedure and Evidence* ed. Roy S. Lee (Ardsley, NY: Transnational Publishers, 2001), 205–207.

243 Lubanga Judgement, para 598.

244 Ibid., para 606.

245 On the role of the elements of crime, see Gabriella Venturini, "War Crimes," in *Essays on the Rome Statute of the International Criminal Court, Volume I*, eds. Flavia Lttanzi, et al. (Ripa di Fagnano Alto: Editrice il Sirente Picoola Societa Cooperative ar.l., 2004), 179.

246 *Report of the Preparatory Committee on the Establishment of an International Criminal Court*, (14 April 1998), 21.

247 The Pre-Trial Chamber also applied this rather strict interpretation of the phrase "participate actively," specifically, that the article does "not apply to food deliveries to an airbase or the use

The ICC Chamber, however, goes on to analyse various decisions, including that of the SCSL, which had a broader understanding: the SCSL Trial Chamber considered that using children to participate actively in the hostilities "encompasses putting their lives directly at risk in combat…any labour or support that gives effect to, or helps maintain, operations in a conflict constitutes active participation." In this interpretation, carrying loads for the fighting faction; finding and/or acquiring food, ammunition, or equipment; acting as decoys; carrying messages; making trails or finding routes; operating checkpoints; and acting as human shields are all examples of active participation as much as actual combat.[248]

The amicus brief submitted in the *Lubanga* case by the SRSG-CAAC makes the point that the term "active" is broader than "direct," incorporating a gender perspective in the distinction and drawing heavily on existing demobilization and reintegration standards.[249] This interpretation would be difficult to sustain, however, because it goes beyond the language contained in the *travaux préparatoires* and does not clearly draw on the statements of the intent of the drafters.

The Chamber continued its consideration by saying that the expression "to participate actively" rather than "direct participation" represents a clear intention to import a wide interpretation to the activities and roles covered by the offence.[250] The Chamber noted the underlying common feature of the child concerned is, at the very least, a potential target. The test therefore is whether the support provided by the child to the combatants exposed him or her to real danger as a potential target. This would have to be done on a case-by-case basis.[251] As such, it differentiates between direct and active, which had been considered one and the same in many understandings, including in previous case law.[252]

---

of domestic staff in married officers' quarters." Yet, the Chamber asserted that the article would apply to the following activities because they were more closely related to hostilities: "if children are used to guard military objectives, such as the military quarters of the various units of the parties to the conflict, or to safeguard the physical safety of military commanders in particular, where children are used as bodyguards." *The Prosecutor v. Thomas Lubanga Dyilo: Decision on the Confirmation of Charges*, International Criminal Court, Case No. ICC-01/04-01/06 ICC (29 January 2007), 262.

248 *Prosecutor v. Morris Kallon (Case No. SCSL-2004-15-AR72(E)) and Brima Bazzy Kamara (Case No. SCSL-2004-16-AR72(E))*, Special Court for Sierra Leone, Appeals Chamber, Decision to Challenge to Jurisdiction: Lomé Accord Amnesty Special Court for Sierra Leone (2004), 736–738.

249 *The Prosecutor v. Thomas Lubanga Dyilo, Written Submission of the United Nations Special Representative of the Secretary-General on Children and Armed Conflict, Submitted in application of Rule 103 of the Rules of Procedure and Evidence*, 18 March 2008. See also *The Prosecutor v. Thomas Lubanga Dyilo*, International Criminal Court, Case No: ICC-01/04-01/06, Transcription No:ICC-01/04-01/06-T-223-ENG ICC (7 January 2010).

250 It also noted that the AP II does not include the word "direct." See further chapter 2 above, section 1.2.

251 Lubanga Judgement, paras. 628 and 629.

252 The International Criminal Tribunal for Rwanda found that the term "direct part in hostilities" had evolved from the phrase "active part in the hostilities" of common article 3,

Even after the Chamber stated that decisions would be made on a case-by-case basis – and despite the fact that its detailed consideration of active versus direct participation indicates that there could be situations where sexual violence led to the child being in danger as a target – its stance on the issue of rape and sexual enslavement was essentially not to consider it because the prosecution had failed to apply to include these charges at the relevant procedural stage. Therefore, rape and sexual enslavement were not considered in the *Lubanga* case. Further, the Chamber said that regardless of whether sexual violence may be included in the scope of using children to participate actively in hostilities as a matter of law, it did not want to consider the issue because sexual violence was not included in the charges.[253]

Rather than trying to broaden the notion of active participation, an alternative approach would be to emphasize the "or" as found in the Rome Statute and argue that "conscripting or enlisting" would be sufficient for a case to be made – regardless of the role that the child played while in association with an armed group or force.[254] However, this is not the route taken by the Chamber. Further analysis into how the Court applied the law in practice indicates that its findings did consider the implications for children beyond defining active participation. But its conclusions did not truly make the point that that there were three different crimes involved, or at least two – one dealing with recruitment (forced and voluntary) and the other dealing with active participation.

It could be argued that a child is never a legitimate target because the child should not have been in the ranks in the first place. But considering how direct participation has been defined in international humanitarian law, when a child is in a role where he or she is directly participating in the conflict, he or she would also be a legitimate target.[255] Other parts of international law would nonetheless continue to apply, as a complement to international humanitarian law, providing for protective measures, with a special focus on children.[256]

---

and concluded that "these phrases are so similar to be synonymous." The Akayesu Judgement, in paragraph 629, concluded, "These phrases are so similar that, for the Chamber's purposes, they may be treated as synonymous". *Prosecutor v. Akayesu*, International Criminal Tribunal for Rwanda, Judgement No. ICTR-96-4-T ICTR (2 September 1998), 629.

253 See also Cecile Aptel, "International Criminal Justice and Child Protection," in *Children and Transitional Justice*, ed. Mindy Jane Roseman Sharanjeet Parmar, Saudamini Siegrist, Theo Sowa (eds.) (Cambridge: Human Rights Program at Harvard Law School, 2010), 82. Aptel highlights the challenge of maximizing the victim's protection while also protecting the rights of the defendant.

254 Matthew Happold, "Child Recruitment as a Crime under the Rome Statute of the International Criminal Court," in *The Legal Regime of the International Criminal Court: Essays in Memory of Igor Blischenko*, eds. José Doria, et al. (Leiden: Brill, 2009), 12.

255 Melzer, *Interpretive Guidance on the Notion of Direct Participation in Hostilities, 60.*

256 Principle IX in the ICRC recommendations on the interpretation of international humanitarian law consider restraints in the use of force in direct attack. Furthermore, "the kind and degree of force which is permissible against persons not entitled to protection

One distinguishing factor between direct and active participation is that anything that would be defined as direct participation would also mean that the child is a legitimate target, though not everything that is considered to be active participation makes the child a legitimate target. This does not negate the importance of distinguishing between what might be protected activities (for example, medical services) in any case under international humanitarian law. A child who is part of the medical services would not be a legitimate target but would be actively participating according to the Rome Statute because of the risk involved if that function takes him or her to the front line. In a role that is not protected under international humanitarian law, such as delivering supplies to the front line, the child would not be directly participating according to a stricter definition, but under the Rome Statute this child would be actively participating because of the danger involved.

Some scholars consider that the Chamber failed to distinguish between international humanitarian law and human rights law, however, it would seem that the Chamber just applied international criminal law, informed by international humanitarian law, and therefore saw no need to specifically point out that it was making that distinction.[257] It does not appear that the Chamber's decision in any way would infringe on the protection accorded by international humanitarian law because it applied a different regime and analysis in contemplating the purpose of the provision as intended by the drafters. The Chamber simply considered that the Rome Statute opened the door for the law to be interpreted in a different way from how aspects of direct and active participation had traditionally been interpreted in international humanitarian law, giving meaning to the provisions of the Rome Statute.

1.3. ESTABLISHING THE FACTS AND APPLICATION OF THE LAW: HOW TO DETERMINE THAT CHILDREN WERE UNDER THE AGE OF 15

The question of age caused major debate during the drafting process of the Rome Statute, in much the same way as other negotiations relevant to child recruitment. During the 1998 deliberations some delegations lobbied to put the age of recruitment at 18. Canadian Minster of Foreign Affairs Lloyd Axworthy

---

against direct attack must not exceed what is actually necessary to accomplish a legitimate military purpose in the prevailing circumstances." See Melzer, 77–82. See also Jean-François Quéguiner, "Direct Participation in Hostilities Under International Humanitarian Law," *International Humanitarian Law Research Initiative, Working Paper* (2003), 8. Quéguiner writes in detail about the distinction between the legal consequence of direct participation within the rules on conduct of hostilities on the one hand, and the legal consequences of direct participation in case of capture on the other hand.

257 Roman Graf, "The International Criminal Court and Child Soldiers," *Journal of International Criminal Justice* 10 (2012): 945–969, 963.

said, "It is my hope that the world will soon recognize 18 as the minimum acceptable age for recruitment and participation in hostilities."[258] And several other delegations supported this age, including Belgium, Brazil, Senegal, and Chile, some referring to "emerging consensus" based on ILO) Convention 182 and the drafting process of the Optional Protocol on the Involvement of Children in Armed Conflict.[259] In the end it was concluded that there was insufficient support for the age of 18 in international customary law.[260]

In looking at how to apply the age of the child in the *Lubanga* case, the ICC was challenged to ensure due diligence as part of the proceedings that children who had been recruited were truly under the age of 15 and that this could be proved beyond reasonable doubt.

From a practitioner's perspective, it would be easy to say that if an armed group or force recruits children under 18 in a conflict setting they are most likely also recruiting children under 15. In addition, if there is no system in place to establish a child's age (such as verification through birth registration), then children much younger than 15 are likely to make it to the ranks of the armed groups and forces, regardless of what age limit is established by law.

For the purposes of criminal law, on the other hand, proof of age is very complex and must answer such questions as: What is sufficient proof that recruitment under the age of 15 took place? What will hold as evidence in an international criminal court? How and by whom could this information be collected in the midst of an armed conflict? The Rome Statute allows for the admission of all relevant and necessary evidence and in determining the facts regarding the age in the *Lubanga* case, the Court did indeed make use of a range of complementary evidence.[261]

The *Lubanga* case demonstrates rigorous adherence to the age limit of 15.[262] The defence repeatedly returned to the question of finding proof that the

258 Ministerial statement by the Honourable Lloyd Axworthy, Minister of Foreign Affairs, to the Preparatory Committee on the Establishment of an International Criminal Court, 3 April 1998.

259 *Report of the Preparatory Committee on the Establishment of an International Criminal Court*, (14 April 1998), 2–91.

260 Otto Triffterer, *Commentary on the Rome Statute of the International Criminal Court: Observers' Notes* (Oxford: Beck/Hart, 1999), 468.

261 For background to the negotiations on evidence, balancing between civil law and common law, see Helen Brady, "The System of Evidence in the Statute of the International Criminal Court," in *Essays on the Rome Statute of the International Criminal Court, Volume I*, eds. Flavia Lattanzi, et al. (Rome: Editrice il Sirente, 2004), 286.

262 See also statements about aspirations beyond 15, which at the moment are not realistic: "Although abjured for child soldiers, international criminal tribunals are invoked to prosecute as war criminals those adults who conscript, enlist, or use children below the age of fifteen as active participants in hostilities. Straight 18 aspirations endeavor to expand this prohibition to cover all children, that is, all persons younger than eighteen." Drumbl, *Reimagining Child Soldiers*, 18–19.

children were younger,[263] confirming that the line has to be drawn somewhere. While this issue will be raised again in future cases, confirmation of charges judgement in the *Lubanga* case used a variety of sources to confirm the evidence, and the pretrial process also used the fact that Mr Lubanga did not enter into any serious effort to release children but rather he conducted a masquerade.[264]

In determining the age of a child, the Trial Chamber made its conclusions according to four criteria: mostly based on physical appearance; comparing with other children; the individual's general physical development (such as breasts, height and voice); and overall behaviour.[265]

The defence approach on age assessment claimed that the methods used did not establish the presence of children under 15 beyond a reasonable doubt. In responding to this concern, the Chamber recognized that it is difficult to distinguish between young people who are close to the age of 15, and exercised caution when considering evidence related to the age of the children.[266]

Even allowing for a wide margin of error in assessing an individual's age, the Chamber concluded:

> It is feasible for non-expert witnesses to differentiate between a child who is undoubtedly less than 15 years old and a child who is undoubtedly over 15. Furthermore, the sheer volume of credible evidence (analysed hereafter) relating to the presence of children below the age of 15 within the ranks of the UPC/FPLC [Union des patriotes congolais/Forces Patriotiques pour la Libération du Congo] has demonstrated conclusively that a significant number were part of the UPC/FPLC army. An appreciable proportion of the prosecution witnesses, as well as D-0004, testified reliably that children under 15 were within the ranks of the UPC/FPLC.[267]

The Chamber then proceeded to review the evidence that had led to this conclusion.

The United Nations Organization Mission in the Democratic Republic of the Congo (MONUC) expert witness's statement was described by the prosecution as "detailed, credible and reliable, particularly when it was based on her personal experience of working with demobilised children in the region." The defence maintained that the witness had insufficient personal knowledge of the events

---

263 See. e.g., the cross-examination of one of the expert witnesses, where she agreed that age determination was not a scientific exercise. *The Prosecutor v. Thomas Lubanga Dyilo*, International Criminal Court, Case No: ICC-01/04-01/06, Transcription No: ICC-01/04-01/06-T-38-EN ICC (20 November 2006), 107. The defence came back to this issue in its reasoning for the entire case. See *The Prosecutor v. Thomas Lubanga Dyilo*, International Criminal Court, Case No: ICC-01/04-01/06, Transcription No: ICC-01/04-01/06-T-43-EN ICC (23 November 2006), 83.

264 Cecile Aptel and Virginie Ladisch, *Through a New Lens: A Child-Sensitive Approach to Transitional Justice*, (2011), 22.

265 Lubanga Judgement, para 641.

266 Ibid., para 642.

267 Ibid, paras 643–644.

because she had not regularly visited the area and suggested that the expert witness was biased towards the prosecution.[268]

The Chamber was satisfied that the witness was able to testify about events and stated that it was "sure the witness has not exaggerated any material facts or otherwise provided biased or unreliable evidence."[269]

The defence also suggested that MONUC colleagues merely collected the statements of children they interviewed and failed to carry out further investigations, thereby casting doubt at the rigour with which this information had been collected. To this the Chamber noted the expert witnesses evidence related to availability of official documentation:[270]

> Identity cards and documents in the Congo are not very common. Very few people have official papers, in particular, children. In fact, I never saw a child with an identity card in Ituri, so carrying out such a verification on the basis of administrative documents was not possible. So when you say independent verification, well, other than the information that the children gave regarding their schooling, that was one way we had to have an idea and to perhaps reinforce the information stated by the children.

It was also considered to be important that the expert witness used other methodology to verify information, such as comparing the dates provided through interviews with children with chronology created by military and political observers from MONUC, along with efforts to seek verification from relevant non-governmental organizations.

For the final determination, the Court took many factors into account to verify that children had indeed been part of the group, building on information compiled and analysed by the MONUC expert witness, including information provided by the children during detailed interviews conducted by trained social workers. Questions were asked about the children's families, their academic records, and the schools they attended, and the children's accounts of recruitment history, date of conscription or enlistment, and the battles in which they participated were recorded. Evaluations were also conducted based on what the children said and how they acted (some cried in the social worker's office or had difficulty discussing their experience).[271]

It is critical to consider the process by which the Chamber elaborates on the credibility of the witness, and that this expert witness testimony is relied upon to a great extent as the Chamber moves to justify its position on the evidence

---

268 For more details regarding the collaboration of the UN in providing information and allowing staff to serve as witnesses and the background put in place, see Larry D. Johnson, "The Lubanga Case and Cooperation between the UN and the ICC," *Journal of International Criminal Justice* 10 (2012): 887–903.

269 Lubanga Judgement, paras 646–648.

270 *The Prosecutor v. Thomas Lubanga Dyilo*, ICC-01/04/-01/06-T-206-ENG ICC (08 July 2009), 9.

271 Lubanga Judgement, paras 651–652.

provided in the case. It has implications for UN staff contributions towards historical justice, maintaining the records, and as in this case, contributing towards trial proceedings.[272]

The Chamber's conclusion regarding the MONUC expert was that the witness's "professional history and personal experience with the children she interviewed enabled her to provide realistic age estimates."[273]

The Chamber also analysed the response of a witness who had worked with the non-governmental organization SOS Grands Lacs, which was funded by UNICEF to work on demobilization and reintegration of child soldiers. The defence challenged this witness by saying that his experience was mostly with issues outside the charges, which is a very important point considering the focus of reintegration programmes being very holistic to cover all children associated with armed groups and forces.

The Chamber then focused only on testimony relevant to the charges and considered that children from UPC who were released were between 8.5 and 18 years old, and some of the same children were later being re-recruited. The conclusion on this witness by the Chamber was that he gave consistent and reliable evidence, noting that he had more than a year's experience working directly with these children, which would have "enabled him to provide first-hand information on how children were re-recruited."[274]

It is interesting that the Chamber here was not focusing on how the witness determined the ages but just on the re-recruitment aspect. This is also where the Chamber quite clearly stated its approach towards the age issue:

> Given the difference in appearance between, for instance, a 9-year-old child and a 15-year-old, the Chamber is persuaded that P-0024 gave credible and reliable evidence that he saw children well below the age of 15, even if the ages of others may have been more difficult to assess.[275]

This means that in the absence of scientific proof through birth certificates or medical records showing that children have been found to be below the age of 15, even if just a few months below, in practice, what is really being dealt with are situations where the children must be much younger than 15 so that age is easy to establish under the circumstances.[276]

---

272 See *Negotiated Relationship Agreement between the International Criminal Court and the UNICEF Nations*, ICC-ASP/3/Res.1 (entered into force 4 October 2004). The agreement deals with the circumstances for the UN to share information with the ICC, including considerations of staff security. Also, it deals with the issue of how the UN could redact its own documentation before giving it to the ICC.

273 Ibid., para 655.

274 Lubanga Judgement., para 661.

275 Ibid., para 663.

276 Age determination is a complex matter, and there is no reliable low-cost medical method that can be applied in non-Western contexts. There is very little written about this question in the

Another witness had been a member of the UPC army (the FPLC) and the Chamber's conclusion shows how this type of non-expert, who might not have thought of these issues before, described the children as being very small, for instance, in relation to the size of the weapons they were carrying. The Chamber decided that this type of testimony is evidence for the children having been below 15, and in assessing the testimony of this particular witness, it concluded:

> The Chamber is persuaded he assessed age reliably, as demonstrated by the details in his testimony which help explain his conclusion that certain children were below the age of 15 (e.g. the difficulties some had carrying weapons), and he was clearly able to evaluate soldiers outside his immediate group. P-0038 was in constant contact with many other soldiers – for instance, during their training – and therefore he was in a position to reach reliable conclusions as to age.[277]

The defence argued that the testimony of many of the witnesses lacked detail, particularly considering how the witnesses assessed the age of the children. However, the Chamber built on the fact that witnesses had observed recruitment of very young children, and as such there could be very little doubt. In reference to one witness the Chamber concluded:

> He estimated the age of a particular five-year-old child at a training centre on the basis that a six-year-old should be able to reach over his head and touch his opposite ear, and this child was unable to do this when asked.[278]

Note that there were also some witnesses who stressed that there were children between 15 and 18, but none below 15. The chamber did not really listen to these witnesses and considered that their "evidence was of less assistance"; some witnesses were also characterized as unreliable.

The Chamber also used video footage as evidence to determine the children's age and determined that "it is possible to draw a safe conclusion based on their appearance."[279]

In addition, the Chamber considered documentary evidence of the presence of child soldiers. For instance, it looked into the evidence provided in the form of logbooks from a demobilization centre, which provided a list that had been made by social workers and contained details for children who were to be placed with host families, including names and ages.[280]

---

academic literature. For further details, see Separated Children In Europe Programme, *Position Paper on Age Assessment in the Context of Separated Children in Europe* (Copenhagen: Save the Children, 2012).

277 Lubanga Judgement, para 691.

278 Ibid., para 708.

279 Ibid., para 711.

280 There were also instances where other logbooks were not considered; for instance, the chamber was unable to rely on the contents of logbook EVD-OTP-00476, notwithstanding

The prosecution pointed out that this demonstrated the systematic nature of the plan that children were conscripted and enlisted into, and used by, the UPC/FPLC. The defence argued that neither the people who collected information for the logbooks nor the individuals who lied at the demobilization centres about their age for material gain could be considered reliable. In this situation, the Chamber concluded, the documents lacked information about the armed group(s) concerned and did not establish the links between the children and the armed group; therefore, the materials could not be relied upon to establish the presence of children in the UPC/FPLC.[281]

The Chamber further considered a letter from the National Secretary for Education to one of the commanders of the FPLC, copied to Mr Lubanga, concerning the selection of 13 officers from the army who were to be trained in a disarmament, demobilization, and reintegration programme. The letter states that the programme is to be applied to those soldiers aged 10–15 or who are 16 and "willing to return to civilian life."[282]

The defence argued that the letter does not prove that child soldiers below the age of 15 were part of the FPLC. The Chamber concluded that the document implies there were children between the ages of 10 and 16 within the FPLC and that the letter validated other evidence significantly.[283]

In discussions about a logbook of radio transmissions provided as evidence, the defence took a new approach in claiming that "children" as used in the logbook is a synonym for soldier, and it does not refer to those who were minors. Here the Chamber concluded, "Given the lack of any reliable guide as to the meaning attributed to the word 'children' in this particular context, the Chamber declines to rely on this document as support for the contention that there were children under the age of 15 within the ranks of the UPC/FPLC armed forces."[284]

The prosecution also provided evidence in the form of a monthly report provided by a person who oversaw awareness-raising campaigns to persuade villagers to send their children for training. Here, too, the defence claimed that the word "children" is used to simply mean FPLC soldiers. The Chamber approached the interpretation in the document with considerable caution and found the evidence unsustainable: it did not sufficiently demonstrate that "children" as used in the report demonstrated those under age 15 because the

the fact that it contains information about the armed groups with which the children were associated, along with their dates of birth, because of the potential unreliability of the information when it was originally provided and the apparent lack of sufficient (or any) verification.

281 Lubanga Judgement, paras 736–739.

282 Ibid., para 741.

283 Ibid., paras 743 and 746–748.

284 Ibid., paras 751–752.

witness's testimony concerned documents that were related only to demobilization.[285]

In the final analysis, the Chamber used such criteria as the "size of the children and their ability to hold a weapon and to participate in training" as factors indicating that recruits were, in fact, children. Given the consistent and cumulative evidence, the Chamber was satisfied that children below age 15 were integrated into the FPLC, the armed wing of the Union des patriotes congolais.[286] It would seem, however, that the Court in referring to the size in the end considered as one of the most important elements in determining the age its own experience in having witnessed the size of the children through the video evidence.[287]

The Chamber also concluded that the evidence supported the contention that children were re-recruited, which is a major aspect in these contexts. Armed groups often want to show goodwill in order to get services delivered to their area of operation, or they might want children to have the opportunity to recover from the war experience and/or allow them to mature over a period of time. It is also common that one part of the organization does not speak to the other, resulting in the problems related to re-recruitment.

The Chamber does not really explain why it gives importance to the issue of re-recruitment, but it is likely to be more of an issue with showing the nexus between the children and the armed group in question. In the interest of other transitional justice efforts, it is useful that the Chamber focuses on re-recruitment rather than on released children in general as a piece of evidence, because this could undermine release and reintegration efforts. It could also alert commanders that they should not be releasing children because such action could be used as evidence that they, in fact, have been recruiting and using children.[288]

Evidence related to the known training centres was also being considered to see if there was sufficient evidence to the effect that children were being trained in those centres. The prosecution claimed that the UPC had 20 training camps, but this could not be substantiated. In this situation, the defence described the evidence as "extremely confused." But the Chamber did not agree with this assessment, and after taking into account evidence by witnesses and video footage, it concluded that children under age 15 were trained by UPC/FPLC at its headquarters, in the Rwampara training camp, in the Mandaro camp, and in the Mongbwalu camp.[289]

Faced with the challenge that there were no proper records such as birth registration or other evidence to firmly establish the children's age, the

285 Ibid., para 753.
286 Ibid., paras 764–769.
287 Ibid, para 644.
288 See Paris Principles p. 36.
289 Ibid., paras 806–819.

Chamber's considerations in determining that there were children under age 15 in the FPLC ranks made use of an extensive variety of evidence.[290] The law in this situation was considered to be clear by the Chamber. What was less clear was how to make use of the evidence gathered in order for the decision to be informed.

1.4. ESTABLISHING THE FACTS AND APPLICATION OF THE LAW: HOW TO DETERMINE THAT CHILDREN WERE CONSCRIPTED, ENLISTED, OR ACTIVELY USED IN CONFLICT

Forced and voluntary recruitment, as previously noted, were considered as one element of the crime for purposes of the Rome Statute as interpreted through the *Lubanga* case. As stated by the Trial Chamber, "In the circumstances of this case, conscription and enlistment are dealt with together, notwithstanding the fact that they constitute separate offences."[291]

From the beginning, it was clear that it would be difficult to distinguish the type of recruitment in this case. For instance, many children joined the ranks to get revenge for their families who had been killed and were very keen to volunteer for the fighting, but they were also compelled to join due to the prevailing situation, the conflict, and the need to get food for the day. The Chamber's approach to this issue indicated that recruitment "does not necessarily involve the conscription of children by force, given the many alternative, non-forceful ways of persuading children to join the military 'voluntarily' that were available."[292]

As noted above, the Court had considered active participation to include situations where children are in danger as a possible target. To the Chamber, it was clear that children who had actively participated in hostilities included those who were involved in roles supporting the combatants as well as those on the front line. Children also played an indirect role, and in these circumstances, active participation was also tested by "whether the support provided by the child to the combatants exposed him or her to real danger by becoming a potential target."[293]

In applying the law, the Chamber identified the various roles that children played, including participation in battles,[294] use of child soldiers as military

290 There was also no procedure in place for those who gathered evidence to determine the age.
291 Lubanga Judgement., para 618.
292 Ibid., paras 759 and 784. See also Graf, "The International Criminal Court and Child Soldiers," 956.
293 Lubanga Judgement, para 820.
294 The Chamber concluded based on the analysis of the evidence that children took direct part in hostilities. The Chamber here looked at the various pieces of information provided by witnesses about how children fought at the front line in active combat. Ibid., para 834.

guards,[295] bodyguards and escorts of commanders,[296] Lubanga's bodyguards,[297] a special *kadogo* ("little ones") unit,[298] and children involved in domestic work.[299] By including these categories, the Chamber considered that its interpretation of "use to actively participate" goes beyond direct participation. Although the Court here did not specifically make a decision about domestic work in an armed group qualifying as use, it did make the conclusion that those involved in domestic work were also involved in other ways during the conflict that put them in danger, which together constituted "use."

Separately, the Chamber considered the use of child soldiers, which was examined more in terms of the conditions rather than the role those children played. One area under review were reports of the type of punishment children were subjected to, including whipping and withholding food. The analysis and reasoning behind including these elements were quite thin, however, and the Chamber concluded "that a number of recruits would have been subjected to a range of punishments during training with the UPC/FPLC, particularly given there is no evidence to suggest they were excluded from this treatment. These punishments are described as part of the context in which children under the age of 15 were conscripted, enlisted and used by the UPC/FPLC."[300]

Sexual violence is another type of condition considered in applying the law. Trainers in the training camps and other guards in the centre took advantage of the situation and raped the recruits; girls who acted as bodyguards were often used to prepare food and to provide sexual services for the commanders. The conclusion on this was that the prosecution failed to include allegations of sexual

---

295 A significant number of children under the age of 15 were used as military guards during the period of the charges. Ibid., para 838.

296 Witness testimony included accounts of children under the age of 15, including girls, among the UPC/FPLC troops, some of whom were in military units, but the majority, particularly the girls, acted as body guards. Children were not considered very demanding and would not cause as many troubles as adult bodyguards would; they were considered to be obedient, yet fearless. Chamber concluded that a significant number of children under the age of 15 were used by the UPC/FPLC as escorts and bodyguards for the main staff and the commanders. Ibid., paras 850–853 and 857.

297 This was concluded as one category based on mix of testimony and video footage. Defence submitted the witness did not explain how he assessed the ages of these guards with the necessary degree of accuracy. However, the Chamber felt confident that Lubanga had used a significant number of children under age 15 within his personal escort and as his bodyguards. Ibid., para 869.

298 Defence submitted that the grouping of *kadogos* within a unit was intended to protect them. The Chamber concluded that the existence of this unit demonstrated the presence of children within the UPC/FPLC, but it did not conclude on their role or the relevance of this particular unit. Ibid., para 877.

299 The Chamber concluded that evidence concerning domestic work by girls under the age of 15 when the support provided by the girl exposed her to danger by becoming a potential target: "a significant number of girls under the age of 15 were used for domestic work, in addition to the other tasks they carried out as UPC/FPLC soldiers, such as involvement in combat, joining patrols and acting as bodyguards." Ibid., para 882.

300 Ibid., para 889.

violence in the charges, and, as a result, there are no findings on this issue, "particularly as to whether responsibility is to be attributed to the accused."[301] The Chamber considered, however, that the issue could possibly be raised when submissions were heard to assist in the sentencing and reparations.

On the issue of sexual violence, the separate and dissenting opinion of Judge Elizabeth Odio Benito disagreed in regard to the legal definition of the crime, arguing that the Chamber should have defined the crime first and then considered what is relevant in a specific case. Judge Benito would have developed a more comprehensive legal definition of use to participate actively in hostilities that would include sexual violence and other ill-treatment suffered by girls and boys.[302] Judge Benito did agree with the majority when it concluded that, regardless of the specific task carried out by the child, it is crucial to determine that he or she could have suffered harm inflicted by the armed group that recruited the child illegally, for example, for the purposes of supporting the combatants through the use of their bodies for sexual violence.[303]

The issue of self-defence forces was also considered, and in this respect there were also some complicated questions. As the self-defence forces were troops active at the village level, with a rather fluid structure, the Chamber had to consider whether these forces were under the control of the UPC/FPLC.

The defence argued that, after September 2002, these groups retained their independence and continued to act autonomously, while the prosecution argued that these forces were able to train with the UPC/FPLC forces.[304]

The Chamber considered it to be "implausible to suggest that the self-defence forces made special arrangements (based on age) as regards the recruits who were sent for training with the UPC/FPLC, when they did not verify the ages of the children who were given weapons and who they allowed to fight." It concluded that some self-defence forces remained independent and that the UPC/FPLC was not responsible for any child below the age of 15 who was recruited or used by these groups. However, the Chamber accepted that there were some children under age 15 who were sent to the UPC/FPLC for training and never returned.[305]

In considering the self-defence forces, the Chamber did not really draw coherent conclusions, saying that on the one hand there was no guidance not to recruit children provided to the self-defence forces, but on the other hand some of them were quite independent so the UPC/FPLC, therefore, was not responsible after all. But the defence also did not use the argument that one could have

301 Ibid., paras 892–896.

302 *The Prosecutor v. Thomas Lubanga Dyilo*, Separate and Dissenting Opinion of Judge Odio Benito, ICC-01/04-01/06-2842 ICC (14 March 2012), 6. See also Graf, "The International Criminal Court and Child Soldiers," 965.

303 Lubanga Judgement, Dissenting Opinion, Judge Benito, 18.

304 Lubanga Judgement, para 899.

305 Ibid., para 902.

expected around self-defence, namely, that this as a concept in international law could fall outside the realm of child recruitment and that it could be legitimate for children to engage in self-defence – and, if so, under what circumstances this might be allowed under international law, considering also that children who do not join forces to defend their own communities may be considered traitors.[306]

The overall conclusions of the Court focused on the crimes of "recruitment" and "use." Regarding recruitment, the Chamber concluded that the UPC/FPLC was responsible for the widespread recruitment of young people, including children under age 15, on an enforced as well as a "voluntary" basis. Certain UPC/FPLC leaders, including the accused, were "particularly active in the mobilisation drives and recruitment campaigns that were directed at persuading Hema families to send their children to serve in the UPC/FPLC army." Hence, the Chamber concluded that the UPC/FPLC forces conscripted and enlisted children under the age of 15, as established by the evidence beyond a reasonable doubt.[307]

It is important to note here that the Chamber puts "voluntary" within quotation marks, indicating once more that there is no true volition in children being recruited by armed groups and forces and recognizing that there are various levels of persuasion and elements of force in the approaches to child recruitment. In its conclusion on recruitment of children, the Chamber also considered that children had endured harsh training and were subject to a variety of severe punishments.

Second, with respect to the use of children, it was clear that children took part in fighting, were military guards, and were part of the *kadogo* unit, used as bodyguards, including those of Lubanga. Hence, "the evidence has established beyond reasonable doubt that children under the age of 15 were conscripted, enlisted and used by the UPC/FPLC to participate actively in hostilities."[308]

2. THE *LUBANGA* CASE: THE SUBJECTIVE CRITERIA

This section reviews the subjective elements of the crime of child recruitment, in which the Court sought to establish the various categories of criminal liability that would apply. The elements of crimes discussion during the drafting of the Rome Statute included the war crime of using, conscripting, or enlisting

[306] *Through a New Lens: A Child-Sensitive Approach to Transitional Justice*, (2011), 23.

[307] Lubanga Judgement, paras 911–914. Awareness-raising campaigns had also been referred to, which were seen as one element of evidence that children were targeted in recruitment efforts; the Chamber concluded, in paragraph 785, "that considerable pressure was exerted on various communities to send young people, including children under the age of 15, to join the UPC/FPLC army during the time frame of the charges."

[308] Ibid., para 916.

children. It highlighted five elements, with the third having particular relevance in the context of a discussion about the subjective criteria (*mens rea*):

1. The perpetrator conscripted or enlisted one or more persons into the national armed forces or used one or more persons to participate actively in hostilities.
2. Such person or persons were under the age of 15.
3. **The perpetrator knew or should have known that such person or persons were under the age of 15 years.** (emphasis added)
4. The conduct took place in the context of and was associated with an international armed conflict.
5. The perpetrator was aware of factual circumstances that established the existence of an armed conflict.[309]

In the *Lubanga* pre-trial decision, the Chamber determined that the test for the "should have known" requirement entailed two aspects: (1) that the accused "did not know that the victims were under the age of fifteen years at the time"; and (2) the accused "lacked such knowledge because he or she did not act with due diligence in the relevant circumstances (one can only say that the suspect 'should have known' if his or her lack of knowledge results from his or her failure to comply with his or her duty to act with due diligence)."[310]

In applying these two aspects, the Pre-Trial Chamber decided, "Thomas Lubanga Dyilo i. was, at the very least, aware that, in the ordinary course of events, the implementation of the common plan would involve: the voluntary recruitment of children under the age of fifteen years into the FPLC; the forcible recruitment of children under the age of fifteen years into the FPLC; the use of children under the age of fifteen years to participate actively in military operations and as bodyguards to protect military objectives; ii. accepted such a result by reconciling himself with it or by condoning it."[311]

2.1. EXISTENCE OF A COMMON PLAN

Article 8 of the Rome Statute establishes that the Court will have jurisdiction in particular in cases where war crimes were "committed as part of a plan or policy or as part of a large-scale commission of such crimes." The considerations in the *Lubanga* case around the question of whether there was a common plan to carry

309 United Nations, *International Criminal Court, Elements of Crimes* UN Doc. PCNICC/2000/1/Add.2 (7 April 2000). See also Happold on a discussion between the language found in the Rome Statute itself and that found in the Elements of Crime. Happold, "Child Recruitment as a Crime under the Rome Statute of the International Criminal Court," 17–19.

310 *The Prosecutor v. Thomas Lubanga Dyilo: Decision on the Confirmation of Charges*, 29 January 2007, 358.

311 Ibid., para 404.

out the crime focused on that there must be at least two individuals involved in the commission of the crime. The Rome Statute requires the responsibility to be established on a "joint" basis. The Pre-Trial Chamber held on the co-perpetrators' plan that:

(i) the co-perpetrators have agreed: (a) to start the implementation of the common plan to achieve a non-criminal goal, and (b) to only commit the crime if certain conditions are met; or
(ii) the co-perpetrators (a) are aware of the risk that implementing the common plan (which is specifically directed at the achievement of a non- criminal goal) will result in the commission of the crime, and (b) accept such outcome.[312]

The prosecution supported this interpretation, while the defence said that the plan must be intrinsically criminal. In other words, the defence argument means that the plan should not be to mobilize recruits generally but to recruit children under the age of 15.

The defence also argued that "the accused can only be guilty of an offence committed jointly with another person rather than committed 'through' another person." It took issue with the Pre-Trial Chamber's formulation of co-perpetration being based on control over the crime. It would not be sufficient, according to the defence, for the prosecution to show that the accused had the power to avert the crime or to punish the perpetrators: the prosecution would need to show "a positive, personal and direct contribution without which the crime would not have existed." The word "commits" in article 25(3)(a) of the Rome Statute means that by his personal acts the accused must have made a contribution without which the crime would not have occurred.[313]

The legal representatives of the V01 group of victims spoke to the phenomenon of child soldiers, stretching back to the mid-1990s. When the UPC army was created, the use of child soldiers in armed groups was a rule not the exception. As such, "it is submitted Mr Lubanga must have known that in order to avoid recruiting child soldiers into this new armed group, strict instructions prohibiting their conscription or enlistment were necessary."[314]

The majority of the Chamber concluded that the prosecution was not required to prove that the plan was specifically directed at committing the crime in question, nor did the plan need to have been intrinsically criminal – "however, it is necessary, as a minimum, for the prosecution to establish the common plan

312 Ibid., para 344. The Rome Statute article 25(3)(a) establishes that a person can be held criminally responsible where the accused: "Commits such a crime, whether as an individual, jointly with another or through another person, regardless of whether that other person is criminally responsible."
313 Lubanga Judgement, paras 955–959.
314 Ibid., para 970.

included a critical element of criminality, namely that, its implementation embodied a sufficient risk that, if events follow the ordinary course, a crime will be committed."[315] Reading articles 25(3)(a) dealing with the commission of the crime individually or jointly and 30 of the Rome Statute dealing with the mental element of intent and knowledge together led the majority to conclude that committing the crime in question does not need to be the overarching goal of the co-perpetrators, but that it could happen as a by-product.[316]

In the view of the majority, the mental requirement that the common plan included the commission of a crime would be satisfied if the co-perpetrators knew that in the ordinary course of events "implementing the plan will lead to that result." In this case, "knowledge" means that the co-perpetrators are aware of the risk that the consequence will occur.[317] The majority concluded that it is not necessary that the agreement or common plan is explicit, but it can be inferred from circumstantial evidence, stating that the objective part of the requirement "means that the agreement on a common plan leads to co-perpetration if its implementation embodies a sufficient risk that, in the ordinary course of events, a crime will be committed."[318]

In concluding that there was an agreement or common plan between the accused and at least one other co-perpetrator that, once implemented, will result in the commission of the relevant crime in the ordinary course of events, the Chamber considered both the fact that the UPC had been organizing training of Hema youths and the events leading up to the emergence of the UPC. Its statement on this issue included the facts that "a declaration dated 14 September 2002 from the UPC/FPLC Presidency, printed on official UPC letterhead and signed by Lubanga, sets out the objectives of the UPC-RP [Union des patriotes congolais pour la reconciliation et la paix] and states 'the UPC-RP has taken [up] arms to remove all the forces that contribute to the destruction of Ituri' and has 'put an end to the management of Ituri by the RCD-ML' [Rassemblement congolais pour la démocratie – Mouvement de libération]."[319]

---

315 Ibid., para 984.

316 This reading of article 25(3) was very much in line with the way that the provision has been understood to date. The first part looks at the contribution to facilitate the criminal activity of a group, while the second part looks at the intention to contribute links to a simple acceptance that there is a risk involved of a criminal outcome as a result of the activity. See also Andrea Sereni, "Individual Criminal Responsibility," in *Essays on the Rome Statute of the International Criminal Court, Volume II*, eds. Flavia Lattanzi, et al. (Ripa di Fagnano Alto: Editrice il Sirente Piccola Societa Cooperative a r.l., 2004), 111.

317 Ibid. para 986. See also Steffen Wirth, "Co-perpetration in the Lubanga Trial Judgment," *Journal of International Criminal Justice* 10 (2012): 971–995.

318 Lubanga Judgement, paras 987–988.

319 Ibid., para. 1103: "The defence contends that all the documents from the UPC archives suggesting that the UPC was involved in securing control of Bunia are unreliable as they were only intended as political propaganda. However, the Chamber does not accept the suggestion that these documents were created, at least in part, for this false purpose. Although they do not demonstrate the UPC had resorted to military action prior to the year 2002, they provide

In this regard, the separate opinion of Judge Adrian Fulford considered that "jointly with another," as presented by the Pre-Trial Chamber, imposed an unnecessary and unfair burden on the prosecution. The Pre-Trial Chamber used the approach of those who "have control over the commission of the offence" as a requirement. Judge Fulford found that the possible modes of commission under article 25(3)(a) of the Statute were not intended to be mutually exclusive, arguing that there is no hierarchy of seriousness in article 25(3)(a) between the crime having been committed "as an individual, jointly with another or through another person." Nothing in the Statute requires that the contribution must involve direct, physical participation at the execution stage of the crime, and, instead, an absent perpetrator may be involved. As such, he concludes, "the prosecution must simply demonstrate that the individual contributed to the crime by committing it with another or others." Judge Fulford therefore argued for a "lesser" test.

The Chamber concluded that Lubanga was a founding member of the UPC, and despite some dispute as to the nature of the UPC's aims in the early days, the founding documents describe the organization's military ambitions as well as a political programme. Regardless of whether the UPC was created as part of a plan to build an army, the UPC-RP was a "political-military movement" that had taken up arms against the RCD-ML, and by the summer of 2002, Lubanga personally intended to take control of Bunia. Recruitment and training were carried out during that year, and Lubanga spoke of the military aims of the UPC/FPLC, for example, when visiting training camps.

It is noteworthy that when portrayed in the media, the visibility of the groups and their leaders and their statements at various occasions to the public can be used as evidence in establishing whether there was a common plan.

The Chamber found that UPC had a military wing, exercised political and military control, and had clear military aims. Lubanga had entered into an agreement with his co-perpetrators to build an effective army in order to ensure political and military control, the Chamber stated, and "this plan resulted in the conscription, enlistment and use of children under the age of 15 to participate actively in hostilities, a consequence which occurred in the ordinary course of events."[320]

2.2. PROVIDING AN ESSENTIAL CONTRIBUTION TO THE CRIME

The next part of the test in determining the individual criminal responsibility of Lubanga was the extent to which his involvement contributed to the crime. With

clear support for the oral evidence of various witnesses linking the armed takeover of Bunia with Thomas Lubanga."

320 Lubanga Judgement, paras 1125–1136.

regard to this aspect, the Pre-Trial Chamber concluded that the contribution had to be essential.

In its submission, the prosecution focused on the requirement of "functional control" over the crime (assigned to a role that was central to the implementation). In other words, according to the prosecution it is enough if the contribution is "substantial" rather than essential; the defence on the other hand stated that the test with a substantial contribution is insufficient.[321]

Two aspects were included according to the majority test: (1) whether it is necessary to establish a connection between the accused's contribution and the crimes that were committed; and (2) the nature of the contribution that gives rise to joint responsibility: should it be described as "more than *de minimis*," "substantial," or "essential."

In line with the language in 25(3)(a), the majority concluded, "None of the participants exercises, individually, control over the crime as a whole but, instead, the control over the crime falls in the hands of a collective as such.'[322] As a result, there was no need to demonstrate that the contribution of the accused, taken alone, caused the crime.

But there is predominance of principal over secondary liability, which thus supports a notion of principal liability that requires a greater contribution than accessory liability: the contribution of a co-perpetrator must be essential. The Chamber then linked the notion of an essential contribution as a minimum threshold to show principal liability of those "persons who are the most responsible for the most serious crimes of international concern."[323]

The Chamber agreed with the prosecution's approach that "it is not necessary that the accused physically perpetrated any of the elements of the crimes or that he was present at the crime scene."[324] Hence, it would not be necessary to show a direct or physical link between the accused's contribution and the commission of the crimes.

The majority concluded that committing a crime jointly with another person involves two objective requirements: (1) the existence of an agreement or common plan between two or more persons that, if implemented, will result in the commission of a crime; and (2) that the accused provided an essential

321 Ibid., para 990.

322 Ibid., para 994.

323 Ibid., para 999. The Court also considered it as a useful test in order to consider the different levels of responsibility, see also Kritz, "Coming to Terms with Atrocities: A Review of Accountability Mechanisms for Mass Violations of Human Rights," 134.

324 Lubanga Judgement, para 1003. See also Wirth, "Co-perpetration in the Lubanga Trial Judgment," 987. Wirth considers that the approach to require that the co-perpetrators must have the "power to frustrate the commission of the crime" is unhelpful as a crime carried out without the withheld contribution would no longer be exactly the same as the one that actually occurred.

contribution to the common plan that resulted in the commission of the relevant crime.[325]

The Chamber then examined Lubanga's position and the entirety of the contribution he made. The position that Mr Lubanga held as the president of the UPC and commander-in-chief of its armed wing, the FPLC, was of importance in considering whether his contribution was essential. There was no one in command above him; he retained the defence and security portfolio for himself; and there is evidence that he was involved substantively in military affairs. Staff planning operations informed the president of their requirements, and Lubanga secured the necessary finances and logistical support.[326]

The defence argued that Lubanga was not always in control, but the Chamber was not persuaded that it established a genuine possibility that his staff had restricted or undermined his authority. The Chamber considered that even if some staff were not in his control, there were others who remained under Lubanga's "ultimate authority."[327] In addition, "the evidence demonstrated that the UPC/FPLC was a well-structured organisation, with the accused and some of his alleged co-perpetrators discharging significant functions. The accused was clearly able to exercise authority over all those within the UPC/FPLC."[328]

The Chamber then considered four elements for the essential role that Lubanga played, examining whether reporting mechanisms were in place to ensure that he was fully informed of developments, had the technical means to run the organization, and was in a position to issue instructions, along with his personal contribution:[329]

1. *Lines of reporting:* The Chamber looked at evidence about how Lubanga regularly received reports, received information on both important and trivial matters, wrote formal letters and issued orders. As such, the Chamber was persuaded that structured and efficient reporting mechanisms were in place to ensure that the accused was informed of all significant developments within the FPLC. He was, therefore, in a position to give relevant instructions, which were distributed as needed down through the FPLC hierarchy.[330]
2. *Technical means:* Here the Chamber considered the availability of short- and long-wave radios, logbooks, call signs, etc., and was satisfied that the UPC/FPLC had the technical means required to ensure that information and instructions could be effectively communicated via the established hierarchy.[331]

325 Lubanga Judgement, para 1006.
326 Ibid., para 1151.
327 Ibid., paras 1159–1169.
328 Ibid., para 1176.
329 Ibid., para 1177.
330 Ibid., para 1182.
331 Ibid., para 1197.

3. *Issuing instructions*: The Chamber reviewed the way attendees for meetings were selected, along with the fact that Lubanga convened meetings with military staff, reprimanded some staff for actions undertaken without the accused being informed, and ordered the removal of a commander. As president of the UPC, he signed a decree regarding demobilization, so that "we would not have difficulties with 'human rights.'"[332]
4. *Personal contribution:* The Chamber was persuaded that Lubanga was actively involved in the exercise of finding recruits, however, whether he was directly and personally involved in recruitment relating to individual children below the age of 15 is difficult to determine. That said, it is certain that he was informed about these activities. The evidence established that he not only condoned the recruitment policy, he played an active part in its implementation and approved the recruitment of children below the age of 15.[333]

The Chamber concluded beyond reasonable doubt that the accused was able to shape the policies of the UPC/FPLC and to direct the activities of his alleged co-perpetrators. The established reporting structures; the lines of communication within the UPC/FPLC; and the meetings and close contact between the accused and at least some of the alleged co-perpetrators, supported the Chamber's conclusion that Lubanga was kept fully informed throughout the relevant period and he issued instructions relating to the implementation of the common plan. Lubanga was involved in planning military operations and he exercised a key role in providing logistical support, by ensuring weapons, ammunition, food, uniforms and military rations and other supplies were available for the troops. As a result, his role was essential to the implementation of the common plan. The role of the accused within the UPC/FPLC and the hierarchical relationship with the other co-perpetrators, viewed in combination with the activities he carried out personally in support of the common plan, led the Chamber to conclude that the implementation of the common plan would not have been possible without Lubanga's contribution.[334]

2.3. THE MENTAL ELEMENT: INTENT AND KNOWLEDGE

The intent and knowledge related to the crime comes from the elements of crime stating that "the perpetrator knew or should have known that such a person or persons were under the age of 15 years."[335] Based on this, the Chamber

[332] Ibid., para 1207.
[333] Ibid., para 1234.
[334] Ibid., para 1270.
[335] See the elements of crime, specifically the third element for the crime related to using, conscripting, and enlisting children. See also William A. Schabas, *An Introduction to the*

established that the mental element must include proof from two perspectives: On the one hand the accused and at least one other perpetrator meant to conscript, enlist or use children under the age of 15 to participate actively in hostilities or they were aware that in implementing their common plan this consequence will occur in the ordinary course of events. On the other hand Lubanga was aware that he provided an essential contribution to the implementation of the common plan. However, in the end the Chamber only seriously considered the second element.

The defence argued that the alleged crimes were not a certain consequence of creating the armed force and thereafter using it in the armed conflict; it also argued that while it was difficult to verify the ages of recruits, a policy requiring verification was in place and was implemented, thereby reducing the risk that underage children would be enlisted. Defence also submitted that since the accused is not prosecuted on the basis of superior responsibility, it has not been established that he condoned or participated in the crimes.[336]

The Chamber made reference to evidence that Lubanga encouraged the population to provide food and to make youngsters available, and that he used child soldiers below the age of 15, including as his bodyguards; he gave speeches at functions where there were children under 15, and such children had contacts with senior staff in the FPLC. It also concluded that he was aware that children under age 15 formed part of the personal escorts for staff. Demobilization efforts were in place, but he did not seek to implement them, and here the Chamber did not consider the fact that he had put some measures in place as a mitigating factor in any event as called for by the defence. Witnesses also said that they had raised the issue of child soldiers with representatives of the UPC at all levels, and also there were attacks on the non-governmental organizations that were there to help these children with reintegration.[337]

Based on this analysis, the Chamber concluded that Lubanga was fully aware of the prohibition on child recruitment and of the concerns of outside bodies as to the recruitment and use of child soldiers, and that this issue was repeatedly raised regardless of the precise nature or context of their meetings. Moreover, the evidence demonstrated that the UPC/FPLC attempted to impede the work of the organizations that were involved with helping child soldiers during the period of the charges.[338]

It is noteworthy that the Chamber made reference to him being "fully aware" of the prohibition on child recruitment, although it did not thoroughly go into the evidence in this regard other than to state that it was raised with Lubanga by different actors, and the connection between that act and the fact that it made

International Criminal Court, Third Edition (Cambridge: Cambridge University Press, 2007), 223–224.

336 Lubanga Judgement, para 1276.

337 Ibid., paras 1277, 1284 and 1288.

338 Ibid., para 1290.

Lubanga aware is not really clarified. The Chamber has clearly identified that Lubanga knew about children in the ranks, but not that he was aware it was a crime. It seems that the one reference to witnesses having raised the issue of child soldiers at "all levels" was considered to be sufficient.

Nonetheless, this is an important aspect for advocates who want to support international criminal justice processes, because it will be important to reach out to commanders and make sure that it is known that they have been made aware of the fact that it is a crime to recruit children under the age of 15.[339] This is also where the development of agreements with armed groups and forces enters in significance, because such agreements could serve as evidence of this awareness and knowledge that it is prohibited under international law, as well as a crime to recruit and use children to participate actively under international criminal law.

The prosecution, however, did rely on the documented letter of 12 February 2003 from the National Secretary for Education to demonstrate that the accused was aware of the presence of children, but the defence suggested the letter demonstrated that the decision for demobilization was being implemented. Apparently, the demobilization decree was not distributed properly, but the Chamber found that it was published in the public domain. There were also many photographs and other media about child soldiers. At one point, a European journalist's interview with a *kadogo* soldier was broadcast on television; the demobilization order was issued within a week of this interview.[340]

In addition, there was reference to a meeting during which witness P-0046 informed Lubanga that MONUC was trying to make a detailed record of the ongoing recruitment of children, including by the UPC/FPLC in particular. P-0046 showed certain documents to Lubanga, including various international resolutions and other instruments concerning the protection of children, and they discussed the Democratic Republic of the Congo's ratification of the Rome Statute. MONUC attempted but was unable to find the official text of the demobilization order. Repeated requests for a meeting with Lubanga to discuss release of children were ignored. Generally, UPC continued to recruit children.[341]

The Rome Statute does not explicitly deal with the issue of *actus reus* although it had been considered in the drafting process, but in the end no provision was included. Some writers have considered that the Statute may

339 The "knowledge" to be passed on through engagement with commanders relates to what both action and inaction may lead to in terms of impact on children, both the act of recruitment itself, but also the consequences of use of children to participate actively. The consequences of action and inaction would be considered as important elements in determining whether the accused has the required "knowledge" of what is the result "in the ordinary course of events." See also Nicola Pisani, "The Mental Element in International Crime," in *Essays on the Rome Statute of the International Criminal Court, Volume II*, eds. Flavia Lattanzi, et al. (Ripa di Fagnano Alto: Editrice il Sirente Picoola Societa Cooperative ar.l., 2004), 126–131.

340 Lubanga Judgement., para 1317.

341 Ibid., paras 1326 and 1327.

include responsibility by omission, and it seems that in this situation did give it some consideration although it was not considered in isolation.[342]

There was a great deal of evidence that young soldiers should have been demobilized, yet the speeches indicate that children below the age of 18 were still being targeted for recruitment and remained within the ranks of the FPLC.[343] Despite the Court being very careful to consider issues related to the age of 15, in this particular instance it mentions 18, indicating the very common approach that if anyone under 18 is allowed to enter, children under 15 will make it to the ranks as well because there is no system in place to limit the entry of children in the armed group or force.

The Chamber also considered that the defence had been imprecise as to whether the demobilization order of 21 October 2002 and the decree of 1 June 2003 lead to the conclusion that the resulting crimes did not occur in the ordinary course of events, or whether it is only suggesting that the accused did not have the "intention" to commit the crimes. The Chamber considered that the lack of cooperation with the non-governmental organization working within the field of demobilization and the threats directed at human rights workers who were involved with children's rights meant that demobilization was never to be implemented.[344]

CONCLUSION

In concluding this chapter on criminal justice, it is important to consider the overall implications of the *Lubanga* case and international criminal justice more broadly on the overall transitional justice process.

While it may not fit all situations, international criminal justice can be an effective approach to depoliticizing the process of bringing criminals to justice, taking the cases away from domestic jurisdictions and bringing them into what may appear to be a more neutral international sphere. It may also allow for other transitional processes to proceed in a more timely fashion and considering the amount of resources going into international criminal proceedings, the level of professionalism is generally also higher than in domestic jurisdictions.[345]

---

342 See Michael Duttwiller, "Liability for Ommission in International Criminal Law," *International Criminal Law Review* 6, no. 1 (2006). More generally on the issue of the drafting history in this regard, see Schabas, *An Introduction to the International Criminal Court, Third Edition*, 225.

343 Lubanga Judgement, para 1344.

344 Ibid., para 1348.

345 Antonio Cassese, "The Rationale for International Criminal Justice," in *The Oxford Companion to International Criminal Justice*, ed. Antonio Cassese (editor-in-chief) (Oxford: Oxford University Press, 2009), 124.

Conversely, criminal justice could internationalize an issue and bring about more sensitivity and political challenges to the transitional justice process at the national level, as has been the case with the charges against Sudan's President Al Bashir by the prosecutor of the International Criminal Court. Following the warrant of arrest, the President and the Government of Sudan undertook a range of activities that were aimed at curtailing international involvement in the transition process in the country.[346]

An important consideration in the area of criminal justice is not just to reflect on the implications of punishment, but also what the implications are if there is no punishment or if there are shortcomings in the punishment. In the *Lubanga* case, there was resentment among communities in affected areas in the Democratic Republic of the Congo due to the exclusive focus on child recruitment, when there had been so many other crimes committed by Lubanga and others.[347]

The proceedings of the ICC in the *Lubanga* case were effective in the sense that they led to the defendant being sentenced, but the procedures were fraught with problems and they took a long time.[348] In addition, pursuing a case through the ICC is very costly, considering what is achieved in the end. Could this money have been better invested in programmes for release and reintegration of children? It is understandably very difficult to measure justice in money or to consider the question of transitional justice over a very short period of time.

Nonetheless, international visibility for the issue of child recruitment has provided entry points for advocacy with commanders. Even since the adoption of the Rome Statute and the arrest warrant itself in 2006, there were points of concern in discussions with rebel leaders, who were not sure about the implications for them. This confirms the importance of viewing the value of criminal justice in transitional processes as progress towards the reconstruction of the rule of law and as having a corrective value.

That said, the international standards may be differently interpreted as well, leading to different legal standards at the national level, but nonetheless there is less likelihood of a complete legal vacuum. The important element here is not that these tribunals have produced cases that are interesting reading to lawyers, but that individuals are not able to completely hide behind domestic jurisdictions in a situation where crimes carried out are recognized as international crimes.

Another dilemma is that while these new procedures provide for an avenue to raise individual criminal responsibility, there is little transparency and scale

346 *The Prosecutor v. Omar Hassan Ahmad Al Bashir*, 4 March 2009.

347 *Through a New Lens: A Child-Sensitive Approach to Transitional Justice*, (2011), 23.

348 On the issue of delay in the proceedings and the timeliness of the decisions, see Heidi L. Hansberry, "Too Much of a Good Thing in Lubanga and Haradinaj: The Danger of Expediency in International Criminal Trials," *Northwestern University Journal on International Human Rights* 9 (2010–2011): 357–401.

as to which cases and who should be brought to justice.[349] There are other indictments that followed the *Lubanga* case that could have included the crime of child recruitment, including the indictment of Al Bashir, but this has not been done.

As the Rome Statute was developed to try those "responsible for the most serious crimes",[350] in the context of ICC proceedings it is critical to consider whether it is those at the highest levels or those who were most involved who should be prosecuted. An example comes from prosecutions of the Berlin Wall shootings, where many low-level guards were brought to trial and convicted, though claiming they were following orders. The lead architects of the country's policy of shoot-to-kill evaded accountability in most cases. When one orders another person to kill, who is responsible? The ICC Statute and the first case of Lubanga has turned things around in this regard, whereby the Court seeks to focus on those who are most responsible rather than those most involved.

But it is not only a question of appropriateness. It also a question of being realistic as to what an international or domestic legal system can achieve with regard to criminal justice during a situation in transition. Key decision makers and those behind child rights violations such as the recruitment and use of children are more often than not protected actors, from the officers to the generals to the president of the country. On the rebel front it will depend on whether the rebels are aligned with the government or totally on their own. Even if they are not aligned with the government, they may still be protected for purposes of domestic peace and other processes of redistributing powers.

Much focus within the transitional justice sphere is on criminal proceedings, holding individuals accountable for the crime of conscripting or enlisting children. This may lead rebel leaders who want to hide from the fact there are children within their ranks refusing to give information in release and reintegration processes that may be used as evidence in criminal proceedings. Children, therefore, may end up in a limbo within an armed force or group. Criminalization and pursuit of war criminals for child recruitment may not ultimately be the best way to ensure release of child soldiers, yet it can serve as an important deterrent to prevent future violations.

In addition to considering the outcome of the case and some of the implications of the judgement, it is critical to take into account the strategies deployed by both the prosecution and the defence in the *Lubanga* case.

349 Antonio Cassese, "On the Current Trends towards Criminal Prosecution and Punishment of Breaches of International Humanitarian Law," *European Journal of International Law* 9 (1998): 2–17, 10.

350 Article 1 of the Rome Statute. Article 1 of the SCSL Statute established that Court for those who were "most responsible." Even if the language has been adjusted in the Rome Statute, the Court did refer to it in the *Lubanga* case (see Lubanga Judgement, para 999), and article 28 goes on to define the applicability to "responsibility of commanders and other superiors."

The prosecution focused on the overall recruitment strategy, reaching out to communities and schools, with coercive campaigns at the village level. This led to conscription, enlistment, and use of children below 15 years of age. There was military training for the children, some were beaten and whipped, and young girls were raped. There was no system to check the ages of the recruits, and Lubanga was aware of the plan leading to the children being recruited and used. He saw children frequently, and he had children as part of his personal protection unit. The prosecution recognized that the use of girl soldiers as sexual slaves existed, even though was not included because it was outside the facts and circumstances described in the charges.[351]

There were few surprises in the arguments put forward by the prosecution, and it could have been useful for the prosecution to dig deeper into the drafting history of the various provisions, as well as how and why the Rome Statute is different from other parts of international law. For instance, the fact that the three crimes of conscripting, enlisting, or using children to actively participate in hostilities are divided by "or" could have benefited from further analysis. In addition, the prosecution could have more carefully considered what it meant to put child soldiers on the stand, and the risks involved in this regard, thereby making an argument that it is not necessary and that evidence can be found through other means – and stating this as a strength and protective measure for affected children rather than a shortcoming in the proceedings, especially in a case that has been internationalized and visible in the way that the *Lubanga* case is.[352]

The other area that could have benefited from further strategies for inclusion in the case was that of sexual violence and the fact that the Chamber did not want to consider this issue except in the context of the reparations discussion. It has certainly not considered this in the context of the notion of the use of children to actively participate. Further work should be done to advocate on the issue of sexual violence in the context of armed conflict and providing information about its widespread practice, thereby showing the implications on children's rights.

Considering the arguments noted above that all that is considered to be active participation is not equal to direct participation should allow for arguments that children who actively participate should not be legitimate targets. Arguments about the significant harm introduced to girls and boys who were raped in the ranks, and the emotional and health consequences of these situations both while in the ranks and afterwards, would have contributed to the level of "real danger as a potential target" – target in this case referring to threats by the very same commanders who had recruited them, not necessarily by other

351 Lubanga Judgement, paras 26–36. Victims' submissions appearing in paragraph 52 onward are not very different from the submissions of the prosecution.

352 See further analysis in this regard in chapter 7 on participatory justice.

armed groups and forces. With a bit more analysis, the Court could have moved in a different direction and included sexual violence in its legal definition of "active participation." Having said that, sexual violence is still part of how children are "used" but not to the same level in bringing about the criminal element as for how children are being used to actively participate in hostilities.

The defence took a two-pronged approach in a rather more advanced strategy to outline its position than that of the prosecution:

The first part of the defence strategy was to challenge the evidence and the testimony of all the prosecution's child soldier witnesses. The key issues included that some of the intermediaries were involved in soliciting false testimony from all the prosecution witnesses; one of the victims solicited false testimony, and the prosecution failed to fulfil its obligations either to investigate all the relevant exculpatory circumstances or to effect timely and appropriate disclosure. The defence requested the Chamber to stay the proceedings as it argued that there were shortcomings with the investigations and the reliability of the evidence.

The second was to focus on the individual criminal responsibility of Lubanga. None of the evidence presented proved beyond reasonable doubt that children under the age of 15 were in the ranks. The prosecution failed to call any former child soldiers who were under 15 at the relevant time, and this on its own cast doubt over the merits of the prosecution's submissions. The defence argued that the UPC was not a military organization, so Lubanga would not have been able to support a "common plan" and he did not play a "central role in the military structure" of the FPLC. It also suggested that while Lubanga visited the camps his involvement did not constitute an "essential contribution" to the process of recruitment. The defence maintained that there was no evidence to suggest that the accused either knew or should have known that there were children under the age of 15 in the ranks and recruitment was taking place, or that he was obliged to ensure that all recruits were over 15. The defence claimed that Mr Lubanga implemented measures prohibiting recruitment of child soldiers and ensuring their demobilization, but that the issue was that demobilization orders were not executed and implementation was difficult.[353]

Indeed, the challenges with the evidence were an easy target for the defence, as this was the first time to collect evidence under very difficult circumstances. Considering that the prosecution had wanted to put child soldiers on the stand, this was also a strong point to put on the table from a defence perspective. Overall, throughout the proceedings, the defence strategy was a strong one.

What could Mr Lubanga have done differently, and what could other commanders learn from this experience? Obviously, ceasing to recruit children is what makes most the sense, but another clear strategy that could have made it more difficult to convict Lubanga would have been to avoid putting the children in harm's way and limiting their participation to auxiliary roles. It would have

---

353 Lubanga Judgement, paras 38–50.

been very difficult to build up a case if the children had not participated in dangerous tasks.

Also, further commitment for the release and reintegration programmes, including announcements and instructions to this effect, along with clear measures to show that there was an effort made to stop the recruitment of children under 15, would have made it easier to tackle the subjective criteria in the case.

The issue of knowledge with regard to age was also emphasized in the adoption of the Paris Commitments, which stress that states endorsing the commitments would "establish mechanisms to ensure that age of entry requirements are fully respected and that responsibility for establishing the age of the recruit rests with the recruiting party."[354] It is also to be read with the provision for *mens rea* as described in article 30 of the Rome Statute, where the perpetrator needs to have "intent" and "knowledge." In other words, the person "means to engage in the conduct"; that person "means to cause the consequence or is aware that it will occur in the ordinary course of events"; and the person must be aware "that a circumstance exists or a consequence will occur in the ordinary course of events."[355]

The provision for "knew or should have known" seems to be stronger than that found in article 30. There may be many issues suggesting that the person should have known that the child was under 15, for instance, because of the appearances of the child, but also that the recruiter had not put in place sufficient procedures for establishing the child's age and did not put the necessary measures in place in order to ensure no child under the age of 15 joins the armed group or force. The provision creates a duty on the part of the accused to take reasonable and feasible safeguards against conscripting, enlisting, or using children to participate actively in hostilities. In the *Lubanga* case, the Chamber certainly found that there was sufficient information available for Lubanga to have understood that he was engaging in a criminal act when children were present within his ranks, but the Chamber also found that not only did he not do anything to address it, efforts to release and reintegrate children were undermined under his leadership.

Finally, what could the humanitarian aid and protection agencies on the ground have done differently? Considering the reasons for recruitment and having better data collection efforts as to why children joined the armed group would be important from a practitioner's point of view. This would provide a better understanding of the wide range of reasons behind recruitment so as to inform recovery and reintegration efforts. It would also have been useful in providing evidence to the process, offering a clear picture of the types of

354 *The Paris Commitments to Protect Children from Unlawful Recruitment or Use by Armed Forces or Armed Groups* (2007).

355 Rome Statute, articles 30(2) and 30(3).

situations that drove children to the ranks of the armed group, including detailed information about the circumstances that they were in while in the armed group. This type of information could also have helped strengthen the case for not separating between voluntary and forced recruitment, as in practice, they cannot be distinguished.

The other issue relates to the age of the child. The age in the Rome Statute cannot be changed, it remains firmly at the age of 15. The Rome Statute in article 21 recognizes the Statute and the Elements of Crime as the key primary sources of law, and as such there would be very little room for interpretation in a question that is as clear as the age below which recruitment of children is a crime. Other parts of international law and general principles of law derived from national jurisdictions are secondary sources, the former of these two likely to include customary international law.[356] However, the Court would only resort to international customary law when something is not clear or when there is a gap in the primary sources available to the Court.

There are situations where treaties have been overridden, but usually in considering a peremptory norm of international law more important than abiding by the rules established through a more general treaty. For instance, in the *Soering* case the European Court of Human Rights considered that the standards found between the two obligations in the European Convention and those found in the extradition treaty. Having considered that the extradition of Soering to the USA would likely expose him to the death row, in violation of article 2, putting Soering at "real risk of exposure to inhuman or degrading treatment of punishment, the Court considered the obligations found in the European Convention as superior to those found in the bilateral extradition treaty."[357] As such, it is unlikely that there would be any way to challenge the parts of the Rome Statute that are quite clear by deferring to other sources of law.

Moving forward it will be useful to see the *Lubanga* judgement in the context of forthcoming deliberations in the Court. Several cases include charges relevant to child recruitment, including the charges against Joseph Kony and Bosco Ntaganda.[358] Child recruitment will continue to be one of the key considerations in the criminal justice agenda.

In chapter 4 on historical justice, the need for systematic data collection carried out through the Security Council mechanism on grave violations against children's rights will be considered in detail.

---

356 Schabas, *An Introduction to the International Criminal Court, Third Edition*, 196.

357 *Case of Soering v. the United Kingdom*, Application no. 14038/88 European Court of Human Rights (07 July 1989), para 88.

358 See *The Prosecutor v. Bosco Ntaganda*, Warrant of Arrest, ICC-01/04-02/06-2-Anx-tENG ICC (22 August 2006), and *The Prosecutor v. Joseph Kony*, Warrant of Arrest for Joseph Kony issued on 8 July 2005 as amended on 27 September 2005, ICC-02/04-01/05-53 ICC (27 September 2005).

CHAPTER 4
CHILD RECRUITMENT AND HISTORICAL JUSTICE
The Security Council Mechanism on Monitoring and Reporting

> *"Could you please write a letter to Mr. Tamil Selvan [head of political wing in the LTTE] to tell him that he had made a mistake. He says all the children have come home, but he has forgotten my child. Please tell him to find my child and send her home."*

INTRODUCTION

Historical justice is about establishing the facts of what has occurred in the past in order to promote the most effective application of justice in the present. This element of transitional justice is often understood to relate to truth commissions, but it draws on several other activities, including those of the criminal justice processes for establishing the facts, distinct fact-finding exercises, and human rights investigations of diverse kinds.[359]

Chapter 4 primarily considers the outcome of the Security Council thematic focus on children and armed conflict as a contribution to historical justice. At the time of the establishment of the monitoring and reporting mechanism of the Security Council in resolution 1612 (2005), it was emphasized that the mechanism was established in order "to collect and provide timely, objective, accurate and reliable information on the recruitment and use of child soldiers in violation of applicable international law and on other violations and abuses committed against children affected by armed conflict."[360] This chapter offers an analysis of the value added by the information gathered through the mechanism and the subsequent conclusions made by the Security Council Working Group

---

[359] Teitel, *Transitional Justice*, 8.

[360] Resolution 1612, para 2(a). See also the Secretary-General's rule of law and transitional justice report from 2011, which references the mechanism as an important aspect of how the Security Council integrates rule of law and transitional justice activities into its work: 12 October 2011 #717, para 11.

(SCWG) on children and armed conflict, as well as action plans developed with armed groups and forces for the release and reintegration of children within the international legal framework for the protection of children during armed conflicts. While the mechanism does much more than gather information, its ultimate purpose is to pave the way for informed action and political transformation in a context of transitional justice.

While there are many options for how to establish the facts, the way that the facts are established and who is behind the fact finding make a great difference.

Key legal questions that are considered in this chapter include:

- What is the objective of historical justice as it relates to the issue of recruitment and use of children?
- Is the information being collected through the Security Council monitoring and reporting mechanism (MRM) on grave violations against children in armed conflict appropriate for other purposes in transitional justice?
- Is the Security Council mechanism used effectively?[361]

Since 1999, the Security Council has demonstrated a keen interest in issues related to conflict-affected children. Although the Security Council has not become involved in setting standards that define the violation of children's rights in armed conflict, it has engaged in translating existing standards into action and in pushing for implementation of those standards.

With respect to historical justice, different situations and different human rights violations will require varying types of facts and truth. In some situations there may be families who need to know the truth in order to be at peace, in others there will be facts needed for a justice process, or the facts may support advocacy efforts to further advance the transitional justice agenda.[362] These records also establish the historical account, and they can in themselves also be a means towards promoting compliance with international human rights and humanitarian law.[363]

To serve the purposes of transitional justice, the historical account must come from a broad and balanced range of sources and encompass descriptions of

---

361 With respect to some of the lessons learned from the mechanism, refer to the review done at the end of SRSG-CAAC Radhika Coomaraswamy's term in 2012. Report prepared by Ambassador Jean-Marc de La Sablière in support of the Special Representative of the Secretary-General on Children and Armed Conflict, *Security Council Engagement on the Protection of Children in Armed Conflict: Progress Achieved and the Way Forward*, (2012), 12–19.

362 See Crocker, "Reckoning with Past Wrongs," 50–51, about knowledge of the past being important in itself, and victims and their descendants having a moral right to information – also, about how some information may be more harmful than good, for instance, by leading to further violence in communities or society as a result of the truth becoming known.

363 Cassese, "On the Current Trends towards Criminal Prosecution and Punishment of Breaches of International Humanitarian Law," 3.

potential violations by both (or all) sides to the conflict. Transitional justice experts, for example, recognize the role of documentation carried out by human rights groups and histories corroborated from victims.[364] At the same time, it is important for those who work on establishing the facts that they remain impartial when collecting information from a human rights perspective, for example: whenever a right has potentially been violated, it will be reported regardless of what actor may have committed the violation.

The truth and historical record of human rights abuses can shape the transition period when established in a transparent way. The literature considering this aspect, however, tends to give only the positive examples of how fact finding led to a successful conclusion, glossing over the drawn-out situations that never seem to come to a conclusion.[365] The realities studied here are quite different as they are primarily based on situations where there is a lack of pre-existing systems, combined with chronic instability and conflict to varying degrees of intensity.

The process for collecting this information and preparing the historical record of children's situation during conflicts, and the policy and practice of the Security Council mechanism, are further analysed below – both in terms of the decisions made by the SCWG and of the action plans developed at the country level, and regarding the way international legal obligations are being implemented through these plans. The work done in the context of truth commissions is not considered here, as this has been studied elsewhere and there is little to add to what has already been researched.[366]

The chapter is divided into two sections: (1) an overview of the way in which the Security Council MRM functions as a tool for historical justice; and (2) an overview and analysis of the Security Council MRM and how it has shaped the approaches to children involved in armed conflict.

1. THE SECURITY COUNCIL'S ENGAGEMENT ON CHILDREN AND ARMED CONFLICT

Between 1999 and 2012, the Security Council adopted nine resolutions on children and armed conflict, which led to the formation of the MRM that addresses grave violations against children's rights. This section looks into its historical development and the type of information being gathered through the mechanism.

---

364 Teitel, *Transitional Justice*, 73.

365 Ibid., 91.

366 See for instance *Through a New Lens: A Child-Sensitive Approach to Transitional Justice*, (2011). This publication includes several articles on truth commissions and their considerations on children's rights, building on the experiences in South Africa, Sierra Leone, Liberia, and Peru.

1.1. THE DEVELOPMENT OF THE SECURITY COUNCIL MECHANISM FOR MONITORING AND REPORTING OF GRAVE VIOLATIONS AGAINST CHILDREN'S RIGHTS

The overall focus of the MRM established under the auspices of the Security Council has been on children affected by armed conflict as broadly defined, with a particular emphasis on six grave violations against children.[367] Security Council engagement began with a focus on child recruitment; recently, it adopted resolution 1882, which expanded the "triggers" for listing violators and concerted action to include the killing and maiming of children, as well as rape and other types of sexual violence against children.[368] Resolution 1998, adopted in July 2011, added attacks on schools and hospitals as another reason for inclusion in the annexes of the list of parties that engage in these violations of international law. These new triggers have not yet benefited from significant implementation in the field, and practice has evolved mainly around the issue of recruitment and use of children, with some general references to the broader framework for children and armed conflict.

In 1998, as the Security Council started its debates on children and armed conflict and adopted its first Presidential Statement on the issue, there was merely a political discussion without any real impact on the ground.[369] The early focus of this initiative was on broad advocacy, on mainstreaming child protection issues, and on ensuring that UN peacekeeping mandates incorporated children's issues, which was also highlighted in the Secretary-General's first report on the issue of children and armed conflict.[370]

---

[367] The six grave violations to be monitored and reported upon are: killing or maiming of children; recruiting or using child soldiers; attacks against schools or hospitals; rape or other grave sexual violence against children; abduction of children; and denial of humanitarian access for children. Also see *Report of the Secretary-General on Children and Armed Conflict*, UN Doc. A/59/695-S/2005/72 (9 February 2005), para 68.

[368] United Nations Security Council, *Security Council Resolution on Children and Armed Conflict* UN Doc. S/RES/1882 (4 August 2009).

[369] United Nations Security Council, *Statement by the President of the Security Council on Children and Armed Conflict* UN Doc. SC/PRST/1998/18 (1998). For a more detailed history of the mechanism, see Bo Viktor Nylund, "From Standard-Setting to Implementation: The Security Council's Thematic Focus on Children and Armed Conflict," *Human Rights & International Legal Discourse* 5: No. 1 (2011): 101–119.

[370] See *Report of the Secretary-General on Children and Armed Conflict*, UN Doc. A/55/163-S/2000/712 (19 July 2000), recommendation 35. The Secretary-General recommended that the Security Council ensure that the mandates of all relevant UN peacekeeping operations include monitoring and reporting on the protection of children. This trend continued in the years following. See, e.g., United Nations Security Council, *Security Council Resolution on Sierra Leone* UN Doc. S/RES/1270 (22 October 1999), para 18, and United Nations Security Council, *Security Council Resolution on the Democratic Republic of Congo* UN Doc. S/RES/1279 (30 November 1999), para 5(e).

The debates became more substantive over time, and the Council initiated the adoption of resolutions on children and armed conflict. The resolutions increasingly focused on making a difference at the field level. The Security Council did not, however, seek to develop new standards under international law relevant to children and armed conflict; rather, it sought to reinforce existing ones.

A few years into the annual debates on children and armed conflict, the Security Council framework began seeking to enhance accountability in three interrelated areas.

The first was monitoring and reporting: since 2001, the Council has sought to establish a mechanism for monitoring and reporting, which would allow it and the UN as a whole to have a better grasp of the actual situation of children in armed conflict situations.[371]

The second was the listing of perpetrators: since 2002, the Secretary-General's reports have been "naming and shaming" actors who were responsible for the recruitment and use of children.[372] In 2003, this list was expanded to include parties that were not on the agenda of the Security Council.[373] In its 2011 resolution, the Council reaffirmed that the MRM would continue be implemented in countries in both annexes.[374]

The third was action on behalf of children: as of 2003, the Council started calling for action plans to be developed at the field level, a kind of legal agreement between the UN and armed forces and groups that sought the release and reintegration of those children back into society.[375]

These were the early days of the work of the Security Council, however, and the three areas of accountability evolved quickly to become interrelated parts of a mechanism. This mechanism was called for in a 2004 resolution requesting the Secretary-General to "devise urgently and preferably within three months, an action plan for a systematic and comprehensive monitoring and reporting

371 *United Nations Security Council Resolution on Children and Armed Conflict*, UN Doc. S/RES/1379 (20 November 2001), para 10(c). This resolution requested the Secretary-General to "continue and intensify, on a case by case basis, monitoring and reporting activities by peacekeeping and peace-building support operations on the situation of children in armed conflict."

372 *Report of the Secretary-General on Children and Armed Conflict*, UN Doc. S/2002/1299 (26 November 2002). S/RES/1379, para 16 included a request for this list.

373 *Report of the Secretary-General on Children and Armed Conflict*, UN Doc. A/58/546-S/2003/1053 (10 November 2003), para 10(3).

374 United Nations Security Council, *Security Council Resolution on Children and Armed Conflict* UN Doc. S/RES/1998 (12 July 2011), para 2. The Council also pointed out that MRM establishment and implementation "shall not prejudge or imply a decision by the Security Council as to whether or not to include a situation on its agenda".

375 United Nations Security Council, *Security Council Resolution on Children and Armed Conflict* UN Doc. S/RES/1460 (30 January 2003), para 4. Recent resolutions also make reference to broader follow-up to the resolutions on children and armed conflict, and efforts to monitor and report progress. See Resolution 1998 (2011) para 12.

mechanism."[376] This led to the adoption of resolution 1612, which endorsed the MRM as designed in the Secretary-General's 2005 report.[377] The mechanism is intended to produce "timely, objective, accurate and reliable information on the recruitment and use of child soldiers in violation of applicable international law and on other violations and abuses committed against children affected by armed conflict."[378]

It was also through resolution 1612 that the Security Council established a working group to review the reports generated through the mechanism and that includes all Council members.[379] These reports have become the key means through which the Security Council remains apprised of the issue of children and armed conflict.

1.2. THE PROCESS FOR COLLECTING INFORMATION

UN offices in situations listed in the annexes of the Secretary-General's annual report are required to establish a task force on monitoring and reporting grave violations. As a result of the established MRM, each task force prepares an annual country-specific report. Based on information emanating from the MRM, a country's annual report is prepared on grave child rights violations that have occurred and it documents, if possible, what party is responsible for them. The country reports also highlight what actions have been undertaken to address and respond to these violations.

This system has given rise to detailed reviews by the Security Council Working Group of different country situations and has resulted in conclusions with respect to each of the situations. The MRM has generated information through more than 40 country reports from 2006–2012.[380]

Security Council resolution 1612 emphasizes the importance of the mechanisms being designed and rolled out in "participation of and in cooperation with" the government.[381] The information gathered is developed based on the mechanism established at the country level, which can be more or less effective depending on the country context and the challenges in gathering information.

It is important to clarify that the information should be vetted by the UN and that the task force on the ground should be led by the organization rather than

376 United Nations Security Council, *Security Council Resolution on Children and Armed Conflict* UN Doc. S/RES/1539 (22 April 2004), para 2.

377 *Report of the Secretary-General on Children and Armed Conflict*, UN Doc. A/59/695-S/2005/72 (9 February 2005).

378 United Nations Security Council, *Security Council Resolution on Children and Armed Conflict* UN Doc. S/RES/1612 (26 July 2005), para 2(a).

379 Ibid., para 8.

380 See bibliography for a full list of the country reports.

381 *Security Council Resolution on Children and Armed Conflict* (26 July 2005), para 2(b)).

by the government. Although there have been situations where a government has insisted that it be part of the mechanism, for purposes of vetting the data so that it is objective and accurate, this must be an exercise within the UN system.[382]

There may be independent bodies affiliated but distinct from government that play a role in the country-level mechanism, such as independent human rights commissions and ombudsmen; however, these bodies may not be as independent as their mandate intends due to a range of political and security considerations on the ground. Having said that, the UN system may not always be able to deliver on protection of human rights as it would be expected.[383]

While the government is not part of the formal mechanism, it is only through cooperation with the government that some of the long-term solutions will be found. It is therefore common practice to establish parallel processes and advocacy discussions with the government, based on the analysis brought forward through the MRM. This can be a more or less formal body depending on the context.[384] Similarly, there may be forums established to have advocacy discussions together with armed groups, although this is not a formal requirement through the Security Council resolutions.

It is not for a national government to decide when a mechanism is put in place and when it ends.[385] The trigger for the mechanism to be established is the listing of parties in the annexes of the annual report of the Secretary-General on children and armed conflict, which also reports on a number of situations of concern, along with the situations of parties listed in the annexes which mandate the UN to put the fully fledged mechanism in place. For other situations of concern, it is also expected that the UN will gather sufficient information to keep monitoring the situation with recommendations as to whether or not it eventually becomes part of the annexes to the Secretary-General's report, which ultimately is the decision of the Secretary-General himself.[386]

A recent example of early engagement comes from the situation in Syria, which has been included in the Security Council MRM. The Syrian authorities have made a commitment to allow the UN to begin independent verification of

382 O/SRSG-CAAC et al., *MRM Field Manual: Monitoring and Reporting Mechanism (MRM) on Grave Violations against Children in Situations of Armed Conflict* (New York: O/SRSG-CAAC, UNICEF, DPKO, April 2010), 5 and 18.

383 The report on how the UN system failed to raise serious human rights concerns during the last months of fighting in Sri Lanka shows that it can be difficult for the UN organizations to fulfil their mandate in complex contexts. *Report of the Secretary-General's Internal Review Panel on United Nations Action in Sri Lanka*, United Nations (2012).

384 O/SRSG-CAAC et al., *MRM Field Manual: Monitoring and Reporting Mechanism (MRM) on Grave Violations against Children in Situations of Armed Conflict*, 7.

385 Annex 2 includes situations that are not on the Security Council agenda, and as such the engagement from the government perspective is more voluntary. Nonetheless, the United Nations needs to have a system in place to gather information for purposes of the Secretary-General annual report on children and armed conflict.

386 Ibid., 5.

alleged violations against children in the ongoing conflict.[387] The principle of working in collaboration with the host government has been applied, while it remains to be seen what will come out of this process of gathering new evidence for purposes of historical and other elements of transitional justice.

The Syrian situation reflects the universal reality that it is tremendously difficult to gather information of this type during armed conflicts, which can make the circumstances even more complex and dangerous than some of the criminal justice processes. The challenge is to collect information about grave violations against children's rights in the midst of armed conflict, including that of recruitment and use of children, among the refugee population as well as communities within Syria. Moreover, with the political complexity of the situation, the information will be scrutinized by many quarters, and it will be almost impossible to expect coherent action by the Security Council because the Council has already been blocked from taking action by political considerations over the past couple of years.

1.3. THE TYPE OF INFORMATION BEING COLLECTED

The mechanism for the monitoring and reporting of grave violations against children's rights was clearly designed to drive accountability and action on behalf of war-affected children, as well as to gather information for its own sake.

As such, the information gathered could be linked to providing a historical account for the purposes of transitional justice mechanisms, and also for the UN human rights apparatus, including the treaty bodies and special procedures. While the data gathered is focused on incidents, it could comprise of incidents involving one or several children, or also incidents that did not directly involve children (such as attacks on schools or hospitals, or denial of humanitarian access).[388] The data also contributes towards the exercise of listing (and delisting) parties to conflict who are responsible for grave violations against children's rights, and for which there is a trigger.[389]

The MRM does not require individual case information, and therefore this information is better held by individual organizations that work with individual children and have expertise in case management. What becomes useful, however, is the overall analysis that provides for an overview of the incidents, the

387 Press release OSRSG-CAAC December 2012.

388 O/SRSG-CAAC et al., *MRM Field Manual: Monitoring and Reporting Mechanism (MRM) on Grave Violations against Children in Situations of Armed Conflict*, 19.

389 Note that the listing and delisting exercises are inherently political, and while they should be independent from the Security Council in the way they are set up, the most recent resolution adopted makes reference to the Council wanting to be briefed on questions relating to the delisting process. United Nations Security Council, *Security Council Resolution on Children and Armed Conflict* UN Doc. S/RES/2068 (19 September 2012), para 4.

locations, the armed forces/groups involved, and the trends over time. This does not downplay the importance of specific data on incidents and release and reintegration efforts in order to plan a response accordingly. As for other human rights information gathering, the number of incidents rising or falling may not necessarily be a trend of more or less children being recruited, but in some circumstances it can be an important indicator of when to reinforce protection through presence initiatives, community advocacy efforts, or advocacy with armed groups and forces.[390]

The MRM Field Manual, which guides staff on how to put in place the mechanism, provides guidance on four focus areas for the data collection exercise:

1. *The child:* The information gathered generally focuses on the victim or survivor of the violence, providing details about the child, including age, origin, gender, etc.
2. *The age:* The process of determining age includes such items as identifying the age of other siblings in order to determine age differences; any significant event that occurred during the year of birth, or before or after; whether he or she has gone to school, and if so in what grade; any other important cultural signposts that the child met; height of the child; and reference to another child who is the same age.
3. *Alleged perpetrators:* Though it may not always be possible to know for certain what force or group perpetrated the violation, this information should be included to the extent possible, along with the way in which the force/group recruited the child and the time, location, circumstances, and other details.
4. *Direct/active participation:* While the guidance provided to UN field staff does not include how to differentiate between different roles played in the armed group/force, it does include a definition that is along the lines of the Paris Commitments to Protect Children from Unlawful Recruitment or Use by Armed Forces or Armed Groups – in other words, a broad definition that is mainly aimed at being as inclusive as possible for recovery and reintegration purposes. What this means is that regardless of the role that the child played, it would be considered a violation under the mechanism and should be recorded as a "case."[391]

Although the MRM is not directly linked to justice mechanisms, information gleaned through the mechanism will be part of the country annual reports,

390 Increase in reports could simply indicate increased awareness that a certain conduct is a violation of children's rights, or awareness of the reporting channels improving over time.

391 O/SRSG-CAAC et al., MRM Field Manual: Monitoring and Reporting Mechanism (MRM) on Grave Violations against Children in Situations of Armed Conflict, 10.

which are public documents and available to any other entity that might want to make use of the information. Also, as was always envisaged in the evidence-gathering schemes developed for the implementation of the Rome Statute, the UN system may contribute with information.[392]

The *Lubanga* case allows for some comparison as to whether the information gathered through the mechanism can be useful in providing evidence in a given case. Considering the outcome, it would be important for the mechanism to go deeper into the circumstances of the child in the armed group or force, detailing not only the role played, but whether at any given time the child felt to be in real danger. The considerations relevant to the age of the child would also benefit from more rigorous approaches, not only detailing the assessed age, but also the means of verification at the time, so that the analysis could outline the key aspects of methodology used in determining the child's age.

The element of "denial of humanitarian access," is also an under-explored area of focus. Since this element involves intentional barring by physical force or administrative barriers of personnel and material, it could clearly include programmes to secure the release and recovery of child soldiers.[393] In addition, this could potentially provide information relevant to the subjective elements for considering liability in a criminal justice case.

2. ANALYSING THE OUTCOME OF THE SECURITY COUNCIL WORKING GROUP'S DELIBERATIONS

By the end of 2012, the Security Council Working Group had adopted 45 sets of formal conclusions covering 20 situations.[394] Currently, 15 situations are listed in the annexes to the Secretary-General's 2014 report because Syria was added in 2012, Mali in 2013 and Nigeria in 2014, and parties in five countries have been delisted: Côte d'Ivoire, in 2008; Burundi, in 2010; Nepal and Sri Lanka, in 2012; and Chad, in 2014.[395] This section looks at the formal outcome of the Security Council MRM, and how it has been used to date.

---

392 Johnson, "The Lubanga Case and Cooperation between the UN and the ICC," 888. Johnson writes from the perspective of balancing between the obligation to disclose, and maintaining confidentiality.

393 O/SRSG-CAAC et al., *MRM Field Manual: Monitoring and Reporting Mechanism (MRM) on Grave Violations against Children in Situations of Armed Conflict*, 11.

394 See annex 1 for a full list of situations and conclusions.

395 See annexes in (15 May 2014 #716) and *Report of the Secretary-General on Children and Armed Conflict*, (26 April 2012). Also, the situation in the Sudan is now divided into two separate processes for the Sudan and South Sudan. Further, Uganda is still listed because of the activities by the Lord's Resistance Army. See also *Security Council Resolution on Children and Armed Conflict* (19 September 2012), paras 9(a) and 9(c). This resolution welcomes the positive developments that have led to the delisting of all parties to the armed conflict, while

2.1. FORMAL CONCLUSIONS AND ACTION PLANS

Equally critical to the monitoring and reporting exercise is the prevention and response – the work implemented to find solutions for children who are caught in conflicts through, for instance, the development of action plans.

Since 2006, the nature of the SCWG's conclusions has evolved. Today, they are fairly rich in recommendations to a range of actors – including the governments concerned, parties listed in the reports of the Secretary-General, the UN, the Security Council, and donors – and they provide guidance on how to move forward in the process for the release, recovery, and reintegration of conflict-affected children. The conclusions also interpret the relevant legal standards applicable to a given situation.

Tools available to better secure the release of children are contained in the information collected by the MRM. These include verified and specific details of the violations that have occurred during a given reporting period, such as information about the nature of the violation, the victim, and the perpetrator. Specific standards of verification and information collection must be met for reports to be deemed accurate, objective, and reliable and thereby realize the overall purpose of the mechanism:

> The purpose of a monitoring, reporting and compliance mechanism is to provide for the systematic gathering of objective, specific and reliable information on grave violations committed against children in situations of armed conflict, leading to well-informed, concerted and effective responses to ensure compliance with international and local children and armed conflict protection norms.[396]

The information collected thus becomes the basis of analysis and advocacy at different levels, with the most important opportunity arising at the country level. Passing the information from the Secretary-General to the Security Council can trigger both action and a response on the political front as well.[397] At the country level, the information gives the country task force a concrete and informed foundation on which to engage with the parties to the conflict. Whereas this engagement is important as a process in itself, by opening up dialogue with the parties to the conflict, the intention is also to secure the commitment and action of the armed forces or group to end the recruitment and use of children in armed conflict as well as other grave child rights violations.

---

asking the Government to continue to investigate violations of children's rights by all parties perpetrated, and that those responsible are held accountable.

396 *Report of the Secretary-General on Children and Armed Conflict*, UN Doc. A/59/695-S/2005/72 (9 February 2005), para 65.

397 Katy Barnett and Anna Jefferys, *Full of promise: How the UN's Monitoring and Reporting Mechanism can better protect children*, Network Paper, Number 62 (September 2008).

As first called for by the Security Council, the commitment explicit in resolution 1460, and reiterated in resolutions 1539 and 1612, should be translated into an action plan to end the recruitment and use of children by armed forces and groups. An action plan is a concrete and time-bound commitment to halt all new recruitment of children and to separate and release all children associated with the group or force. Typically developed jointly by the country task force and the armed force or group, the action plan outlines the commitments and operational steps to be taken to ensure the release of all children, including programmatic reintegration activities to assist the children in making the transition from military to civilian life.

While the action plans developed within the Security Council framework and other agreements developed together with armed groups and forces are different in nature, they all build on international law relevant to child recruitment.[398] To date there have been more than 20 different action plans covering 12 situations; these plans are generally signed by both the relevant armed group or force and the UN.[399] In some instances, armed groups have also made unilateral statements.[400]

Out of the six grave violations covered by the monitoring and reporting mechanism, four now trigger "name and shame" listing in the annexes of the Secretary-General's report. The original trigger was that of "recruitment and use of children", while "sexual violence" and "killing and maiming" were added in 2009, and "attacks on schools and hospitals" was added in 2011. At the recent debate of the Security Council, several governments advocated for "abductions of children" to be added as a trigger. In the early days of implementing the triggers introduced in 2009 and 2011, few countries were listed. However, the listings for the new triggers are more prominent in the most recent annual report of the Secretary-General of May 2014, and it is now quite common for parties to be listed for more than one violation.[401]

The list of key perpetrators is by no means all-inclusive at this point in time, considering also the fact that the new triggers would not have retroactive effect and could not, for instance, take into account the surge of violence in Sri Lanka or Palestine during the early part of 2009. To date, only one action plan, which was concluded in Somalia, focuses on killing and maiming, while the action plan developed in Afghanistan has an annex that makes reference to taking

398 Note that some qualify as a measure for delisting, while others do not.

399 See the bibliography for the complete list of action plans concluded to date.

400 Plan d'action des Forces Armées des Forces Nouvelles pour mettre fin à l'utilisation des Enfants fréquentant les lieux de rassemblement militaires, Côte d'Ivoire (10 October 2005), and Plan d'Action contre l'utilisation des enfant associés aux conflit armés. Forces de Résistance du Grand Ouest de la Côte d'Ivoire. (14 September 2006), and Deed of Commitment, Office of the Supreme Headquarters, Karen National Union, Kawthoolei (4 March 2007), and Deed of Commitment: Chin National Front/Army (15 March 2009).

401 See annexes to the *Report of the Secretary-General on Children and Armed Conflict*, UN Doc. A/68/878-S/2014/339 (15 May 2014).

action to address killing and maiming, as well as rape and sexual violence.[402] In the future, the development of additional action plans for addressing these three additional grave violations can be expected.

2.2. PERSONAL SCOPE: CHILDREN AFFECTED BY ARMED CONFLICT, CHILD RECRUITMENT, AND THE QUESTION OF AGE IN THE SECURITY COUNCIL MECHANISM

Although the Security Council framework applies to children affected by armed conflict generally, the development of the MRM prioritized six grave violations. Several of those violations are also broad in application, for example, the denial of humanitarian access, attacks on schools and hospitals (especially when giving a broad reading to the term "attacks"), and the provision for killing and maiming. These violations may take many forms and they affect larger groups of children.

With regard to the age for the prohibition of recruitment, several conclusions refer to age 18, albeit in different ways. In the context of Nepal, the SCWG urged the Government to "provide full support to the United Nations Mission in Nepal in separating children under the age of 18 from combatants...with a view to reintegrating those children into their families as a matter of priority."[403] In the context of Sri Lanka, the Working Group urged both the Liberation Tigers of Tamil Eelam (LTTE) and the Tamil Makkal Viduthalai Pulikal (TMVP) to "immediately end the practice of abduction, use and recruitment of children under the age of 18."[404]

Similarly, in its 2008 conclusions, the SCWG was concerned that children were not being released, including those who were adults at the time but had been recruited when they were under 18.[405] In its conclusions on Uganda, the

402 See Somali National Armed Forces (SNAF) Transitional Federal Government of Somalia. "Action Plan between the Transitional Federal Government of Somalia, Somali National Armed Forces and the United Nations to eliminate killing and maiming of children in contravention of international law." 6 August 2012 and "Action Plan between the Government of the Islamic Republic of Afghanistan and the United Nations Country Task Force on Monitoring and Reporting regarding children associated with National Security Forces in Afghanistan." 30 January 2011.

403 United Nations Security Council Working Group on Children and Armed Conflict, *Conclusions on Children and Armed Conflict in Nepal* UN Doc. S/AC.51/2007/8 (12 June 2007), para 15(b(ii)).

404 United Nations Security Council Working Group on Children and Armed Conflict, *Conclusions on Children and Armed Conflict in Sri Lanka* UN Doc. S/AC.51/2007/9 (13 June 2007), paras 10(c(i)) and 10(e(i)).

405 United Nations Security Council Working Group on Children and Armed Conflict, *Conclusions on Children and Armed Conflict in Sri Lanka* UN Doc. S/AC.51/2008/11 (21 October 2008), para 7(b). Mentioned again in United Nations Security Council Working

SCWG again referred to the age of 18, this time building on standards found in national legislation and referring to the prohibition against recruiting anyone under 18 years old included in the Uganda People's Defence Forces Act.[406] In its 2010 conclusions on Uganda, the SCWG refers to "children under 18 years of age" in discussing commitments made by the Lord's Resistance Army during previous years.[407] As can be seen from the examples above, while the Working Group is not making consistent use of age 18 for the prohibition of child recruitment, whenever it has referred to an age it is 18. Similarly, in action plans and agreements where an age is referred to, it is the age of 18.[408] On a few occasions "child soldier" is not defined,[409] and in the case of Nepal the action plan does not mention the words "child" or "child soldier," but it does refer to the Comprehensive Peace Agreement, which stated that the signatories were "not to conscript or use children who are aged 18 or below in the armed force. Children thus affected shall be rescued immediately and appropriate assistance as may be needed shall be provided for their rehabilitation."[410]

In its 2009 conclusions on Afghanistan, the SCWG provided an interpretation of "direct participation" that urged the parties to take measures "to ensure that children are not used in any military operation or any other violent action, [and to] proceed with the immediate and unconditional release of all children associated with them *in any capacity*."[411] (emphasis added)

Generally developed to focus on the release and reintegration process, the action plans and other agreements have taken an inclusive approach in defining "child soldier" by referring to the full range of activities that children may have

---

Group on Children and Armed Conflict, *Conclusions on Children and Armed Conflict in Sri Lanka* UN Doc. S/AC.51/2010/2 (3 June 2010), para 7(b).

406 United Nations Security Council Working Group on Children and Armed Conflict, *Conclusions on Children and Armed Conflict in Uganda* UN Doc. S/AC.51/2010/1 (16 June 2010), para 13(c).

407 Ibid., para 5(c).

408 The Front pour la libération du grand ouest, Karen, SLM/A, TMVP, Uganda, Moro Islamic Liberation Front, SPLA, and JEM agreements all refer to age 18.

409 See Plan d'action des Forces Armées des Forces Nouvelles pour mettre fin à l'utilisation des Enfants fréquentant les lieux de rassemblement militaires, Côte d'Ivoire (10 October 2005).

410 See Action Plan between the Government of Nepal, the Unified Communist Party of Nepal – Maoist, and the United Nations in Nepal regarding the Discharge of Disqualified Maoist Army Personnel and Related Tasks (16 December 2009). For the language of the peace agreement see 'Unofficial Translation of the Comprehensive Peace Agreement concluded between the Government of Nepal and the Communist Party of Nepal (Maoist),' (21 November 2006), article 7(6(1)).

411 United Nations Security Council Working Group on Children and Armed Conflict, *Conclusions on Children and Armed Conflict in Afghanistan* UN Doc. S/AC.51/2009/1 (13 July 2009), para 15(d(iii)). See also Chad Conclusions of 2007 speaking of urging to 'release unconditionally children present in their ranks in any capacity': United Nations Security Council Working Group on Children and Armed Conflict, *Conclusions on Children and Armed Conflict in Chad* UN Doc. S/AC.51/2007/16 (24 September 2007), para 16(b(ii)). United Nations Security Council Working Group on Children and Armed Conflict, *Conclusions on Children and Armed Conflict in the Philippines* UN Doc. S/AC.51/2008/10 (3 October 2008).

been involved in while associated with armed groups and forces. Several agreements take the definition from the Cape Town Principles,[412] while other agreements have a more simplified definition.[413]

As a result, looking at the above practice of the Security Council conclusions and the way that it has endorsed the signing of action plans, the Security Council framework appears to take on a broad notion of children recruited or used under the age of 18. It is significant that the Council has adopted this broad notion of which groups of children should be included because girls in particular tend to be overlooked since they serve in auxiliary roles, which leaders of armed forces and groups tend to oversee as being part of their cadre.

Among the six grave violations, child recruitment has received the greatest attention. The strong focus of the Security Council on child recruitment is most likely linked to the fact that it is the most developed element of the international legal framework relevant to children in armed conflict. Moreover, child recruitment has proved to be an area that can be monitored and reported on by child protection agencies with greater success than some of the other violations such as gender-based violence. Child recruitment has also been a focus of advocacy groups and organizations working with conflict-affected children.

While this narrow focus could be seen as a shortcoming, it would also seem to be a strength in the sense that child recruitment has become an entry point to negotiation with armed groups and forces. In dealing with children who have been recruited and used by armed forces and groups it is also possible to address broader socio-economic issues and develop programmes for broader recovery and reintegration programming.

2.3. FOCUS ON STATE AND NON-STATE ACTORS IN THE SECURITY COUNCIL MECHANISM

The Security Council framework provides an equal focus on both state and non-state actors and does not distinguish in its practice between the different actors

412 This is the case with the Moro Islamic Liberation Front, Front pour la libération du grand ouest, Chin, and Karen agreements.

413 This is the case with the JEM agreement. See also *Cape Town Principles and Best Practices, adopted at a symposium on the prevention of the recruitment of children into armed conflicts and on demobilization and on social reintegration of child soldiers in Africa*, (Cape Town, 30 April 1997). The Cape Town Principles were antecedents to the Paris Principles, adopted at a symposium on the prevention of recruitment of children and demobilization and social reintegration of child soldiers in Africa. They became widely referenced after their adoption in 1997 because they were the first advocacy tool recognizing the need for a broad definition of "child soldiers" to include children in various roles within armed groups and forces. Compared to the Paris Principles, however, the Cape Town Principles were different in legal nature in that they were adopted by an expert group and not by governments. See *The Paris Principles and Guidelines on Children Associated with Armed Forces or Armed Groups*, (February 2007).

to which it is providing feedback. However, at the stage of holding its deliberations to develop and adopt the conclusions, the SCWG is primarily dealing with the governments concerned, and hence the guidance provided by the Security Council tends to be more government-oriented. At the same time, in situations where governments are reluctant to allow the UN to develop action plans with non-state armed groups, the Council consistently makes reference to this as a necessary means of achieving results for children and calls on governments to permit contacts with those actors.[414]

In terms of the focus of the action plans, some two-thirds of those plans have to date focused on armed groups. This clearly shows that the Security Council is willing to apply the legal standards to non-state actors in all types of situations, as well as the commitments made by these armed groups for the release and reintegration of children.

The MRM designed for the Security Council framework takes a child-centred approach, as it focuses on the impact of the situation on children and does not necessarily designate a particular context as an armed conflict, nor does it distinguish situations as international or non-international armed conflict. In so doing, the Secretary-General has stated that:

> In the performance of her mandate, my Special Representative has adopted a pragmatic and cooperative approach to this issue, with a humanitarian emphasis, aimed at ensuring broad and effective protection for children exposed and affected by conflict in situations of concern. Reference to a situation of concern is not a legal determination and reference to a non-State party does not affect its legal status.[415]

The listing exercise does not make any distinction as to an armed group's level of organization; it is the fact that there is verified information that children are implicated by a situation which warrants the listing. In the context of children and armed conflict, this makes it possible for the listing exercise to include situations that are not necessarily armed conflicts with all that implies. It is also not necessary for the situations listed under this mechanism to be a threat to international peace and security, which is normally the trigger for Security Council engagement. For the purposes of addressing the issues at stake, the fact that the Security Council mechanism has looked at the impact on children rather than at the level of organization has allowed groups that are not well organized and easily identifiable to become the object of critical attention. It remains important, nonetheless, that there is a certain level of organization and structure within the armed group in order to have meaningful negotiations with

---

414 See, e.g., United Nations Security Council Working Group on Children and Armed Conflict, *Conclusions on Children and Armed Conflict in Colombia* UN Doc. S/AC.51/2010/3 (30 September 2010), para 5(d).

415 *Report of the Secretary-General on Children and Armed Conflict*, UN Doc. A/64/742-S/2010/181 (13 April 2010), para 7.

decision makers on the release and reintegration of children and to develop programmes for humanitarian action.[416]

The Security Council Working Group also makes use of similar language in dealing with situations that are not an agenda item, so as to make sure that they are not labelling a situation as a threat to international peace and security and therefore entering into the political realm of discussing the applicability of sanctions and other enforcement mechanisms.[417]

2.4. TEMPORAL FOCUS OF THE SECURITY COUNCIL: FROM PREVENTION TO RECOVERY AND REINTEGRATION

The Security Council MRM is a mechanism for the implementation of accountability at all its different levels, both during and after conflict, and primarily in situations that are of concern in maintaining international peace and security. In situations covered by its mandate, the Council emphasizes preventive child protection systems, such as legislation and measures implemented to ensure that the intake into armed forces abides by existing standards. It also includes recommendations for the release and reintegration of children and for the types of programmes that need to be established for these children.

Of the 18 situations of concern within the Security Council framework, 16 states have endorsed the Paris Commitments.[418] This is likely to be the result of the fact that signing onto these Commitments indicates a willingness to engage in the release and reintegration of children, and may provide more support to those governments for recovery and reintegration programming. The Commitments were developed to support the release and reintegration of children who have been recruited and used, not as a tool to develop new standards in international law but to further advance the prohibition of recruitment and use in operational terms, particularly during the release, recovery, and reintegration phase. The state-endorsed Paris Commitments are high-level standards applicable to prevent and respond to child recruitment, and were adopted in 2007, with an annual event seeking to obtain further endorsements. As of Spring 2015, 105 states have endorsed the Commitments.

---

416 See Andrew Clapham, "Human Rights Obligations of Non-State Actors in Conflict Situations," *International Review of the Red Cross* 88, no. 863 (2007): 491–523.

417 See, e.g., the recently adopted Colombia conclusions: United Nations Security Council Working Group on Children and Armed Conflict, *Conclusions on the Situation of Children and Armed Conflict in Colombia* UN Doc. S/AC.51/2012/4 (21 December 2012).

418 *The Paris Commitments to Protect Children from Unlawful Recruitment or Use by Armed Forces or Armed Groups* (2007).

The Paris Principles: Principles and Guidelines on Children Associated with Armed Forces or Armed Groups constitute an accompanying document for humanitarian and child protection agencies. They were designed under UNICEF leadership as a practical tool to guide release and reintegration programming for children and to identify best practices that can be applied in all contexts.[419]

Regarding the question of age, in adopting the Paris Commitments, governments agreed, according to article 1, "to spare no effort to end the unlawful recruitment and use of children by armed forces or groups in all regions of the world." Although article 1 of the Commitments does not include an age specification, article 4 expresses the commitment "to take all feasible measures, including legal and administrative measures, to prevent *armed groups* within the jurisdiction of our State *that are distinct from our armed forces* from recruiting or using children under 18 years of age in hostilities" (emphasis added). This leaves some issues open, however, including what age restrictions actually apply to government forces, rather than non-state groups. And though article 6 describes the commitment to "effectively investigate and prosecute those persons who have unlawfully recruited children under 18 years of age into armed forces or groups, or used them to participate actively in hostilities," the issue is not entirely resolved in the Commitments.

The Principles, on other hand, are more specific. As noted in article 1, "While recognising that States have different obligations under international law, a majority of child protection actors will continue advocating for States to strive to raise the minimum age of recruitment or use to 18 in all circumstances."[420] In addition, article 2(1) is both specific and comprehensive:

> **"A child associated with an armed force or armed group"** refers to any person below 18 years of age who is or who has been recruited or used by an armed force or armed group in any capacity, including but not limited to children, boys and girls, used as fighters, cooks, porters, messengers, spies or for sexual purposes. It does not only refer to a child who is taking or has taken a direct part in hostilities. (emphasis in the original)

The fact that most countries listed in the Security Council MRM have endorsed the Principles is of legal significance in that it shows the application of a relatively strong standard by these governments. This indicates a strong commitment to the broader definition of child recruitment, which in a pragmatic way seeks to

---

419 *The Paris Principles and Guidelines on Children Associated with Armed Forces or Armed Groups* (February 2007).

420 The Paris Principles article 1(14). See also the Sri Lanka conclusions of 2012 as an example of the SCWG welcoming the Government's acknowledgement of the Paris Principles, and treating children formerly associated with armed groups primarily as victims. United Nations Security Council Working Group on Children and Armed Conflict, *Conclusions on the Situation of Children and Armed Conflict in Sri Lanka* UN Doc. S/AC.51/2012/3 (21 December 2012).

benefit all children in reintegration programming. Four of the five permanent members of the Security Council have also endorsed the Paris Commitments, showing strong political support for the inclusive approach of the reintegration phase, the United States being the sole hold-out.[421]

The fact that some very important and powerful governments remain outside this framework means there is less room for interpretation of legal standards that go above and beyond what is in the existing legal frameworks through international human rights, humanitarian, and criminal law. At a practical level, the inclusion of children who have not "directly" participated in the conflict has been accepted, but it would be difficult to draw broader conclusions based on the Security Council mechanism and practice for legal debates concerning individual criminal responsibility going beyond direct participation.

2.5. THE NATURE OF OBLIGATIONS WITH RESPECT TO THE SECURITY COUNCIL'S THEMATIC FOCUS

The Security Council is the forum for questions of peace and security within the UN, and it can take legally binding decisions through resolutions adopted under chapter VII of the UN Charter. It is not, however, representative of the full UN membership, and as a result, the law-making force from a customary law point of view is to be considered with great care.

The legal value of the work undertaken within the Security Council MRM varies from tool to tool. Although the thematic resolutions themselves are not legally binding, they are strong interpretative statements, and they certainly push the UN system to do its utmost for war-affected children.

The SCWG conclusions have lesser legal value but go into each specific country situation in more detail; they are more or less like the concluding observations of one of the treaty bodies, although certainly more politically loaded because the Security Council is a political body, not a body of independent experts. Nonetheless, most governments appear to take the SCWG conclusions seriously and make efforts to implement changes in their practices that undermine the protection of children. Hence, they can be considered a type of soft law that certainly has implications at the field level. What will be interesting to see in the years to come is whether these agreements will be considered legal obligations in international jurisdictions such as the ICC. Having signed up to an action plan brings about an important legal dilemma, as it demonstrates that the leader of the armed group or force concerned has accepted the fact that there are children within the ranks and that it is the right of these children to be released and reintegrated.

421 The United States did, however, ratify OPAC, which contains a detailed provision on recovery and reintegration.

The Security Council activities related to child recruitment can establish some level of practice to form the basis for emergence of international customary law; however, the fact that most agreements relate to non-state actors make the law-making force *vis-à-vis* states more complex.[422] The situations where the Security Council steps in to enhance the implementation of existing international standards are those where child recruitment is the biggest problem and where the implementation of international standards is an issue. It can be argued that in those contexts, the application of a straight 18 standard has been virtually uniform. As far as *opinio juris* is concerned, this relates to the legal conviction that the practice carried out is law. In the context of addressing child recruitment, the practice and the *opinio juris* often are one and the same act carried out by states in the context of the implementation of the mechanism.[423]

The nature of action plans and other agreements under international law is not totally clear since they are not agreements between states. Some are agreements between a government (when signed for the purposes of armed forces) and the UN, while others are agreements between non-state entities and the UN. These types of agreements have not been widely studied in the international legal arena and can have different legal meanings depending on how they have been crafted and who has been part of the signatory process.[424] With the exception of the Nepal action plan, all agreements refer to relevant international law, which makes a stronger case for those provisions to have the kind of legal relevance that is reflective of international law and is legally binding on the signatories.

For state actors this may not be of significant value, but for non-state actors it demonstrates an acceptance of these bodies of law as relevant to them. The Optional Protocol on the Involvement of Children in Armed Conflict is referenced in the Karen National Union deed of commitment, in the Sudan agreement signed with the Sudan Liberation Movement/Army (SLM/A), the Sri Lanka TMVP action plan, the Moro Islamic Liberation Front action plan, the Chin National Front deed of commitment, and the Sudan People's Liberation Army (SPLA) action plan, as well as the Sudan Justice and Equality Movement

---

422 In the ICRC study on customary law the practice of armed groups such as codes of conduct and other commitments to observe the rules of international humanitarian law were determined not to "constitute State practice as such." Since its legal significance is unclear, this practice was not relied upon to prove the existence of customary international law. Henckaerts, "The ICRC Study on Customary International Humanitarian Law: Characteristics, Conclusions and Practical Relevance," 232.

423 See, for instance, the 2013 Myanmar conclusions, Conclusions on Children and Armed Conflict in Myanmar, Conflict, United Nations Security Council Working Group on Children and Armed, UN Doc. S/AC.51/2013/2 (16 August 2013), para 7(a(i)).

424 While the legal nature of these types of agreement has not been widely studied, some similarities can be seen with peace agreements, which have received some attention. See further Christine Bell, *Peace Agreements and Human Rights* (Oxford University Press, USA, 2000).

(JEM) memorandum of understanding. The Convention on the Rights of the Child is referenced in the SLM/A, TMVP, and JEM agreements.

Nonetheless, the legal value of these agreements can be debated. To date, they have generally been mostly programmatic in nature, and while drawing on prevailing standards through reference to existing international law, the main focus has been on release and reintegration programmes and how those programmes were to be implemented. The MRM could still be considered successful in that many action plans have resulted from it, and thousands of children have been released during the recent past.[425] A problem of attribution remains, and whether that is as a result of Security Council involvement can be debated, but most of the situations where children were released had an action plan in place, so there is certainly a strong link.

CONCLUSION

The MRM is a significant contribution towards historical justice in the context of providing information relevant to child recruitment. It is a comparatively rigorous mechanism that has been established with the key tenets of providing objective and verified information related to grave violations against children's rights. The mechanism is very political, which provides for good entry points and stronger advocacy in the field. At the Security Council level, however, it can mean that certain discussions, topics, and situations are not as transparently considered as would be warranted from a historical justice perspective. A case in point is the fact that there is no sign of the mechanism having made any difference during the final months of fighting between the LTTE and the Government in Sri Lanka, despite the fact that the mechanism was operating on the ground and producing important information at the time.[426] The SCWG is not sufficiently empowered to truly take action in the midst of armed conflict, and has yet to show that it would be able to stimulate action by the Security Council itself, or other transitional justice mechanisms, so as to respond at the height of conflict.

For many situations where child recruitment is rampant, the mechanism is establishing a solid historical record of the events from the perspective of specific grave violations against children's rights. To date, the public reports are the main forum for capturing this information – though it is conceivable that much more specific data could be made available to authorities for transitional justice purposes through this mechanism, as long as the individual data on children is managed in a way that is in their best interests. It is disconcerting that the

425 UNICEF, *Thematic Report 2009: Child Protection from Violence, Exploitation and Abuse*, (2010), 22. Some 5,000 children were released in 2009 alone.

426 *Conclusions on the Situation of Children and Armed Conflict in Sri Lanka* (21 December 2012).

information generated has mainly been used for the mechanism itself, and references made to the information in other forums are still very limited. Likewise, the listing of parties who are engaged in these violations is not used much beyond the mechanism itself.

In listing parties to armed conflict, the Secretary-General's report is not using the threshold "beyond reasonable doubt"; the verification process for becoming listed is based on a pattern of violations rather than on crimes that would have to be investigated and proved based on evidence.[427] It would be interesting to find from a future case of the International Criminal Court, for example, whether the listing of an armed group in the annexes to the report would be considered as evidence.

The MRM is a tool for historical justice that applies the age of 18 in considering recruitment and use of children as a grave violation of international law. Again, it is not a mechanism that per se is looking to prove guilt of an international crime, the level of verification does not fulfil the criteria for a criminal investigation, although the information could be used to probe further and as an element of a pattern of abuse. But the fact that it is the only comprehensive system in place with a focus on child recruitment does place certain expectations on the mechanism. If, for example, the MRM is intended to be as useful as possible for the purposes of criminal justice, it is necessary to be able to distinguish between what is happening to children under age 15 and what is happening to children in the older age range of 15–18.

The primary objective of the MRM is not only to inform criminal justice processes but to establish the historical record that can help develop a response, which could include prosecutions and criminal justice though more likely would inform advocacy and programme work relevant to child recruitment, release, and reintegration.[428] Establishing the objective of the effort to develop a historical account is critical because this will determine the impact that is desired with the effort, as well as what type of information is gathered. The information may be used to make a public apology and promote reconciliation, to inform advocacy and action, and to support criminal investigation, or it can inform the process of deciding about political positions in the aftermath of a conflict. At a certain point in time, establishing facts can be an aim in itself, but this would generally come after the conflict and does not necessarily apply to the MRM, which is active during the midst of armed conflict.

---

427 *Report of the Secretary-General on Children and Armed Conflict*, UN Doc. A/64/742-S/2010/181 (13 April 2010), para 174.

428 For the time being, the nature of the links to criminal justice remains more as a deterrent rather than as the establishment of a link between the MRM and criminal justice processes. See, for instance, the DRC conclusions of 2014: *Conclusions on Children and Armed Conflict in the Democratic Republic of the Congo, Conflict, United Nations Security Council Working Group on Children and Armed*, UN Doc. S/AC.51/2014/3 (19 September 2014), para 6(d).

While the Security Council's mechanism focuses on monitoring and reporting of grave violations against children's rights, it also begins to deal with informed action in a more effective way than many other exercises to address historical justice – though not in as comprehensive a manner as an otherwise rigorous mechanism could allow for. For these purposes, the action plans are a key feature of the MRM. The strong focus on child recruitment as an initial attempt to strengthen the effective implementation of international law has proved to be useful in terms of providing a clear mandate to those who are implementing the mechanism on the ground. The SCWG mechanism has allowed for a pragmatic approach to the applicable law, especially at the country level through the action plans that have been adopted.

Importantly, the action plans can demonstrate a commitment to release children, but they can also be evidence of a group having children in the ranks. It would seem from the reasoning in the *Lubanga* case that it is better for an individual to have made the effort of putting such systems in place, because that would help prove the intention to address the situation by both limiting the intake of children into the ranks and putting measures for their release and reintegration in place. To date, the information has not been used by the ICC. During the time covered by the *Lubanga* case, the MRM was in its very early days and only limited information was available.[429]

Action plans developed with armed groups and forces have yielded important results in terms of children actually being released and now taking part in reintegration programmes in different parts of the world. At the same time, many of those negotiated processes have taken a long time, and there are still many situations where armed forces and groups do not seem to take the standards in place, and the emphasis added by the Security Council, seriously enough to do something about the situation.

Under the French presidency, the SCWG developed a "toolkit" in the form of a document containing the range of possible actions in response to violations and including the option of referring the information to transitional justice mechanisms.[430] There is no evidence, however, that Security Council members have made further use of this toolkit in lending support to relevant transitional justice mechanisms, not only international criminal tribunals but also truth-seeking mechanisms and human rights investigations. For instance, in referring

429 The period covered through the charges in the *Lubanga* case occurred between 1 July 2002 and 31 December 2003, and hence preceded the monitoring and reporting mechanism. However, there were already at that time Child Protection Advisors with peacekeeping missions and an effort to collect information at the field level, albeit not through a formal monitoring and reporting mechanism.

430 United Nations Security Council Working Group on Children and Armed Conflict, *Letter Dated 8 September 2006 from the Permanent Representative of France to the United Nations Addressed to the President of the Security Council (Conclusions on Democratic Republic of Congo)* (11 September 2006).

the Darfur situation to the International Criminal Court, the reports on children and armed conflict in Sudan could have informed the Court by adding accounts based on crimes against children at the same time. This could have led to a more serious consideration of children's issues relevant to the case against President Al-Bashir.[431]

The Special Representative of the Secretary-General for Children and Armed Conflict has played a role in linking with the International Criminal Tribunal, but mainly in connection with legal issues at stake, and has not made submissions highlighting available information related to international crimes through the country-specific or annual reports of the Secretary-General.[432] There are also many other actors who could make transitional justice mechanisms more informed of pre-existing initiatives and the wealth of information that is generated through the Security Council mechanism.

The MRM is only 10 years into implementation, so only partial success could be expected. It has certainly succeeded with some tangible results for conflict-affected children. The mechanism is quite holistic in its approach, given its strong focus on the monitoring and reporting exercise on the ground, linked with the naming and shaming of actors who carry out crimes against children, as well as the response in addressing grave violations against children.

Reviewing the guidance available to UN offices putting this mechanism in place, little is said about the archives and the management of the information relevant to how children have been recruited and used, and how this data should be maintained and saved over the years. This is a crucial issue, because the sensitivities around the information changes over time, and having the relevant data may sometimes become useful years and years after the facts were established. Someone may be looking for a child who was recruited and never released, for example, and just having the records may help establish certain facts and circumstances. This aspect is not featured strongly enough in the current guidance on documentation related to the MRM.

Finally, while there has been some progress in certain situations considered as part of the child-focused Security Council agenda, there is inconsistency in that some situations are only "situations of concern" and not listed in the annexes of the Secretary-General's report. The listing criteria are to some extent

---

431 Resolution 1612 also "notes that information compiled by this mechanism, for reporting by the Secretary-General to the General Assembly and the Security Council, may be considered by other international, regional and national bodies, within their mandates and the scope of their work, in order to ensure the protection, rights and well-being of children affected by armed conflict." *Security Council Resolution on Children and Armed Conflict* (26 July 2005), 6.

432 *Submission of the Observations of the Special Representative of the Secretary General of the United Nations for Children and Armed Conflict pursuant to Rule 103 of the Rules of Procedure and Evidence* (ICC-01/04-01/06-1229 (2008)).

considered in a political context. Also, there is significant delay and inconsistency in terms of follow-up and adopting conclusions in the Working Group.[433]

Chapter 5, on reparatory justice, focuses on the rights of victims to rehabilitation or compensation for harm with an emphasis on disarmament, demobilization, and reintegration programmes on the one hand, and reparations as developed through the *Lubanga* case on the other. The chapter analyses how the notion of repair has developed from the perspective of child recruitment and how it fits with other components of transitional justice.

433 Jean-Marc de La Sablière, *Security Council Engagement on the Protection of Children in Armed Conflict: Progress Achieved and the Way Forward*, (2012), 23.

CHAPTER 5
CHILD RECRUITMENT AND REPARATORY JUSTICE
Recovery and Reintegration of War-Affected Children

"When we first came back, the people did not want us. But now it is OK. Now it is good. They like the projects we are doing for the village."

INTRODUCTION

Reparatory justice is an integral part of transitional justice and builds on the obligation of states to make restitution whenever international legal obligations have been violated. The Basic Principles and Guidelines on the Right to a Remedy and Reparation, adopted by the UN General Assembly in 2006, form the basis of what today is considered a framework for reparations – defining that victims of human rights and humanitarian law violations have the right to "adequate, effective, prompt and appropriate remedies, including reparation."[434] In addition:

> Restitution should, whenever possible, restore the victim to the original situation before the gross violations of international human rights law or serious violations of international humanitarian law occurred. Restitution includes, as appropriate: restoration of liberty, enjoyment of human rights, identity, family life and citizenship, return to one's place of residence, restoration of employment and return of property.[435]

The Basic Principles and Guidelines further state that compensation should consider the circumstances for each case and be provided in proportion to the severity of the violation.[436]

---

434 *Basic Principles and Guidelines on the Right to a Remedy and Reparation for Victims of Gross Violations of International Human Rights Law and Serious Violations of International Humanitarian Law*, UN Doc. A/Res/60/147 (21 March 2006), para 2(c). [hereinafter "Basic Principles and Guidelines"].

435 Ibid., para 19.

436 Ibid., para 20.

Reparatory justice includes many dimensions and forms: reparations, services, damages, remedies, redress, restitution, compensation, rehabilitation, official apology, tribute.[437] In transitional contexts, reparatory justice enables recognition of individual rights violations and the harm that followed, and the fact that someone did wrong, in addition to a commitment for non-repetition of the crime. This element looks back at what the violations were, and even if it is not the same actor who repairs, the obligation remains. It also looks forward in a political and transitional sense, repairing so as to be able to move forward.

Key legal questions that are covered in this chapter include:

- What does reparatory justice mean in the context of recruitment and use of children in armed conflicts? How can we ensure that reparations are in the best interests of the child?
- What legal protection is accorded to children ensuring that this element of transitional justice is accorded the necessary importance?
- What lessons have been learned from reparatory justice processes relevant to the recruitment and use of children, and how can those inform how this element fits into a broader transitional justice approach?
- Who repairs?

Reparations for war guilt and treaties adopted after the Second World War outlined the reparations that would follow. These were obligations of states, which would mobilize to pay back the war debts years after the conflict.

Addressing reparatory justice in the context of child recruitment is different and less developed, at least as a consideration of justice for children. On the whole, the release and reintegration programmes for former child soldiers are a type of reparation and fit well within the overall framework for reparatory justice. The process of recovery and reintegration and approaches to DDR programmes for children who have been involved in armed conflict are designed to be applicable to the conditions on the ground, and therefore can address many of the aspects considered under reparatory justice when it is well applied.[438]

The concept of reparations is also included in the outcome of decisions before the International Criminal Court, and as such, the *Lubanga* case has given rise to considerations by the Court. While the reparations scheme has not yet been implemented, the case provides a useful study into the principles and approaches that apply.

Because the issue of whether a child soldier should be held accountable for crimes is dealt with rather unprofessionally, it is not always clear whether

437 Teitel, *Transitional Justice*, 119. See also Basic Principles and Guidelines cited above.

438 See also United Nations, *IDDRS Module: Transitional Justice and DDR* (2009). The Module considers the following for primary approaches to transitional justice in a context of disarmament, demobilization, and reintegration: prosecutions, reparations, truth commissions, and institutional reform.

reparations are appropriate for these children. Are they are "free to go," or should they take on responsibility to repair the harm of others? Part of this issue is dealt with in this chapter, while other relevant topics are considered in chapter 7 on participatory justice.

An important aspect of reparatory justice is consultation with affected communities, including children, in the design of the reparations. The meaning and message behind providing reparation in an individual case go much beyond singular concerns: they provide a signal that society as a whole is moving forward and repairing for the past to the benefit of entire societies.[439]

This chapter considers the issues of reparatory justice in three sections: (1) an analysis of the international legal framework applicable to recovery and reintegration for war-affected children; (2) the application of a reparations scheme through the ICC in the *Lubanga* case; and (3) an overview of reparations provided to child soldiers through recovery and reintegration programmes.

1. THE RIGHT TO RECOVERY AND REINTEGRATION IN INTERNATIONAL LAW

This section considers the law applicable to recovery and reintegration of war-affected children broadly, and child soldiers specifically, as well as how recovery and reintegration programmes have been implemented in practice.

1.1. BROAD PROTECTION: THE CONVENTION ON THE RIGHTS OF THE CHILD

As highlighted above, the Convention on the Rights of the Child (CRC) is unique not only because it has received nearly universal ratification (only Somalia and the United States have not ratified the Convention), but also because it applies throughout the cycle of peace to conflict through post-conflict and the return to peace. The CRC, contrary to some other human rights instruments, does not have a derogation clause that would allow States parties to identify rights that can be deviated from during armed conflicts or other emergency situations.

The CRC is also unusual in that it specifically refers to international humanitarian law in article 38 and has several other articles that are particularly relevant to armed conflict situations, although not necessarily exclusively so. In other words, the Convention is more conflict-sensitive than other human rights instruments because it has looked to address at least some of the central issues facing children in armed conflicts. While the CRC is the only human rights law

439 Teitel, *Transitional Justice*, 147.

instrument that makes reference to international humanitarian law, it is still very much focused on the obligations of States parties (not extending to warring parties or armed groups in the way that international humanitarian law does), even if it could be argued that at least some of the provisions might be applicable to non-state actors as well.[440]

When discussing the recovery and reintegration needs of war-affected children, the most relevant item in the CRC is article 39. Prior to the introduction of article 39, this concept of a right to recovery and reintegration had not been recognized in international law. The end result of this provision introduced by the Norwegian delegation reads:

> States Parties shall take all appropriate measures to promote physical and psychological recovery and social reintegration of a child victim of: any form of neglect, exploitation, or abuse; torture or any other form of cruel, inhuman or degrading treatment or punishment; or armed conflicts. Such recovery and reintegration shall take place in an environment which fosters the health, self-respect and dignity of the child.[441]

Regarding States parties' legal obligations, some of the early drafts had stronger language than the version finally adopted.[442] Delegations to the drafting also had dissimilar views about the words "recovery" and "reintegration." The original text included rehabilitation only; in the end, delegates agreed to include recovery as well. The Canadian delegation, however, wanted the records to reflect that it would have preferred only the word "reintegration."[443] This type of controversy would have arisen from concerns that children who have fled from their place or country of origin would have a right to recovery anywhere, not only in their original place.

As far as "social reintegration" is concerned, the term speaks to action on behalf of the family and the community, allowing the child to be reintegrated in a society that is familiar to him or her. This aim cannot be achieved unless action

---

440 The Optional Protocol on the Involvement of Children in Armed Conflict goes in a different direction as it also establishes obligations for non-state actors. The CRC itself also speaks of the responsibility of the family, and hence is somewhat different from other human rights instruments. General Comment No. 16: On State obligations regarding the impact of the business sector on children's rights, Committee on the Rights of the Child, UN Doc. CRC/C/GC/10 (15 March 2013).

441 There are no reservations to article 39.

442 During the considerations of the 1988 Working Group, the words "legal, administrative and other measures" were exchanged for "all measures," and in the 1989 Working Group, the word "appropriate" was inserted between "all" and "measures" so as not to put an unduly strong obligation on the State. See *Considerations of the 1988 Working Group* E/CN.4/1988/28, pp. 17–18 10th Session and E/CN.4/1988/WG.1/WP.1/Rev.2, p. 23 for the work of the 1988 Working Group, and E/CN.4/1989/48, pp. 93–94 for the 1989 Working Group. The word "appropriate" was inserted as a result of a suggestion made by the US Government, which was supported by the representative of the Federal Republic of Germany and Norway.

443 Considerations of the 1988 Working Group, E/CN.4/1988/28, 17.

for recovery is taken at the same time: one right cannot be fulfilled without the other.

In this context, it is also interesting to note that the language relevant to "armed conflicts" as triggering the need for special consideration was not included until proposed in the 1989 working group.[444] During the deliberations, the representative of Norway argued that the article failing to include this aspect would leave armed conflicts uncovered in the Convention.

Looking more closely at the provisions of article 39, it is first necessary to note that it has two main parts: recovery and reintegration; and the type of environment in which activities to that end should take place. Physical recovery would cover the essential rights of a child to food, water, health, and sanitation. Psychological recovery may include services that restore normalcy, such as education and psychosocial support activities through recreation and play.[445]

The second sentence of article 39 reads as follows: "Such recovery and reintegration shall take place in an environment which fosters the health, self-respect and dignity of the child." This obligation can be read together with other principles found in the Convention, such as taking into account the best interests of the child and ensuring non-discrimination in undertaking activities for recovery and reintegration.[446] Non-discrimination would also apply to gender and to providing specific services for girls that provide for their needs.

The provision focusing on the environment in article 39 is to set a framework for a certain level of quality of the action, in war contexts often with the support from international organizations.[447] It should therefore place an obligation on the state and the international community to strive towards establishing a sound environment to deal appropriately with a broad range of children's recovery and reintegration needs.

1.2. SPECIFIC PROTECTION: OPAC AND THE COMMITTEE ON THE RIGHTS OF THE CHILD

While the legal obligation in article 39 of the CRC is rather vague, it does cover a basic level of protection on behalf of war-affected children's need for recovery

---

444 *Considerations of the 1989 Working Group*, E/CN.4/1989/WG.1/WP.57. This proposal was submitted by a drafting group consisting of Argentina.

445 In reviewing the report of Liberia the Committee speaks of those who have been directly or indirectly affected by the traumatic experiences of the war. Committee on the Rights of the Child, *Consideration of Reports Submitted by States Parties under Article 8 of the Optional Protocol to the Convention on the Rights of the Child on the Involvement of Children in Armed Conflict, Concluding Observations: Sri Lanka* UN Doc. CRC/C/15/Add.207 (2 July 2003).

446 Committee on the Rights of the Child, *Consideration of Reports Submitted by States Parties under Article 44 of the Convention, Concluding Observations: Liberia* UN Doc. CRC/C/15/Add.236 (1 July 2004).

447 Considerations of the 1988 Working Group, E/CN.4/1988/28, p. 17.

and reintegration. It can also be used in conjunction with other provisions in the Convention, especially when considering specific protection issues – survivors of torture, refugee children, children separated from their families, or survivors of gender-based violence – as well as the obligation to foster an environment of respect, taking into account, for example, provisions that promote child participation.[448]

The Committee on the Rights of the Child has encouraged system-building through such measures as undertaking studies and training service providers.[449] During recovery and reintegration, it is difficult to care for individual children unless there are some systems that can serve a large number of children. For instance, establishing a strong juvenile justice system in a war-affected country can serve children who have been prosecuted for participating in the conflict or girls who are survivors of gender-based violence.[450]

In terms of specific provisions for the recovery and reintegration of war-affected children, the Optional Protocol on the Involvement of Children in Armed Conflict (OPAC) covers these issues for children who have been recruited or used by armed forces or groups in article 6(3):

> States Parties shall take all feasible measures to ensure that persons within their jurisdiction recruited or used in hostilities contrary to the present Protocol are demobilized or otherwise released from service. States Parties shall, when necessary, accord to such persons all appropriate assistance for their physical and psychological recovery and their social reintegration.

Article 7 provides additional focus on cooperation among States parties in rehabilitation and social reintegration, technical cooperation, and financial assistance "in consultation" between the governments concerned and relevant international organizations.[451]

The drafting history of this provision makes interesting reading. At its first session, the working group drafting OPAC considered that it was necessary to have some text in addition to what had been proposed by the Committee on the Rights of the Child, and "some members of the working group felt that new

448 Rachel Hodgkin and Peter Newell, *Implementation Handbook for the Convention on the Rights of the Child* (Geneva: UNICEF, 2008 (Third Edition)), p. 591.

449 Ibid., p. 589.

450 The most recent report of the Secretary-General calls upon national and international actors to support and expand programmes to ensure that children who are victims of violations have access to appropriate services and response. Committee on the Rights of the Child, *Consideration of Reports Submitted by States Parties under Article 8 of the Optional Protocol to the Convention on the Rights of the Child on the Involvement of Children in Armed Conflict, Concluding Observations: Croatia* UN Doc. CRC/C/15/Add.243 (3 November 2004).

451 For instance, UNICEF's Board approved policies addressing the recovery and reintegration for children who have been released from armed groups and forces. See *Core Commitments for Children in Emergencies*, UNICEF 2005, and *UNICEF Child Protection Strategy*, E/ICEF/2008/5/Rev.1, 20 May 2008.

articles were needed to address issues such as the physical and psychological reintegration of child victims of armed conflicts."[452] The representative of Cuba proposed language to cover "rehabilitation and reintegration," specifying that it would guarantee medical care and adequate nutrition.[453]

However, at the working group's second session, when the provision was being considered, this was changed into a preambular paragraph, providing a much less structured focus. This paragraph was proposed by the delegations of Australia and Cameroon, and was placed before the original seventh preambular paragraph: "Convinced of the need to strengthen international cooperation regarding the physical and psychosocial rehabilitation and social reintegration of children who are victims of armed conflicts."[454]

The matter was then left aside for the subsequent working groups, and it was not until the sixth and final session that a more serious discussion on the topic was held, when "several delegations supported the idea of including in the optional protocol a separate provision on cooperation in implementing the protocol, including through international assistance for the rehabilitation and social reintegration of child soldiers."[455]

Canada and Norway put forward a proposal that brought the language on recovery and reintegration back into the operative paragraphs; however, the *travaux préparatoires* do not shed any light on what happened during the negotiation process between the proposed version and the one adopted, which completely reflects the language of the CRC itself.[456] Nor is further clarity provided in terms of what might be meant by these words in a legal sense, although further obligations are placed on the action of releasing the children, and it is interesting that article 7(1) not only prohibits any negative acts that may hinder recovery and reintegration, it also binds states to consult "relevant international organizations."

1.3. COUNTRY REPORTS AND COMMITTEE REVIEWS OF RECOVERY AND REINTEGRATION EFFORTS

In reviewing the progress of States parties to OPAC, the Committee on the Rights of the Child has paid particular attention to "information on the

452 Report of the Working Group on a Draft Optional Protocol to the Convention on the Rights of the Child on Involvement of Children in Armed Conflicts, UN Doc. E/CN.4/1995/96 (10 February 1995), para 29.

453 Ibid., para 147.

454 Report of the Working Group on a Draft Optional Protocol to the Convention on the Rights of the Child on Involvement of Children in Armed Conflicts on Its Second Session, UN Doc. 21 March 1996, paras 89,128–130.

455 Report of the Working Group on a Draft Optional Protocol to the Convention on the Rights of the Child on Involvement of Children in Armed Conflicts on Its Sixth Session, 27 March 2000, para 44.

456 Ibid., para 46.

measures adopted ... with a view to ensuring that the rights and best interests of children who have been the victims of the practices prohibited under the Optional Protocol are fully recognized."[457] In submitting their reports, states are requested to specify the steps they have taken to make sure that legal, psychological, and other types of training are provided to those who work with children whose rights have been violated. These reports should also portray "existing public and private demobilization programmes that provide child victims of recruitment with assistance in social reintegration, paying special attention to family reunification, and physical and psychological recovery."[458]

The Committee has also requested States parties to report on the remedies and reparations that child victims of recruitment may seek, while paying particular attention to the role of the government in enforcing these measures. It is interesting to note that little emphasis is placed on the extent to which consultation has been undertaken with relevant international organizations, although there is a request for information as to whether the State party has cooperated with the Office of the SRSG-CAAC.[459] This is a shortcoming in dealing, for instance, with former child recruits who have been prosecuted under domestic jurisdictions, wherein governments should be encouraged to seek the advice of child protection agencies on how to deal with such matters in a child-friendly way.

In reviewing State party reports, the Committee has looked at the question of assistance for physical and psychological recovery. As stated in its review of Chile's report, for example:

> The Committee welcomes the information that the State Party has implemented a resettlement programme as a tool to ensure protection for Colombian refugees, as well as its commitment to receive Palestinian refugees coming from Iraq, including children affected by armed conflict. It also notes with appreciation the projects aiming at the regularization of all children entering into the State party's territory, irrespective of the migratory status of their parents, in order to guarantee access to education and health to them on an equal footing as Chilean nationals. However, the Committee notes that no specific measures have been taken to identify children who may have been recruited or used in hostilities abroad and that no specific programmes are available for their recovery and reintegration.[460]

---

457 *Revised Guidelines Regarding Initial Reports to Be Submitted by States Parties under Article 8, Paragraph 1, of the Optional Protocol to the Convention on the Rights of the Child on Involvement of Children in Armed Conflict*, UN Doc. CRC/C/OPAC/2. 19 October 2007, para 27.

458 Ibid., para 29.

459 Ibid., para 35.

460 Consideration of Reports Submitted by States Parties under Article 8 of the Optional Protocol to the Convention on the Rights of the Child on the Involvement of Children in Armed Conflict, Concluding Observations: Chile, 13 February 2008, para 21.

It should be noted that only a few countries where child recruitment has been a significant problem have reported to the Committee to date. Uganda, however, is one example where the issue was both reported and considered, in detail, in the Committee's concluding observations:

> The Committee, while noting the valuable reintegration efforts undertaken by NGOs to provide physical and psychological recovery for demobilised children, is concerned that such efforts are primarily short-term and are hampered by the lack of adequate resources and State party support. The Committee also notes with concern that demobilised children may be recruited into the armed forces, in particular when the reconciliation process with kin and local community lacks assistance. The Committee is concerned that customary reconciliation practices may re-victimise children who have been recruited or used in hostilities, especially girls who have suffered sexual violence. The Committee recommends that the State party strengthen long-term efforts to provide reintegration measures in order to provide all children who have been recruited or used in hostilities with immediate and child and gender-sensitive multidisciplinary assistance for their physical and psychological recovery, in accordance with article 6, paragraph 3, of the Optional Protocol. The State party is recommended to significantly increase its support for reintegration and recovery measures, ensure that they are accessible in affected regions and develop such programmes in consultation with concerned communities.[461]

Such advice provided by the Committee to the Government can be particularly useful for follow-up advocacy by child protection agencies.

In dealing with donor governments, the Committee has also commended State parties for providing support to reintegration programmes.[462] Similar to the Chilean case, the Committee' review of Sweden's report promoted the establishment of services for children who may come from other countries: "The State party should ensure that all unaccompanied asylum-seeking children have access to adequate services, including social and health services and accommodation, irrespective of the municipality in which they are accommodated." The Committee urged "that asylum-seeking children who have been involved in armed conflict receive all appropriate assistance for their physical and psychological recovery and social reintegration."[463]

---

461 Consideration of Reports Submitted by States Parties under Article 8 of the Optional Protocol to the Convention on the Rights of the Child on the Involvement of Children in Armed Conflict, Concluding Observations: Uganda, UN Doc no. CRC/C/OPAC/UGA/CO/1 (17 October 2008), paras 30 and 31.

462 Sweden is one such example: Consideration of Reports Submitted by States Parties under Article 8 of the Optional Protocol to the Convention on the Rights of the Child on the Involvement of Children in Armed Conflict. Committee on the Rights of the Child, *Consideration of Reports Submitted by States Parties under Article 8 of the Optional Protocol to the Convention on the Rights of the Child on the Involvement of Children in Armed Conflict, Concluding Observations: Sweden* UN Doc. CRC/C/OPAC/SWE/CO/1 (6 July 2007).

463 Ibid., paras 24 and 25.

In the case of the Philippines, the Committee recommended that "the State party ensure that special and adequate attention is paid to children who have been recruited or used in hostilities when entering into negotiation and talks with armed groups, especially in the area of prevention, physical and psychological recovery and social reintegration."[464] It is noteworthy that the Moro Islamic Liberation Front and UNICEF recently signed an action plan focusing, among other issues, on the recovery and reintegration of children recruited or used by the Liberation Front.[465]

The fact that States parties, in line with article 4(2), "shall take all feasible measures to prevent such recruitment and use, including the adoption of legal measures necessary to prohibit and criminalize such practices" provides a safeguard as far as transitional justice measures are concerned under national jurisdictions. However, pieces of implementing legislation are still few and far between, and when they have been established, there are often shortcomings. Hence, this is an area still calling for major advocacy and support to governments to start drafting such laws, as they are not just a legislative act but provide an opportunity to raise awareness and address issues of accountability in the long term. Such legislation not only needs to criminalize the recruitment or use of children, it must address questions of universal jurisdiction, the criminal responsibility of children themselves, and the recovery and reintegration needs of former child soldiers.

It is also important to note that in negotiating the release of children, many armed groups make the release conditional because as they claim, and often rightly so, the children have ended up with the armed group because services such as education were not available in their communities. This again emphasizes the point that reintegration does not work without recovery. Unless solid recovery and reintegration programmes are in place, efforts such as effective political advocacy for upholding the legal standards against the recruitment of children are difficult to maintain.

Social reintegration acquires a very specific meaning when it involves children who have been associated with armed groups and forces. Returning such children to their home communities may sometimes require specific awareness-raising or trust-building activities. Generally, in language relevant to children recruited or used by armed forces and groups there is reference to "release and reintegration" as one coherent whole. The release process is part of and adds value to the reintegration process if done correctly.

---

464 Consideration of Reports Submitted by States Parties under Article 8 of the Optional Protocol to the Convention on the Rights of the Child on the Involvement of Children in Armed Conflict, Concluding Observations: The Philippines, 15 July 2008, para 21.

465 Action Plan between the Moro Islamic Liberation Front and the United Nations in the Philippines regarding the Issue of Recruitment and Use of Child Soldiers in the Armed Conflict in Mindanao, 1 August 2009.

1.4. THE PARIS COMMITMENTS AND PRINCIPLES: PLACING A FOCUS ON REINTEGRATION

The Paris Commitments, as mentioned above, are state-endorsed commitments, adopted in 2007, with an annual event seeking to obtain further endorsements.[466] As of Spring 2015, 105 states had endorsed the Paris Commitments. The Commitments were not established to create new standards in international law, but to further develop the prohibition of recruitment and use in operational terms, particularly during the release, recovery, and reintegration phase. The idea behind developing these Commitments, and the Paris Principles, was to learn from experience in release and reintegration programme, and to codify that experience so it could be applied by the governments, UN agencies, and non-governmental organizations that implement those programmes.

In adopting the Paris Commitments governments agreed, in article 1, to "spare no effort to end the unlawful recruitment and use of children by armed forces or groups in all regions of the world." Although this article does not specify age, the Commitments make reference to unlawful recruitment under the age of 18, and states agree to "fight against impunity, and to effectively investigate and prosecute those persons who have unlawfully recruited children under 18 years of age into armed forces or groups, or used them to participate actively in hostilities."[467]

The Paris Principles, an accompanying document for humanitarian and child protection agencies, were designed under UNICEF leadership as a further practical tool to guide release and reintegration programming for children associated with armed groups and forces and to identify best practice that can be applied in all contexts.[468] The Principles' language on age includes the following, in article 1.14: "While recognising that States have different obligations under international law, a majority of child protection actors will continue advocating for States to strive to raise the minimum age of recruitment or use to 18 in all circumstances."[469]

It is critical that the programmes developed for former child soldiers consider the specific protection issues that children may face as they leave armed groups and forces. Depending on the context, they may be at great risk of retaliation, they may be at risk of re-recruitment, and they may be harassed by the authorities or brought in for questioning. Reintegration programmes need to be

---

466 *The Paris Commitments to Protect Children from Unlawful Recruitment or Use by Armed Forces or Armed Groups* (2007).

467 Ibid., para 6.

468 UNICEF, *Machel Study 10-Year Strategic Review: Children and Conflict in a Changing World*, 69.

469 *The Paris Principles and Guidelines on Children Associated with Armed Forces or Armed Groups* (February 2007), art. 1.14.

able to consider these distinct vulnerabilities and deal with them. As such, the integrated approach is not an end in itself.[470]

Links through social welfare programmes are also important to ensuring that children and families can be connected with various services that may already be available in their community, such as income generation and vocational training.[471]

The Paris Principles place specific emphasis on what is called the "inclusive approach to reintegration," in other words, making sure that children associated with armed forces or groups are not given services that are not available to other children and families in the same community, thereby further stigmatizing these children. This approach begins to tackle the issue of child soldiers returning home with more support than other children in the community.[472]

1.5. ADDRESSING ACCOUNTABILITY: THE SECURITY COUNCIL'S INVOLVEMENT

While chapter 4 dealt with the MRM in detail, the purpose here is to look at this mechanism from the perspective of establishing a framework for the recovery and reintegration of war-affected children.

One aspect that is of relevance to recovery and reintegration efforts is that Security Council resolutions have continued to highlight the importance of incorporating child protection within peacekeeping missions, including an emphasis on supporting programmes for recovery and reintegration. In 1999, the Security Council adopted two country-specific resolutions underscoring not only the plight of children in Sierra Leone and the Democratic Republic of the Congo, but also the need to engage particular child rights and protection expertise in support of the respective Special Representatives.[473] This was to

470 See also United Nations, *IDDRS Module: Children and DDR* (2006).

471 See, e.g., *Independent Evaluation of Special Projects for Child Soldiers in the Democratic Republic of Congo*, Final Report Presented to the World Bank's Multi-country Demobilization and Reintegration Program (5 February 2007). Andrew Brooks, *The Disarmarment, Demobilisation and Reintegration of Children Associated with Fighting Forces* (Dakar: UNICEF, 2005). UNICEF, *Assessment of UNICEF Supported Programmes for Reintegration of Children Formerly Associated with Armed Groups and Forces in Sudan*, (2008).

472 Roger Duthie and Irma Specht, "DDR, Transitional Justice, and the Reintegration of Former Child Combatants," in *Disarming the past: Transitional justice and ex-combatants*, ed. Pablo de Greiff, Ana Cutter Patel, and Lars Waldorf (New York: Social Science Research Council, 2009), 204.

473 See Security Council Resolution on the Democratic Republic of Congo, United Nations Security Council, UN Doc. S/RES/1279 (30 November 1999), para 5(e). The resolution asked the Special Representative "[t]o maintain liaison with all parties to the Ceasefire Agreement to facilitate the delivery of humanitarian assistance to displaced persons, refugees, children, and other affected persons, and assist in the protection of human rights, including the rights of children." The resolution for Sierra Leone was rather more detailed. The Security Council emphasized "that the plight of children is among the most pressing challenges facing Sierra

become standard practice during the years when new UN peace mission mandates are established or when existing mandates are being reviewed. Country-specific resolutions, as far as children are concerned, focus on several distinct issues: they emphasize the impact of armed conflict on children; they highlight specific issues related to child recruitment and the disarmament, demobilization, and rehabilitation (DDR) processes; and they include child protection aspects in peacekeeping mandates and provide for the deployment of child protection advisers.[474]

As noted in chapter 4, the Security Council resolution in 2004 requested the Secretary-General to "devise ... an action plan for a systematic and comprehensive monitoring and reporting mechanism."[475] This development culminated in the system that was developed subsequent to the 2005 report of the Secretary-General and the adoption of Security Council resolution 1612 focusing on countries listed in the annexes to the Secretary-General's report.

In resolution 1612, the Security Council acknowledges that the process "has generated progress, resulting in the release and reintegration of children into their families and communities." The resolution also highlights the importance of implementing action plans and "stresses that effective disarmament, demobilization and reintegration programmes for children, building on best practices identified by UNICEF and other relevant child protection actors, are crucial for the well-being of all children who ... have been recruited or used by armed forces and groups." In addition, it urges both governments and donors to make certain that community-based DDR programmes "receive timely, sustained and adequate resources and funding."[476]

The situations listed in the annexes of the Secretary-General's annual report also benefit from the annual country-specific reports on grave child rights violations, and the SCWG's reviews provide recommendations to the respective countries for follow-up and action.

As the lack of access and the volatile security situation on the ground in many countries often affect the ability to develop recovery and reintegration programmes, the importance of linking the monitoring and reporting activities

Leone, welcomes the continued commitment of the Government of Sierra Leone to work with the United Nations Children's Fund, the Office of the Special Representative of the Secretary-General for Children and Armed Conflict and other international agencies to give particular attention to the long-term rehabilitation of child combatants in Sierra Leone, and reiterates its encouragement of those involved to address the special needs of all children affected by the conflict." See Security Council Resolution on Sierra Leone, United Nations Security Council, UN Doc. S/RES/1270 (22 October 1999), para 18.

474 *Security Council Resolution on the Situation in Chad* UN Doc. S/RES/1861 (14 January 2009), para 23.

475 *Security Council Resolution on Children and Armed Conflict (22 April 2004), para 2.*

476 *Security Council Resolution on Children and Armed Conflict* (4 August 2009), para 13.

to concrete action cannot be emphasized strongly enough.[477] It is crucial that operational agencies on the ground, such as UNICEF, UNHCR, and the Office of the High Commissioner for Human Rights, stick to their mandated approaches in delivering humanitarian action or human rights activities relevant to children and civilian populations in need. While the monitoring and reporting work can inform their activities on the ground, they have a most important role in enhancing the opportunities for advocacy with warring parties. The risk, otherwise, is that the agencies' work in light of the mandate received through the Secretary-General to implement Security Council resolution 1612 becomes politicized, seen mainly through the lens of the political processes before the Council.

The MRM is not an end in itself: it must lead to advocacy and action on the ground. As far as the Security Council framework helps advance the agenda for recovery and reintegration it is useful, but when this is not the case, other work should go ahead. It is therefore important that while such operational agencies contribute towards the body of information at the global level, they do so only to the extent that is useful to their operational goals.

The information collected becomes the basis of analysis and advocacy at different levels, with the most important opportunity arising at the country level. As the information is passed by the Secretary-General to the Security Council, this can trigger both action and a response at the very highest level.[478] However, at the country level, the information gives the country task force and child protection agencies a concrete and informed foundation on which to engage with the parties to the conflict.

As first called for by Security Council resolution 1460 and reiterated in 1539 and 1612, a commitment should be translated into an action plan to end the recruitment and use of children by the armed forces and groups involved. An action plan is a concrete and time-bound commitment to halt all new recruitment of children and to separate and release all children associated with the group or force. It is normally developed jointly by the country task force and the armed force or group and outlines commitments and the operational steps to ensure the release of all children, including programmatic reintegration activities to assist the children in making the transition from military to civilian life.

The importance of an action plan is related to the fact that it constitutes a concrete tool whereby the country task force and the Security Council Working

---

477 *Report of the Secretary-General on Children and Armed Conflict*, UN Document A/63/785-S/2009/158 (26 March 2009). The report highlights that "measures to achieve sustainable reintegration of children affected by conflict" is identified as an "emerging concern".

478 Katy Barnett and Anna Jefferys, *Full of Promise: How the UN's Monitoring and Reporting Mechanism Can Better Protect Children*, Humanitarian Practice Network Paper, no. 62, September 2008.

Group can monitor the progress of implementation in releasing children, thus enabling them to hold the signatory to the plan accountable for its commitments through continuous dialogue and engagement. To date, almost 20 action plans and deeds of commitment have been signed with a number of armed forces and groups. The following paragraphs highlight the two action plans, Nepal and Sudan, and briefly describe the results of their action plans as relevant to recovery and reintegration.

The lengthy negotiations for the release of children in Nepal followed the successful peace process in 2006, which had led to the Comprehensive Peace Agreement between the Government of Nepal and the Communist Party of Nepal (Maoist) – perhaps providing an example of a mechanism that took enough time to become successful. But it was not until the end of 2009 that the UN was able to secure the release of children, many of whom by then had become adults. While the development of an action plan was fruitful in the end, this shows how political these processes can become, leading to a host of other child protection concerns as a result.[479]

The case of Sudan illustrates well how the Security Council's involvement with the issue of children and armed conflict can be used as a platform for advocacy. Following the publication of the Secretary-General's second Annual Report on Children and Armed Conflict in Sudan, in 2007, a joint UN-Government Committee was established to initiate dialogue on the reported violations. This represents a significant step forward in terms of the Government's engagement. Moreover, following the signing of an action plan with SLM/A in 2007 on the release of children associated with its armed group, additional groups came forward expressing their interest in dialogue and in signing similar plans, leading to the signature of an action plan by the Government of Southern Sudan in 2009.[480] Despite these political developments and successes in establishing appropriate frameworks for action, the actual numbers of released children remain small.[481]

The format and key principles of an action plan are not yet standardized across countries with established monitoring and reporting mechanisms; a

---

479 Action Plan between the Government of Nepal, the Unified Communist Party of Nepal – Maoist, and the United Nations in Nepal Regarding the Discharge of Disqualified Maoist Army Personnel and Related Tasks, 16 December 2009. Child protection issues that arose in the meantime include keeping children together with adults, limited freedom of movement, and the right to recovery and reintegration not being fulfilled. With respect to some of the other issues that arose as part of the recovery and reintegration process in Nepal, see Sophie Hodgson, "Whose Action Plan? An Analysis of the UN Security Council Resolution 1612 Action Plan and Monitoring and Reporting Mechanisms in Nepal," *Journal of Human Rights Practice* 4, no. 2 (2012): 164–186.

480 Action Plan between the Sudan People's Liberation Army (SPLA) and the United Nations Regarding Children Associated with the SPLA in Southern Sudan, 20 November 2009.

481 Report of the Secretary-General on Children and Armed Conflict in Sudan, UN Doc. S/2009/84 (10 February 2009), para 51 and 52.

unified approach to what type of response measures will be included also remains to be determined. While this may not be a problem per se, it could be exploited by some parties to conflict. The MRM has only been fully operational in a small number of countries since 2005, and the examples described above illustrate many problems in terms of implementation and making the action plans a reality for children on the ground. There is a risk that parties to conflict will seek to develop such plans just to be seen as collaborating and in order to gain status internationally. The short time frame has made it difficult to assess the extent of the direct impact of the work on children's lives. Whereas children have been released in some of the countries under consideration, reports of new recruitment cases and other grave child rights violations continue to be documented. Notable progress has nonetheless been achieved in raising the profile of the monitoring and reporting work and thereby the plight of children affected by armed conflicts, and strong political commitment has resulted in frameworks for addressing these issues.

2. REPARATIONS TO FORMER CHILD SOLDIERS: INTERNATIONAL HUMAN RIGHTS AND HUMANITARIAN LAW AS APPLIED IN THE *LUBANGA* CASE

While there is growing recognition in international human rights law that victims and groups of victims – including children – have a right to reparation for grave violations of human rights and serious violations of international humanitarian law, it is less clear what such reparations should look like in practice, and how they could be implemented in situations where there are many levels and types of harm that have been inflicted.[482] This section looks at the application of a reparations scheme in the *Lubanga* case.

2.1. CONSIDERING REPARATIONS IN THE *LUBANGA* CASE

Moving to the reparations stage after its verdict, the Chamber for the *Lubanga* case considered that "the ICC Statute and the Rules introduce a system of

482 See, e.g., the *Basic Principles and Guidelines on the Right to a Remedy and Reparation for Victims of Gross Violations of International Human Rights Law and Serious Violations of International Humanitarian Law* (21 March 2006), principles 8 and 13. (hereinafter "the Basic Principles on Remedy and Reparation") Case law of the European Convention on Human Rights and the American Convention of Human Rights, which both allow groups and individuals to claim reparations for violation of their rights. See also Lisa Magarrell, *Reparations in Theory and Practice*, Reparations Justice Series (New York: International Center for Transitional Justice, 2007).

reparation that reflects the growing recognition in international criminal law that there is a need to go beyond the notion of punitive justice, towards a solution which is more inclusive, encourages participation and recognizes the need to provide effective remedies for victims."[483]

The findings on reparations in this case have begun to define the principles and processes that should apply, and what reparations could look like in practice for war-affected children. In the process following the verdict, the ICC invited organizations to make presentations during the reparations proceedings so as to bring in their perspectives and those of the victims. This aspect of consultation with those affected, including the victims, applies to decisions on the basic principles for reparations, and also to application of the basic principles in a specific context.[484] As the *Lubanga* case is the first case of the ICC, and the ensuing decision about reparations also its first, the Court was careful in reviewing in detail the submissions of each of the organizations that wanted to contribute towards the proceedings.[485]

In these situations, the harm that victims have suffered is the result of gross violations of human rights and serious violations of international humanitarian law. The harm can be physical or mental, lost opportunities, material damages, moral damage, and costs required for legal or expert assistance.

In determining whether there is a sufficient causal link between the crime and the relevant harm, international law does not provide much guidance on how to approach this. However, the Chamber did consider that reparations should not be limited to "direct" harm, but should also apply a standard of "proximate" cause. As the Court had alluded to already during the consideration of the case itself when dealing with the issue of sexual violence, in considering the framework for reparations, it has gone beyond strict definitions as defined by international criminal law to also consider the Basic Principles and Guidelines on Remedy and Reparation, the Paris Commitments and Principles, and the Nairobi Declaration on Women's and Girls' Right to a Remedy and Reparation.

It is also clear that the standard of criminal law of proof beyond reasonable doubt does not apply, and hence the Chamber decided to apply the standard of "a balance of probabilities" when it is directed against the convicted person, adopting a flexible approach to determining factual matters, "taking into account the extensive and systematic nature of the crimes and the number of victims involved."

483 Lubanga Reparations Decision, para 177. See also *Guidance Note of the Secretary-General: UN Approach to Justice for Children*, (New York: United Nations, September 2008), para 6. The Guidance Note focuses on the involvement of victims in the design and implementation of transitional justice processes and mechanisms.

484 *The Prosecutor v. Thomas Lubanga Dyilo*, Decision Granting Leave to Make Representations in the Reparations Proceedings, ICC-01/04-01/06-2870 ICC (20 April 2012).

485 Lubanga Reparations Decisions, para 8.

In the decision establishing the principles and procedures to be applied to reparations, the ICC considered several other key issues, including: who should have access to the reparations procedures; the type of reparations, whether individual or collective; who should be eligible as a beneficiary; and implementation of a scheme for reparations. These areas are covered in the following sections.

2.2. ACCESSIBILITY AND NON-DISCRIMINATION

In determining who will benefit from reparations, the process should be considered as important as the decision itself.[486] This way, it can be ensured that the reparations live up to expectations and that their impact is maximized. This is critical because reparations are not just about the material benefit for those who receive them: they have important symbolic value for society as a whole.[487] Consequently, if the reparations are not appropriate or handed out in way that is considered prompt, adequate, and effective by the victims and the community as a whole, they may undermine any effort for reconciliation and reintegration.

It is also necessary to consider that in a situation with widespread violations against human rights and humanitarian law, it will not be possible to focus reparations on all victims. Some type of targeting or prioritization must be done, while allowing access to reparations as a forum to as many victims as possible.[488] From a child rights perspective, the best interests of the child must be considered in application of reparations, and as noted in the first part of this chapter, the physical and psychological recovery and social reintegration "shall take place in an environment which fosters the health, self-respect and dignity of the child."[489]

In the context of child recruitment, it is very important to consider what society thinks about individual benefits being given to former child soldiers, especially in contexts where they may have carried out violations in the communities and where reparations may be seen as a reward for a group of

486 Magarrell, *Reparations in Theory and Practice*, 9. The importance of the process cannot be underestimated when seeking to make the reparations scheme fair and legitimate as viewed by the victims, and the society as a whole, including any part of the population that may consider themselves to have been left out.

487 Ibid., 4. See also submissions by the Trust Fund for Victims, Lubanga Reparations Decision, paras 30–31.

488 Anja Wiersing, "Lubanga and its Implications for Victims Seeking Reparations at the International Criminal Court " *Amsterdam Law Forum* 4: 39 (2012): 21–39.

489 CRC Article 3 and 39. In the Decision on the Reparations process the Chamber also concluded that these principles would guide the Court and that the decisions should reflect a gender-inclusive perspective. Lubanga Reparations Decision, para 211–212.

children who really do not deserve compensation.[490] It is noteworthy that every group that contributed towards the proceedings in the *Lubanga* case highlighted the risk of perpetrators benefiting from a reparations scheme and how this would not be appropriate for the Democratic Republic of the Congo context. While the principles for reparations have not yet been implemented, the intention of the Court was also to make reparations appropriate to the context. This is why it may be more appropriate to implement reparation schemes that are community-based and have a broader focus than just former child soldiers.[491]

The gender perspective and sexual violence are other significant aspects in this context, as girls and women are likely to have been marginalized during the reintegration efforts. Frequently, women and girls who are returning home from an armed force or group have come home pregnant or with a little baby. The baby may not be considered to be part of the society due to having been fathered by rebel leaders who have brought harm to the community.[492]

The Nairobi Declaration on Women's and Girls Right to a Remedy and Reparation also recognizes the importance of the gender perspective and participation of women and girls in every stage of the reparation process. In addition, the Declaration highlights that "reintegration and restitution by themselves are not sufficient goals of reparations, since the origins of violations of women's and girls' human rights predate the conflict situation." Reparations in this context therefore need to go beyond considering just the harm done, must seek to address the root causes of discriminatory practices in society.[493]

Considering how to best put in place a reparations scheme is a process that should include participation of the community for purposes of aligning the reparations with what is acceptable in the community. The purpose is also to ensure that the reparations are non-discriminatory and that victims who might not otherwise be known or heard of have a chance to make their situation known during the reparations proceedings.

In considering reparations for the *Lubanga* case, the Chamber considered the importance of children's participation and of seeking the views of the child victims when decisions are made about individual or collective reparations

490 *Through a New Lens: A Child-Sensitive Approach to Transitional Justice*, (2011), 29. Aptel/Ladisch provide an example of a girl receiving money as part of the reparations scheme, and the message that it portrays, asking why she would get money for causing harm to others.

491 See, e.g., *The Prosecutor v. Thomas Lubanga Dyilo*, International Criminal Court, Case No: ICC-01/04-01/06, UNICEF Submission on the principles to be applied, and the procedure to be followed by the Chamber with regard to reparations, ICC-01/04-01/06-2878 (10 May 2012). See Lubanga Reparations Decision, para 192.

492 Helen Liebling et al., *Bearing Children through Rape in Eastern Congo: Community and State Responses*, (17 April 2012).

493 *Nairobi Declaration on Women's and Girls' Right to a Remedy and Reparation*, (2007), para 3. See section on access to reparation.

concerning them, bearing in mind their circumstances, age, and level of maturity.[494]

2.3. INDIVIDUAL AND COLLECTIVE REPARATIONS

Reparations may be focused on individuals, a group of individuals, or collectives, such as communities or certain parts of a country.

In the context of child recruitment, it may not be appropriate to focus on individual reparations, as experience shows that individual support in the context of recovery and reintegration can lead to stigmatization and bad feelings in the community. However, it may still be relevant for certain types of cases to provide individual reparations, and to tailor such cases in a way that they focus on the most excluded, such as the victims of sexual violence. Cash payments, however, can be a challenge in any society, due to patriarchal structures, organizing methods for payment, and imbalances between those who have the means and those who do not.[495]

Collective reparations will be very important in this context and have proved to be much easier to manage. They may also avoid stigmatization, by promoting reconciliation in the community, as well as individual reintegration, when focused on services that support the recovery and reintegration process for children and simultaneously benefit the community as a whole. At the same time, reparations between communities must be balanced equally to avoid fuelling discontent between, for instance, different ethnic groups.[496]

One concern in this regard in the implementation of reparations in the *Lubanga* case will be to ensure that the reparations put in place are not separate and different from what is already in place, or that they at least do not undermine existing efforts, as this will prove to be difficult from a coordination and implementation perspective. The Chamber ruled on the type of collective reparations that may be appropriate in the context, including medical services, such as psychiatric and psychological services, along with assistance towards general rehabilitation, housing, education, and training. However, psychiatric care may not be appropriate to the circumstances, and it will not be possible to find actors in the local context who would be able to implement this type of reparations. Providing housing may also cause problems because it is not really collective, but aimed to benefit individual families. Unless carefully considered, such activities can cause discontent within or among communities rather than build reconciliation.

---

494 Lubanga Decision on Reparations, para 215.

495 Magarrell, *Reparations in Theory and Practice*, 6. Magarrell notes examples from Chile and Peru where individual payments had a negative impact on the internal harmony in the communities.

496 Lubanga Reparations Decision, para 63.

2.4. DEFINING THE BENEFICIARIES

A reparations initiative needs to define the universe of victims, and then specific groups within that who may need to receive reparations.[497] This will partly be determined through the participatory process that leads to the reparations decisions. Some victims may have more exposure to the process and opportunities to apply for reparations, while others may not have the information or it may be otherwise difficult for them to apply. The Chamber in the *Lubanga* case was very careful to not exclude anyone who could be considered a victim at this stage, and wanted recommendations to come forth during the consultative process.

Important questions inevitably arise in relation to who could be considered a victim.[498] The UN Basic Principles identify victims as those persons "who individually or collectively suffered harm ... the term 'victim' also includes the immediate family or dependants of the direct victim and person who have suffered harm in intervening to assist victims in distress or to prevent victimization."[499] ICC rule 85 also considers reparations for both direct and indirect victims. In the *Lubanga* case, the organizations participating in the proceedings clearly argued that the reparations should not just focus on victims who participated during the trial.

The level of proof that a person can be considered a victim is complex and will likely lead to interesting debates in the procedures to be applied to reparations. The Chamber considered that both direct and indirect victims should be able to participate in the reparations process and be provided with support to make their participation substantive and effective.[500] Soliciting such inputs to the proceedings requires active outreach, across gender and ethnic groups, in a sensitive and proactive manner that allows access to victims who may otherwise not seek reparations or provide contributions to the process.[501] Outreach activities will require specialist support, especially due to questions on how children may safely contribute to this process and in order to bring in expertise on how to best deal with the situation of sexual violence. It may even be

---

497 Magarrell, *Reparations in Theory and Practice*, 7.

498 In the context of the ICC, Rule nr. 85, which considers: " 'Victims' means natural persons who have suffered harm as a result of the commission of any crime within the jurisdiction of the Court." See *Rules of Procedure and Evidence*, UN Doc. PCNICC/2000/1/Add.1 (2000).

499 *Basic Principles and Guidelines on the Right to a Remedy and Reparation for Victims of Gross Violations of International Human Rights Law and Serious Violations of International Humanitarian Law* (21 March 2006), para 8.

500 Lubanga Reparations Decision, para 203.

501 Ibid., para 205. See also ICTJ publication: International Center for Transitional Justice Clara Ramirez-Barat, *Engaging Children and Youth in Transitional Justice Processes: Guidance for Outreach Programs*, (2012).

useful to confer with children about the consultation, in order to determine the most effective forms of outreach and maximize children's participation.[502]

The dilemma of reaching out to marginalized groups is not a new one in trying to reach former child soldiers. The same is true for programmes that focus on recovery and reintegration, sometimes incorporated in larger DDR programmes with a focus on children. Many children return home not knowing about the existing programmes or how to access them, or they may themselves consider themselves to be unsafe because the programmes might give them exposure they do not want.[503] It is also common for groups of children not to be considered part of release and reintegration programmes because the groups did not consider them to be child soldiers. This is why it is very important to make sure to highlight that advocacy for release relates to all children associated with the group or force in one way or another. The Court is also open to reparations schemes being broadened beyond the functions that were considered active participation in armed conflicts.

2.5. ESTABLISHING THE TYPE OF REPARATION

Reparation includes a range of forms: restitution, restoring victims to their original situation; compensation for economically assessable damage; rehabilitation, supporting recovery and reintegrate; satisfaction, for example, through public apologies by the perpetrators; as well as guarantees of non-repetition, strengthening of the rule of law and related institutions to uphold the law. In the case of the International Criminal Court, the Court "may make an order directly against a convicted person specifying appropriate reparations" or it may make an order for "restitution, compensation and rehabilitation."[504]

Many of the submissions in the *Lubanga* case focused on education and reintegration activities. A critical question that arises is the extent to which the reparations scheme in the form of rehabilitation and reintegration activities builds up new initiatives or feeds into the existing ones.[505] The Chamber also considered in this case that the principles decided upon were limited to the circumstances of the present case, but should afford justice to the victims and

---

502 *Key Principles for Children and Transitional Justice: Involvement of Children and Considerations of Children's Rights in Truth, Justice and Reconciliation Processes* (2009), section on outreach and consultations. See section on outreach and consultation.

503 Specht, "DDR, Transitional Justice, and the Reintegration of Former Child Combatants," 196–197.

504 Rome Statute, article 75(1). See also Schabas, *An Introduction to the International Criminal Court, Third Edition*, 338.

505 See, for instance, the UNICEF submission suggesting the Court support particular current initiatives directed at the practice of recruiting and using children. *The Prosecutor v. Thomas Lubanga Dyilo*, 10 May 2012, paras 19–20.

aim to relieve the suffering while providing effective reintegration and promoting reconciliation.[506]

The Chamber considered rehabilitation activities to include medical, psychological, psychiatric, and social assistance; any relevant legal and social services; and education and vocational training, along with sustainable work opportunities. An important point is raised by the Nairobi Declaration, namely, not to undertake development instead of reparation. As stated in the Declaration, "There is a distinct need for both reconstruction and development, of which reparations programmes are a distinct part."[507] This is also where the link between DDR programmes and transitional justice comes in, with two considerations:

First, in general, mainstream DDR programmes are considered to be quite separate from transitional justice and reparations schemes, mainly because it would be difficult to see an immediate fit between former adult soldiers as "victims" of crimes and hence having a right to reparation. The nexus between peace and justice is strong in the development of DDR programmes, and while there is not an immediate fit in a reparations way of thinking, they certainly both pull in the same direction.[508]

Second, this particular issue of defining the beneficiaries and the type of support to be received is even more challenging when it comes to child soldiers. Children are considered to be victims in this context, because they should not have been in the armed group in the first place. Also, in a DDR programme, while there is risk of children being forgotten, they do not await formal disarmament, demobilization, and rehabilitation to start: advocacy for their release begins even in the midst of armed conflict.

Regardless of these shortcomings, in the absence of any formal transitional justice process that defines reparations, a DDR programme for children is already a way of repairing for the harm done. As such, it is very important that linkages are created between programmes established through the ICC and pre-existing DDR programmes for children. It is not useful for the ICC to begin a new mode of reparations programmes that neglect these years of lessons learned or perhaps even undermine existing programmes.[509]

In addition, the Chamber considered rehabilitation measures that include means of addressing the shame that child victims may feel. This is particularly

---

506 Lubanga Reparations Decision, paras 179–181.

507 *Nairobi Declaration on Women's and Girls' Right to a Remedy and Reparation* (2007), section 3.

508 Specht, "DDR, Transitional Justice, and the Reintegration of Former Child Combatants," 139. Pablo de Greiff in 'Disarming the Past', p. 139.

509 Drumbl considers the implication of the current approach to release and reintegration as being very delinked from justice, though the process put in place for reparations in the *Lubanga* case provide an opportunity to begin to address some of this dilemma. Drumbl, *Reimagining Child Soldiers in International Law and Policy*, 113.

relevant for children who have perpetrated crimes while in the ranks of the armed groups and forces. Symbolic reparations, such as commemorations and tributes, are also considered relevant.[510]

2.6. IMPLEMENTING A REPARATIONS SCHEME

Ultimately, it is the state that has the responsibility to establish programmes for reparation and enforce domestic judgements. Nonetheless, in situations where individual criminal responsibility arises, the individual in question may also be asked to take on a role in reparation, such as publicly giving an apology or, depending on available assets, paying a nominal sum to make a contribution to the reparations.

In the context of the ICC, there is a Trust Fund for Victims through which funds can be channelled for purposes of reparations. In the *Lubanga* case, the Chamber considered a voluntary apology to individual victims or to groups of victims to be appropriate, but since Lubanga has no assets or property that can be used for purposes of reparations, it invoked the concept of "reparations through the Trust Fund" and drawing on the resources of the Fund in implementing the award.[511] The reparations will be dealt with principally by the Trust Fund for Victims, which is monitored and overseen by a differently composed Chamber that will deal with any contested issues.[512]

On the ICC Registry's proposal, the Chamber also recommended the establishment of a multidisciplinary team of experts to provide assistance to the Court in the following areas:

- an assessment of the harm suffered by the victims in this case;
- the effect that the crimes had on their families and communities;
- identifying the most appropriate form of reparations, in consultation with the victims and their communities;
- establishing those individuals, bodies, groups, and communities that should be awarded reparations; and
- accessing funds for these purposes.[513]

The task of finding members for this team was delegated to the Trust Fund for Victims, although the Chamber did consider that experts in the field of child soldiers, violence against girls and boys, and gender issues should be among

510 Lubanga Reparations Decision, paras 233–236.

511 Lubanga Reparations Decision, paras 241, 269 and 270.

512 Ibid., para 261. The ICC Statute in Article 75 provides for reparations, but it does not specify the body that is to monitor and supervise this part of the proceedings. The Chamber, however, considered that this was within the responsibilities of the Judiciary.

513 Ibid., para 263.

those appointed by the Trust.[514] It is very promising to see that the Chamber made this decision about the multidisciplinary team, and hopefully it can help with some of the issues raised above related to reparations schemes of the ICC linking with programmes for recovery and reintegration that are already in place.

It will be interesting to follow the process as the reparations scheme is implemented. To begin with, the localities to be involved in the reparations process need to be established and then those communities engaged in a process of consultation to allow for an assessment of harm. According to the decision by the Chamber, the assessment of harm should be carried out by the team of experts. It is important in this regard to consider the multiple ways in which children have been affected and to make sure that children are not being stigmatized when they are made eligible for reparations.

Following the assessment of harm, there will be public debates held in each locality to explain the reparations principles and procedures and to address the victims' expectations. Proposals for collective reparations will then be developed in each locality and presented to the Chamber for approval.

CONCLUSION

This chapter has considered the child's right to reparation following grave violations with a view to support the recovery and reintegration of war-affected children. Although comprehensive frameworks are in place for children who have been recruited or used by armed groups or forces, there is a need to place the release and reintegration programmes for children squarely within a reparations and justice approach, as to date the different regimes are not connecting.

The arguments found in international law are compelling and can be used more proactively in advocacy at the international and national levels in order to bring the same focus found in the CRC and the Optional Protocol into other initiatives. Such normative standards do not need to come in the form of treaties – they can also be introduced through peace agreements, action plans, and other forms of agreement that provide for practical approaches to addressing the recovery and reintegration needs of children.

Although the area of reparations in international criminal law is quite well defined from a principles point of view, it still needs to be applied and considered in each context. It is also crucial that the reparations schemes now developed for criminal justice processes pick up the lessons learned in the area of recovery and reintegration for child soldiers, as these institutions are neither well placed to

514 The Key Principles for Children and Transitional Justice in discussing reparations schemes also focused on the need to coordinate reparations programmes with child protection agencies, experts, and representatives from key sectors.

consider the appropriate forms of reparations in an informed manner, nor are the reparations predictable to the victims. Therefore, the reparations schemes being designed by international criminal tribunals can be questioned.

The *Lubanga* reparations decision will begin to bring compensation for harm to the victims. However, it is very important that the reparations component of the judgement is not dealt with in isolation, but that the schemes link up with the programmes already initiated on the ground. Only then can the different aspects of transitional justice that support reparations become mutually reinforcing.

A key question in the context of reparatory justice is that of timing and the consequences of time passing before coming to the point of providing reparations through transitional justice processes. Reparations following from criminal law cases will be made long after the actual events, and the communities and individuals receiving reparations may not even agree on the charges or consider the charges to be only partial. Recovery and reintegration programmes, on the other hand, are generally timely and start even before other elements of transitional justice are up and running.

The two areas of reparations that have been considered in this chapter come at very different times in the transitional justice process, and while they need to connect, it may not be the best way to go about a reparations scheme that results from a criminal justice case to just do "more of the same." This may be an opportunity to think of new and different approaches, which are initiated much later than the support that is provided through recovery and reintegration programmes following children's release from armed groups and forces.

Former child soldiers run the risk of falling through the cracks on many occasions in the transitional process. Not only might they be waiting for years to get support, but when programmes for recovery and reintegration are set up, because they are children, they may be sidelined in mainstream DDR processes, or they may not get the same level of support. Alternatively, they might have grown older than 18 years of age and may not qualify for release even if they had been recruited as children.

Over time, reparation becomes increasingly symbolic, a gesture saying that what happened was wrong, accompanied by provision of a little compensation. Over the years, most of the children will have moved on and it becomes increasingly difficult to find a specific target group that should be reached. They may not even want to be reminded about certain events. But if former child soldiers who are adults and had a more difficult time reintegrating can be found and supported as a specific group, this would be a good way to focus the support, in consultation with the group and their communities at large.

Reparations for child soldiers, and child protection programming in general, are as much about social considerations and approaches as they are about legal considerations and approaches. Lessons show that individually focused support is not easily provided without provoking misgivings in the community among other children and families who do not get the same support. Individual support also needs to be carefully monitored and supervised, and targeted to reach those children and families who need it most. This means that there must be a social or case work component that allows constant follow-up and monitoring. Only then can a focus on the individual be targeted towards those who need it, while considering any negative impact that the individualized support may lead to.

Reparation may also take place in an approach that provides for affirmative action. This could be a situation where a particular part of the population has been sidelined during the conflict and long before, and where transition will greatly benefit from that part of the population being positively considered for law enforcement positions, roles in government, and formal functions that will support a society moving forward.

In the case of child recruitment, the point has been made that these children may receive support far more sophisticated than other children, and in some situations, these children have carried out crimes, at times even against their own communities. This is when it becomes difficult to reconcile affirmative action for people who have possibly committed crimes. At the same time, unless they are dealt with in a very proactive way, there is a large risk of former child recruits becoming more of a problem than a solution. And at the end of the day, it is the fault of adults that they ended up in the fighting ranks to begin with.

While it is important to distinguish between reconstruction programmes and reparations, conflict brings about very visible and tangible impacts on infrastructure and services that provide for the basic necessities to ensure the right to life and development for children. Not all support for a community coming out of war needs to be designed specifically for children in order to serve children. This includes access to water, food, health, and education. But children are also affected emotionally and sometimes psychosocially, which needs to be considered not only in the immediate response to humanitarian crises but also in their long-term development. Specific protection issues may have arisen due to the conflict and need professional handling.

Generally, the area of transitional justice and children, and how it relates to their successful recovery and reintegration, is under-explored, with many issues remaining difficult because agreement has not been reached on some of the approaches. While there is no "one size fits all" solution, it would be useful to study further the linkages between transitional justice and the psychosocial well-being of children, in other words, how different procedures may or may not feed into the recovery process for a child.

Throughout reparations processes, it is critical to bring in the children and young people more proactively, exploring how they can participate in the recovery of their own society and how they can influence the peace or transitional justice processes. It is more easily said than done, but in the reparatory justice phase it is likely more important than any other aspect, as if that fails, all fails.

Chapter 6 on child recruitment and institutional justice focuses on how institutional change can address the situation of child soldiers, and how judicial and non-judicial mechanisms and institutional reform processes can protect the rights of child soldiers.

CHAPTER 6

CHILD RECRUITMENT AND INSTITUTIONAL JUSTICE

"If I were the president, I would talk to the rebel group leaders and build peace amongst the different ethnic groups. It does not make sense to fight this war."

INTRODUCTION

Institutional justice considers reform of "public institutions that helped perpetuate conflict or repressive rule."[515] The laws and policies implemented through institutions at various levels are themselves the engine of change. Law can help distribute power more effectively and build or reform fair and efficient public institutions.

While criminal sanctions are generally predicated on individual criminal responsibility, civil sanctions of an administrative nature are based on exclusionary conditions, chiefly of political loyalty, which, for example, systematically disqualifies certain groups of people from participation in the new government.[516] But changes of an institutional and administrative nature may also be part of an overall effort to change the way institutions operate and interrelate. In the Secretary-General's report taking stock of progress made in the rule of law and transitional justice arenas, emphasis is placed on institution building that provides for greater levels of national ownership, more concerted efforts at sector-wide approaches, and more emphasis on initiatives to facilitate access to justice.[517]

Key legal questions that are considered in this chapter include:

- What does institutional justice signify in the context of the recruitment and use of children? What institutions are most important to safeguarding their rights?

[515] *Guidance Note of the Secretary-General: UN Approach to Justice for Children*, 9. For Teitel, this area covers both administrative justice and constitutional justice. Teitel, *Transitional Justice*, 149–212.

[516] Teitel, *Transitional Justice*, 150.

[517] *Report of the Secretary-General on the Rule of Law and Transitional Justice in Conflict and Post-Conflict Societies*, UN Doc. S/2011/634 (12 October 2011), para 33.

- What areas of law in current contexts of child recruitment have developed during recent years, and how have they evolved?
- What role could business play in respecting and supporting children's rights within a context of child recruitment and transitional justice?
- What are the entry points in this otherwise big-picture area of transitional justice for issues related to children?

Much of what is implemented as part of institutional justice often has its beginning in early parts of the peace process, including ceasefire and peace agreements. An example of this type of transformation is the signing, in 2006, of the peace agreement for Darfur, where the Sudan Liberation Army leader became a vice-president as part of the peace agreement discussions. Although this decision was made in the interest of peace for the region, this leader did not have influence over all of Darfur, so there were many other rebel leaders who would have needed to be considered in a new power-sharing offer – revealing the potentially negative effects of early negotiations on long-term institutional justice.

Another type of action that could be included under institutional justice is the redirecting or redistribution of public goods if certain areas in a country are receiving more support than others. During the 2003–2005 period of the ceasefire agreement in Sri Lanka, the Action Plan for Children Affected by War aimed to bridge the gap between children in the southern parts of the country and those living in the northern and eastern areas that were affected by the armed conflict.[518] This type of action can be a central factor in the overall effort for recovery and reintegration of war-affected children.[519]

While these examples are widely different, they reflect upon how positive impact on children's rights can be achieved through peace negotiations and peace agreements in many various ways, not only through means that are directly geared towards children.

In situations with widespread child recruitment, there are notable limitations, particularly with respect to the rule of law and institutional capacity, because there has usually been little investment in child protection systems and the structures for implementing justice are weak. This makes some aspects of the organizational framework and long-term institutional infrastructure, such as administrative justice and security sector reform, very difficult to realize.[520] It is

518 Action Plan: Addressing the Needs and Care for the Children in the North East Affected by War, Sri Lanka (22 April 2003).

519 'Agreement on a ceasefire between the Government of the Democratic Socialist Republic of Sri Lanka and the Liberation Tigers of Tamil Eelam,' (22 February 2002).

520 Such scholars as Teitel also recognize this fact, although most of her examples come from the post WW II situations, as well as the perestroika period. See Teitel, *Transitional Justice*, 220. See also United Nations, *Integrated Disarmament, Demobilization and Reintegration Standards: Module 6.10 DDR and Security Sector Reform* (New York: United Nations, 2009).

important not to build capacity in the wrong place so as to undermine the transition process, but at the same time, it is only by developing the national justice system that the necessary institutions can have the capacity and tools necessary to support the rule of law and transition process.[521] Institutional justice and reform will be studied in detail in this chapter, with a focus on building child protection systems in the context of armed conflict and how this needs to be accompanied by extensive training on applicable legal standards to support the overall rule of law.

Constitutionalism in transition is commonly included in this element of transitional justice and can have many facets. Constitutions build the underpinnings of a new democracy, as the transition period is often a move from a military and/or totalitarian regime to democracy. Different aspects of constitutional justice in the transitional justice process balance between the rights of the individual and the power of the state. Constitutional justice determines the function and structure of the state, while simultaneously delineating the obligations of the state to protect the rights of individuals.[522] This is why constitutions play such a critical role in constructing the foundations of the transition. However, since the relevance of constitutionalism is quite limited when it comes to child recruitment, this will not be considered further in this chapter.

Chapter 6 is divided in two parts: (1) an analysis of the normative provisions and how children's concerns have been integrated into peace processes; and (2) an overview of the child protection systems that are needed within institutional justice structures and the type of reform that will be necessary in order for child protection actors to successfully respond to the release and reintegration of child soldiers.

1. PEACE AGREEMENTS AND CHILDREN'S ISSUES

This section reflects on how peace and ceasefire agreements to date have considered issues related to children, with a focus on child recruitment.

1.1. ANALYSIS OF THE PROVISIONS RELATED TO CHILDREN

A serious effort to include children's issues in peace agreements began only during the late 1990s, largely prompted by the 1996 Machel study, which

521 *Report of the Secretary-General on the Rule of Law and Transitional Justice in Conflict and Post-Conflict Societies*, UN Doc. S/2004/616 (23 August 2004), 12.

522 Teitel, *Transitional Justice*, 193.

emphasized the importance of bringing children's issues into peace negotiations and paved the way for the creation of institutional arrangements that would secure the release and reintegration of former child soldiers.

Early examples of the inclusion of provisions specifically related to children include the conclusion of the 1994 Washington Agreement on the situation in Bosnia and Herzegovina, which refers to the Convention on the Rights of the Child; and commitments made in the State of Chiapas, Mexico, in 1996, which encompasses language relevant to survival rights, basic services, and the right to education.[523] As early as 1976, the Tripoli Agreement (Philippines) referred to the right to education as a specific issue relevant to children. In Guatemala, in 1996, special attention to children was cited in the peace agreement that stated, "The programme [of overall reconstruction] shall treat former combatants, women, young people and disabled persons as sectors requiring specific priority attention."[524]

Although peace agreements have made a number of general references to children, child recruitment has been the most common specific feature. Other issues are raised in a very ad hoc manner.

Since 1996, out of 11 peace agreements with some mention of children's issues, 8 have addressed child recruitment. The fact that child recruitment is prohibited under international law makes it inherently difficult to get parties to agree to address this issue in peace agreements, and hence, the language has not been direct and clear. The table below compares provisions included in various peace agreements.[525]

523 'Washington Agreement Signed by Bosnian Prime Minister Haris Silajdzic, Croatian Foreign Minister Mate Granic, Bosnian Croat Representative Kresimir Zubak: Confederation Agreement between the Bosnian Government and Bosnian Croats,' (1 March 1994), 'Actions and Measures for Chiapas Joint Commitments and Proposals from the State and Federal Governments and the Ezln,' (16 February 1996), www.usip.org/library/pa/chiapas/agreement_960216.html (accessed 5 January 2009).

524 'The Final Agreement on the Implementation of the 1976 Tripoli Agreement between the Government of the Republic of the Philippines (GRP) and the Moro National Liberation Front (MNLF) with the Participation of the Organization of Islamic Conference Ministerial Committee of Six and the Secretary General of the Organization of Islamic Conference,' (2 September 1996). 'Agreement on Social and Economic Aspects and Agrarian Situation Concluded on 6 May 1996 between the Presidential Peace Commission of the Government of Guatemala and the Unidad Revolucionaria Nacional Guatemalteca,' (6 May 1996).

525 Central African Republic (CAR), 'Accord de cessation des hostilities en Rėpublique Centrafricaine,' (2015). 'Democratic Republic of the Congo (DRC), Ceasefire Agreement,' (1999), www.usip.org/library/pa/drc/drc_07101999.html. 'Comprehensive Peace Agreement between the Government of Liberia and the Liberians United for Reconciliation and Democracy (LURD) and the Movement for Democracy in Liberia (MODEL) and Political Parties,' (18 August 2003), 'Unofficial Translation of the Comprehensive Peace Agreement Concluded between the Government of Nepal and the Communist Party of Nepal (Maoist),' (21 November 2006), 'The Government of the Republic of Sierra Leone and the Revolutionary United Front of Sierra Leone (RUF/SL),' (7 July 1999), 'Agreement between the Governments of Sudan and Uganda,' (1999), 'Agreement on Permanent Ceasefire and Security Arrangements Implementation Modalities During the Pre-Interim and the Interim Periods

Agreement	Language Referring to Child Recruitment, Demobilization, and Reintegration
Central African Republic, Ceasefire Agreement, 2014	The parties commit not to recruit children as combatants, in conformity with the African Charter and the Convention on the Rights of the Child and its Optional Protocol on the Involvement of Children in Armed Conflict.
Democratic Republic of the Congo, Ceasefire Agreement, 1999	Article I (3[c]): The Ceasefire shall entail the cessation of … recruitment and use of child soldiers.
Sierra Leone, 1999	Article XXX: The Government shall accord particular attention to the issue of child soldiers. It shall, accordingly, mobilize resources, both within the country and from the International Community, and especially through the Office of the UN Special Representative for Children in Armed Conflict, UNICEF and other agencies, to address the special needs of these children in the existing disarmament, demobilization and reintegration processes.
Sudan-Uganda, 1999	Article 8: … especially children, who have been abducted in the past and return them to their families
Liberia, 2003	Article XXXI (a): '… accord special attention to the issue of child combatants.' (b): 'It shall, accordingly, mobilize resources with the assistance of the International Community, especially in cooperation with the Office of the U.N. Special Representative for Children in Armed Conflict, UNICEF, the African Committee of Experts on the Rights and Welfare of the Child and other relevant agencies, to address their special demobilization and re-integration needs'
Sudan, Comprehensive Peace Agreement, 2005	Article 10.1: The following acts shall constitute violations to this Agreement: … 'recruitment of child soldiers.' Article 24: Guiding principles: … 'The demobilization of all child soldiers within six months of the signature of the Comprehensive Peace Agreement.' Article 24.11: "UNICEF, ICRC and other international organizations are called upon to assist in the child component of the DDR in the Sudan."
Nepal, 2006	Article 7(6): … not to conscript or use children who are aged 18 or below in the armed force. Children thus affected shall be rescued immediately and appropriate assistance as may be needed shall be provided for their rehabilitation.
Sudan, Darfur Peace Agreement, 2006	Article 275. The Parties shall release all boys and girls associated with armed forces and groups. UNICEF, UNHCR, and the ICRC shall be called upon to assist in the identification, removal, family unification and reintegration of children associated with armed forces and groups. UNICEF and other child protection organizations shall be called upon to support and assist in the identification, removal, family reunification and reintegration of children associated with armed forces and armed groups.

between the Government of the Sudan (GoS) and the Sudan People's Liberation Movement/ Sudan People's Liberation Army (SPLM/SPLA),' (31 December 2004), and 'Darfur Peace Agreement,' (5 May 2006).

Together, these provisions lend themselves to some useful analysis. Given the legal vacuum common in the aftermath of armed conflicts, and even when relevant customary law may be in place, recognition of children's issues through peace agreements can draw attention to recruitment and use of children as a violation that needs to be rectified. Peace agreements also serve as an important advocacy opportunity to put the issue of child recruitment on the peace negotiations agenda and compel parties to the conflict to understand and accept them as legal obligations.

Regarding the question of age, peace agreements with provisions for child recruitment have almost entirely referred to "children" without including an age. The Nepal peace agreement, which specifies the age of 18, is the only exception.

Generally, peace agreements have also given superficial attention to the issue of children's participation, viewing child recruitment as an issue in which they are looking for practical solutions and for ways to include these children in programming that will address their situation. The Liberia agreement of 2003, for example, is largely a programmatic statement that provides a "hook" for the development of reintegration programmes for children, and the language it uses is very similar to that found in the Sierra Leone agreement of 1999.

Once parties to conflict are aware of their legal obligations, they can acknowledge the need to put in place programmes for recovery and reintegration of children. This acknowledgement is critically important for the successful reintegration of children because international law does not deal with such practical matters or understand what good reintegration programmes should entail.[526]

Several agreements, however, including the Sudan Comprehensive Peace Agreement (CPA), make reference to child recruitment as a ceasefire violation, and this is an important feature. In the case of Sudan, it was consistently referred to in programmatic documentation that followed.[527]

The Darfur Peace Agreement, adopted in May 2006, is the most comprehensive of all agreements in dealing with children's issues. The agreement included provisions related to identification, removal, family unification, and reintegration of children associated with armed forces and groups. It also included provisions related to sexual and gender-based violence, as well as special protection measures for women and children in the camps, including services provided by police specific to women and children.[528]

526 Anatole N. Ayissi, "Protecting Children in Armed Conflict: from Commitment to Compliance," *Disarmament Forum*, no. 3 (2002): 5–16, 5. See also the Paris Principles and Guidelines on Children Associated with Armed Forces or Armed Groups, (February 2007).

527 See, for instance, *Assessment of UNICEF Supported Programmes for Reintegration of Children Formerly Associated with Armed Groups and Forces in Sudan*, (2008).

528 In the Darfur Peace Agreement Articles 3, 17, 21, 22, 25, 26, 27 and 29 all have relevance to children. 'Darfur Peace Agreement,' (5 May 2006).

The gender aspect is significant. International law concerning the recruitment and use of children in armed forces and groups is not gender sensitive. However, peace agreements can add that element, as was done with the Darfur Peace Agreement, in which paragraph 275 states:

> The Parties shall release all boys and girls associated with armed forces and groups. UNICEF, UNHCR, and the ICRC shall be called upon to assist in the identification, removal, family unification and reintegration of children associated with armed forces and groups.

Gender sensitivity is important in this context, as is the definition of who is a child soldier, because girls are frequently forgotten in recovery and reintegration initiatives. Sometimes, girls carry guns just like boys and are easily recognized as "child soldiers," but in other situations they are involved as cooks or used for the purposes of forced sex. During the release process, girls have often been excluded from reintegration programmes, either because they were not armed and not considered "child soldiers" or because no one thought to include them. Although the Darfur Peace Agreement did not sustain peace, it nevertheless provided, and continues to provide to date, a forum for discussion on addressing the situation of both girls and boys.[529]

The terminology used in many peace agreements is often broader than that found in international law because it is dealing directly with child recruitment issues without the need to define "direct participation" nor to distinguish between whether a child has participated "voluntarily" or due to force. When a peace agreement was developed in a situation where child recruitment was an issue, the coverage of provisions is fairly good. However, there are situations where provisions could have been included for the release of children, in addition to identifying the practice as a violation of the agreement, but for one reason or another they were not.

Peace agreements add detail and enable contextual interpretation, which can enhance the legal standard in a given situation, both towards states and non-state actors. However, allocating a legal nature to peace agreements is a complex undertaking as these agreements do not fit neatly in traditional legal categories. If an agreement is made between two states, then it could obviously be an agreement in the form of a treaty. However, peace agreements are most often entered into between the State and one or several armed groups, and then

[529] The Action Plan between the Sudan Liberation Movement/Army (SLM/A) and the United Nations Children's Fund regarding Children associated with the SLM/A, 11 June 2007, is an example of such an undertaking. The SLM/A is a signatory to the Darfur Peace Agreement, and in the Action Plan the Agreement is consistently referred to. The *Sudan Tribune* reported that 36 children were released on 27 July 2009.

immediately there are complex considerations of the nature of the obligations.[530] Also, the language itself does not always lend itself to legal consideration.[531] During the time of the activities of the SCSL, it was not as clear what the law stated, and the SCSL did consider the value of the legal status of the agreements in place and the value of the amnesty provisions.[532]

With respect to many provisions relating to children's rights, and child recruitment specifically, they reflect international legal obligations that are already in place both at the treaty and customary law level. As such, these peace agreements add another level of political importance to the issue rather than legal relevance. This can nonetheless be equally important for making progress in the release and reintegration efforts. However, as part of the process it is important to show the legal value of these provisions, so that even if the peace agreement otherwise ceases to be relevant for one reason or another, the provision can nonetheless be introduced into other transitional processes or domestic legislation.

Regarding the individual responsibilities of child soldiers, while peace agreements have not explicitly dealt with children as perpetrators of crimes, child soldiers have been included in arrangements for disarmament, demobilization, rehabilitation, and reintegration, and are covered by general amnesties. Child soldiers are considered primarily as victims, and therefore, the general approach has been that children should be channelled back to their families and communities as a matter of priority, diverting them from judicial processes.

Peace agreements typically place equal weight on armed groups and armed forces, making no distinction in the sense that one party would have a different obligation from the other. There is no specific reference to sources of international law in the peace agreements, although in several agreements the language reflects either relevant international law, or in the Paris Commitments or the Cape Town Principles.

1.2. RECOVERY AND REINTEGRATION

The peace process is part of an effort to promote recovery and reintegration following an armed conflict. To what extent the peace agreements have been

530 Cassese makes the point about the Lomé agreement that it was an international legal agreement, due to the status of the non-state actors, but also due to the fact that in signing the agreement, the parties had that intention of making a legally binding international agreement. Antonio Cassese, "Special Court and International Law – The Decision Concerning the Leone Agreement Amnesty," *Journal of International Criminal Justice* 2 (2004): 1130. Sometimes, Security Council action and resolutions can also bring added legal value to the agreements.

531 Bell, *Peace Agreements and Human Rights*, 398.

532 *Prosecutor v. Morris Kallon (Case No. SCSL-2004-15-AR72(E)) and Brima Bazzy Kamara (Case No. SCSL-2004-16-AR72(E))*, 2004, para 48.

successful is not the focus of this thesis; rather, it concentrates on the legal implications, as well as the implications for programmes related to the recovery and reintegration of children, which to varying degrees highlight successes.[533]

A good example of recognition of the need for a release and reintegration programme for children is the Sudan Comprehensive Peace Agreement. The civil war between North and South Sudan began in 1983 and raged for more than 20 years, ending with the adoption of the CPA – which covers the southern third of Sudan's territory and includes agreements on the sharing of political power and national resources between two governments within one country. All groups had to align themselves with either the Government or the Sudan People's Liberation Movement/Army (SPLM/A) following the signing of the Peace Agreement. This seems to have more or less worked, although it took some time for some groups.

The CPA encompasses substantive provisions concerning children, including a general reference to the CRC and a provision on the general rights of children. It also has specific provisions relating to the release of child soldiers within six months of the signature of the agreement. A specific provision was also made for children separated from their families in order to facilitate the tracing of their families and family reunification. UNICEF and the ICRC were called upon to assist in the child component of disarmament, demobilization, and rehabilitation in Sudan.

The CPA was the backbone for child release and reintegration in the areas covered by the agreement. In this context, it was consistently referred to by both the Government of Southern Sudan and the Government of National Unity.[534] There were areas in which it was not clear how child DDR would be implemented, especially in the three areas between the North and the South, nor was it implemented within the required time frame. But without any doubt, the CPA was the "body of law" that was referred to for the specific provisions. It was also complemented by an Interim Constitution, which had the bearing of prime law in the national legal system and provided backing for the CPA.[535]

Another example of where the peace agreement led to further processes for child soldiers is in Nepal, where the action plan at the end of 2009 built on and referred to the 2006 Comprehensive Peace Agreement. In this particularly context, no other instruments such as the OPAC or the CRC were referred to in

533 The question of how to make peace agreements more successful is dealt with in detail in the *Report of the Secretary-General: In Larger Freedom: Towards Development, Security and Human Rights for All*, UN Doc. A/59/2005 (2005).

534 See, for instance, 'Agreement on Permanent Ceasefire and Security Arrangements Implementation Modalities During the Pre-Interim and the Interim Periods Between the Government of the Sudan (GoS) and the Sudan People's Liberation Movement/Sudan People's Liberation Army (SPLM/SPLA),' (31 December 2004).

535 *Assessment of UNICEF Supported Programmes for Reintegration of Children Formerly Associated with Armed Groups and Forces in Sudan*, (2008).

the action plan, but the peace agreement remained the sole authority for moving forward with the release of children.[536]

Although these examples indicate of progress, overall, there is still room for making the child dimensions of peace agreements more comprehensive, considering the vast recovery and reintegration needs that exist and go beyond the needs of children who have been recruited or used by armed groups and forces. However, considering the overall trend in reduction of peace negotiations and peace agreements, there is currently not much room for influencing those discussions.

2. INSTITUTIONAL JUSTICE AND CHILD PROTECTION

The following section describes the institutional justice aspects of building child protection systems in post-conflict environments, followed by considerations applying to non-state actors as well as governments. This section also considers the need for awareness raising on the issue of child recruitment, so as to ensure that the services provided through a child protection system are truly accessible to affected children and families, and that they are reaching out to get the necessary support.

2.1. CHILD PROTECTION SYSTEMS IN POST-CONFLICT ENVIRONMENTS

In humanitarian contexts, it is often difficult to justify work on strengthening systems during an emergency, and donor governments frequently do not see bolstering such structures as warranted during situations of armed conflict. Nonetheless, advocacy and release of children from armed groups and forces often happens while the conflict is ongoing, and it is important to also build up the systems that can respond to the recovery and reintegration needs of those children, along with the needs of other war-affected children.[537]

---

536 Action Plan between the Government of Nepal, the Unified Communist Party of Nepal – Maoist, and the United Nations in Nepal regarding the Discharge of Disqualified Maoist Army Personnel and Related Tasks (16 December 2009).

537 Note that article 39 of the CRC recognizes, in addition to overall recovery and reintegration, that "such recovery and reintegration shall take place in an environment which fosters the health, self-respect and dignity of the child." The need for development of national institutions to support the response towards addressing grave violations of children's rights is also recognized by the Security Council in recent years in that it recommends support by Member States, United Nations entities, and financial institutions to help put in place such systems. See *Security Council Resolution on Children and Armed Conflict, Council*, UN Doc. S/RES/2143 (7 March 2014), para 14.

Such systems can also help prevent violations from taking place, building capacity among service providers and awareness about child protection risks and how they can be addressed in a systematic way. Also, while it is hard to claim sustainability in the context of armed conflict, systems that have been built up during the emergency phase normally remain active after the emergency and can work for the protection of all children.[538]

Such initiatives to build child protection systems could include:

- Strengthening the legislature, including its implementation of the law through strengthened capacities in the police, social workers, and judiciary.
- Social work, with capacity to link children to the various services and to manage cases of child protection effectively, with records and information kept on file for easy follow-up.
- Coordination of actors involved in child protection work and the building of the systems.[539] Specific to child recruitment there may also be a national authority coordinating overall national demobilization and reintegration activities. However, it is important not to over-invest in temporary structures of this type because they may not be sustainable and, in any case, should not be part of developing the expertise for implementation that should be based in other parts of government that need to have this capacity and the resources in the long term.
- Results orientation, both in terms of seeing the effect of the interventions and establishing records of cases of abuse and violence, and in engaging with all the various stakeholders to advocate and discuss the response. It is quite common for government actors to be hesitant in accepting that there are child protection issues in the country, and even if they keep the numbers to themselves, they are important indicators with respect to the problem at hand and also the effectiveness of the response.

In addition, there are some considerations specific to child soldiers that need to be taken into account as part of the systems-building approach. Family tracing and reunification is one central component that is directly affected by armed conflicts. If children are likely to know where their families are living, family tracing efforts can be easy enough. Situations of armed conflict, however, will

538 Agreement on Permanent Ceasefire and Security Arrangements Implementation Modalities During the Pre-Interim and the Interim Periods Between the Government of the Sudan (GoS) and the Sudan People's Liberation Movement/Sudan People's Liberation Army (SPLM/SPLA), 31 December 2004. The discussion paper prepared by Save the Children also recognized that there was a need to begin pulling in the same direction on these issues and hence initiated the preparation of the paper on behalf of the Child Protection Working Group. See also www.cpwg.net.

539 See also The Save the Children Fund, *Child Protetion Systems in Emergencies – a Discussion Paper*, (2010).

most likely have led to extensive displacement, the relocation of families, and many situations where immediate family members have been killed and it will be necessary to trace more distant relatives.

The difficulties of reunifying children with their families in these circumstances highlight the usefulness of birth registration, which is an essential part of protecting children before, during, and after an armed conflict. The lack of birth registration is a major obstacle in addressing ongoing recruitment by government armed forces and armed groups, especially in currently conflict-affected countries. Comprehensive birth registration can help prevent the reoccurrence of child-rights violations, including recruitment and use of children by the armed forces.[540]

During the process of demobilization, former child soldiers may be in need of interim care. The key here is "interim," as it is important not to make the care situation more comfortable than the child's home environment, possibly leading to little success in finding the families of some of the children and endless efforts to close down the operation. Depending on the situation and the relationship with the armed forces or groups, and on the current conflict scenarios, it may even be a better option to keep the children with the armed group or force during the duration of searching for their families. This may serve children's long-term interests in that they may already have their basic needs provided for, and more efforts can be placed on undertaking the family search and reunification, along with making investments in the reintegration programmes once the child has returned home.

Mental health support is not typically a major component of recovery and reintegration programmes. In general, there is a misunderstanding that former child soldiers suffer from trauma and that this problem needs to be dealt with clinically,[541] but it is usually not the approach of humanitarian organizations to focus on trauma.[542] Because we are speaking of large numbers of children, it is generally not appropriate to set up services to deal with trauma and individual children, but to focus on strengthening coping mechanisms and resilience. This can be done by reinforcing the capacity of relevant community workers;

540 Jonathan Todres, "Birth Registration: An Essential First Step Toward Ensuring the Rights of All Children," *Human Rights Brief* 10, no. 3 (2003): 32–35.

541 See, for instance, Drumbl noting that "[r]emedial efforts currently undertaken for former child soldiers accentuate medicalized trauma recovery and psychotherapy," and that the "conventional wisdom is that former child soldiers suffer from high rates of post-traumatic stress disorder (PTSD) and related afflictions because of their experiences of extreme violence, their immaturity, their fragility, and the effects of drug ingestion." Drumbl, *Reimagining Child Soldiers in International Law and Policy*, 2 and 53.

542 Child Protection Working Group, *Minimum Standards for Child Protection in Humanitarian Action* (2012), 97. See also Inter-Agency Standing Committee, *Mental Health and Pscyhosocial Support in Humanitarian Emergencies: What Should Humanitarian Health Actors Know?* (Geneva: IASC Reference Group for Mental Health and Psychosocial Support in Emergency Settings, 2010).

providing activities in the communities, including recreation and sports; and offering follow-up and referral mechanisms to children who experience severe difficulty in recovery and reintegration.[543]

Child protection systems – the network of services for children who need support for the prevention or response to violence, abuse, exploitation, and neglect – can encompass a range of initiatives carried out by many different actors; they can also vary in terms of scale and scope. These systems are generally national, or depending on the size of the country, regional, and focus on services among actors both in government and the non-formal sector, with strong interlinkages between the services. In post-conflict situations, a child protection system is not rebuilt or established overnight, and it can never be expected to be perfect. But in response to children who have been recruited and used by armed forces and groups, it is important to begin with the services that will be most critical in each context.

2.2. BUILDING CAPACITIES AMONG NON-STATE ACTORS

One complex and highly political consideration is whether to make an attempt to build child protection systems in rebel-held territory. There are certain rebel groups that are well developed and have begun to build government-like infrastructure, such as the LTTE in Sri Lanka, which had its own military, police, and judiciary. At the same time, some government infrastructure, such as the health and education system, continued to exist within territory held by the LTTE.

Here it is important to continue working through existing government structures, and it could also be reasonable to work on some of the rebel-group systems, with a focus on "software" components for the police, military, and judiciary, including awareness raising on child rights and protection issues. Software elements are those that generally do not provide physical infrastructure, but could include providing training to the police on child-friendly procedures or providing copies of human rights treaties to the judiciary. If members of armed groups are not informed about what the standards in international law are, they will also not be able to implement them in times of hostilities.[544]

---

543 Michael G. Wessells, "Psychosocial Well-being and the Integration of War-affected Children: Towards a Community Resilience Approach," in *Re-member: Rehabilitation, reintegration and reconciliation of war-affected children*, ed. Cindy Mels, Ilse Derluyn, Stephan Parmentier and Wouter Vandenhole (Cambridge: Intersentia, 2012), 62–63.

544 The Geneva Conventions and the Additional Protocols expressly impose a legal obligation on States parties to take all necessary measures to make the treaty provisions known to people likely to be in situations in which they must be applied. Additional Protocol 1 even puts an obligation forward that "any military or civilian authorities who, in time of armed conflict, assume responsibilities in respect of the application of the Convention and this Protocol shall be fully acquainted with the text thereof." Article 83. See further Jean-Jacques Surbeck, "Dissemination of International Humanitarian Law," *The American University Law Review*,

However, institutional capacity building with physical infrastructure, for instance a child-friendly court room, would not be easy to support in a conflict setting, as it may be construed as physical support for one or more of the warring parties.

In terms of being a non-state actor that has taken on human rights obligations that mimic a state, the LTTE had begun implementing a state-like level of responsibility following the signature of the ceasefire agreement in 2002. Although it had not been recognized as a state, it nonetheless formed many of the entities that a state forms, including separate structures for military and police, along with a judiciary.[545]

These developments slowly began to change with the changes occurring after 9/11 in 2001, when many countries began implementing antiterrorist measures and the LTTE was labelled as a terrorist group due to some of its practices. Not long after the signing of the ceasefire agreement, delegations from the LTTE were no longer being received in any of the European Union Member States, which added the LTTE to its terrorist list on 26 September 2005, through a declaration by the Presidency on behalf of the European Union. This meant that it would not have access to any such forums for a long time. The European Union also repeated its concern about the "continuing recruitment and retention of child soldier cadres by the LTTE."[546]

The return of conflict and the defeat of the LTTE in 2008 finally brought an end to the movement as a whole, but it still provides an interesting case study of the nature of an armed group and its desire to become more state-like, providing opportunities for capacity development to enhance the protection of children's rights. Also, in some situations, the armed groups may eventually take power and become the leaders of the state, and therefore it can be important to have entry points with non-state actors from the outset, considering that they may be in a very different situation later on.

2.3. THE NEED TO RAISE AWARENESS OF THE NEGATIVE IMPACTS OF CHILD RECRUITMENT

Effective child protection systems provide a range of services, with each actor knowing where to refer a child for a different type of service. These systems take

---

33 (1983): 125–143. The OPAC only refers to the state obligation to: "undertake to make the principles and provisions of the present Protocol widely known and promoted by appropriate means, to adults and children alike." (CRC article 6(2)) This OPAC provision does not lend itself to arguing for space to raise awareness with non-state actors as readily as the Additional Protocol provision does.

545 Agreement on a ceasefire between the Government of the Democratic Socialist Republic of Sri Lanka and the Liberation Tigers of Tamil Eelam, 22 February 2002.

546 Council of the European Union, *Declaration by the Presidency on Behalf of the European Union Concerning Listing of the LTTE as a Terrorist Organisation (9962/06)*, (31 May 2006).

time to build up, and depending on the level of awareness among the actors, it may even be necessary to begin by raising awareness so as to ensure that the different issues are accepted as problems for a specific society. Otherwise, there is a risk of practices being hidden and when they are hidden, no children or families will be looking for support from service providers.[547]

In addition to building the systems, it is equally important to build awareness and knowledge about child protection problems and issues, both among service providers and the communities.[548]

When monitoring systems are implemented for the first time, it is important to recognize, at least initially, that it is a good indicator if the numbers of violations are going up: it means that the monitoring system is working and that there is an effective way of recording those violations. Over time, as the response is improving, the numbers of violations may also go down, depending on the situation in the country.

Strengthening the protective environment needs to build on respective strengths and weaknesses of different actors on the ground. Some will have good access to senior-level government officials and can influence the entire agenda for protective systems, while others are better at providing community-based services and setting up local coordination and referral mechanisms.[549]

Taking child protection systems to scale is costly and requires a substantial amount of funding in post-conflict reconstruction. It is costly both in terms of developing the approach or adapting it to local circumstances, and may even require physical structures and mobility that has not been in place before.

The reporting framework within the Committee on the Rights of the Child, and the emphasis on child protection in the country reports as well as the deliberations of the Committee, along with the focus on inter-ministerial dialogue and collaboration in the Security Council monitoring and reporting mechanism, have been extremely useful in engaging with governments on the issues, as were the follow-up and concluding recommendations made by the Committee and the Security Council Working Group.[550]

It is also very important to raise awareness with service providers, including the police, social welfare authorities, and the judiciary, who ultimately, with the help of international actors, provide the support for responses to children's rights

547 Gerry Mackie and Francesca Moneti, *What are Social Norms? How are they Measured?*, (2012).

548 Brooks, *The Disarmarment, Demobilisation and Reintegration of Children Associated with Fighting Forces.*

549 For further information on the background of the protective environment approach, see Karin Landgren, "The Protective Environment: Development Support for Child Protection," *Human Rights Quarterly* 27, no. 1 (2005): 214–248.

550 The 2014 Security Council Resolution on Children and Armed Conflict recognizes the "interministerial committees as a successful framework for partnership with concerned Governments to discuss and follow-up on child protection commitments." (Council, 7 March 2014 #720) para 3.

violations, including sexual and gender-based violence; child DDR programming; and services for unaccompanied or separated children.

2.4. ADDRESSING THE IMPACT OF PRIVATE MILITARY SECURITY COMPANIES AND OTHER BUSINESSES

Business is becoming an increasingly strong force in driving sustainable development.[551] In 2011, official development assistance dropped by 2.7 per cent; excluding debt cancellation, this fall-off, breaks 14 years of growth since 1997. Additionally, between 2003 and 2011, official development assistance was reduced from 54 per cent of capital flows to 26 per cent of total capital flows to the developing world as compared to private investment.[552] Since private capital flows to developing countries are now more significant than official aid flows, private spending has become a greater contributor to development than official aid. Such power cannot come without responsibility.

The business and human rights agenda has a much longer history than can be fully considered here, but in 2005, the UN Commission on Human Rights (replaced with the UN Human Rights Council in 2006), considered the topic of business and human rights. The Commission was responsible for approving the mandate of the Special Representative, who guided the process for developing the fundamental standard for discussion around this topic: the Guiding Principles on Business and Human Rights: Implementing the UN "Protect, Respect and Remedy" Framework.[553]

The Guiding Principles, adopted in June 2012, apply to all states and business. Although every business needs to consider its impact on human rights, and as relevant with a specific focus on children's rights, certain industries are more closely linked to human rights risks than others, including in situations of armed conflict. For instance, extractive companies often operate in communities and countries with a high level of export of primary commodities that are significantly more at risk of conflict.[554] The extractive industries are also a known contractor of private military security companies (PMSCs).

---

551 See the outcome of the High Level panel that has been working on the future post millennium development goals agenda has considered business as an important actor in the coming period. See United Nations, *A New Global Partnership: Eradicate Poverty and Transform Economies Through Sustainable Development* (New York: United Nations Publications, 2013).

552 See Organization for Economic Cooperation and Development (OECD) statistics at http://stats.oecd.org/Index.aspx?DatasetCode=TABLE1.

553 United Nations, Guiding Principles on Business and Human Rights: Implementing the United Nations "Protect, Respect and Remedy" Framework, UN Doc. A/HRC/17/31 (21 March 2011).

554 World Bank, The Economic Cause of Civil Conflict and their Implications for Policy, UN Doc. E/CN.4/2000/74 (2000), 6.

Under the Montreux Document, adopted in 2006 and which provides guidance to PMSCs on responsible conduct in armed conflict situations, these companies "are private business entities that provide military and/or security services, irrespective of how they describe themselves."[555] According to the Montreux Document, "military and security services include, in particular, armed guarding and protection of persons and objects, such as convoys, buildings and other places; maintenance and operation of weapons systems; prisoner detention; and advice to or training of local forces and security personnel." Personnel recruited for these companies are frequently working in resource-rich countries and conflict-affected contexts around the world.

An important element in establishing the link between child recruitment and business activities is to consider the extent to which PMSCs recruit and use children in their operations, many of which take place in the midst of armed conflict.

In a review of 15 countries, based on 41 country reports since 2006 (see annex 2 to this thesis), there is no mention of any type of private security company, including PMSCs. The focus is exclusively on state actors, armed groups, or other less easily defined entities. More generally, there is no mention of the presence of businesses or their practices affecting children, let alone any forms of private security arrangements. An effort to review whether PMSCs recruit children reveals that it is an almost impossible task. At the field level where these troops are active, it is difficult to know whether a recruit comes from a PMSC or from the armed group or force itself, which seriously complicates the process of determining the extent to which such recruitment is taking place.

Nonetheless, outside the specific country reports, the Report of the Secretary-General to the General Assembly and Security Council in 2009 briefly discussed the presence of private military and security companies in Iraq. In the report, it is noted that on 16 September 2007, at least one child was killed when Blackwater security guards fired into a group of civilians in Baghdad's Nisoor Square.[556] In reports on children and armed conflict to the Security Council dating back to 2000, this was the only specific reference to a PMSC or private company involved in the provision of security services.

This leads to a separate and different consideration of the importance of PMSCs to exercise restraint in the use of force in direct attack, particularly as related to considering child soldiers who are part of armed groups and forces, some of which may not be military targets for purposes of what is "actually

---

555 Montreux Document on Pertinent International Legal Obligations and Good Practices for States Related to Operations of Private Military and Security Companies During Armed Conflict, Swiss Initiative in Cooperation with the International Committee of the Red Cross, (17 September 2008).

556 Report of the Secretary-General on Children and Armed Conflict, UN Document A/63/785-S/2009/158 (26 March 2009), para 65.

necessary to accomplish a legitimate military purpose in the prevailing circumstances."[557]

Some situations of armed conflict, such as those in Syria and Iraq, which involve armed extremist groups being aided by external actors, do not neatly fit the PMSC framework. These groups reach out to potential recruits, including children, in third countries to join their ranks, but they cannot be characterized as private business entities. They are also not easily defined as mercenary activities because the recruitment of children in these situations is not dictated by "personal gain" as defined in the Additional Protocol to the Geneva Conventions.[558] In order to shed some light on the grey zone between PMSCs and mercenaries, the UN Working Group on the use of mercenaries as a means of violating human rights and impeding the exercise of the rights of peoples to self-determination has recommended a legally binding treaty be developed to regulate the work of PMSCs.[559]

The voluntariness of business conduct *vis-à-vis* human rights has been emphasized through various initiatives that seek to strengthen the behaviour of business, beginning with the creation of the UN Global Compact. The types of mechanisms that are being set in place draw links between business and human rights and challenge many of the traditional approaches to international law. Voluntary standards are being developed; investors provide portfolios based on the ethical performance of companies; businesses are developing human rights policies, some with a specific focus on children's rights; and reporting is being seen as an increasingly important element for stakeholders to evaluate and hold companies accountable for their business behaviour and impacts on human rights and humanitarian law.[560]

---

557 Nils Melzer, *Interpretive Guidance on the Notion of Direct Participation in Hostilities* (Geneva: International Committee of the Red Cross, 2009), 77.

558 See AP 1, article 47. The Protocol identifies monetary gain that is substantially more than what local fighters would get as a key determinant of mercenary activities. See also the work of the UN Working Group on the use of mercenaries as a means of violating human rights and impeding the exercise of the rights of peoples to self-determination, which was established in July 2005. It succeeded the mandate of the Special Rapporteur on the use of mercenaries, which had been in existence since 1987.

559 The UN Working Group on the use of mercenaries as a means of violating human rights and impeding the exercise of the rights of peoples to self-determination, which was established in July 2005. It succeeded the mandate of the Special Rapporteur on the use of mercenaries, which had been in existence since 1987. The Working Group has played a role in providing inputs and recommendations for the possible development of an oversight mechanism for the Code of Conduct mentioned above, and also advocates for a new treaty to be developed. The position of the Working Group has been to say that voluntary schemes alone are insufficient to regulate this area of work. See Report of the Working Group on the use of mercenaries as a means of violating human rights and impeding the exercise of the rights of people to self-determination, A/HRC/21/43 (2 July 2012), paras 69–70.

560 See KPMG Global Reporting Initiative, Unit for Corporate Governance in Africa, United Nations Environment Programme, Carrots and Sticks – Promoting Transparency and

The Voluntary Principles on Security and Human Rights released in 2000 address how companies evaluate and monitoring the provision of security at their business premises, and the 2010 International Code of Conduct for private security providers took a further step towards encouraging companies to voluntarily sign up to making commitments towards human rights.[561] The International Code of Conduct includes a provision prohibiting the worst forms of child labour in paragraph 45:

Signatory Companies will respect the rights of children (anyone under the age of 18) to be protected from the worst forms of child labour, including:

(a) all forms of slavery or practices similar to slavery, such as the sale and trafficking of children, debt bondage and serfdom and forced or compulsory labour, including forced or compulsory recruitment of children for use in provision of armed services;
(b) the use, procuring or offering of a child for prostitution, for the production of pornography or for pornographic performances;
(c) the use, procuring or offering of a child for illicit activities, in particular for the production and trafficking of drugs;
(d) work which, by its nature or the circumstances in which it is carried out, is likely to harm the health, safety or morals of children.

Signatory Companies will, and will require their Personnel to, report any instances of the activities referenced above that they know of, or have reasonable suspicion of, to Competent Authorities.

Although this provision sets the age at 18, as per ILO standards (and placing it within a labour conditions framework), it focuses on forced or compulsory recruitment and does not consider levels of "voluntariness" or the concept of direct participation. An oversight mechanism is now being put in place for the Code of Conduct, which could support is implementation and help ensure that companies comply with the standards once they have signed up.[562]

The Children's Rights and Business Principles (CRBP), which were developed in a process led by UNICEF, the Global Compact, and Save the Children, and

Sustainability: An update on trends in Voluntary and Mandatory Approaches to Sustainability Reporting (2010).

561 The Voluntary Principles on Security and Human Rights, (December 2000), see further www.voluntaryprinciples.org, and The International Code of Conduct for Private Security Service Providers, (2010) at www.icoc-psp.org. The Code of Conduct now has more than 600 private security company signatories.

562 See further The International Code of Conduct for Private Security Service Providers' Association: Articles of Association (2013).

released in March 2012 provide further focus on the issue of child recruitment.[563] Principle 7, which focuses on the need for companies to respect and support children's rights in security arrangements, provides the following guidance:

i. When making and implementing security arrangements, whether with public or private security service providers, conduct human rights due diligence with particular attention to any adverse impact on the rights of children.
ii. Ensure that respect for the rights of children is explicitly addressed in the business's security contracts.
iii. Do not recruit or use children in security arrangements either directly or through private or public security service providers.

This provision is broader in application than that found in the International Code of Conduct, and places the onus on those who procure services for the company, as well as the private military security company itself.

The CRBP build on the UN Guiding Principles on Business and Human Rights, and outlines a framework for action based on the corporate responsibility to respect and the corporate commitment to support children's rights, with a focus on integration of child rights into business management and due diligence processes.[564] The General Comment on state obligations regarding the impact of the business sector on children's rights, adopted by the Committee on the Rights of the Child in March 2013, complements the CRBP in considering the state responsibility to protect, respect and fulfil children's rights.[565] The General Comment makes a call for states to implement legislation that "includes a specific prohibition on such companies recruiting children or using them in hostilities; requirements for effective measures to protect children from violence and exploitation; and mechanisms for holding personnel accountable for abuses of children's rights."[566]

As the Montreux Document is also aimed at guiding states on good practices for implementation, several of these initiatives are aligned. But in order to

---

563 The Children's Rights and Business Principles, UN Global Compact UNICEF, and Save the Children, (12 March 2012).

564 The due diligence process is outlined in Principle 1 of the CRBP, and in the Guiding Principles para 17 onwards outline the way in which human rights due diligence is to "identify, prevent, mitigate and account for how [companies] address their adverse human rights impacts." This process includes tracking of impact and progress, and transparency in reporting about the impact as well as the activities and actions taken to address that impact. UNICEF has engaged in a process of piloting due diligence tools, such as a Children's Rights Checklist developed together with the Danish Institute for Human Rights, as well as a reporting tool. See further www.unicef.org/csr.

565 General Comment No. 16: On State obligations regarding the impact of the business sector on children's rights, Committee on the Rights of the Child, UN Doc. CRC/C/GC/10 (15 March 2013).

566 Ibid para 51.

address child recruitment by PMSCs, it would be important that national legislation to prohibit the recruitment and use of children applies not only to state and non-state actors as called for by OPAC, but that it clearly applies to the private security companies as well. However, there are reasons why some states (and non-state actors for that matter) would prefer to maintain a weak legal relationship with these entities and to maintain weak legal responsibilities for any violations against international humanitarian and human rights law by these entities.[567] There are situations where states make use of security outfits to carry out tasks that they are not comfortable doing themselves. Nonetheless, some of the recent voluntary initiatives help set the stage for a future of a more regularized business conduct in relation to security services, and over time these voluntary schemes gain the force of law in some jurisdictions. There is a range of complicating factors though, including the fact that PMSCs do not only recruit personnel from the countries where they are based, but from a wide range of countries. This makes the effort to hold individuals accountable for any violations against human rights complex and challenging.

In addition, the prohibition of recruitment and use of children under international human rights and humanitarian law, and the way that this prohibition has now made its way into the realm of criminal law, extend the prohibited act to individuals working for these companies. As such, it seems that the complementarity between voluntary schemes and more strictly legal approaches should be further explored and strengthened.[568]

The emphasis placed here on PMSCs does not factor out the significant role that businesses more generally can have in supporting the recovery and reintegration of child soldiers. The extractive industries, for example, often have considerable influence in relation to governments in situations where such companies are major investors and a source of fiscal revenue. These companies may have a role in promoting equitable investments in social services based on their payment of taxes and royalties. The responsibility to support children's rights – which is highlighted in the CRBP, though not as much in the UN Guiding Principles – can be taken on by companies in any industry. However, considering that extractive companies would be particularly concerned about reintegration efforts for children who have been recruited and used, they might

567 E.L. Gaston. "Mercenarism 2.0 – The Rise of the Modern Private Security Industry and Its Implications for International Humanitarian Law Enforcement." *Harvard International Law Journal* 49, no. 1 (2008): 221–248, 222.

568 Gillard draws a very strong distinction between voluntary mechanisms and the responsibilities derived from international humanitarian law, however, what she is referring to is actually the responsibility of the state to take measures to prepare implementing legislation, criminalize as appropriate, and enforce the law. See Emanuela-Chiara Gillard. "Business and Humanitarian and Human Rights Obligations: The Position with Regard to International Humanitarian Law." *American Society of International Law Proceedings* 100, (2006): 129–140.

be particularly well placed to support such initiatives in the areas of education or other community services.[569]

Overall, business practices can have a positive impact on institution building, and in many of the situations where governments are challenged with issues of child recruitment, recovery, and reintegration, business is in a good position to pay the taxes that are due; provide technical expertise and advice; and engage in advocacy for the purposes of child-friendly budgeting that provides the services needed for conflict-affected children.

CONCLUSION

The two areas – peace agreements and institutional justice as relates to child protection – covered above are quite different, but equally important when it comes to institution building in post-conflict environments. The work related to peace agreements remains at a higher policy level, but for decision makers and implementers alike, peace agreements are critical tools in the transitional justice phase, and continuously referred to as a justification for taking action and moving forward with what has been agreed to as part of the peace negotiations. But raising concerns for children from a transitional justice perspective in peace agreements is not just about coming up with a standard language on child recruitment to be used in a cookie-cutter approach. Each situation is different.

The common elements that do need to be considered as part of any peace negotiation include:

- recognition of the recruitment of children as a violation of international law and a violation of the agreement in question;
- identification of a procedure through which children in the ranks will be identified for purposes of release from the armed group(s) and force(s);
- allocation of responsibilities of who will be responsible for the different steps of identification, registration, release, and reintegration, as those actors will need that as part of the implementation process when difficult situations arise; and
- recognition of any other supportive action that will be critical to success, such as legal reform, reform of the justice sector, education reform, with priority given to children's issues during the reconstruction process.

In some cases, the possibility of children having perpetrated international crimes while in the ranks may be considered – depending on how international

569 See further Principle 10 of the CRBP and UNICEF, *Children are Everyone's Business: A practical workbook to help companies understand and address their impact on children's rights.* Geneva: UNICEF, (2012), 83.

crimes by adults are dealt with, and focusing on a restorative justice approach as far as children are concerned. And there will clearly be a need to identify other critical child rights issues, such as child recruitment. Actors focused on child recruitment may not be involved in measures related to redistribution of power; however, they will certainly need to pay attention to the outcomes of those discussions and make sure to align their activities with the new power structures in the given situation.

Child protection systems are not always appreciated as an emergency response, but they are sorely needed in the provision of services to children, and can also facilitate the prevention of child rights violations from happening in the first place. Institutional justice and the rule of law are very closely linked, in fact, the rule of law element can be seen as the area for setting the standards, while institutional justice focuses on the implementation of those standards. There are some distinct areas of expertise needed, however, as institutional justice requires an understanding of how the different pieces fit together and take on a very human element of making the standards relevant to people.

How to engage with non-state actors in the context of institutional justice is a complex matter, which will largely depend on the context and the extent to which the armed group is serious about taking the rule of law on the ground as a matter of priority. It is normally helpful that peace negotiations are moving forward to be able to entertain any other element of institutional justice with an armed group; otherwise, the group will still be considered illegitimate and therefore difficult to engage with without putting relationships with government at stake.

The area of business and human rights is still an evolving field of work, yet governments are increasingly considering the responsibilities of business to respect and support human rights through requirements in reporting on sustainability initiatives, platforms, and sign-up mechanisms. At the same time, states must address the impact of business on children's rights through legislation and regulatory initiatives.

While examples of business addressing children's rights are now commonplace, the extractive industries and PMSCs have generally limited their attention to children's rights to philanthropic approaches and to issues of child labour, including but not limited to the worst forms of child labour. Although it may appear that there is a proliferation of standards and tools, the voluntary frameworks that are in place, along with guidance developed for governments to implement, provide good avenues for strengthened action to hold business accountable – including in addressing issues related to child recruitment. The conduct of private military security companies working in the context of armed conflict remains a concern that needs to be continuously followed through the monitoring and reporting mechanism and other instruments, so as to scrutinize the practices of these companies. Overall, it is important for the business and human rights world to link up more closely with the humanitarian and development worlds in order to find synergies and ways to better build on the potential of business to protect children's rights.

Chapter 7 on participatory justice establishes that children have a right to participate in decisions that affect them. The chapter puts forward an analysis of how children as victims or survivors, as well as witnesses or alleged perpetrators of crimes, have engaged in transitional justice processes and how their rights are protected in these contexts.

CHAPTER 7

CHILDREN INVOLVED IN ARMED CONFLICT AND PARTICIPATORY JUSTICE

Balancing Rights and Responsibilities

> *"They made you chop off an arm or kill someone in your family, then they gave you drugs to make you feel better, and then you did not care and you killed many more people."*

INTRODUCTION

Participatory justice is an area of transitional justice that includes elements of administrative and constitutional justice, but it has recently been viewed as a distinct field deserving focused attention.[570] Although this field could be seen as a cross-cutting theme in transitional justice settings, participatory justice requires separate consideration in the context of child recruitment.

Participatory justice offers an opportunity for children to make a significant contribution to the various processes related to transitional justice. It is every child's right to be heard and to express her or his views and opinions, but participatory justice not only conveys rights to an individual child, it confers responsibilities.

The topic of child recruitment offers a particularly interesting paradox in the field of transitional justice: while child recruitment is defined as a war crime, children themselves may perpetrate human rights violations while serving as child soldiers.

Key legal questions that are considered in this chapter include:

- What does the law provide for more generally that can be applied to support children's participation in justice processes in a transitional justice context?

---

[570] For specific work related to children's participation in outreach programmes, see, e.g., *Engaging Children and Youth in Transitional Justice Processes: Guidance for Outreach Programs*, (2012). See also for broader issues related to participation of affected communities: *Transitional Justice and Development: Making Connections*, ed. Pablo de Greiff et al., Advancing Transitional Justice Series (New York: Social Science Research Council, 2009).

- What is the situation of children who have participated in the conflict and who may have carried out crimes while in the ranks of an armed group or force?
- In both those instances, what approaches are in the best interests of children and society as a whole, inclusive of protecting the rights of children while also considering their responsibilities?

It is critical to be clear about the objectives in the processes of participatory justice. Are we seeking ways and means through which children can recover and reintegrate, or looking for ways to hold children accountable? Do we want to warn future child soldiers against participating in armed conflicts? Or do we want to achieve all of the above? It is in the best interests of the child and the wider society that justice is approached with a view to restore and recover so that child soldiers are able to reintegrate. But it is important to remember that justice also entails possible violations that children may have perpetrated. Children and society on the whole will not benefit from justice being overlooked.

Many scholars have considered these issues, but the debate has often been based on opinions that come to a conclusion without fully considering all sides of the argument.

Chapter 7 aims to bring a new perspective to these issues by considering the implications of making children true stakeholders in transitional justice processes. It provides an in-depth focus on various aspects of children's participation and considers the issues from two focal points: (1) the rights and responsibilities of children when participating in criminal justice processes as victims/survivors and witnesses; and (2) children as alleged perpetrators of war crimes, with an analysis of the specific applicable standards. focal

1. THE PARTICIPATION OF CHILDREN IN CRIMINAL JUSTICE PROCESSES

In considering the child's contribution to society, the Committee on the Rights of the Child specified that "recognizing the right of the child to express views and to participate in various activities, according to her/his evolving capacities, is beneficial for the child, for the family, for the community, the school, the State, [and] for democracy."[571] This recognition of a child's worth in processes from small to big can be applied in the context of transitional justice, where children have traditionally not played a role, as is discussed in the following sections.

[571] Committee on the Rights of the Child, *Report on the forty-third session*, September 2006, Day of General Discussion. The concept of evolving capacities comes from article 5 and 14 of the Convention and is strongly related to the age and maturity of the child.

1.1. CHILDREN AS SURVIVORS, VICTIMS, AND WITNESSES OF INTERNATIONAL CRIMES DURING ARMED CONFLICTS

Every child "who is capable of forming his or her own views [has] the right to express those views freely in all matters affecting the child, the views of the child being given due weight in accordance with the age of maturity of the child," according to the Convention on the Rights of the Child.[572] This provision does not cease to apply during emergencies or other difficult contexts, including during criminal justice proceedings that result from armed conflicts.[573]

The key ramification that follows is whether children who generally do not have access to most of the transitional justice processes really can make their voices heard and become genuine stakeholders in a criminal justice process as a victim/survivor or a witness. Most justice processes are not fit to consider children's issues in earnest, and criminal justice processes are no different in that respect. But, in addition, criminal justice processes often receive a great deal of political attention, and as a result, it may be even more difficult to introduce child-friendly approaches in these proceedings.

Much in the same way that children have a right to express their opinions, in connection with criminal justice proceedings, a child should be asked whether she or he wants to take part: this must be a voluntary effort, with informed consent from the child and parents or guardians.[574]

The right to information is a central aspect throughout the process, ensuring that information is given in the child's language, in appropriate language for his/her age, and covering essential details, such as the place and the times the child is expected to appear. This includes information about the implications of the child's involvement in the process, and also the implications if the child decides not to be involved, based on the engagement as a victim or witness being voluntary.

Investigations that seek to secure information from children should similarly be focused on how this can be done while pursuing the best interests of the child. Those who work with children in any part of this process must be trained in child-friendly procedures and understand how to interview children and what

---

572 Convention on the Rights of the Child article 12. Child Protection Working Group, *Child Protection in Emergencies Coordinator's Handbook* (2009). These Guidelines further elaborate by stating in 8(d): *Right to participation.* "Every child has, subject to national procedural law, the right to express his or her views, opinions and beliefs freely, in his or her own words, and to contribute especially to the decisions affecting his or her life, including those taken in any judicial processes, and to have those views taken into consideration according to his or her abilities, age, intellectual maturity and evolving capacity."

573 See also *The Participation of Children and Young People in Emergencies*, (October 2007).

574 See also *Key Principles for Children and Transitional Justice: Involvement of Children and Considerations of Children's Rights in Truth, Justice and Reconciliation Processes* (2009), section on judicial mechanisms.

type of information is appropriate to ask them about. All interviews, examinations, and other forms of investigation should be conducted by trained professionals who proceed in a sensitive, respectful, and thorough manner, keeping in mind the evolving capabilities of the child.[575]

Children who provide information for investigations or judicial procedures may need special protection measures following this experience. It is therefore imperative that the child's identity is not known, and the accused should not be able to see the child and vice versa. Gender considerations must also be integral to these protection measures as girls and boys may have very distinct needs during the various stages of the process.[576]

Involving a child in justice procedures should not be excessive and should remain at the level of obtaining necessary information from the child. This is often where coordination and effective collaboration between different service providers will be of assistance; for example, information that has been obtained by a social worker can be useful for a psychologist and a judge without necessarily asking the child to go through the same information again. Another option could be to record evidence provided by the child, so that the child does not need to appear in court.

As a witness or a victim providing testimony, a child would normally give testimony or in some way provide information that can become part of the criminal justice process. In the context of international crimes, it is hard to imagine information that could not have been witnessed by adults or represented by organizations that speak in the interests of children. Since these crimes are usually widespread and systematic, and a vast range of individuals will have witnessed grave violations, it would be the rare exception that a child would need to be a witness in a proceeding.

Should an individual child agree to give evidence for a criminal investigation or in court, the protection issues that may follow are substantial. Safety considerations for children are therefore paramount before, during, and after the proceedings. A child victim or witness will not necessarily know what is in his or her best interests from a security perspective and, again, trained professionals need to consider the implications of a child's involvement in the proceedings and what measures need to be put in place for this purpose.[577] Oftentimes the witnesses live in conditions that are precarious from a safety point of view, and while it is not for the prosecution or the Court to take responsibility for the overall safety of those who provide evidence, it is certainly their responsibility to

575 *Guidelines on Justice Matters Involving Child Victims and Witnesses of Crime*, UN Doc. Economic and Social Council Resolution 2005/20 (22 July 2005), para 13.

576 See Smith, "Basic Assumptions of Tranitional Justice and Children," 50.

577 *Basic Principles and Guidelines on the Right to a Remedy and Reparation for Victims of Gross Violations of International Human Rights Law and Serious Violations of International Humanitarian Law* (21 March 2006), paras 10 and 22.

ensure that they are not put at further risk because they have supported the evidence-gathering exercise.[578]

1.2. THE IMPLICATIONS OF CHILDREN'S PARTICIPATION IN THE *LUBANGA* CASE

In international transitional justice mechanisms, children have sometimes been engaged as witnesses in relation to crimes against children, or children's issues have been presented by their representatives, taking into account appropriate measures as recognized by the CRC.[579] The appearance of child witnesses in international criminal proceedings started with the Special Court for Sierra Leone, in 2005, and developments there informed the way that the International Criminal Court began to practise the inclusion of children in its proceedings.[580]

Although victims' participation in the context of the International Criminal Court is seen as a great innovation,[581] the participation of children in international justice forums is a relatively new field, with standards and practices still to be solidly codified. Among the elements that could be included, and have been implemented in some cases, are hiring specialized staff; assessing and addressing any particular vulnerabilities of children who are coming forward as witnesses; and providing counselling to the child before, during, and after the

---

578 Schabas, *An Introduction to the International Criminal Court, Third Edition*, 334. Schabas also cites an interesting debate between former prosecutor Moreno-Ocampo and Professor Cassese, which concerned the security conditions in Darfur and some general comments about the role of the Court in the protection of victims. See further *Situation in Darfur*, ICC-02/05, Prosecutor's Observations to Cassese's Observations on Issues Concerning the Protection of Victims and the Preservation of Evidence in the Proceedings on Darfur Pending Before the ICC International Criminal Court (11 September 2006), para 8.

579 For instance, in the *Lubanga* case the Special Representative of the Secretary-General provided an amicus brief and appeared as a witness before the International Criminal Court on the issue of how children are conscripted or enlisted into armed groups in light of the crime of child recruitment as listed in the Rome Statute. See *The Prosecutor V. Thomas Lubanga Dyilo, Written Submission of the United Nations Special Representative of the Secretary-General on Children and Armed Conflict, Submitted in Application of Rule 103 of the Rules of Procedure and Evidence*, (18 March 2008), and *Press Statement of the Special Representative on Children and Armed Conflict: International Criminal Court – UN Official testifies on the Lubanga case*, The Hague/New York, 6 January 2010.

580 Siegrist, "Child Rights and Transitional Justice," 12. The engagement of the children in the SCSL proceedings was based on the *Principles and Procedures for the Protection of Children in the Special Court*, which later informed the development of similar approaches in the ICC. For a detailed account of the experiences in putting five children on the witness stand in Sierra Leone,, see Kyra Sanin and Anna Stirnemann, *Child Witnesses at the Special Court for Sierra Leone* (California: University of California, War Crimes Studies Center, 2006).

581 Schabas, *An Introduction to the International Criminal Court, Third Edition*, 328.

testimony, as well as follow-up and referrals as appropriate to safeguard the return and continued well-being of the child.[582]

The introduction of a system for the participation of victims in the Rome Statute has been considered as ground-breaking in that it gives the victims an opportunity to tell their stories and to be key stakeholders in decisions about reparations as well as the receipt of recompense.[583] Article 68(3) of the Statute states:

> Where the personal interests of the victims are affected, the Court shall permit their views and concerns to be presented and considered at stages of the proceedings determined to be appropriate by the Court and in a manner which is not prejudicial to or inconsistent with the rights of the accused and a fair and impartial trial. Such views and concerns may be presented by the legal representatives of the victims where the Court considers it appropriate, in accordance with the Rules of Procedure and Evidence.

As the ICC's first case, the Lubanga trial proceedings allow for analysis that considers a number of procedural questions that point to the challenge of engaging witnesses and gathering evidence in post-conflict situations, and the extent to which it is necessary and useful to promote the participation of children.[584] Such issues pose important questions from the child rights and transitional justice perspectives.

As a criminal justice process, the evidence was at the base of proving Lubanga's guilt, and for a conviction, each element of the particular offence

---

582 See An Michels, "Psychosocial Support for Children: Protecting the Rights of the Child Victims and Witnesses in Transitional Justice Processes," *Innocenti Working Paper* 2010-14 (2009). This paper builds on the experiences gained from both international tribunals as well as truth commissions.

583 Lucia Catani, "Victims at the International Criminal Court: Some Lessons Learned from the Lubanga Case," *Journal of International Criminal Justice* 10 (2012): 905-922.

584 Participation of witnesses is considered in the Rome Statute in articles 15(3) and 19(3), whereby victims may make representations to the pre-trial chamber and victims may also submit observations in the context of considering the admissibility and jurisdiction of the Court. Given that this was the first case of the ICC, it gave rise to a great deal of procedural considerations and short-comings, many of which would have been specific to the issue at hand, while others would have been more generic for the operating of the Court. Four major procedural events had an impact on the course of the proceedings: the first related to the Office of the Prosecutor failing to disclose a significant body of potentially exculpatory evidence covered by certain confidentiality agreements; the second related to a notification by the Chamber that the legal characterisation of the facts may be subject to change; the third related to the Trial Chamber imposing a second stay of proceedings because of the prosecution's non-compliance with an order to disclose the names of a specific intermediary; and finally the defence seeking a permanent stay of proceedings raising among other issues claims that the Prosecution had used some intermediaries who had prepared false evidence. With respect to the issue of stay in proceedings related to issues of collaboration between the UN and the ICC, see Johnson, "The Lubanga Case and Cooperation between the UN and the ICC."

charged had to be established "beyond reasonable doubt."[585] The process did not prove to be without difficulties. Children are not well suited to consider their own well-being and interests in providing testimony in a trial or any justice process. And the fact that alleged war criminals may be able to go free between lengthy trials does not bode well for witness protection.

The first child to serve as a witness in the *Lubanga* case was a former child soldier testifying against a former rebel leader from the Democratic Republic of the Congo. The defendant was charged by the ICC with the war crime of conscripting or enlisting children under the age of 15. This child, like all the other witnesses, had requested to remain anonymous.[586] After seeing, and being seen by, the defendant in court, the witness recanted his testimony due to fear of reprisals arising from this lack of child-friendly procedures and other shortcomings in procedural standards to protect witnesses.

There were also issues related to showing faces of children waving at the camera on videotape, where there had been no consent given by those children or their families. This footage had been secured by the Office of the Prosecutor from a producer of a television documentary. The identity of the children in this footage was not hidden until after one of the witnesses raised concerns over the tapes being shown in Court.[587]

Before the trials even began, the prosecution had a number of challenges in putting together the investigative team and finding investigators who had the necessary background and skills. There were also difficulties with the missions to the field, due to a lack of external support and the UN sometimes declining to help or imposing excessive constraints.

The requirement on the prosecution by the Rome Statute is to investigate both incriminating and exculpatory evidence.[588] Evidence included oral, written, and audio-visual forms. Much effort went into the Chamber assessing the reliability of individual pieces of evidence and their probative value in the context of any other admissible and probative material.[589] Evidence must have

---

585 Rome Statute Article 66(1 3). In terms of balancing between children's participation in such proceedings, focusing attention on the rights of child victims and witnesses of crime should not happen at the expense of the alleged offender(s). See *Guidelines on Justice Matters Involving Child Victims and Witnesses of Crime* (22 July 2005), para 7(j).

586 Catani, "Victims at the International Criminal Court: Some Lessons Learned from the Lubanga Case," 912.

587 *The Prosecutor v. Thomas Lubanga Dyilo*, 08 July 2009, 15, lines 15 to 20.

588 *Guidelines on Justice Matters Involving Child Victims and Witnesses of Crime* (22 July 2005), paras 130–131. See also Robert Cryer, "Means of Gathering Evidence and Arresting Suspects in Situations of States' Failure to Cooperate," in *The Oxford Companion to International Criminal Justice*, ed. editor-in-chief Antonio Cassese (Oxford: Oxford University Press, 2009), 203.

589 *The Prosecutor v. Thomas Lubanga Dyilo*, ICC-01/04-01/06-T-342-ENG International Criminal Court (01 April 2011), 64–65. At the same time, the Prosecution and the Defence were requested to flag parts that they consider be relevant. *The Prosecutor v. Thomas Lubanga Dyilo*, 14 March 2012, para 94.

been submitted, discussed at trial, and found to be admissible by the Chamber: only materials that satisfied these three criteria were considered.[590]

This is a key consideration, because in its final submission, the defence asserted that the prosecution failed to fulfil its obligations in regard to disclosure and the investigation of exculpatory circumstances. As a result, this arguably weakened the reliability of the entire body of evidence presented by the prosecution at the trial, to the extent that it might not have provided findings beyond all reasonable doubt.[591] However, it was finally considered that "throughout the trial, the Chamber addressed any potential prejudice to the accused arising from incomplete or late disclosure."[592]

At the very start of the investigations, in late 2004, debate had taken place within the Office of the Prosecutor on the problem of determining children's age, once the forensic expert raised the issue. The approach was to ask for civil status documents, or a doctor saw the children in order to estimate the age based on physical development; however, for security reasons, the prosecutor's office could not speak to the families or contact schools. This policy applied to all witnesses and was only varied on an exceptional basis. In the final analysis, the Chamber concluded that the "failure to investigate the children's histories has significantly undermined some of the evidence called by the prosecution."[593]

There was also a specific issue related to the child soldiers who had been called by the prosecution, and nine witnesses were not accepted.[594] The Chamber stated that the prosecution should not have delegated its investigative responsibilities to the intermediaries, notwithstanding the security challenges faced. As a result, the prosecution's negligence in failing to verify and scrutinize this material sufficiently before it was introduced led to significant expenditure on the part of the Court. In addition, the alleged former child soldiers would have been vulnerable to manipulation in that process.[595] Considering this result, perhaps the Office of the Prosecutor should have reconsidered the value of interviewing children themselves.

As the Chamber concluded its discussion on the evidence, it appears that it relied heavily on expert witnesses, as well as other witnesses, and video evidence.

---

590 *The Prosecutor v. Thomas Lubanga Dyilo*, 14 March 2012, para 101.

591 Ibid., 119.

592 Ibid., para 121. It then went on to explain how it addressed incomplete disclosure, late disclosure, and violations of the prosecution's statutory obligations.

593 Ibid., para 172.

594 Six victims testified before the Chamber as prosecution witnesses, while three witnesses were called upon at the request of legal representatives. Some of the victims were still children when they submitted their applications, and their parents, relatives, or others have acted on their behalf. A legal guardian could also represent the child, and it was permitted for children to participate directly without an adult representing them. *The Prosecutor v. Thomas Lubanga Dyilo*, Public Annex 1 to Corrigendum to "Decision on the applications by victims to participate in the proceedings", ICC-01/04-01/06-1556-Corr-Anx1 International Criminal Court (13 January 2009), paras 67–72.

595 Ibid., para 482.

In the end, it was satisfied to have achieved the standard of "beyond reasonable doubt" through the evidence that was before the Chamber.

The handling of evidence and how it was obtained in the *Lubanga* case raises a critical question for future investigations: Considering the security implications for children and families on the ground, should they have aimed at speaking to the children at all? Obviously, no context is the same as another, but there are certain practices that were not appreciated by the Chamber. As a result, not only did this lead to the validity of the children's histories being questioned, it becomes clear that the investigations could have been undertaken differently or the prosecution could have relied on a different set of investigatory material as far children's testimony was concerned. In fact, it may not have been in the child's best interest to be interviewed at all, and the evidence could have been gathered mainly through adults who are able to make decisions about their own protection.

In this regard, it is important to consider the extent to which an issue, or a process or a response to an issue, is affecting the child and how relevant it will be to engage children and young people in the process. In other words, it is not just about children exercising their rights, but involves weighing this against the necessity for doing so. Likewise, if the same result can be achieved without putting children on the spot, then perhaps it is better to consider alternative modes of getting inputs so as to uphold children's rights, keeping in mind the best interests of the child.

The main point for child protection practitioners is to be proactive about what type of evidence should be considered imperative under these circumstances. In addition, practitioners can be more professional about gathering information that can be analysed and digested without putting individual children into the limelight, for instance, through the monitoring and reporting mechanism developed by the Security Council.

2. STANDARDS ON CHILDREN AS POSSIBLE PERPETRATORS OF WAR CRIMES

This section analyses the law and practice so as to achieve an informed conclusion about how to best respect the rights and responsibilities of children as alleged offenders. It begins by reviewing the standards on children's criminal responsibility in general and then moves on to analyse the issue against three levels of due diligence as defined under international law: children engaged in international and national jurisdictions, including considerations of the standard "beyond reasonable doubt"; applications of the "serious grounds for believing" standards, which has been used in considering exclusion of asylum seekers; and, finally, recovery and reintegration of child soldiers and the standards applied in restorative justice.

2.1. THE MINIMUM AGE OF CRIMINAL RESPONSIBILITY

According to a popular saying, "If you're old enough to commit a crime you are old enough to do the time." Legal procedures, however, must take a far more nuanced approach, though the exact age of criminal responsibility has historically been contentious in international law and has yet to be standardized across countries.

For purposes of defining the minimum age of criminal responsibility, states are applying ages ranging from 7–18 years old.[596] Although the issue was debated during drafting of the CRC the drafters could only agree to disagree. As a result, the provision in the Convention was left open and identifies the duty to establish a minimum age through States parties' policies and procedures, without giving guidance as to what the age should be.

Article 40(3[a]) of the CRC requires States parties to "promote the establishment of a minimum age below which children shall be presumed not to have the capacity to infringe the penal law." What this means in practice is that children below that age limit cannot be held liable under penal law – and children above that age can be formally charged and subject to penal law procedures. In all cases, these procedures, including the final outcome, must provide for child-friendly procedures that are in line with the Convention.[597]

In its General Comment 10, the Committee on the Rights of the Child considered that given the wide range of minimum ages for criminal responsibility in place, and that some countries have a disturbingly low age, it would be necessary to provide some guidance in this regard. Rule 4.1 of the Beijing Rules recognizes that "the beginning of that age shall not be fixed at too low an age level, bearing in mind the facts of emotional, mental and intellectual maturity."[598] As such, the Committee has considered that states should not set the age of criminal responsibility below 12, and it encourages setting the standard at 14 or 16. Also, "if there is no proof of age and it cannot be established that the child is at or above the minimum age of criminal responsibility, the child shall not be held criminally responsible."[599]

---

596 See UNICEF, *Innocenti Digest: Juvenile Justice* (Florence: UNICEF Innocenti, 1998).

597 Committee on the Rights of the Child, *General Comment No. 10: Children's Rights in Juvenile Justice* UN Doc. CRC/C/GC/10 (25 April 2007), para 31.

598 The Commentary of the Beijing Rules goes on to say: "The minimum age of criminal responsibility differs widely owing to history and culture. The modern approach would be to consider whether a child can live up to the moral and psychological components of criminal responsibility; that is, whether a child, by virtue of her or his individual discernment and understanding, can be held responsible for essentially antisocial behaviour. If the age of criminal responsibility is fixed too low or if there is no lower age limit at all, the notion of responsibility would become meaningless." General Assembly, *United Nations Standard Minimum Rules for the Administration of Juvenile Justice ("The Beijing Rules")* UN Doc. A/40/53 (29 November 1985).

599 *General Comment No. 10: Children's Rights in Juvenile Justice* (25 April 2007), 35. See also Don Cipriani's comprehensive study on the issue of minimum age of criminal responsibility.

The question of children as alleged perpetrators was considered in the drafting of the Additional Protocols to the Geneva Conventions. Viet Nam's delegation wanted to include a provision related to the responsibilities of those children who have been involved with armed groups and forces, to be added to paragraph 1: "Persons under eighteen who have been arrested for their patriotism or for their political non-submission shall be set free as soon as possible and before other civilians."[600] This was supported by the Byelorussian Soviet Socialist Republic, the Union of Soviet Socialist Republics, and Yugoslavia, but not by the United Kingdom, and such a provision never made it to the final document.

The Brazilian delegation advocated for adding language to make the third paragraph refer to penal proceedings in general: "Penal proceedings shall not be taken against, and sentence shall not be pronounced on, persons who were under sixteen years of age at the time the offence was committed."[601] A few delegations supported this (such as Yugoslavia); Japan suggested the age be lowered to 14, considering that the minimum age for criminal responsibility might be lower in some situations; and Canada thought it was a matter of sovereign responsibility to set such standards.[602]

In the end, this matter prevailed within the sovereign realm and no reference was made to criminal responsibility for children other than to the fact that children under age 15 who might have taken part in armed conflicts are to be provided with special protection and the provision prohibiting the death penalty under age 18.[603] While there is no age limit for providing prisoner-of-war status

Cipriani suggests there is no one optimal age limit applicable to all countries, however, he draws the conclusion that international consensus draws the limit at 12. Don Cipriani, *Children's Rights and the Minimum Age of Criminal Responsibility.* Surrey: Ashgate Publishing, (2009),.

600 'Official Records of the Diplomatic Conference on the Reaffirmation and Development of International Humanitarian Law Applicable in Armed Conflicts, Geneva (1974–1977): Volume III,' 300.

601 'Official Records of the Diplomatic Conference on the Reaffirmation and Development of International Humanitarian Law Applicable in Armed Conflicts, Geneva (1974–1977): Volume XV,' 66. See also 'Official Records of the Diplomatic Conference on the Reaffirmation and Development of International Humanitarian Law Applicable in Armed Conflicts, Geneva (1974–1977): Volume III,' 301.

602 'Official Records of the Diplomatic Conference on the Reaffirmation and Development of International Humanitarian Law Applicable in Armed Conflicts, Geneva (1974–1977): Volume XV,' 68. See also feed-back from the Report to Committee III on the Work of the Working Group submitted by the Rapporteur: "One representative wished to have it noted in the report that he would have preferred to add a new paragraph 6 prohibiting any penal prosecution and punishment of a child who was not old enough at the time the offence was committed to understand the implications of his acts. The Working Group, however, decided that the definition of such standards was better left to national law." See Ibid., 522.

603 This was considered by the III Committee, which stated, "The Committee recognized that it was a principle of general international law that no person could be convicted of a criminal offence if, at the time the offence was committed, he was unable to understand the consequence of his act." The Committee nevertheless decided that the application of this principle should be left to national legislation. See Ibid., 222.

in international armed conflicts, the special protection measures would continue to apply to children.[604] This protection is important in situations where children have been captured because their situation can be used to advocate for child-friendly procedures to be applied, for instance, in situations where children are being prosecuted for their participation in a conflict.[605] If a child soldier falls into the power of an adverse party, for example, they will continue to benefit from special protection, including special respect and protection against any form of indecent assault, but also provision of the care and aid they require, whether because of their age or for any other reason.[606]

2.2. CHILDREN'S POTENTIAL RESPONSIBILITY FOR WAR CRIMES IN INTERNATIONAL AND NATIONAL JURISDICTIONS

Before attempting to resolve the questions of whether and how children should be held responsible for their own acts, it is necessary to first consider the reasoning that has led to a trend of excluding children from international jurisdictions.

The issue of child responsibility for international crimes in international forums was deliberated during the creation of the SCSL. At this time, while the Court's statute allowed for prosecution of children above 15, the prosecutor decided not to prosecute any children below the age of 18, building on the statute that mandated the prosecution to focus on individuals who bear the greatest responsibilities for war crimes. In general, this responsibility would apply to those who "forced thousands of children to commit unspeakable crimes," not the children.[607]

---

604 "With respect to paragraph 3, it should be noted that prisoner of war status cannot be denied on the grounds of age but that, whether a child under 15 is a PW or not, he should continue to benefit from the special protection accorded by this article." Rapporteur for working group during Diplomatic Conference. See Ibid., 522.

605 See Nils Melzer at 60, stating that as soon as children regain protection against direct attack, they also regain their special protection status.

606 AP I article 77(1), referred to in article 77(3). See also article 70(1) on privileged treatment and special protection of children in relief actions.

607 Press Release, Special Court for Sierra Leone, Public Affairs Office, Special Court Prosecutor Says He Will Not Prosecute Children (November 2, 2002). There were also two other hybrid courts that allowed for prosecution of children below the age of 18, namely the Special Panels for Serious Crimes in Timor-Leste, having jurisdiction for persons over 12 years of age, and the War Crimes Chamber in the Court of Bosnia and Herzegovina, having jurisdiction for persons over age 14. The former dealt with one case which is considered further below. For further details see Aptel, "International Criminal Justice and Child Protection," 102–103. See also Diane Marie Amann, "Calling Children to Account: The Proposal for a Juvenile Chamber in the Special Court for Sierra Leone," *Pepperdine Law Review* 29 (2001–2002): 167–186.

The deliberations that led to the adoption of the Rome Statute provide some interesting background for understanding the issue of age of criminal responsibility for international crimes. Article 26 of the Rome Statute determines that "the Court shall have no jurisdiction over any person who was under the age of 18 at the time of the alleged commission of a crime." This presents several challenging dilemmas, as the enlistment and conscription of children under the age of 15 is a crime in itself, and a reality in many circumstances.

The first challenge relates to whether article 26 could lead to armed groups exploiting the fact that children between 16 and 18 cannot be held criminally responsible, making use of such children in their efforts to recruit younger children and carry out other international crimes.[608] Several governments thought the discrepancy between 15 and 18 could "open the door to abuse."[609] However, it keeps the focus on holding those "most responsible" accountable for their crimes. Also, it was made clear by many delegations that this did not mean that child soldiers would go unpunished or be "legalized," but that it would be up to the national systems to take action in such cases.[610]

A second challenge is the fact that to some extent this meant that governments avoided seeking consensus on the age of criminal responsibility for international crimes. In the early drafts of the Rome Statute, the idea had been to determine when a child could be held criminally responsible for an international crime. In national jurisdictions, it proved difficult to find any common standards on the minimum age of criminal responsibility, not only because it varies from country to country, but also because the age of criminal responsibility within a country is sometimes broken up into different categories depending on the nature of the crime.[611]

---

608 The 17 June 1998, message from Olara A. Otunnu, SRSG-CAAC, sought consistency between the age of criminal responsibility under the Statute and the age when recruitment of children becomes illegal. This was in order to avoid the deliberate use of children in committing crimes, as they would be de jure immune from the Court's jurisdiction. See also Antonio Cassese, *International Criminal Law, Second Edition* (Oxford University Press, 2008), 267.

609 A/CONF.183/C.1/SR.220 November 1998, statements made by Jordan, USA, Israel, Republic of Korea, paras 6–30.

610 Committee of the whole, A/CONF.183/C.1/SR.220 November 1998, statements made by New Zealand, Mexico, El Salvador, Venezuela, Lebanon, paras 5–37.

611 Preparatory Committe on the Establishment of an International Criminal Court, *Proceedings of the Preparatory Committee during the Period 25 March – 12 April 1996*, UN Doc. A/AC.249/ CRP.3/Add.1 (8 April 1996), para 13. The need for including a provision setting an age limit at which an individual could be regarded as not having the requisite *mens rea* was widely supported. The question of at what age, however, would require common agreement. There was support for various proposals to this effect, including one that would give the court discretion to evaluate an offender – within a certain age range – as to his or her maturity at the time of the commission of the crime. Attention was also drawn to a number of international instruments relevant to this issue, including the Convention on the Rights of the Child.

The options at hand were threefold:

1. Include a low age where a person under that age had no criminal responsibility.
2. Include a high age above which a person would be held fully responsible or at the discretion of the prosecutor (from age 16 for some delegations, including Austria, Côte d'Ivoire, Iran, Madagascar, and Slovenia).[612]
3. Include an age range somewhere in the middle where child-friendly procedures would need to be applied, with tremendous resource implications in establishing the Court and considering that it is a punitive body rather than a restorative one.

In the end, states considered the jurisdiction of the court rather than the age of criminal responsibility, as introduced by the United Kingdom as an alternative. This would delink the provision from the question of age of responsibility and consider the question as a jurisdictional issue. This approach was supported by several states and received support from several child protection agencies, as well, including UNICEF.[613] Following the introduction of this compromise, several governments noted that they still saw the age of criminal responsibility for international crimes not being applicable below 18, including in their domestic jurisdictions.[614]

While there is no customary rule that has been distinctly defined on this matter yet, there is emerging consensus that children should not be held responsible for international crimes in international jurisdictions, while they may be held responsible for international crimes in domestic jurisdictions if that is provided for under national law.[615]

Holding children accountable at the domestic level raises significant issues regarding the appropriateness and effectiveness of participatory justice. One

---

612 Preparatory Committee on the Establishment of an International Criminal Court, *Decisions Taken by the Preparatory Committee at Its Session Held from 11 to 21 February 1997*, UN Doc. A/AC.249/1997/L.5 (12 March 1997). Proposal 2 read: Age of persons liable to punishment: [Persons aged 13 to 18 years at the time of the facts shall be criminally responsible but their prosecution, trial and sentence and the regime under which they serve their sentence may give rise to the application of special modalities specified in the Statute.].

613 Roy S. Lee (Ed.), *The International Criminal Court: The Making of the Rome Statute, Issues, Negotiations, Results* (Kluwer Law International, 1999), 200–201. See also statement of 18 June 1998, by UNICEF Deputy Executive Director Stephen Lewis, asking for 18 years in terms of the age for age of recruitment, and no jurisdiction under 18 years.

614 This includes statements made by Italy, Portugal, Uruguay, Malta, Syrian Arab Republic, Algeria, Kenya, and Oman. *Committee of the Whole: Summary Record of the 35th Meeting*, UN Doc. A/CONF.183/C.1/SR.35 (20 November 1998), paras 8–35.

615 Cassese, *International Criminal Law, Second Edition*, 267. Note the Key Principles, which state, "In principle, children should not be held criminally responsible under an international jurisdiction." Also, the ad hoc tribunal for Rwanda and Yugoslavia set the age at 18 in articles 23(2) and 24(2), respectively.

issue that is recognized in the Paris Commitments is the question of whether a child can be prosecuted as a deserter. The answer is covered in article XX: "Children who have been unlawfully recruited or used by armed forces are not considered as deserters under applicable domestic law." In other words, their membership in an armed group or force is not a crime of desertion in itself.

What actually occurs in today's conflict situations is that children are not being prosecuted for international crimes, but they do fall victim to political divides for which adults bear responsibility. The issues of desertion, treason, or crimes against the state are the reasons children are being prosecuted, mostly under laws that have been adopted to fight terrorism. Research found that there is no single case to date in which a child has been prosecuted and/or convicted for a war crime, one case of a prosecution for crimes against humanity, and quite a number of cases in which children were tried for the crime of genocide, following the Rwanda events in 1994.[616]

The Security Council consideration of children affected by armed conflicts has taken a proactive stance in supporting children who have been part of armed forces and groups, and who face detention or prosecution following release or capture. Security Council engagement on this issue in general aims to ensure that child-friendly procedures prevail and that children are seen as victims rather than perpetrators of crimes.

In its 2008 Burundi conclusions, the SCWG encouraged the release of children who were illegally detained under suspicion of being associated with the Palipehutu-FNL (Parti pour la liberation du peuple hutu – Forces nationales de liberation).[617] In the case of Myanmar, it made a similar reference, urging the Government to "cease the arrest of children for desertion, if any, and to ensure their swift release."[618] In its 2009 Burundi conclusions, the SCWG went even further, requesting the Government to:

616 There is one case where a child was prosecuted for crimes against humanity through acts carried out at the age of 14; however, in the end the sentence passed was not for an international crime. See The Case of X: A Child Prosecuted for Crimes against Humanity, Special Panels for Serious Crimes, Dili, Timor Leste Judicial System Monitoring Programme (2005). Drumbl, *Reimagining Child Soldiers in International Law and Policy*, 125. For experiences related to the Gacaca, see e.g. Peter E. Harrell, *Rwanda's Gamble: Gacaca and a New Model of Transitional Justice* (iUniverse, 2003), and Allison Corey and Sandra F. Joireman, "Retributive Justice: The Gacaca Courts in Rwanda," *African Affairs* 103, no. 410 (2004): 73–89, and Phil Clark, "Hybridity, Holism and Traditional Justice: The Case of the Gacaca Courts in Post-Genocide Rwanda," *George Washington International Law Review* 39, no. 4 (2007): 765–838.

617 United Nations Security Concil Working Group on Children and Armed Conflict, *Conclusions on Parties to the Situation of Armed Conflict in Burundi* UN Doc. S/AC.51/2008/6 (5 February 2008), para 12(iv).

618 SCWG, Conclusion on Children and Armed Conflict in Myanmar (S/AC.51/2008/8) (25 July 2008), para. 5(g(vi)).

> Consider the protection of children in the application of transitional justice mechanisms ... [and] ensure that children who are prosecuted for associations with armed groups and crimes are treated in accordance with Burundi's international obligations specific to the rights of child, in particular with regard to the age of criminal responsibility, due process and the principle of deprivation of liberty as a measure of last resort.[619]

In the Sudan, there were issues around children who had fought with the Justice and Equality Movement in the May 2008 attack on Omdurman and were caught by the Government and detained, most likely under antiterrorist legislation. One child was sentenced to death. The SCWG responded to this, urging the Government to "implement the national laws and international obligations derived from the CRC that prohibit the death penalty of any person below the age of eighteen, if this penalty exists, in all of its jurisdictions and regardless of the offence."[620]

In article 4 of its 2009 conclusions on children and armed conflict in Afghanistan, the SCWG referred to the issue of children being trained for engagement in acts of terrorism for the first time:

> The members of the Working Group strongly condemned the training and use of children to commit terrorist acts by several armed groups, in particular the Taliban, and other violations and abuses committed by such groups against children.

In article 11, it further expressed concern "about the situation of children detained by the authorities of Afghanistan and international military forces because of their alleged association with armed groups, emphasizing the need for full respect for relevant provisions of international law." The SCWG has also consistently sought to address impunity, the development of implementing legislation, and the criminalization of child recruitment in domestic law.[621]

One case that helps exemplify the things that can go wrong with pursuing adult justice procedures for former child soldiers is the military judicial tribunal against Omar Khadr, who was 15 at the time of his capture in Afghanistan.[622] Pre-trial detention and proceedings alone took some nine years. The US Military Commission convicted Khadr in October 2010 through a plea bargain of charges, among them violations of the laws of war. Khadr pleaded guilty to five

---

619 SCWG, Conclusions on Children and Armed Conflict in Burundi (S/AC.51/2009/6), para. 6(c(i and iii)).

620 SCWG, Conclusions on Children and Armed Conflict in the Sudan (S/AC.51/2009/5) (21 December 2009), para. 15(d(viii)).

621 See, for instance, SCWG Conclusions on Children and Armed Conflict in the Central African Republic (S/AC.51/2009/2) (13 July 2009), para 16(v); Conclusions on Parties in the Armed Conflict in the Sudan (S/AC.51/2008/7) (5 February 2008), para 13(e(iii)).

622 Charlie Savege, "U.S. Wary of Example Set by Tribunal Case," 27 August 2010.

charges, including throwing a grenade in a 2002 firefight that killed a US combatant, in addition to crimes in connection with terrorist activity.

Such examples show that while it is not a bad principle per se to promote the responsibility of child soldiers for crimes they have been involved in, including through national judicial processes, in practice, children end up being dragged into military legal and terrorist-related procedures – which under no means are appropriate for children because there are never any efforts to make them child-friendly. Another challenging context is the situation when governments have emergency laws that allow for detention and questioning of adults and children alike under circumstances that are far from ideal.[623]

In considering the issue of children as perpetrators of international crimes, it is necessary to understand the political and societal context within which these violations have taken place. Following armed conflicts, the children who have actively participated in hostilities will either be on the winning side or the losing side. How they are treated will be manipulated and politicized and, in the overall interests of transitional justice, is not useful to push for children's accountability at all, because it ends up being considered based on legislation and in forums that are not appropriate for the child.

2.3. APPLYING THE STANDARD OF REASONABLE DOUBT

Based on the approach of international jurisdictions not to consider cases of children, domestic jurisdictions generally do not charge children with international crimes. Certainly, the decision by the prosecutor in the SCSL referred to above stemmed from a situation where the prosecutor considered that there were shortcomings in the procedures that would make it difficult to convict children "beyond reasonable doubt."

Assuming, however, that a child were to be prosecuted for international crimes in a court that can apply child-friendly procedures in line with the procedures identified for victims and witnesses above, it is useful to pause for a moment and consider what type of evidence would be needed in order to prove "beyond reasonable doubt" that a child carried out an international crime.

The *Lubanga* case is just a first taste of the type of scrutiny and the kind of tests that the ICC will deploy, and the elements of crime are different depending on the crime in question. However, in a situation where domestic courts were to consider similar issues in order to prove guilt beyond reasonable doubt, it would

623 See, e.g., Committee on the Rights of the Child, *Consideration of Reports Submitted by States Parties under Article 8 of the Optional Protocol to the Convention on the Rights of the Child on the Involvement of Children in Armed Conflict, Concluding Observations: Sri Lanka* CRC/C/OPAC/LKA/CO/1 (19 October 2010).

need to be a rather strict test safeguarding the rights of the perpetrator while justice is fulfilled.

It would also be difficult to expect success in a proceeding that seeks to prove that a child "knew or should have known" about the crime carried out; developed actions as part of a "common plan" with military and political objectives; and then provided an "essential contribution" by taking the lead on reporting, technical means, issuing instructions, and providing a personal contribution. While these were the considerations in the *Lubanga* case, many of the crimes listed in the Rome Statute include similar aspects as part of the elements of crime.[624]

Although the proceedings differ depending on the type of crime, there are at least four common issues to contemplate:

- First, it is difficult for children to provide testimony and remain firm under pressure about what it is they did and what they did not do. They can easily be manipulated.
- Second, children were not supposed to be in the ranks in the first place, and there are many other people to pursue. There will be exceptions to this approach, but in general, it holds: begin with the big bad guys, and then move to the little bad guys.
- Third, there is hardly any case law to learn from, and there is a reason for that. When there is a case, the end result is often plea bargains and the like. Yet the debate goes on as if it were a solution to prosecute child soldiers.
- Fourth, a consideration is required around whether children really can be tried against the standard of "know or should have known" about the criminal impact of activities that they were involved in when they are not yet able to fully form their knowledge

Certainly, there could be a sliding scale, in line with the principle of engaging the child based on his or her maturity, and as the child gets older it is possible to expect more responsibility. However, there are few safeguards to ensure appropriate procedures for children in conflict with the law in countries affected by armed conflicts, as well as limited focus on building national child-protection systems to address any and all child protection issues, including future child recruitment.

In the absence of any justice process that determines whether a child was involved in carrying out crimes while with an armed group or force, would it, perhaps, be appropriate to withhold support to that child through the programmes that have been established for children's recovery and reintegration?[625]

---

624 See *International Criminal Court, Elements of Crimes* (7 April 2000).

625 Specht, "DDR, Transitional Justice, and the Reintegration of Former Child Combatants," 207. Duthie and Specht, in their article on former child combatants, also write about these questions and refer to the considerations depending on context-specific factors.

This is a very complex question. To begin with, if criminal liability is not determined through appropriate due process, how could the child's exclusion be justified? Second, if the programme is designed to enable young people to contribute to society, what will happen if the most difficult children are excluded from these programmes?

It can be an interesting issue to debate, but in practice, it would be very difficult for the resources to be in place to make such a determination. What would be worthwhile considering, however, is what distinct support and processes may be needed for children who could be expected to have been involved in crimes as outlined above.

2.4. EXCLUSIONARY CRITERIA AND FORMER CHILD SOLDIERS SEEKING ASYLUM

International refugee law lays out the criteria for granting refugee status. At the same time, individuals may also be excluded from international protection. This concept of exclusion was introduced in order to protect the humanitarian nature of the institution of asylum and ensure that it is not available to those who do not deserve it.[626] Article 1(F) of the 1950 Refugee Convention provides that asylum:

> Shall not apply to any person with respect to whom there are serious reasons for considering that:
> (a) he has committed a crime against peace, a war crime, or a crime against humanity, as defined in the international instruments drawn up to make provision in respect of such crimes;
> (b) he has committed a serious non-political crime outside the country of refuge prior to his admission to that country as a refugee;
> (c) he has been guilty of acts contrary to the purposes and principles of the United Nations.

In making reference to "any person," this article does not distinguish between adult and child asylum seekers, which means that the provision must be carefully considered against standards that provide guidance on how to deal with the criminal responsibility of children.[627]

---

626 Executive Committee of the High Commissioner's Programme, *Note on the Exclusion Clauses* UN Doc. EC/47/SC/CRP.29 (30 May 1997), para 3.

627 See UNHCR, *Guidelines on International Protection: Child Asylum Claims under Articles 1(A)2 and 1(F) of the 1951 Convention relating to the Status of Refugees* UN Doc. HCR/GIP/09/08 (22 December 2009). See also Matthew Happold, "Excluding Children from Refugee Status: Child Soldiers and Article 1F of the Refugee Convention," *American University International Law Review* Volume 17, Issue 6 (2002): 1131–1176, 1136. Happold considers that the drafters of the Convention did not really consider that the article might apply to children when crafting it.

The first guiding standard relates to the minimum age of criminal responsibility, which is actually not much of a standard in international law because there is no globally recognized minimum age. Children seeking asylum find themselves in further complexity regarding the age of minimum criminal responsibility because they can be subject to either the age applicable in the country of asylum or the age applicable in the country of origin.

In applying the exclusionary criteria listed above, the question becomes: What would need to be considered in a case concerning a child soldier who may have committed an international crime? There is a three-step analysis relevant to conduct that may give rise to exclusion:[628]

1. The acts themselves must be considered against the exclusion grounds. This step of the analysis focuses on the determination of the subjective criteria and individual responsibility, and the issue is whether the child has the necessary mental state (*mens rea*). In other words, the process needs to determine whether the child acted with the sufficient intent and knowledge to be held individually responsible for an act that warrants exclusion. This is where the provisions of the Beijing rules become particularly useful, whereby the maturity of the child must be considered. Case law on this aspect of mens rea focuses on situations where children have acted in groups that are blacklisted, and based on their membership they have been excluded. Also, most of the case law involves situations in which the act could have been committed by someone was a child at the time but sought asylum after the age of 18.[629]
2. The objective criteria focus on a determination that the child in fact committed a crime in a manner that gives rise to criminal liability in accordance with internationally applicable standards. In addition to establishing the facts, it is important to consider other grounds for rejecting individual responsibility, such as whether the child acted under duress, coercion, or in defence of self or others. This is where the events leading to the recruitment of the child are considered, and the circumstances of the active participation of the child, along with the mental health and status of the child.[630]

---

628 See also UNHCR, *Advisory Opinion Regarding the International Standards for Exclusion from Refugee Status as Applied to Child Soldiers* (12 September 2005).

629 See, for instance, the case of *Penate v. Canada* Minister of Employment and Immigration, Trial Division, Reed J. (26 November 1993). This was a case of an asylum seeker having joined an armed group at the age of 13, but he had then remained in the armed group for 10 years, and during that time grown in ranks and was involved in a range of crimes. At the time that the asylum claim was considered, this person was no longer a child. Complicity where applicant was aware is also involved in a case concerning the Salvadoran army, of which member, committing international offences, not dissociating himself from army, and accepting positions of higher responsibility such as teaching, planning, and executing counter-insurgency operations.

630 See also UNHCR, *Guidelines on International Protection: Application of the Exclusion Clauses: Article 1F of the 1951 Convention relating to the Status of Refugees* UN Doc. HCR/GIP/03/05 (4 September 2003), paras 21–23.

3. Once individual responsibility has been established, it must be determined whether the consequences of exclusion from refugee status are proportional to the seriousness of the act committed. UNHCR guidance points out the need for a balance between the risk of persecution upon return and the crime committed. This is also where reprisals for having left the armed group may be considered as a mitigating factor.[631]

As noted in earlier sections of this chapter regarding the context of whether children could be prosecuted for international crimes, it is important that analysis to determine grounds for exclusion from asylum respect the rights of the child, in particular the best interests of the child as per the CRC, and consider the mental capacity of children and their ability to understand and consent to acts that they are requested or ordered to undertake, as outlined in the Beijing Rules. The detailed considerations of the above-mentioned three-step analysis are not dissimilar from those in a criminal offence, however, there is no requirement of beyond reasonable doubt; rather, the standard is one of establishing that "there are serious reasons for considering" that the exclusion clause may be invoked.

While in making an application for asylum, the burden of proof lies with the applicant, in the case of developing the case for exclusion, the burden of proof falls back to decision maker. Even in the asylum application, the decision maker may need to establish many of the facts in order to consider the case. The above 3 steps consider what test goes into making a determination for having "serious reasons for considering", however, it would seem that the level of evidence and the process required to come to a successful conclusion will be difficult to take to a successful conclusion with child asylum seekers.[632]

The critical question is whether the type of rigorous determination required in this approach can be applied to children.[633] Although the proceedings would theoretically not be as rigorous as in a criminal trial, and therefore the exclusion clause would be easier to apply to children, there are few cases where these issues have actually been tested. While it could happen that a child was denied asylum, or denied other international protection, there are still provisions in

631 *Guidelines on International Protection: Child Asylum Claims under Articles 1(A)2 and 1(F) of the 1951 Convention relating to the Status of Refugees* (22 December 2009), para 64. See also *Poshteh v. Canada* Minister of Citizenship and Immigration, Federal Court of Appeal, Rothstein, Noel and Malone JJ. A Ottawa (8 April 2005). In this case the applicant requested special consideration because of being a child, which was rejected.

632 See Michael Bliss, "'Serious Reasons for Considering': Minimum Standards of Procedural Fairness in the Application of the Article 1F," *International Journal of Refugee Law* 12 (suppl 1) (2000): 92–132. Bliss considers the different elements of due process that should be in place in determining "serious reasons for considering" and also goes into considering what test might apply.

633 The position of the European Council on Refugees and Exiles is that the exclusion should not apply to children under 18 because of the best interest consideration and the ICC statute.

international law and domestic jurisdictions that protect persons against *refoulement*, as established in the Convention Against Torture.[634] The child who is on death row in the Sudan for having been part of an armed group, for example, could certainly benefit from this type of protection.

2.5. RECOVERY AND REINTEGRATION OF CHILD SOLDIERS: APPLYING THE STANDARDS OF RESTORATIVE JUSTICE

Restorative justice as applied to children refers to a concept for holding children responsible, while at the same time considering their specific needs and rights in the process of recovery and reintegration. It may often include attempts to avoid delegating a child to the justice system by seeking alternatives to criminal trials, incarceration, and other actions that would impede a child's return to society. As established by the CRC, States parties should seek to apply, "whenever appropriate and desirable, measures for dealing with such children without resorting to judicial proceedings, providing that human rights and legal safeguards are fully respected."[635]

However, the best interests of children who have been involved in situations of armed conflict are not best served by pursuing reintegration activities without addressing their criminal responsibility.[636] Children need to take responsibility for these acts, and avenues to provide appropriate consideration and, sometimes, legal action in line with international juvenile justice standards for any crimes carried out while in the ranks need to be pursued. It is critical that children, their families and communities, or representatives thereof are part of this process and also part of the decision-making exercise for what type of punishment should be exacted and/or what type of compensation may need to follow.

Restorative justice allows for this approach because it does not assume innocence or guilt; rather, it enables a process that addresses possible criminal responsibility while beginning with an assumption that whatever the finding,

634 Article 3(1) of the Convention against Torture.

635 The Convention on the Rights of the Child, article 40(3(b)).

636 See, for instance, studies cited by Martien Schotsmans, "No Return Home: The (non-) Reintegration of Youth Ex-combatants in Sierra Leone as a Challenge to the Contextualisation of DDR and Transitional Justice," in *Re-member: rehabilitation, reintegration and reconciliation of war-affected children*, ed. Cindy Mels, Ilse Derluyn, Stephan Parmentier and Wouter Vandenhole (Cambridge: Intersentia, 2012), 226. Schotsmans describes the situation in Sierra Leone as leaving ex-combatants fearful of revenge for years after the war. See also Andrew Mawson, "Children, Impunity and Justice: some Dilemmas from Northern Uganda," in *Children in Extreme Situations: Proceedings from the 1998 Alistair Berkley Memorial Lecture*, eds. Lisa Carlson et al. (London: London School of Economics and Political Science, 2000).

the solution will seek to restore and, if necessary, rehabilitate. It is also an approach that can be adapted to be sensitive towards the child's situation and background.[637]

In considering a former child soldier's responsibility, it is vital to recognize that children should not have been in the ranks in the first place, and that the children having been recruited is the prior crime. This line of thinking does not exclude children taking responsibility for their acts, but in the context of armed conflict, it considers that they have been victimized. It also acknowledges that support for any child who may have carried out crimes should be provided in line with international juvenile justice standards, within a framework of restorative justice and social rehabilitation.[638] The response will depend on the context, and the law can give an indication of the direction in which to take the response to these complex issues.[639]

The best way forward is frequently to keep children outside judicial proceedings for international crimes that seek to hold actors accountable for the patterns of violence that took place during an armed conflict. This avoids the cases of abuse and politicization that occur in situations where children have been released from armed forces or groups. The restorative justice approach is also more effective and timely than processes in most justice systems, and does not leave children waiting for years to have a solution to their case.

It is a great challenge that in the countries where most child soldiers can be found, the juvenile justice system is not in line with international standards or, as noted above, children are held responsible for having belonged to an armed group under terrorism laws. In situations where there are no guarantees of child-friendly procedures, child protection agencies need to make sure that children are channelled through a restorative justice process so they do not remain in jail for years to come. In such situations, it may be necessary to advocate for some type of amnesty or pardon, in line with the best interests of the child.[640]

---

637 *Guidelines on Justice Matters Involving Child Victims and Witnesses of Crime* (22 July 2005), 10. "Child victims and witnesses should be treated in a caring and sensitive manner throughout the justice process, taking into account their personal situation and immediate needs, age, gender, disability and level of maturity and fully respecting their physical, mental and moral integrity."

638 See *Report of the Secretary-General on Children and Armed Conflict*, UN Doc A/63/785-S/2009/158 (26 March 2009), para 171. See also O/SRSG-CAAC et al., *MRM Field Manual: Monitoring and Reporting Mechanism (MRM) on Grave Violations against Children in Situations of Armed Conflict*, 42–44. The Key Principles also highlight that: "There is emerging consensus that children associated with armed forces or groups who may have been involved in the commission of crimes under international law shall be considered primarily as victims, not only as perpetrators." Key Principles, section IV on specific principles and programmatic recommendations relevant to judicial mechanisms.

639 Angela McIntyre et al., "Politics, War and Youth Culture in Sierra Leone," *African Security Studies* 11.3 (2002): 6–15.

640 This was, for instance, the situation following the capture of nearly 100 children in Sudan following the attack by the Justice and Equality Movement on Omdurman. Republican Decree No 276 for the year 2008 allowed for a presidential pardon so the children could be

Less formal and less visible approaches can benefit children's participation. In this context, it should be noted how children's participation has been promoted in truth commissions as particularly appropriate because of the non-judicial and consultative nature of such forums.[641] To be successful, the messages developed by truth commissions also need to be communicated back to children in order to make their participation meaningful.[642] These elements can become integrated into a restorative justice approach, but considerations of children's rights in the context of a restorative justice approach require attention to issues beyond participation, and must meaningfully respond to children's social, economic, civil and political rights.[643]

CONCLUSION

Based on the above analysis, it is clear that children's participation in transitional justice processes needs to be carefully considered both in terms of the potential benefits for children as agents in determining their own fates and in terms of the possible protection and security considerations that may follow. Children's participation in criminal justice processes needs to be prudently planned, with systems put in place to safeguard their rights before, during, and after the events. Planning must include a determination of whether it is appropriate and effective for children to contribute towards a criminal justice process or if other options should be found.

The lessons from the *Lubanga* case need to be kept in mind. It is a new forum, and it was the first case to be investigated and considered by the International Criminal Court. However, if professionals with the type of resources that have been put in place for the ICC are not able to do a good job, how could justice mechanisms in war-affected countries be expected to do a good job? Also, as a forum for children as witnesses, the great visibility and politicization of the process make children vulnerable in this context, even when safeguards are put in place to protect the identity of those children.

While the discussions on the minimum age of criminal responsibility are inconclusive, children can under no circumstances be considered to bear the

---

channelled back to their families and communities. See also Katherine Fallah, "Perpetrators and Victims: Prosecuting Children for the Commission of International Crimes," *African Journal of International and Comparative Law* 14, no. 1 (2006): 83–103.

641 UNICEF, *Children and Truth Commissions* (Florence: UNICEF, 2010).

642 Truth and Reconciliation Commission Report for the Children of Sierra Leone: Child-Friendly Version, (2004).

643 For further analysis see Don Cipriani, *Children's Rights and the Minimum Age of Criminal Responsibility*. See also Godfrey M. Musila, "Challenges in Establishing the accountability of Child Soldiers for Human Rights Violations: Restorative Justice as an Option," *African Human Rights Law Journal* 5 (2005): 321–334.

greatest responsibility for the crimes carried out in the context of armed conflicts.

It is clear that for international jurisdictions, children are not the ones who should be brought to justice, considering the aim and focus of these tribunals. There is the inherent dilemma of children between the ages of 15 and 18 being sent by commanders to carry out horrendous missions, with the aspect of children's impunity in mind, or children themselves may feel invulnerable to prosecution. However, this is not an approach that has become evident in conflicts to date, and it would not necessarily reduce the responsibilities for crimes of the commanders.

While there is no minimum age standard that could universally apply to domestic jurisdictions, practice is certainly leaning in a direction that children rarely get charged with war crimes – and when children have ended up in contact with the law related to international or domestic crimes, the case law takes multiple directions and does not lead to many coherent conclusions. One exception is the situation of children being charged under terrorism and treason laws, which lead to processes that are never well suited for the protection of children's rights. Children who have participated actively in hostilities should clearly not be assumed guilty and must not be punished solely for their involvement with an armed force or group.

It is imperative to examine the purpose of participatory justice with an open mind. Considering it as part of a transitional justice approach, the purpose is to carefully weigh the value of peace and justice, in the interest of moving forward as a society. In situations of armed conflict, while individual child soldiers have individual needs, rights, and responsibilities, it is important to consider them as a group as well. From the justice perspective, it would be difficult to be effective with an individualistic approach, and this is where restorative justice can promote innovative ways of dealing with groups of children.

Restorative justice can be linked to recovery and reintegration programmes for children. Depending on the context, it may be important to recognize that children have been involved in crimes while they were in the armed group or force, and that this could be considered as part of restorative justice activities that feed into the overall transitional justice process. Given the fact that in these situations, justice systems generally do not have child-friendly procedures in place, it is essential to set up effective mechanisms that aim to divert children from the normal judicial process and reconcile them with their families and communities.

A restorative justice approach considers children as participants in the transitional justice process, rather than faultless and passive victims. It recognizes the crimes that children may have committed, but with a view to bringing them back home to their communities, where they can live and thrive. The foundation of restorative justice, as reflected in the Convention on the Rights of the Child, is an approach that promotes every "child's sense of dignity and worth, which reinforces the child's respect for the human rights and fundamental freedoms of others and which takes into account the child's age and the desirability of promoting the child's reintegration and the child's assuming a constructive role in society."[644]

Chapter 8 provides overall conclusions on the law relevant to child recruitment and the way forward in applying the transitional justice framework to end child recruitment.

644 Convention on the Rights of the Child, article 40(1).

CHAPTER 8
CONCLUSIONS
Transitional Justice and the Potential for Stronger Protection of the Rights of Children Involved in Armed Conflicts

"I hope my family wants me back."

INTRODUCTION

The number of child soldiers appears to have decreased slightly during the past several years, due to solutions in some long-term conflicts and significant releases of children. This is no doubt partly the result of the consistent advocacy and action taken by actors in the different spheres of transitional justice. Recently escalating conflicts, however, have generated significant reports of new recruitments of children under varying degrees of coercion to be used by armed forces and groups to wage war. There is still significant work to be done: the 2014 report includes the listing of eight government forces and 51 armed groups.

Approaching the issue of child recruitment from the perspective of transitional justice provides a fresh perspective on ways to prevent and redress this grave violation of children's rights. This approach aims to systematize the law, knowledge, and practice across a wide range of legal fields. It allows for a synthesis of legal debate, a greater understanding of the established law and principles, and a more informed basis for practical engagement with transitional justice mechanisms.

This concluding chapter focuses on two main streams: (1) it undertakes a final legal analysis of the law related to child recruitment, and (2) it makes suggestions about the way forward and how the different aspects of transitional justice can more successfully come together.

1. ANALYSING INTERNATIONAL LAW RELEVANT TO CHILD RECRUITMENT THROUGH THE TRANSITIONAL JUSTICE FRAMEWORK

This section brings together the lessons from having used the transitional justice framework as the point of departure. It begins with an exploration of the outcomes of having used the framework and then considers the conclusions that can be made on the state of the art with respect to international law related to child recruitment.

1.1. ADVANTAGES OF AN OVERALL FRAMEWORK

The key advantage of looking at children's issues through the lens of transitional justice rather than a single area of law is that it is possible to consider the entire "life cycle" of the event of child recruitment, from root causes and prevention to the nature of the violation itself, along with the options and solutions to address the violation. In addition, the holistic nature of this type of assessment enables identification of some of the gaps and opportunities in the way that child recruitment is currently being addressed.

While the transitional justice framework emerged out of an era looking to make democratic governance the ultimate goal, the framework has the necessary flexibility and interpretation of transitional justice to focus on situations moving from worse to better, sometimes back again to worse, and then to better again. While the aim is to constantly push towards an increasingly protective environment for children's rights, transition does not only move in one direction, but it is still possible to apply the transitional justice framework.

Through the analysis employing the transitional justice approach, it has been possible to consider all the aspects of the law separately and to consider how they fit together (or do not fit, as the case may be) and how they can reinforce each other. The approach also allowed for going beyond the law, which is very important in the context of children's rights because situations that affect children are often solved through extrajudicial measures that build on the law, but go beyond in very practical ways to find solutions.

Going deep into the *travaux préparatoires* for each of the legal instruments has brought new knowledge to the study of the law related to child recruitment. Little of the records from the discussions during the drafting of the Optional Protocol on the Involvement of Children in Armed Conflict (OPAC) has been made publicly available, but during the research that formed the foundations of this book, these records were recovered from the Quaker United Nations Office in Geneva and made use of for the first time in academic writing. Although there is a great deal published with respect to the *Lubanga* case, to date the work developed in this regard has not considered the angles presented in this work, including the aspects of relating the Lubanga reparations decision with a link to disarmament, demobilization, and rehabilitation (DDR) programming. Likewise, the Security Council mechanism and children's rights in the context of peace agreements have not been studied by others from this perspective.

There is a trend towards a narrow focus on the event of recruitment and use of the child, while ignoring the surrounding circumstances that need to be addressed in order to prevent and respond to child recruitment more effectively; to raise awareness about its damaging impact on children; and to offer the child a chance of recovery, reconciliation, and reintegration – the complete set of rights to which a child soldier is entitled.

This book challenges that narrow focus while aiming to contribute to the world of experts on transitional justice. The approach focuses on the comprehensive use of a framework that was developed by academics and practitioners to take societies through transitions, balancing carefully between peace and justice. It also brings in elements to the transitional justice framework that may otherwise not have been considered in this context, for instance, the Security Council framework and peace agreements, taking the flexible notion of transitional justice to the level where it can be useful for academics and practitioners alike.

Transitional justice processes are not an end in themselves, but their significance in the post-conflict context contributes towards a society coming to terms with violations of international law while prudently considering the need for justice and the need for transition. The emphasis placed on these sometimes temporary institutions makes it important to ensure appropriate consideration of the recruitment and use of children. It is also important to support mainstream, long-term systems building that goes beyond the temporary nature of some of the transitional justice mechanisms. As such, the findings have highlighted some of the tools and arguments for placing child recruitment and other child protection issues firmly on the transitional justice agenda.

1.2. ESTABLISHED PRACTICE AND APPLICATION OF THE LAW

This work has demonstrated how the various areas of law have taken both similar and varying approaches to child recruitment. It is a complex consideration, spanning many areas: humanitarian law, human rights law, criminal law, and other aspects of public law, some of which are difficult to categorize, such as peace agreements and action plans developed with armed groups and forces. The objectives of the different areas are also different, with international humanitarian law seeking to put in place the rules of warfare; human rights law introducing a long-term development and justice perspective that spans war and peace promoting the rule of law; and international criminal law bringing to justice those who have carried out serious violations of international law.

The law and practice related to child recruitment are sufficiently flexible to provide for the necessary arguments to be made in the face of violations against the law.

The broadest terminology of "children associated with armed groups and forces" applies to providing for children's right to reparations, recovery, and reintegration. In this context, there is no doubt that not only does the age of 18 apply, but children serving any role with an armed group or force would also be included. Practice since the adoption of the Paris Commitments and Principles has consistently taken this inclusive approach, including through the 105 states that have endorsed the Principles, but also through consistent practice employed by the Security Council and the signature of peace agreements and action plans developed with armed groups and forces. The Convention on the Rights of the Child and OPAC provide the foundation for this evolving practice, although more often the Paris Commitments are more widely known and understood than the treaties themselves in the context of practical implementation.

Of the 15 situations listed within the Security Council framework based on the 2012 listing exercise in the annexes to the Secretary-General's report, 10 endorsed the Paris Commitments (see annex 3). This shows a strong commitment to the broader definition of child recruitment, which in a very pragmatic way seeks to benefit all children in reintegration programming. Four of the five permanent members of the Security Council endorsed the Paris Commitments, also showing strong political commitment to the inclusive approach of the reintegration phase, the US being the sole hold-out.[645]

Forced recruitment has a strong prohibition founded in international law, and the standard prohibiting forced recruitment of children under age 18 can now be considered a peremptory norm in international law. This standard has been recognized by nearly all states in the world through the ratification of the OPAC and the ILO Convention 182. The language included in legal instruments for forced recruitment is also stronger than that relevant to voluntary recruitment or direct participation, with OPAC, for instance, using the word "ensure" rather than "shall take all feasible measures," which is the language used for direct participation. Forced recruitment is also recognized in some voluntary schemes applicable to private military security companies, while more recent developments in the business and human rights arena go beyond to consider all forms of recruitment and the direct participation of children.

The facts that the provision of forced recruitment came first in considerations of international criminal law and child recruitment, and that it was found in the Special Court for Sierra Leone (SCSL) statute, demonstrate that this element has

[645] The United States did, however, ratify OPAC, which contains a detailed provision on recovery and reintegration.

a stronger foundation in the law. However, the SCSL applied the age limit of 15 in the context of international criminal law, which is dealt with further below.

The prohibition of voluntary recruitment is also rapidly moving towards 18 years. Increasingly, states ratifying OPAC declare that they have prohibited voluntary recruitment of children below the age of 18, while others have indicated age 17, and some the age of 16 for recruitment into armed forces. Nonetheless, the military schools provide for loopholes of several kinds, whereby children under age 18 make decisions at a young age that will affect them in adulthood, whether or not they truly had a choice at the time.

As a result, voluntary recruitment in the context of armed forces is still in the 16–18 range. However, even if voluntary recruitment cannot yet be said to have reached the level where it would be prohibited under international law to recruit children who are 16 and 17 years old, a stronger case can be made for direct participation in hostilities. Not only is the seriousness of the active participation coming out in the case law under international criminal law for any activity that is potentially dangerous to children, but the restrictive nature of participation in hostilities is also being recognized in OPAC and the Security Council, as well, has come down hard on direct participation of children.

In terms of international criminal law, the age standard of 15 for international criminal law stands firmly at what has been codified through the Rome Statute. While there were some doubts about whether this standard truly represented customary law at the time it was introduced, the increased focus and attention on international criminal responsibility for child recruitment, along with the court decisions that have followed, has helped reinforce it. In terms of increasing the standard from 15 to a higher age, it will only be supported by further strengthening of the standard for prohibition of recruitment (forced and voluntary) going firmly to age 18. While the International Criminal Court (ICC) standard of 15 cannot change without an amendment to the treaty, what could change is the consideration of whether children have to be visibly below the age of 15 as the standard firms up through future case law. In the *Lubanga* case, children had to be visibly below the age of 15; it was not possible to consider that they were around the age of 15. Some domestic laws already consider the age of 18 for individual criminal responsibility, and case law should consistently be pushing in this direction in domestic jurisdictions. While the Rome Statute standard is not yet out of date, it is certainly going to be challenged in the years to come.

Age verification is key to success in this aspect. Not only should protection and human rights organization have better mechanisms for determining age, To begin with, it should not be necessary to only consider a case if children are visibly under the age of 15; in addition, protection and human rights organizations should have better mechanisms for determining age. Although regional variation and local contexts frequently make age verification difficult, this does not preclude further investment in finding good methodologies for the process. This would help tremendously in strengthening the base for the evidence in these court proceedings.

In a consideration of what intensity of conflict and how organized an armed group needs to be, it will be difficult to argue a situation where no standard applies to an armed group or force. In practice, the provision of the OPAC that focuses on armed groups is applied with the same force as those relevant to state actors: there is no distinction being made between the non-state actor standard of "should" carrying less legal value that the standard of "shall" for state actors. On the contrary, states are quite pleased in referring to the fact that it is a straight 18 provision, allowing for a very categorical approach. On no occasion is the "should" raised as an issue in creating legal accountability for non-state actors as evidenced through the practice to date. In addition, OPAC sets no standard for how organized the group needs to be, while Additional Protocol II requires that it be an organized armed group under responsible command. Nonetheless, including "should" as a qualifier in the OPAC has a legal significance in that it highlights the fact that non-state actors are not on equal footing with states. However, even if it is difficult to prove the law through mere practice in the Security Council framework it would be rather difficult for an armed group to claim that it is not legally bound by these provisions considering this practice. In the context of the Security Council mechanism, the Secretary-General has listed all types of groups, not only those "under responsible command," thereby holding them accountable for grave violations against children's rights, notably child recruitment.

Regarding the issue of "direct participation," there seem to be four levels currently in place depending on the type of law and practice applied:

- One level is a strictly applied "direct participation" that refers to children with guns and those directly involved in the fighting. This is the standard that could be derived from international humanitarian law regarding loss of immunity from attack. It is generally recognized today that the law now operates on other additional levels.
- A second level broadens the coverage beyond children who have guns to include those in direct involvement with the armed activities, such as spies, porters, or messengers. This is the standard that would apply for a broader interpretation of international human rights and humanitarian law, which is the standard reading of the provisions found in international humanitarian law today.
- A third level refers to "active participation" in international criminal law, which currently is interpreted based on the level of danger involved in carrying out the task or role that the child has. It is not so important what the role is, rather the extent to which the child was in danger while serving in the ranks of armed groups or forces.

- A fourth level is based on the Paris Commitments and includes all children associated with the armed group or force, including those who may not have a link to the activities that contribute to the hostilities: girls and boys being sexually exploited, cooks, abducted children, cleaners, etc. This is the standard being applied for purposes of release, recovery, and reintegration of child soldiers.

Considering that the first two levels belong to the same category, there are three basic approaches to considering the issue of the implications of the child's participation in hostilities, and it is important to consider each within its own legal sphere.

For purposes of targeting within international humanitarian law, a narrow level-one interpretation provides better protection to a higher number of children as civilians (and the protective standard for below age 15). As a result, it would be better to have a tight definition that focuses on children with guns, so as to allow for a protective regime for the remainder.

The ICC interpretation of the provision found in international criminal law is more nebulous. The Court has considered that children who are in "real danger as a potential target" is focusing on the level of danger involved *vis-à-vis* the children. However, it has only thought of real danger being applied by external forces. So even in applying something of a child-sensitive approach, the Court has failed to consider the fact that real danger to children comes from both within and outside the ranks and could include sexual exploitation. One challenge here though, is the nexus to armed conflict, and how close that has to be to the actual violation. However, it should be sufficient to consider, as the Court did, that the overall context constituted an armed conflict.

The test introduced by the ICC of being in "real danger as a potential target" was, as stated, to be determined on a case-by-case basis. The Court did not want to go into this issue because it was not raised in the charges by the prosecution. But might the Court also not have wanted to add further confusion to the distinction between "direct" and "active" participation? In the way that the Court distinguished quite clearly between those two aspects of participation, making the considerations in international criminal law somewhat different from those in international humanitarian law, it would not have been a very far stretch – and is perhaps an even further illustration of how different the two terms were – that the threat for being in "real danger as a potential target" could even come from the same warring side. In this case, any act constituting a grave violation of children's rights would have been considered "use to actively participate."

While through this interpretation, criminal law currently stands with a slightly wider interpretation for individual criminal responsibility to arise than could be expected from a traditional interpretation of international humanitarian law had the two terms been coined to mean the same thing, it is actually not useful to compare the two because they come from different bodies of law and their objective of protection has different purposes.

Much in the same way that international humanitarian law prohibits the act and ICC raises individual criminal responsibility, so the difference between active and direct also are from different bodies of law that apply in different contexts. While the notion of active participation exists in humanitarian law, in the context of child recruitment, the direct participation issue concerns targeting.

More generally, the gender aspects are poorly considered in international legal instruments and domestic-level implementation. Practice strongly indicates a problematic exclusion of girls who have been associated with armed groups and forces; the language introduced is often insensitive to the fact that girls also take direct part in hostilities and are left out of mainstream DDR processes as a result. The lack of gender considerations also tends to exclude the possibility that boys may have suffered from sexual and other forms of exploitation and abuse in the ranks.

Within the Rome Statute, there are two additional issues that are still open for further interpretation: the first is to make more out of the disjunctive reading between conscription, enrolment, and use for active participation and to maximize the protective standards; the second is that there is currently no difference between forced and voluntary recruitment in the interpretation of the Statute's language, which can be used to further strengthen overall prohibition against child recruitment.

With respect to the three different crimes: conscription, enrolment, and use – or as the Court now seems to have determined, two different crimes because it is practically impossible to distinguish between forced and voluntary recruitment – this would render useless the introduction of the words "actively participate" by the drafters of the Rome Statute. Nonetheless, it is somewhat like the argument around the difficulties in distinguishing between forced and voluntary, equally difficult to distinguish between what is real danger and what is not in the context of hostilities. Thus, an argument could be construed to state that regardless of how they came into this situation, and regardless of what role they are playing, bringing children into the ranks of an armed group or force is a criminal offence. However, such an argument is still another step behind successfully making the argument related to the issue of sexual violence above.

The attention of the Security Council is helping to build and maintain momentum. While not developing international law, it continues to apply the law in a way that strengthens the standards and pushes the agenda forward, including awareness about child recruitment. This in itself is a driving force towards preventing and addressing the use of children during armed conflicts, and provides a forum for continued attention to the issue. In addition, the

Security Council Working Group conclusions and action plans have made use of the age of 18 in all aspects of its work.

It is useful to draw some conclusions about the application of the law in countries where the Secretary-General's annual report on children and armed conflict raised the issue of child recruitment, because there is evidence that application of the law would be particularly relevant in those situations. Out of the 18 countries where parties have either been listed or included as situations of concern, 13 have ratified the Optional Protocol, and nine have adopted age 18 as admissible for voluntary recruitment. In most situations the armed groups, not the armed forces, are recruiting and using children.

By contrast, of the permanent five members of the Security Council, none have opted for the 18-year limit for voluntary recruitment: three have declared 17 years (Russia pointing out it is for purposes of education under article 3(2) of the Optional Protocol) and two have declared age 16 the legal age for voluntary recruitment. This leaves some "persistent objectors" to a standard for child recruitment of all types moving towards 18.

Among the 18 countries within the Security Council framework, 16 have ratified the ILO Convention 182, only India and Myanmar have not. The standard prohibiting forced recruitment is consistently applied through the Security Council framework both in its action plans and conclusions.

The protection of the rights of children who are recruited and used by armed forces and groups has evolved rapidly in international law over the past 30–40 years and continues to advance with increased intensity. The law is alive and developing and becoming more detailed through practice focused on the ultimate goal of eliminating all recruitment and use of children by armed forces and groups.

2. MOVING FORWARD IN A TRANSITIONAL JUSTICE APPROACH: KEY AREAS FOR COLLABORATIVE AND POLICY/LEGAL ACTION

This section considers the gaps and untapped potential in the interactions between different areas of transitional justice and makes recommendations for key opportunities for collaboration, as well as legal and policy development that should be pursued.

2.1. DOMESTIC IMPLEMENTATION OF THE LAW AND THE COMMITTEE ON THE RIGHTS OF THE CHILD

Considering child recruitment against a transitional justice framework enables a detailed understanding of the components: rule of law, criminal justice, historical justice, reparatory justice, institutional justice, and participatory justice. A holistic approach makes it possible for these areas to reinforce each other, leading to a more effective response to child recruitment.

Building on the current state of the law, the focus now needs to be on implementation, including at the domestic level. This is the sphere within which the law can continue to be strengthened in terms of the standards put in place at the global level, which allow for states to adapt their own laws to a certain extent. This is what needs to be pushed, beginning with putting in place a solid legal framework and systems that can allow for implementation at the domestic level as a critical priority.

Because of the complexities inherent in the different types of issues that arise, the laws and the understanding of these issues need to be strengthened in situations where child recruitment is not necessarily at the forefront. While there are some good domestic legislative approaches, many gaps remain in making the type of law that has evolved at the international level a reality at the domestic level. For instance, the aspect of direct participation may not be sufficiently noted, or the applicability of legislation to armed groups.

The Committee on the Rights of the Child is following up with signatories to OPAC, now a significant number of 150 States parties, each country every few years. But it is not enough, and it is not systematic enough. There needs to be a more concerted effort of giving legal advice and guiding countries on how to prepare implementing frameworks for OPAC.

To date, a General Comment on either of the Optional Protocols has not been considered, but even if a General Comment is far from practical, it can provide a key tool for guiding legal and policy development at the domestic level, and draw out common themes and issues among the countries that have already reported to the Committee regarding the OPAC. The human rights organizations, along with more operational child protection agencies, need to take more of a rule-of-law approach and become leaders in providing legal advice and legal drafting, along with pushing for universal jurisdiction in domestic legislation, as this will also help internationalize increasingly strong legal standards relevant to child recruitment.

Overall, the treaty-based bodies such as the Committee on the Rights of the Child have huge backlogs and very limited capacity between sessions to follow up and carry out important tasks identified in the guidance provided to states through the concluding observations and general comments. This is left for other organizations to do. However, in addition to making a stronger link with the work of the Committee, it would be important for the Committee to prioritize the issues it would want to drive if it wanted to make progress in the various contexts and along thematic streams that have been considered through its concluding observations.

2.2. CRIMINAL JUSTICE

Throughout this study, there have been elements of how other areas of justice could both contribute towards and draw upon the area of criminal justice. For those working in areas related to child recruitment, it is ultimately a good thing that the first case of the ICC focused exclusively on the issue of child recruitment because it provides entry points for how transitional justice with a view to ending child recruitment can be pushed further.

The *Lubanga* case, after all, must be considered a great victory for the cause of transitional justice. Certainly, there are shortcomings in procedural aspects, and considering the overall cost and impact of the judgement, it can be questioned if in the long run this is money best placed to find solutions to child recruitment. However, it is about not losing sight of what is ahead. It is necessary to tackle international crimes through criminal justice procedures as one of many approaches to address grave violations, and child recruitment is a case in point. Many more cases are now following, and though they will not be able to deal with child recruitment in such detail, they will continue to come back to the issue and further elaborate on the law and consider each specific situation according to the details of the case.

The interfaces between different areas of justice do not just impact positively on one another, they also need to consider their potential negative impact so as to minimize it. Even then, transitional justice is a tight balancing act between peace and justice and, as a result, full of compromises. One example would be the danger of an overly strong push for criminal justice to be applied, likely leading to armed groups and forces not wanting to admit that children exist within their ranks, most likely due to the increased negative attention their leaders are receiving.

It is reassuring, however, to note that the *Lubanga* case judgement viewed the absence of a commitment to release children as a contributing factor towards Lubanga's criminal responsibilities, rather than as evidence that there were no children to release. A failure of real effort to identify and release children in the ranks would serve only to prove that the leader knew that the problem existed and that it constituted a war crime, but did nothing to address the issue. While it is difficult to show evidence that leaders of armed groups and forces are concerned about international criminal proceedings, anecdotal information indicates that several commanders have voiced concern over the possibility of being prosecuted for having recruited children.

There is still very limited activity in domestic jurisdictions to bring individuals to justice for child recruitment. Perhaps the experience and analysis brought forward through the *Lubanga* case will change this, but at the same time it is also one of the bargaining chips between peace and justice. In other words, if some of those warlords were to be charged with this type of crime, it would be less likely that the process for transitional justice can move forward. However, as the issue becomes more known, and as institutional capacity is further strengthened to take these issues into account, there will likely be cases in domestic jurisdictions as well, whereby it will be important to further build the capacities of all those involved, including defence lawyers, in dealing with such cases so as to keep the standard of "beyond reasonable doubt."

There is potential for a much stronger link to be made between aspects of historical justice and criminal and reparatory justice. Oftentimes, monitoring and reporting on child rights violations becomes an end in itself, and the operational aspects of addressing those violations are only considered in abstract. Therefore, it is important that operational organizations are involved in monitoring and reporting and vice versa. Although these are two areas with distinct expertise, being involved does not necessarily mean that one has to take over the other, rather that they are engaged and consider the benefits of what the other actors are doing. To move this forward, further efforts should be made to ensure the information on grave violations on children's rights that is already publicly available is highlighted as a source of evidence for international criminal tribunals.

While there are concerns about the very limited nature of the counts in the case against Lubanga, compared to the crimes that he had committed, from a macro justice perspective it can still make sense that there was only one count. Whose justice is justice through the *Lubanga* case? It has been found that the crimes related to child recruitment were not that much of a priority for people on the ground. Obviously, it would have been good to find a better match between what people consider as the key crimes carried out by Lubanga and what the charges were, but at the same time, this judgement is not only applicable to this context. Its ramifications will be far broader than just in the context of the Democratic Republic of the Congo. The case law will be used and interpreted again by the ICC, it will be used by other courts, and it will influence decisions of commanders in other wars.

2.3. THE SECURITY COUNCIL MONITORING AND REPORTING MECHANISM

The information gleaned through the Security Council monitoring and reporting mechanism (MRM) is not currently used in any comprehensive way for broader transitional justice purposes – other than the mechanism itself. In this regard, the issue of child recruitment through the mechanism receives attention at both the Security Council and country level through direct contact with armed forces and groups through the UN system.

Much more can be done to promote the link between the MRM and formal and informal transitional justice mechanisms, including the UN human rights machinery. Unfortunately, the political nature of the mechanism does not lend itself to big progressive steps forward, especially while there are very complex conflicts raging in the Middle East and vast differences in the political agendas of the permanent five members of the Security Council. But on the ground, where the mechanism is effective, the mere connection to the Security Council can be used as a great motivator in getting things done.

Further arguments need to be construed around the issue of forced and voluntary recruitment based on real-time historical evidence from the field. As suggested in the chapter on historical justice, the monitoring and reporting exercise would benefit from gathering data on this aspect, so as to develop trends and analysis of what the situation is on the ground. There will always be grey zones, and this if anything is context specific, yet that analysis would be important input into any other transitional justice process.

Historical justice can be an effective way to identify the key gaps in institutional justice and to develop some type of priorities in what institutions will be most needed in the transitional justice process. The evidence gathered through the Security Council mechanism, for instance, furnishes useful information and direction for action to be taken when it is analysed over time.

The monitoring and reporting mechanism brings in a unique mix of historical justice with politics and action to address the violations. It begins to compare situations and draw up criteria that can allow one situation to be measured against another. It provides background information useful for many purposes. But it is constrained by international politics in addition to local politics, and it is constrained by security considerations both for those who collect the information and those who give the information.

2.4. RECOVERY AND REINTEGRATION

The reparations scheme developed through the *Lubanga* case is exciting yet frightening. Again, as a matter of principle, it should be seen as a great victory to those who work in different areas of transitional justice, as it is often a much overlooked element or partial response. This is the beginning of the ICC making the most out of a reparations scheme, and it is promising to note that the Chamber requested outreach to experts as part of the implementation process.

What is recovery and reintegration for these children? As already noted in the introduction, "rehabilitation" programmes for children affected by war started during the late 1980s. Through more than 25 years of programming experience, many lessons have shaped what is good practice and how this work can be successfully carried out. There are many factors, however, and there is great danger in the ICC reparations schemes coming up with new types of reparations that may just be relearning the old lessons and not have much success, or even worse, undermine existing recovery and reintegration programming. Even in the reparations decision by the Court, there was little effort to reach out and consider those lessons learned, which would have been an important element for both the prosecution and the defence to prepare an informed perspective.

Certainly, the point should be considered of not being seen to provide support to child soldiers with individual gains, leading potentially to resentment and even more children joining in case where there is re-recruitment because there are more opportunities to get benefits once out of the ranks. These types of hidden messages need to be carefully considered in a recovery and reintegration process if they are going to make sense from a justice perspective. Justice is both about the actual event and action, and the perceived action or inaction.

Guidance prepared for child DDR has some limited references to transitional justice and what should be done in situations where it may be better not to just send the children home, but to go through some type of justice process that recognizes any wrongdoing they might have been involved in. There is some experience in this area, but it would be worth considering further, including through research and how children and communities alike have come to terms with the reconciliation processes and the need to take into account children's responsibilities in the release process.

Depending on the context, this is an area that could be further considered in the context of developing peace agreements; if there were a clear process in place already at that level, it would be easier to argue for its case in the implementation.

Some response to address child recruitment can be done through international organizations of one type or another, but at the end of the day, it is the national institutions that need to be able to protect and fulfil the rights of the child, and therefore, this is where investments must be made.

The institutions involved in responding to the overall needs of children will be the same ones that will be helpful in setting up reparations schemes and informing the orientation of those schemes, so there is a very close link between these areas of work. As we have seen from the *Lubanga* case reparations process, there is important outreach to both communities and service providers as part of deciding on the implementation of the reparations.

The power of business is not to be underestimated in light of the current downturn of public expenditure and the increased role of business in sustainable development. While the exploration of business responsibilities vis-à-vis human rights is a relatively new undertaking, businesses are non-state entities that enter into voluntary arrangements at the global level. Such arrangements can also be turned into domestic initiatives, including legislation that will make these companies bound by their "voluntary commitments." Hence, it is important to develop implementing legislation that concerns private military security companies' responsibility to respect children's rights and not recruit children to become part of their forces.

Peace agreements used to be an important trademark in conflict situations, but recent years have not produced the same level of outcome. This has led to great concern among practitioners who have developed expertise in this area of work, and while it will be important to keep children's issues on the agenda of ceasefire and peace talks, the current potential seems to be somewhat limited. The contemporary complexities in politics of the conflicts that are raging, and the fact that the armed groups fighting the wars are on the United States' list of terrorist groups, makes gathering around the table to discuss peace and transition much more difficult.

Linking up the treaty bodies and other actors working in this space with national human rights institutions to identify key priorities would be another important avenue to consider. This could be a matter of identifying long-term thematic priorities along with few country-specific priorities with a number of countries.

2.5. CHILDREN'S PARTICIPATION

Participation of children in transitional justice processes must be approached with caution. Some processes are by nature less child-friendly than others. Any judicial setting does not have a great potential of becoming a child-friendly forum, nor have recent efforts in the SCSL and the ICC turned out to be great success. Perhaps the experience is still insufficient to draw conclusions, but it would certainly for the moment lead to the conclusion that it is not worth the effort.

Evidence related to violations against children's rights can be established through other means than the physical presence of children in courtrooms. Also, it should be carefully considered if it is necessary to speak to children as witnesses at all. Is it in their best interests? Is it strictly indispensable for the case? Since there are so many other tests applied in these cases, it would be most effective to introduce a "strictly necessary" and "best interests" test before engaging children in international criminal justice processes. This could usefully be done in consultation with children.

Forums for adjudging international crimes and identifying those most responsible are not venues for children to be considered as perpetrators of crimes. International law establishes, and the Paris Commitments strengthen, the protective framework for children who are captured by or surrender to a warring party. In the context of international crimes, children are to be primarily considered as victims.

Based on working with these issues for the past 20 years, the concept for this study was to approach the issue of participatory justice and children as alleged perpetrators of international crimes with an open mind, without overlooking the situations where children have been caught in trials lacking due process with the end verdict being a death sentence. It has been mentioned many times before, but once more it should be emphasized that each situation is unique, and each child is unique, even though some issues need to be addressed in responding to the needs of most children in the group concerned.

When all the considerations of how to hold a child accountable for international crimes are taken to their logical conclusion, it does not make sense to charge children with international crimes in any forum. This does not preclude the necessity of children taking responsibility for their crimes, but is rather based on the evidence that the international and national justice systems are not ready to handle such charges against children appropriately. It is far from the best interests of the children to involve them when both they and the judicial systems are not properly prepared for the process. In addition, in the context of armed conflict, the inherently political dimensions come to play and, generally, children are not charged under the appropriate jurisdictions.

A restorative justice approach considers children as participants in the transitional justice process, rather than faultless and passive victims. It recognizes the crimes that children may have committed, but with a view to bringing them back home to their communities, where they can live and thrive. The foundation of restorative justice, as reflected in the Convention on the Rights of the Child, is an approach that promotes every "child's sense of dignity and worth, which reinforces the child's respect for the human rights and fundamental freedoms of others and which takes into account the child's age and the desirability of promoting the child's reintegration and the child's assuming a constructive role in society."[646]

Child recruitment is not only one of the most developed areas of law in the child rights arena, it is also one of the more popular areas of research related to children in armed conflicts. Perhaps following this focus on child recruitment, it may also be possible to develop further research in other areas affecting children in the years to come using the same approach.

The Key Principles for Children and Transitional Justice: Involvement of Children and Considerations of Children's Rights in Truth, Justice and Reconciliation Processes constitute an important instrument. This "soft law" instrument is particularly useful for the processes involved. However, the Key Principles can benefit from an accompanying practical guide and broader stakeholder consultation among a wide range of practitioners coming from beyond the traditional transitional justice field. A practical guide could also help address some of the misguided authors who have been quite vocal about children's responsibility for international crimes over the past several years. The reason it has come up as such a big issue is partly that it has not been well addressed by the actors involved.

---

[646] Convention on the Rights of the Child, article 40(1).

Yes, more can be done to make restorative justice processes accessible to children, but formal justice processes dealing with international crimes are not a good place for children to exercise their right to recovery and reintegration. At the end of the day, children should not have needed to be in the ranks of the armed forces and groups in the first place.

The current political context is not very promising for making big advances in addressing the issue of child recruitment. Continued emphasis on the fight against terrorism and the raging conflicts in the Middle East, Central Asia, and Africa deepen both political and religious divides, making it difficult to address even specific and relatively well-defined issues such as child recruitment in a comprehensive way. Nonetheless, there are continued efforts to monitor, report, and take action to address child recruitment across the globe, with the ultimate goal of each girl and boy in the ranks of armed groups and forces being released and able to return back to their families and communities. And the answer then, to the question about whether transitional justice is realized only when and if it is successful, is that even if the process fails to achieve the expected outcome it is transition, sometimes for the better, sometimes for the worse, but constantly with a push in applying the law for the situation to get better.

ANNEXES

ANNEX 1. SECURITY COUNCIL WORKING GROUP CONCLUSIONS AS OF SPRING 2015

	Country	2006	2007	2008	2009	2010	2011	2012	2013	2014
1	Afghanistan			S/2008/695			S/2011/55			
2	Burundi	S/2006/851	S/2007/686		S/2009/450	Delisted				
3	CAR				S/2009/66		S/2011/241	S/2012/365 (LRA)		
4	Chad		S/2007/400	S/2008/532			S/2011/64			
5	Colombia				S/2009/434			S/2012/171		
6	Côte d'Ivoire	S/2006/835	S/2007/515	Delisted						
7	DRC	S/2006/389	S/2007/391	S/2008/693		S/2010/369		S/2012/365 (LRA)		S/2014/453
8	Iraq						S/2011/366			
9	Mali (2013)									S/2014/267
10	Myanmar		S/2007/666		S/2009/278				S/2013/258	
11	Nepal	S/2006/1007		S/2008/259		S/2010/183		Delisted		
12	Philippines			S/2008/272		S/2010/36			S/2013/419	
13	Somalia		S/2007/259	S/2008/352		S/2010/577				
14	Sri Lanka	S/2006/1006	S/2007/758		S/2009/325		S/2011/793	Delisted		
15	Sudan	S/2006/662	S/2007/520		S/2009/84		S/2011/413	S/2012/365 (LRA)		
16	South Sudan									S/2014/884
17	Syria (2012)									2/2014/31
18	Uganda		S/2007/250	S/2008/409	S/2009/462			S/2012/365 (LRA)		
19	Yemen								S/2013/383	

ANNEX 2. COUNTRY REPORTS AS OF SPRING 2015

	Country	2006-2007	2008	2009	2010	2011	2012-2013	2014
1	Afghanistan			S/AC.51/2009/1		S/AC.51/2011/3		
2	Burundi	S/2007/92	S/AC.51/2008/6	S/AC.51/2009/6	Delisted			
3	CAR			S/AC.51/2009/2				
4	Chad	S/AC.51/2007/16	S/AC.51/2008/15			S/AC.51/2012/4		
5	Colombia				S/AC.51/2010/3		S/AC.51/2012/4	
6	Cote d'Ivoire	S/2007/93	S/AC.51/2008/5 Delisted					
7	DRC	S/2006/724		S/AC.51/2009/3		S/AC.51/2011/1		S/AC.51/2014/4
8	Iraq					S/AC.51/2011/6		
9	Mali (2013)							S/AC.51/2014/2
10	Myanmar		S/AC.51/2008/8	S/AC.51/2009/4			S/AC.51/2013/2	
11	Nepal	S/AC.51/2007/8	S/AC.51/2008/12		S/AC.51/2010/4		Delisted	
12	Philippines		S/AC.51/2008/10					S/AC.51/2014/1
13	Somalia	S/AC.51/2007/14	S/AC.51/2008/14			S/AC.51/2011/2		
14	Sri Lanka	S/AC.51/2007/9	S/AC.51/2008/11		S/AC.51/2010/2		S/AC.51/2012/3 Delisted	
15	Sudan	S/2006/971	S/AC.51/2008/7	S/AC.51/2009/5			S/AC.51/2012/1	
16	South Sudan						S/AC.51/2012/2	
17	Syria							S/AC.51/2014/4
18	Uganda	S/AC.51/2007/12	S/AC.51/2008/13		S/AC.51/2010/1			
19	Yemen						S/AC.51/2013/3	
	LRA						S/AC.51/2013/1	

ANNEX 3. OVERVIEW OF RATIFICATIONS/ ENDORSEMENTS MADE IN RELATION TO CHILD RECRUITMENT FOR COUNTRIES RELEVANT TO THE MRM

Country	Listed/country of concern in S-G's Report	CRC and OP-CAAC	Paris Commitments: a) Attendance b) Endorsement	a) GCs b) AP 1, c) AP 2	Rome Statute ratification / ILO 182
Afghanistan	Listed and on SC Agenda	a. 1994 (CRC) b. 2003 (OP) (a) Art. 3(2): 22	a) Attended b) Endorsed (2007)	a. 1956 (GC) b. 2009 (API) c. 2009 (APII)	10.02.2003 07.04.2010
Burundi	Delisted 2010	a. 1990 (CRC) b. 2008 (OP) Art. 3(2): 18	a) Attended b) Endorsed (2007)	a. 1971 (GC) b. 1993 (API) c. 1993 (APII)	21.09.2004 11.06.2002
CAR	Listed and on SC Agenda	a. 1992 (CRC) b. ------ (OP)	a) Did not attend b) Endorsed (2009)	a. 1966 (GC) b. 1984 (API) c. 1984 (APII)	03.10.2001 28.06.2000
Chad	Listed and on SC Agenda	a. 1990 (CRC) b. 2002 (OP) Art. 3(2): 18	a) Attended b) Endorsed (2007)	a. 1970 (GC) b. 1997 (API) c. 1997 (APII)	01.11.2006 06.11.2000
Colombia	Listed (in Annex II) and not on SC Agenda	a. 1991 (CRC) b. 2005 (OP) Art. 3(2): 18	a) Attended b) Endorsed (2007)	a. 1961 (GC) b. 1993 (API) c. 1995 (APII)	05.08.2002 28.01.2005
Cote d'Ivoire	Delisted 2008 but on SC Agenda	a. 1991 (CRC) b 2012 (OP) (a) Art. 3:2: 18 ex training	a) Attended b) Endorsed (2007)	a. 1961 (GC) b. 1989 (API) c. 1989 (APII)	------ 07.02.2003
DRC	Listed and on SC Agenda	a. 1990 (CRC) b. 2001 (OP) Art. 3(2): 18 / 20	a) Attended b) Endorsed (2007)	a. 1961 (GC) b. 1982 (API) c. 2002 (APII)	11.04.2002 20.06.2001
India	Situation of concern	a. 1992 (CRC) (a) b. 2005 (OP) Art. 3(2): 16 recr; 18 ops	a) Did not attend b) Did not endorse	a. 1950 (GC) b. ------- (API) c. ------- (APII)	------ ------

Country	Listed/country of concern in S-G's Report	CRC and OP-CAAC	Paris Commitments: a) Attendance b) Endorsement	a) GCs b) AP 1, c) AP 2	Rome Statute ratification / ILO 182
Iraq	Listed and on SC Agenda	a. 1994 (CRC) (a) b. 2008 (OP) Art. 3(2): 18	a) Did not attend b) Did not endorse	a. 1956 (GC) b. 2010 (API) c. ------- (APII)	------ 09.07.2001
OPT / Israel	Situation of concern and on SC Agenda	a. 1991 (CRC) b. 2005 (OP) Art. 3(2): 18 (combat) / 17 (recruit)	a) Did not attend b) Did not endorse (2009)	a. 1951 (GC) b. -------- (API) c. -------- (APII)	------ 15.03.2005
Lebanon	Not listed in in Annexes but on the SC Agenda	a. 1991 (CRC) b. ------ (OP)	a) Did not attend b) Did not endorse		------ 11.09.2001
Libya	Not listed in Annexes but on the SC Agenda	a. 1993 (CRC) (a) b. 2004 (OP) Art. 3(2): 18	a) Did not attend b) Did not endorse		------ 04.10.2000
Mali	Listed and on SC Agenda	a. 1990 (CRC) b. 2002 Art. 3(2): 18	a) Attended b) Endorsed (2007)	a. 1965 (GC) b. 1989 (API) c. 1989 (APII)	16.08.2000 14.07.2000
Myanmar	Listed and on SC Agenda	a. 1991 (CRC) (a) b. ------ (OP)	a) Did not attend b) Did not endorse	a. 1992 (GC) b. ------ (API) c. ------ (APII)	------ ------ ------ ------
Nepal	Delisted 2012	a. 1990 (CRC) b. 2007 (OP) Art. 3(2): 18	a) Attended b) Endorsed (2007)	a. 1964 (GC) b. ------- (API) c. ------- (APII)	------ 03.01.2002
Pakistan	Situation of concern	a. 1990 (CRC) b. ------ (OP)	a) Did not attend b) Did not endorse	a. 1951 (GC) b. -------- (API) c. -------- (APII)	------ 11.10.2001
Philippines	Listed (in Annex II) and not on the SC Agenda	a. 1990 (CRC) b. 2003 (OP) Art. 3(2): 18 (except for training)	a) Did not attend b) Did not endorse	a. 1952 (GC) b. 2012 (API) c. 1986 (APII)	30.08.2011 28.11.2000

Country	Listed/country of concern in S-G's Report	CRC and OP-CAAC	Paris Commitments: a) Attendance b) Endorsement	a) GCs b) AP 1, c) AP 2	Rome Statute ratification / ILO 182
Somalia	Listed and on SC Agenda	a. ------- (CRC) b. -------- (OP)	a) Attended b) Endorsed (2007)	a. 1962 (GC) b. ------ (API) c. ------ (APII)	------ ------ ------ ------
South Sudan	Listed and on SC Agenda	a. ------- (CRC) b. -------- (OP)	a) Did not attend b) Did not endorse	a. 2013 b. 2013 c. 2013	------ 29.04.2012
Sri Lanka	Delisted 2012	a. 1991 (CRC) b. 2000 (OP) Art. 3(2): 18	a) Attended b) Endorsed (2007)	a. 1959 (GC) b. ---- (API) c. ---- (APII)	------ 01.03.2001
Sudan	Listed and on SC Agenda	a. 1990 (CRC) b. 2005 (OP) Art. 3(2): 18	a) Attended b) Endorsed (2007)	a. 1957 (GC) b. 2006 (API) c. 2006 (APII)	------ 07.03.2003
Syria	Listed and on the SC Agenda	a. 1993 (CRC) b. 2003 (OP) (a) Art. 3(2): 18	a) Did not attend b) Did not endorse	a. 1953 b. 1983 c. ------	------ 22.05.2003
Thailand	Situation of concern	a. 1992 (CRC) (a) b. 2006 (OP) Art. 3(2): 18	a) Did not attend b) Did not endorse	a. 1954 b. ------ c. ------	------ 16.02.2001
Uganda	Listed and on SC Agenda: LRA	a. 1990 (CRC) b. 2002 (OP) Art. 3(2): 18	a) Attended b) Endorsed (2007)	a. 1964 (GC) b. 1991 (API) c. 1991 (APII)	14.06.2002 21.06.2001
Yemen	Listed and on SC Agenda	a. 1991 (CRC) b. 2007 (OP)	a) Did not attend b) Endorsed (2012)	a. 1970 b. 1990 c. 1990	------ 15.06.2000
China	Not included	a. 1992 (CRC) b. 2008 (OP) Art. 3(2): 17	a) Attended b) Endorsed (2007)	a. 1956 (GC) b. 1983 (API) c. 1983 (APII)	------ 08.08.2002
France	Not included	a. 1990 (CRC) b. 2003 (OP) Art. 3(2): 17	a) Attended b) Endorsed (2007)	a. 1951 (GC) b. 2001 (API) c. 1984 (APII)	09.06.2000 11.09.2001

Country	Listed/country of concern in S-G's Report	CRC and OP-CAAC	Paris Commitments: a) Attendance b) Endorsement	a) GCs b) AP 1, c) AP 2	Rome Statute ratification / ILO 182
Russia	Not included	a. 1990 (CRC) b. 2008 (OP) Art. 3(2): 18 / 16 (military academy)	a) Attended b) Endorsed (2007)	a. 1954 (GC) b. 1989 (API) c. 1989 (APII)	------ 25.03.2003
UK	Not included	a. 1991 (CRC) b. 2003 (OP) Art. 3(2): 16	a) Attended b) Endorsed (2007)	a. 1957 (GC) b. 1998 (API) c. 1998 (APII)	04.10.2001 22.03.2000
US	Not included	a. ------- (CRC) – s b. 2002 (OP) Art. 3(2): 17	a) Did not attend b) Did not endorse	a. 1955 (GC) b. ------ (API) – s c. ------ (APII) – s	------ 02.12.1999

BIBLIOGRAPHY

DOMESTIC LEGISLATION

Australia, Australia: Criminal Code Act. 1995, amended 2007.

Australia, International Criminal Court (Consequential Amendments) Act. 2002.

Azerbaijan, Criminal Code. 1999.

Belgium, Act on Serious Violations of International Humanitarian Law. 5 August 2003.

Canada, Crimes against Humanity and War Crimes Act. 2000.

Canada, National Defence Act. 1985, amended 2000.

China, Military Service Law of the People's Republic of China. Adopted in 1984 and amended in 1998.

Colombia, Code for Infants and Adolescents. 2006.

Colombia, Criminal Code, Law No. 599. 2000.

Croatia, Penal Code. 2002.

Democratic Republic of Congo, Child Protection Code. 2009.

Eritrea, Proclamation 11/1991. 1991.

Finland, Act 365/2000 Amendment of Conscription Act. 2000.

Germany, Act to Introduce the Code of Crimes against International Law. 26 June 2002.

Guatemala, Integral Law for the Protection of Children and Adolescents. 2003.

Indonesia, Law Number 23 Year 2002 on Child Protection. 2002.

Ireland, International Criminal Court Act. 2006.

Israel, Israel Defence Service Law 5746. 1986.

Kazakhstan, Children's Rights Act. 2002.

Moldova, Law No. 162-XVI on the Status of Military Personnel. 22 July 2005.

Netherlands, International Crimes Act. 19 June 2003.

Norway, General Civil Penal Code No 54. 28 June 2002.

Pakistan, The Pakistan National Service Ordinance. 1970.

Portugal, Law Adapting Criminal Legislation to ICC Statute. 2004.

South Africa, Implementation of the Rome Statute of the International Criminal Court, Act No 27. 2002.

Sri Lanka, Penal Code (Amendment) Act, No. 16 of 2006. 24 April 2006.

Sudan, The Child Act. 2010.

Switzerland, Military Penal Code. 23 December 2003.

The Interim National Constitution of the Republic of Sudan (2005). 2005.

The Philippines, Republic Act No. 9231: Act Providing for the Elimination of the Worst Forms of Child Labor and Affording Stronger Protection for the Working Child, amending for this purpose republic Act No. 7610, as amended, otherwise known as the "special Protection of Children against Child Abuse, Exploitation and Discrimination Act. December 19, 2003.

United Kingdom, International Criminal Court Act. 2001.
United States of America, Child Soldiers Accountability Act. 2008.
United States of America, US War Crimes Statute. 2008.
Yemen, Law No. 45 on Child Rights. 2002.

TREATIES

African Charter on the Rights and Welfare of the Child, 1990, Organization of African Unity, African Charter on the Rights and Welfare of the Child, 11 July 1990, CAB/LEG/24.9/49.
Convention Against Torture and Other Cruel, Inhuman or Degrading Treatment or Punishment 10 December 1984, United Nations, Treaty Series, vol. 1465, p. 85.
Convention on the Rights of the Child, 1989, 28 I. L. M. 1448 (1989).
Convention Relating to the Status of Refugees, 1951, United Nations, Treaty Series, vol. 189, p. 137.
Council of Europe, European Convention for the Protection of Human Rights and Fundamental Freedoms, as amended by Protocols Nos. 11 and 14, 4 November 1950, ETS 5.
Geneva Convention relative to the Protection of Civilian Persons in Time of War, 12 August 1949, 75 U.N.T.S. 287.
Geneva Convention relative to the Treatment of Prisoners of War, 12 August 1949,
ILO Convention No. 182: Worst Forms of Child Labour Convention, 1999,
Optional Protocol to the Convention on the Rights of the Child on the Involvement of Children in Armed Conflict, 2000, 39 ILM 1286 (2000).
Optional Protocol to the Convention on the Rights of the Child on a Communications Procedure, Adopted by the UN General Assembly on 19 December 2012 (A/RES/66/138), and opened for signature on 28 February 2012. Not yet in force.
Organization of American States, American Convention on Human Rights, "Pact of San Jose", Costa Rica, 22 November 1969,
Protocol Additional to the Geneva Conventions of 12 August 1949, and Relating to the Protection of Victims of International Armed Conflicts (Protocol I), 1125 U.N.T.S. 3.
Protocol Additional to the Geneva Conventions of 12 August 1949, and Relating to the Protection of Victims of Non-International Armed Conflicts (Protocol II), 1125 U.N.T.S. 609.
Protocol I Additional to the Geneva Conventions of 12 August 1949, 1977.
Protocol II Additional to the Geneva Conventions of 12 August 1949, 1977.
The Rome Statute of the International Criminal Court, 1998.
Vienna Convention on the Law of Treaties, 1969.

SECURITY COUNCIL MATERIALS

Conclusions on Children and Armed Conflict in Afghanistan, United Nations Security Council Working Group on Children and Armed, UN Doc. S/AC.51/2011/3 (03 May 2011).

Conclusions on Children and Armed Conflict in Afghanistan, —, UN Doc. S/AC.51/2009/1 (13 July 2009).
Conclusions on Children and Armed Conflict in Burundi, —, UN Doc. S/AC.51/2009/6 (S/AC.51/2009/6).
Conclusions on Children and Armed Conflict in Chad, —, UN Doc. S/AC.51/2011/4 (03 May 2011).
Conclusions on Children and Armed Conflict in Chad, —, UN Doc. S/AC.51/2008/15 (5 December 2008).
Conclusions on Children and Armed Conflict in Chad, —, UN Doc. S/AC.51/2007/16 (24 September 2007).
Conclusions on Children and Armed Conflict in Colombia, —, UN Doc. S/AC.51/2010/3 (30 September 2010).
Conclusions on Children and Armed Conflict in Cote d'Ivoire, Conflict, —, UN Doc. S/AC.51/2008/5 (1 February 2008).
Conclusions on Children and Armed Conflict in Iraq, —, UN Doc. S/AC.51/2011/6 (03 October 2011).
Conclusions on Children and Armed Conflict in Mali, —, UN Doc. S/AC.51/2014/2 (7 July 2014).
Conclusions on Children and Armed Conflict in Myanmar, —, UN Doc. S/AC.51/2013/2 (16 August 2013).
Conclusions on Children and Armed Conflict in Myanmar, —, UN Doc. S/AC.51/2009/4 (28 October 2009).
Conclusions on Children and Armed Conflict in Myanmar, —, UN Doc. S/AC.51/2008/8 (25 July 2008).
Conclusions on Children and Armed Conflict in Nepal, —, UN Doc. S/AC.51/2008/12 (5 December 2008).
Conclusions on Children and Armed Conflict in Nepal, —, UN Doc. S/AC.51/2007/8 (12 June 2007).
Conclusions on Children and Armed Conflict in Somalia, —, UN Doc. S/AC.51/2011/2 (1 March 2011).
Conclusions on Children and Armed Conflict in Somalia, —, UN Doc. S/AC.51/2008/14 (5 December 2008)
Conclusions on Children and Armed Conflict in Somalia, —, UN Doc. S/AC.51/2007/14 (20 July 2007).
Conclusions on the Situation of Children and Armed Conflict in Sri Lanka, —, UN Doc. S/AC.51/2012/3 (21 December 2012).
Conclusions on Children and Armed Conflict in Sri Lanka, —, UN Doc. S/AC.51/2010/2 (3 June 2010).
Conclusions on Children and Armed Conflict in Sri Lanka, —, UN Doc. S/AC.51/2008/11 (21 October 2008).
Conclusions on Children and Armed Conflict in Sri Lanka, —, UN Doc. S/AC.51/2007/9 (13 June 2007).
Conclusions on Children and Armed Conflict in the Central African Republic, —, UN Doc. S/AC.51/2009/2 (13 July 2009).
Conclusions on Children and Armed Conflict in the Democratic Republic of the Congo, —, UN Doc. S/AC.51/2014/3 (19 September 2014).

Conclusions on Children and Armed Conflict in the Democratic Republic of the Congo, —, UN Doc. S/AC.51/2011/1 (1 March 2011).

Conclusions on Children and Armed Conflict in the Democratic Republic of Congo, —, UN Doc. S/AC.51/2009/3 (13 July 2009).

Conclusions on Children and Armed Conflict in the Philippines, —, UN Doc. S/AC.51/2008/10 (3 October 2008).

Conclusions on Children and Armed Conflict in the Philippines, —, UN Doc. S/AC.51/2014/1 (19 February 2014).

Conclusions on Children and Armed Conflict in the Sudan, —, UN Doc. S/AC.51/2008/7 (5 February 2008).

Conclusions on Children and Armed Conflict in the Sudan, —, UN Doc. S/AC.51/2012/1 (11 October 2012).

Conclusions on Children and Armed Conflict in the Sudan, —, UN Doc. S/AC.51/2009/5 (21 December 2009).

Conclusions on Children and Armed Conflict in the Syrian Arab Republic, —, UN Doc. S/AC.51/2014/4 (26 November 2014).

Conclusions on Children and Armed Conflict in Uganda, —, UN Doc. S/AC.51/2010/1 (16 June 2010).

Conclusions on Children and Armed Conflict in Uganda, —, UN Doc. S/AC.51/2008/13 (5 December 2008).

Conclusions on Children and Armed Conflict in Uganda, —, UN Doc. S/AC.51/2007/12 (20 July 2007).

Conclusions on Children and Armed Conflict in Yemen, —, UN Doc. S/AC.51/2013/3 (9 December 2013).

Conclusions on the Situation of Children and Armed Conflict Affected by the Lord's Resistance Army, —, UN Doc. S/AC.51/2013/1 (22 April 2013).

Conclusions on the Situation of Children and Armed Conflict in Colombia, —, UN Doc. S/AC.51/2012/4 (21 December 2012).

Conclusions on the Situation of Children and Armed Conflict in South Sudan, —, UN Doc. S/AC.51/2012/2 (11 October 2012).

Letter Dated 1 December 2006 from the Permanent Representative of France to the United Nations Addressed to the President of the Security Council (Conclusions on Sudan), —, (13 December 2006).

Letter Dated 13 February 2007 from the Permanent Representative of France to the United Nations Addressed to the President of the Security Council (Conclusions on Children and Armed Conflict in Burundi), —, (15 February 2007).

Letter Dated 13 February 2007 from the Permanent Representative of France to the United Nations Addressed to the President of the Security Council (Conclusions on Cote d'Ivoire), —, (15 February 2007).

Letter Dated 14 January 2008 from the President of the Security Council to the Chairman of the Security Council Committee Established Pursuant to Resolution 1533 (2004) Concerning the Democratic Republic of Congo, —, (14 January 2008).

Letter Dated 2 May 2006 from the Permanent Representative of France to the United Nations Addressed to the President of the Security Council (Terms of Reference of the Working Group of the Security Council on Children and Armed Conflict), Council, United Nations Security, (3 May 2006).

Letter Dated 22 December 2000 from the President of the Security Council Addressed to the Secretary-General, —, S/2000/1234 (22 December 2000).
Letter dated 4 April 2007 from the Permanent Representatives of Myanmar, Nepal, the Philippines, Sri Lanka, the Sudan and Uganda to the United Nations addressed to the Secretary-General, (9 April 2007).
Letter Dated 4 April 2007 from the Permanent Representatives of Myanmar, Nepal, the Philippines, Sri Lanka, the Sudan and Uganda to the United Nations Addressed to the Secretary-General, —, (9 April 2007).
Letter Dated 8 September 2006 from the Permanent Representative of France to the United Nations Addressed to the President of the Security Council (Conclusions on Democratic Republic of Congo), Conflict, United Nations Security Council Working Group on Children and Armed, (11 September 2006).
Message to the Head of the Lord's Resistance Army Delegation to the Juba Peace Talks through a Public Statement by the Chairman of the Working Group to be Transmitted by the Special Envoy for the Areas Affected by the Lord's Resistance Army, —, (20 July 2007).
Security Council Resolution on Children and Armed Conflict, Council, United Nations Security, UN Doc. S/RES/1882 (4 August 2009).
Security Council Resolution on Women and Peace and Security, —, UN Doc. S/RES/1889 (2009) (5 October 2009).
Security Council Resolution on Children and Armed Conflict, —, UN Doc. S/RES/1314 (11 August 2000).
Security Council Resolution on Children and Armed Conflict, —, UN Doc. S/RES/1998 (12 July 2011).
Security Council Resolution on the Situation in Chad, —, UN Doc. S/RES/1861 (14 January 2009).
Security Council Resolution on Protection of Civilians, —, UN Doc. S/RES/1296 (19 April 2000).
Security Council Resolution on Women and Peace and Security, —, UN Doc. S/RES/1820 (19 June 2008).
Security Council Resolution on Children and Armed Conflict, —, UN Doc. S/RES/2068 (19 September 2012).
Security Council Resolution on Children and Armed Conflict, —, UN Doc. S/RES/1539 (22 April 2004).
Security Council Resolution on Sierra Leone, —, UN Doc. S/RES/1270 (22 October 1999).
Security Council Resolution on Children and Armed Conflict, —, UN Doc. S/RES/1612 (26 July 2005).
Statement by the President of the Security Council on Children and Armed Conflict, —, UN Doc. S/PRST/2009/9 (29 April 2009).
Security Council Resolution on Children and Armed Conflict, —, UN Doc. S/RES/1261 (30 August 1999).
Security Council Resolution on Children and Armed Conflict, —, UN Doc. S/RES/1460 (30 January 2003).
Security Council Resolution on the Democratic Republic of Congo, —, UN Doc. S/RES/1279 (30 November 1999).

Security Council Resolution on Women and Peace and Security, —, UN Doc. S/RES/1888 (2009) (30 September 2009).
Security Council Resolution on Sudan, —, UN Doc S/RES/1706 (31 August 2006).
Security Council Resolution on Women and Peace and Security, —, UN Doc. S/RES/1325 (31 October 2000).
Statement by the President of the Security Council on Children and Armed Conflict, —, S/PRST/1999/21 (8 July 1999).
Statement by HE Mr. Than Swe, Permanent Representative of the Union of Myanmar to the United Nations at the Open Debate on Children and Armed Conflict at the United Nations Security Council, Myanmar, Government of, (29 April 2009).
Statement by Mrs. Sansanee Sahussarungsi, Charge d'affaires, a.i. Permanent Mission of Thailand to the United Nations at the Open Debate of the Security Council on Agenda Item "Children and Armed Conflict", Thailand, Government of, (29 April 2009).
Statement by the Chairman Addressed to the Leadership of the Liberation Tigers of Tamil Eelam, —, UN Doc. S/AC.51/2007/10 (13 June 2007).
Statement by the Chariman Addressed to the Leadership of the Tamil Makkal Viduthalai Puligal and its Military Wing, the Karuna Faction, —, UN Doc.
Statement by the President of the Security Council on Children and Armed Conflict, —, UN Doc. SC/PRST/1998/18 (1998).
Statement Delivered by HE Mr. Jean-Maurice Ripert, Ambassador, Permanent Representative of France to the United Nations, France, Government of, (29 April 2009).

COMMITTEE ON THE RIGHTS OF THE CHILD

Concluding observations on the initial report of Burkina Faso submitted under article 8, paragraph 1, of the Optional Protocol to the Convention on the Rights of the Child on the involvement of children in armed conflict, adopted by the Committee at its sixty-second session, Committee on the Rights of the Child, UN Doc. CRC/C/OPAC/BFA/CO/1, (26 June 2013).
Concluding observations on the initial report of China submitted under article 8, paragraph 1, of the Optional Protocol to the Convention on the Rights of the Child on the involvement of children in armed conflict, adopted by the Committee at its sixty-fourth session, —, UN Doc. CRC/C/OPAC/CHN/CO/1, (29 October 2013).
Concluding observations on the initial report of Paraguay submitted under article 8, paragraph 1, of the Optional Protocol to the Convention on the Rights of the Child on the involvement of children in armed conflict, adopted by the Committee at its sixty-fourth session, —, UN Doc. CRC/C/OPAC/PRY/CO/1, (25 October 2013).
Concluding observations on the initial report of Slovakia submitted under article 8, paragraph 1, of the Optional Protocol to the Convention on the Rights of the Child on the involvement of children in armed conflict, adopted by the Committee at its sixty-second session, —, UN Doc. CRC/C/OPAC/SVK/CO/1, (26 June 2013).
Concluding observations on the initial report of Uzbekistan submitted under article 8, paragraph 1, of the Optional Protocol to the Convention on the Rights of the Child

on the involvement of children in armed conflict, adopted by the Committee at its sixty-third session, —, UN Doc. CRC/C/OPAC/UZB/CO/1, (8 July 2013).

Concluding observations on the report submitted by Bolivarian Republic of Venezuela under article 8, paragraph 1, of the Optional Protocol to the Convention on the Rights of the Child on the involvement of children in armed conflict, —, UN Doc. CRC/C/OPAC/VEN/CO/1, (3 November 2014).

Concluding observations on the report submitted by Cambodia under article 8, paragraph 1, of the Optional Protocol to the Convention on the Rights of the Child on the involvement of children in armed conflict, —, UN Doc. UN Doc. CRC/C/OPAC/KHM/CO/1, (23 February 2015).

Concluding observations on the report submitted by Hungary under article 8, paragraph 1, of the Optional Protocol to the Convention on the Rights of the Child on the involvement of children in armed conflict, —, UN Doc. CRC/C/OPAC/HUN/CO/1, (3 November 2014).

Concluding observations on the report submitted by India under article 8, paragraph 1, of the Optional Protocol to the Convention on the Rights of the Child on the involvement of children in armed conflict, —, UN Doc. CRC/C/OPAC/IND/CO/1, (7 July 2014).

Concluding observations on the report submitted by Jordan under article 8, paragraph 1, of the Optional Protocol to the Convention on the Rights of the Child on the involvement of children in armed conflict, —, UN Doc. CRC/C/OPAC/JOR/CO/1 (7 July 2014).

Concluding observations on the report submitted by Morocco under article 8, paragraph 1, of the Optional Protocol to the Convention on the Rights of the Child on the involvement of children in armed conflict, —, UN Doc. CRC/C/OPAC/MAR/CO/1 (13 November 2014).

Concluding observations on the report submitted by Portugal under article 8, paragraph 1, of the Optional Protocol to the Convention on the Rights of the Child on the involvement of children in armed conflict, —, UN Doc. CRC/C/OPAC/PRT/CO/1, (24 February 2014).

Concluding observations on the report submitted by Singapore under article 8, paragraph 1, of the Optional Protocol to the Convention on the Rights of the Child on the involvement of children in armed conflict, —, UN Doc. CRC/C/OPAC/SGP/CO/1, (13 October 2014).

Concluding observations on the report submitted by the Holy See under article 8, paragraph 1, of the Optional Protocol to the Convention on the Rights of the Child on the involvement of children in armed conflict, —, UN Doc. CRC/C/OPAC/VAT/CO/1 (25 February 2014).

Concluding observations on the report submitted by the Russian Federation under article 8, paragraph 1, of the Optional Protocol to the Convention on the Rights of the Child on the involvement of children in armed conflict, —, UN Doc. CRC/C/OPAC/RUS/CO/1 (25 February 2014).

Concluding observations on the report submitted by Yemen under article 8, paragraph 1, of the Optional Protocol to the Convention on the Rights of the Child on the involvement of children in armed conflict, —, UN Doc. CRC/C/OPAC/YEM/CO/1 (26 February 2014).

Concluding observations on the second report of United States of America submitted under article 8, paragraph 1, of the Optional Protocol to the Convention on the Rights of the Child on the involvement of children in armed conflict, adopted by the Committee at its sixty-second session, —, UN Doc. CRC/C/OPAC/USA/CO/2, (26 June 2013).

Consideration of Reports Submitted by States Parties under Article 44 of the Convention, Concluding Observations: Liberia, —, UN Doc. CRC/C/15/Add.236 (1 July 2004).

Consideration of Reports Submitted by States Parties under Article 8 of the Optional Protocol to the Convention on the Rights of the Child on the Involvement of Children in Armed Conflict, Concluding Observations: Costa Rica, —, UN Doc. CRC/C/OPAC/CRI/CO/1 (1 May 2007).

Consideration of Reports Submitted by States Parties under Article 8 of the Optional Protocol to the Convention on the Rights of the Child on the Involvement of Children in Armed Conflict, Concluding Observations: Sri Lanka, —, UN Doc. CRC/C/15/Add.207 (2 July 2003).

Consideration of Reports Submitted by States Parties under Article 8 of the Optional Protocol to the Convention on the Rights of the Child on the Involvement of Children in Armed Conflict, Concluding Observations: El Salvador, —, UN Doc. CRC/C/OPAC/SLV/CO/1 (2 June 2006).

Consideration of Reports Submitted by States Parties under Article 8 of the Optional Protocol to the Convention on the Rights of the Child on the Involvement of Children in Armed Conflict, Concluding Observations: Kyrgyzstan, —, UN Doc. CRC/C/OPAC/KGZ/CO/1 (2 May 2007).

Consideration of Reports Submitted by States Parties under Article 8 of the Optional Protocol to the Convention on the Rights of the Child on the Involvement of Children in Armed Conflict, Concluding Observations: Croatia, —, UN Doc. CRC/C/15/Add.243 (3 November 2004).

Consideration of Reports Submitted by States Parties under Article 8 of the Optional Protocol to the Convention on the Rights of the Child on the Involvement of Children in Armed Conflict, Concluding Observations: The Republic of the Maldives, —, UN Doc. CRC/C/OPAC/MDV/CO/1 (4 March 2009).

Consideration of Reports Submitted by States Parties under Article 8 of the Optional Protocol to the Convention on the Rights of the Child on the Involvement of Children in Armed Conflict, Concluding Observations: Israel, —, UN Doc. CRC/C/OPAC/ISR/CO/1, (4 March 2010).

Consideration of Reports Submitted by States Parties under Article 8 of the Optional Protocol to the Convention on the Rights of the Child on the Involvement of Children in Armed Conflict, Concluding Observations: Sweden, —, UN Doc. CRC/C/OPAC/SWE/CO/1 (6 July 2007).

Consideration of Reports Submitted by States Parties under Article 8 of the Optional Protocol to the Convention on the Rights of the Child on the Involvement of Children in Armed Conflict, Concluding Observations: Norway, —, UN Doc. CRC/C/OPAC/NOR/CO/1 (6 July 2007).

Consideration of Reports Submitted by States Parties under Article 8 of the Optional Protocol to the Convention on the Rights of the Child on the Involvement of

Children in Armed Conflict, Concluding Observations: Sudan, —, UN Doc. CRC/C/OPAC/SDN/CO/1 (8 October 2010).

Consideration of Reports Submitted by States Parties under Article 8 of the Optional Protocol to the Convention on the Rights of the Child on the Involvement of Children in Armed Conflict, Concluding Observations: Sudan, —, UN Doc. CRC/C/OPAC/SDN/CO/1 (8 October 2010).

Consideration of Reports Submitted by States Parties under Article 8 of the Optional Protocol to the Convention on the Rights of the Child on the Involvement of Children in Armed Conflict, Concluding Observations: Belgium, —, UN Doc. CRC/C/OPAC/BEL/CO/1 (9 June 2006).

Consideration of Reports Submitted by States Parties under Article 8 of the Optional Protocol to the Convention on the Rights of the Child on the Involvement of Children in Armed Conflict, Concluding Observations: Canada, —, UN Doc. CRC/C/OPAC/CAN/CO/1 (9 June 2006).

Consideration of Reports Submitted by States Parties under Article 8 of the Optional Protocol to the Convention on the Rights of the Child on the Involvement of Children in Armed Conflict, Concluding Observations: United-Republic of Tanzania, —, UN Doc. CRC/C/OPAC/TZA/CO/1 (10 October 2008).

Consideration of Reports Submitted by States Parties under Article 8 of the Optional Protocol to the Convention on the Rights of the Child on the Involvement of Children in Armed Conflict, Concluding Observations: Australia, —, UN Doc. CRC/OPAC/AUS/CO/1 (11 July 2012).

Consideration of Reports Submitted by States Parties under Article 8 of the Optional Protocol to the Convention on the Rights of the Child on the Involvement of Children in Armed Conflict, Concluding Observations: Guatemala, —, UN Doc. CRC/C/OPAC/GTM/CO/1 (12 June 2007).

Consideration of Reports Submitted by States Parties under Article 8 of the Optional Protocol to the Convention on the Rights of the Child on the Involvement of Children in Armed Conflict, Concluding Observations: Oman, —, UN Doc. CRC/C/OPAC/OMN/CO/1 (12 June 2009).

Consideration of Reports Submitted by States Parties under Article 8 of the Optional Protocol to the Convention on the Rights of the Child on the Involvement of Children in Armed Conflict, Concluding Observations: Slovenia, —, UN Doc. CRC/C/OPAC/SVN/CO/1 (12 June 2009).

Consideration of Reports Submitted by States Parties under Article 8 of the Optional Protocol to the Convention on the Rights of the Child on the Involvement of Children in Armed Conflict, Concluding Observations: Chile, —, UN Doc. CRC/C/OPAC/CHL/CO/1 (13 February 2008).

Consideration of Reports Submitted by States Parties under Article 8 of the Optional Protocol to the Convention on the Rights of the Child on the Involvement of Children in Armed Conflict, Concluding Observations: Germany, —, UN Doc. CRC/C/OPAC/DEU/CO/1 (13 February 2008).

Consideration of Reports Submitted by States Parties under Article 8 of the Optional Protocol to the Convention on the Rights of the Child on the Involvement of Children in Armed Conflict, Concluding Observations: Kuwait, —, UN Doc. CRC/C/OPAC/KWT/CO/1 (13 February 2008).

Consideration of Reports Submitted by States Parties under Article 8 of the Optional Protocol to the Convention on the Rights of the Child on the Involvement of Children in Armed Conflict, Concluding Observations: Ireland, —, UN Doc. CRC/C/OPAC/IRL/CO/1 (14 February 2008).
Consideration of Reports Submitted by States Parties under Article 8 of the Optional Protocol to the Convention on the Rights of the Child on the Involvement of Children in Armed Conflict, Concluding Observations: Timor-Leste, —, UN Doc. CRC/C/OPAC/TLS/CO/1 (14 February 2008).
Consideration of Reports Submitted by States Parties under Article 8 of the Optional Protocol to the Convention on the Rights of the Child on the Involvement of Children in Armed Conflict, Concluding Observations: Sierra Leone, —, CRC/C/OPAC/SLE/CO/1 (14 October 2010).
Consideration of Reports Submitted by States Parties under Article 8 of the Optional Protocol to the Convention on the Rights of the Child on the Involvement of Children in Armed Conflict, Concluding Observations: The Philippines, —, UN Doc. CRC/C/OPAC/PHL/CO/1 (15 July 2008).
Consideration of Reports Submitted by States Parties under Article 8 of the Optional Protocol to the Convention on the Rights of the Child on the Involvement of Children in Armed Conflict, Concluding Observations: France, —, UN Doc. CRC/C/OPAC/FRA/CO/1 (15 October 2007).
Consideration of Reports Submitted by States Parties under Article 8 of the Optional Protocol to the Convention on the Rights of the Child on the Involvement of Children in Armed Conflict, Concluding Observations: Luxembourg, —, UN Doc. CRC/C/OPAC/LUX/CO/1 (15 October 2007).
Consideration of Reports Submitted by States Parties under Article 8 of the Optional Protocol to the Convention on the Rights of the Child on the Involvement of Children in Armed Conflict, Concluding Observations: Andorra, —, UN Doc. CRC/C/OPAC/AND/CO/1 (17 March 2006).
Consideration of Reports Submitted by States Parties under Article 8 of the Optional Protocol to the Convention on the Rights of the Child on the Involvement of Children in Armed Conflict, Concluding Observations: Bangladesh, —, UN Doc. CRC/C/OPAC/BGD/CO/1 (17 March 2006).
Consideration of Reports Submitted by States Parties under Article 8 of the Optional Protocol to the Convention on the Rights of the Child on the Involvement of Children in Armed Conflict, Concluding Observations: Switzerland, —, UN Doc. CRC/C/OPAC/CHE/CO/1 (17 March 2006).
Consideration of Reports Submitted by States Parties under Article 8 of the Optional Protocol to the Convention on the Rights of the Child on the Involvement of Children in Armed Conflict, Concluding Observations: Kazakhstan, —, CRC/C/OPAC/KAZ/CO/1 (17 October 2006).
Consideration of Reports Submitted by States Parties under Article 8 of the Optional Protocol to the Convention on the Rights of the Child on the Involvement of Children in Armed Conflict, Concluding Observations: Malta, —, UN Doc. CRC/C/OPAC/MLT/CO/1 (17 October 2006).
Consideration of Reports Submitted by States Parties under Article 8 of the Optional Protocol to the Convention on the Rights of the Child on the Involvement of

Children in Armed Conflict, Concluding Observations: Viet Nam, —, UN Doc. CRC/C/OPAC/VNM/CO/1 (17 October 2006).
Consideration of Reports Submitted by States Parties under Article 8 of the Optional Protocol to the Convention on the Rights of the Child on the Involvement of Children in Armed Conflict, Concluding Observations: Qatar, —, UN Doc. CRC/C/OPAC/QAT/CO/1 (17 October 2007).
Consideration of Reports Submitted by States Parties under Article 8 of the Optional Protocol to the Convention on the Rights of the Child on the Involvement of Children in Armed Conflict, Concluding Observations: Spain, —, UN Doc. CRC/C/OPAC/ESP/CO/1 (17 October 2007).
Consideration of Reports Submitted by States Parties under Article 8 of the Optional Protocol to the Convention on the Rights of the Child on the Involvement of Children in Armed Conflict, Concluding Observations: Syrian Arab Republic, —, UN Doc. CRC/C/OPAC/SYR/CO/1 (17 October 2007).
Consideration of Reports Submitted by States Parties under Article 8 of the Optional Protocol to the Convention on the Rights of the Child on the Involvement of Children in Armed Conflict, Concluding Observations: Uganda, —, UN Doc. CRC/C/OPAC/UGA/CO/1 (17 October 2008).
Consideration of Reports Submitted by States Parties under Article 8 of the Optional Protocol to the Convention on the Rights of the Child on the Involvement of Children in Armed Conflict, Concluding Observations: United Kingdom of Great Britain and Northern Ireland, —, UN Doc. CRC/C/OPAC/GBR/CO/1 (17 October 2008).
Consideration of Reports Submitted by States Parties under Article 8 of the Optional Protocol to the Convention on the Rights of the Child on the Involvement of Children in Armed Conflict, Concluding Observations: Sri Lanka, —, CRC/C/OPAC/LKA/CO/1 (19 October 2010).
Consideration of Reports Submitted by States Parties under Article 8 of the Optional Protocol to the Convention on the Rights of the Child on the Involvement of Children in Armed Conflict, Concluding Observations: Republic of Moldova, —, UN Doc. CRC/C/OPAC/MDA/CO/1 (20 February 2009).
Consideration of Reports Submitted by States Parties under Article 8 of the Optional Protocol to the Convention on the Rights of the Child on the Involvement of Children in Armed Conflict, Concluding Observations: Thailand, —, CRC/C/OPAC/THA/CO/1 (21 February 2012).
Consideration of Reports Submitted by States Parties under Article 8 of the Optional Protocol to the Convention on the Rights of the Child on the Involvement of Children in Armed Conflict, Concluding Observations: Czech Republic, —, UN Doc. CRC/C/OPAC/CZE/CO/1 (21 June 2006).
Consideration of Reports Submitted by States Parties under Article 8 of the Optional Protocol to the Convention on the Rights of the Child on the Involvement of Children in Armed Conflict, Concluding Observations: Iceland, —, UN Doc. CRC/C/OPAC/ISL/CO/1 (21 June 2006).
Consideration of Reports Submitted by States Parties under Article 8 of the Optional Protocol to the Convention on the Rights of the Child on the Involvement of Children in Armed Conflict, Concluding Observations: Colombia, —, CRC/C/OPAC/COL/CO/1 (21 June 2010).

Consideration of Reports Submitted by States Parties under Article 8 of the Optional Protocol to the Convention on the Rights of the Child on the Involvement of Children in Armed Conflict, Concluding Observations: Finland, —, UN Doc. CRC/C/OPAC/FIN/CO/1 (21 October 2005).
Consideration of Reports Submitted by States Parties under Article 8 of the Optional Protocol to the Convention on the Rights of the Child on the Involvement of Children in Armed Conflict, Concluding Observations: Italy, —, UN Doc. CRC/C/OPAC/ITA/CO/1 (23 June 2006).
Consideration of Reports Submitted by States Parties under Article 8 of the Optional Protocol to the Convention on the Rights of the Child on the Involvement of Children in Armed Conflict, Concluding Observations: Bulgaria, —, UN Doc. CRC/C/OPAC/BGR/CO/1 (23 October 2007).
Consideration of Reports Submitted by States Parties under Article 8 of the Optional Protocol to the Convention on the Rights of the Child on the Involvement of Children in Armed Conflict, Concluding Observations: CROATIA, —, UN Doc. CRC/C/OPAC/HRV/CO/1 (23 October 2007).
Consideration of Reports Submitted by States Parties under Article 8 of the Optional Protocol to the Convention on the Rights of the Child on the Involvement of Children in Armed Conflict, Concluding Observations: Denmark, —, UN Doc. CRC/C/OPAC/DNK/CO/1 (24 November 2005).
Consideration of Reports Submitted by States Parties under Article 8 of the Optional Protocol to the Convention on the Rights of the Child on the Involvement of Children in Armed Conflict, Concluding Observations: United States of America —, UN Doc. CRC/C/OPAC/USA/CO/1 (25 June 2008).
Consideration of Reports Submitted by States Parties under Article 8 of the Optional Protocol to the Convention on the Rights of the Child on the Involvement of Children in Armed Conflict, Concluding Observations: Republic of Korea, —, UN Doc. CRC/C/OPAC/KOR/CO/1 (27 June 2008).
Day of General Discussion on Children in Armed Conflict, Committee on the Rights of the Child, UN Doc. CRC/C/10 (1992).
General Comment No. 16: On State obligations regarding the impact of the business sector on children's rights, Child, Committee on the Rights of the, UN Doc. CRC/C/GC/10 (15 March 2013).
General Comment No. 12: The Right of the Child to be Heard, —, UN Doc. CRC/C/GC/12 (20 July 2009).
General Comment No. 10: Children's Rights in Juvenile Justice, —, UN Doc. CRC/C/GC/10 (25 April 2007).
General Comment No. 5 (2003), —, UN Doc. CRC/GC/2003/5 (27 November 2003).
General Comment 17, The Rights of the Child, Article 24 (Thirty-fifth session, 1989), Human Rights Committee, UN Doc. HRI/GEN/Rev.1 (1994).
General Guidelines regarding the Form and Content of Period Reports to be Submitted by States Parties under Article 44, Paragraph 1 (b), of the Convention, —, UN Doc. CRC/C/58/Rev.1 (29 November 2005).
Revised Guidelines regarding Initial Reports to be Submitted by States Parties under Article 8, Paragraph 1, of the Optional Protocol to the Convention on the Rights of

the Child on Involvement of Children in Armed Conflict, Committee on the Rights of the Child, —, UN Doc. CRC/C/OPAC/2 (19 October 2007).

SOFT LAW, GUIDELINES AND RESOLUTIONS

Advisory Opinion Regarding the International Standards for Exclusion from Refugee Status as Applied to Child Soldiers, —, (12 September 2005).

Basic Principles and Guidelines on the Right to a Remedy and Reparation for Victims of Gross Violations of International Human Rights Law and Serious Violations of International Humanitarian Law, UN Doc. A/Res/60/147 (21 March 2006).

Cape Town Principles and Best Practices, adopted at a symposium on the prevention of the recruitment of children into armed conflicts and on demobilization and on social reintegration of child soldiers in Africa, (Cape Town, 30 April 1997).

Code of conduct for the International Red Cross and Red Crescent Movement and non-governmental organisations in Disaster Relief, (1994).

Declaration on the Protection of Women and Children in Emergencies and Armed Conflicts, UN Doc. 3318(XXIX) (1974).

Guidelines on International Protection: Application of the Exclusion Clauses: Article 1F of the 1951 Convention relating to the Status of Refugees, UNHCR, UN Doc. HCR/GIP/03/05 (4 September 2003).

Guidelines on International Protection: Child Asylum Claims under Articles 1(A)2 and 1(F) of the 1951 Convention relating to the Status of Refugees, —, UN Doc. HCR/GIP/09/08 (22 December 2009).

Guidelines on Justice Matters Involving Child Victims and Witnesses of Crime, UN Doc. Economic and Social Council Resolution 2005/20 (22 July 2005).

International Criminal Court, Elements of Crimes, Nations, United, UN Doc. PCNICC/2000/1/Add.2 (7 April 2000).

Key Principles for Children and Transitional Justice: Involvement of Children and Considerations of Children's Rights in Truth, Justice and Reconciliation Processes, (2009).

Montreux Document on Pertinent International Legal Obligations and Good Practices for States Related to Operations of Private Military and Security Companies During Armed Conflict, Swiss Initiative, in Cooperation with the International Committee of the Red Cross, (17 September 2008).

Nairobi Declaration on Women's and Girls' Right to a Remedy and Reparation, (2007).

Negotiated Relationship Agreement between the International Criminal Court and the UNICEF Nations, ICC-ASP/3/Res.1 (entered into force 4 October 2004).

Note on the Exclusion Clauses, Programme, Executive Committee of the High Commissioner's, UN Doc. EC/47/SC/CRP.29 (30 May 1997).

On the Establishment of Panels with Exclusive Jurisdiction over Serious Criminal Offences, Timor, United Nations Transitional Administration in East, UN Doc. UNTAET/REG/200/15 (6 June 2000).

Protection of Children in Armed Conflicts, Resolution 9, 25th International Conference of the Red Cross (Geneva 23 to 31 October 1986).

Resolution on Protection of Children Affected by Armed Conflicts, UN Doc. A/RES/48/157 (20 December 1993).
Resolution XIV: Civil War, Conference, Xth International Red Cross, (Geneva 1921).
Resolution XIV: Role and Activity of the Red Cross in time of Civil War, Conference, XVIth International Red Cross, (London, 1938).
Rules of Procedure and Evidence, UN Doc. PCNICC/2000/1/Add.1 (2000).
The Children's Rights and Business Principles, UNICEF, UN Global Compact, and Save the Children, (12 March 2012).
The International Code of Conduct for Private Security Service Providers, (2010).
The International Code of Conduct for Private Security Service Providers' Association: Articles of Association, (2013).
The Paris Commitments to Protect Children from Unlawful Recruitment or Use by Armed Forces or Armed Groups, (2007).
The Paris Principles and Guidelines on Children Associated with Armed Forces or Armed Groups, (February 2007).
The Voluntary Principles on Security and Human Rights, (December 2000).
UNICEF Child Protection Strategy, UNICEF, E/ICEF/2008/5/Rev.1 (20 May 2008).
United Nations General Assembly Resolution on the Rights of the Child, UN Doc. A/RES/51/77 (20 February 1997).
United Nations Security Council Resolution on Children and Armed Conflict, UN Doc. S/RES/1379 (20 November 2001).
United Nations Standard Minimum Rules for the Administration of Juvenile Justice ("The Beijing Rules"), Assembly, General, UN Doc. A/40/53 (29 November 1985).
Vienna Declaration and Programme of Action, UN Doc. A/Conf.157/23 (12 July 1993).

ACTION PLANS

"Afghanistan: Action Plan between the Government of the Islamic Republic of Afghanistan and the United Nations Country Task Force on Monitoring and Reporting regarding children associated with National Security Forces in Afghanistan." 30 January 2011.
"Central African Republic: Accord pour l'elimination de l'enrolment et de l'utilisation des enfants soldats leur demobilisation et reintegration entre Le Gouvernement de la République Centrafricaine, UNICEF, et Le Mouvement Politico-Militaire Union des Forces Démocratiques pour le Rassemblement (UFDR)." 16 June 2007.
"Central African Republic: Engagements des groupes politcio-militaires participant au forum de Bangui pour mettre fin au recrtement et a l'utilisation des enfants ainsi que les autres violations graves des droits de l'enfant." 4 May 2015.
"Central African Republic: Plan d'action entre Convention of Patriots for Justice and Peace (CPJP) et l'Equipe speciale des Nations Unies chargée du mécanisme de surveillance et de communication de l'information en République Centrafricaine sur les enfants associés à la CPJP." 20 November 2011.
"Central African Republic: Plan d'action entre L'Armée Populaire pour la Restauration de la Démocratic (ARPD) et l'Equipe speciale des Nations Unies chargée du

mécanisme de surveillance et de communication de l'information en République Centrafricaine sur les enfants associés aux l'APRD". 19 October 2011.
"Chad: Plan d'action sur les enfants associés aux force et groups armés au Tchad entre le Government du Tchad et l'Equipe special des Nations Unies chargée du mécanisme de surveillance et de communication de l'information sur les violations grave des droits de l'enfant dans les conflits armés." 14 June 2011.
"Chad: Protocole d'accord sur la protection des Enfant victimes des conflits armés et leur réinsertion durable entre le Ministre des Relations Extérieures et Le Bureau des Fonds des Nations Unies pour L'Enfance au Tchad (UNICEF)." 9 May 2007.
"Democratic Republic of Congo: Plan d'action pour la lutte contre le recrutement et l'utilisation d'enfant ainsi que les autres violations graves des droits de l'enfant par les forces armées et les services de sécurité de la République Démocratique du Congo entre le Gouvernement de la République Démocratique du Congo et l'Equipe Spéciale des Nations Unies sur les enfants et les conflits armés." 4 October 2012.
"Ivory Coast: Plan d'Action contre l'utilisation des enfant associés aux conflit armés. Forces de Résistance du Grand Ouest de la Côte d'Ivoire." 14 September 2006.
"Ivory Coast: Plan d'action des Forces Armées des Forces Nouvelles pour mettre fin à l'utilisation des Enfants fréquentant les lieux de rassemblement militaires, Côte d'Ivoire." 10 October 2005.
"Myanmar: Deed of Commitment, Office of the Supreme Headquarters, Karen National Union, Kawthoolei." 4 March 2007.
"Myanmar: Deed of Commitment: Chin National Front/Army." 15 March 2009.
"Myanmar: Memorandum of Understanding and the Signing Ceremony of Plan of Action between the Republic of Myanmar of the Union of Myanmar and the Country Task Force on Monitoring and Reporting." 27 June 2012.
"Nepal: Action Plan between the Government of Nepal, the Unified Communist Party of Nepal – Maoist, and the United Nations in Nepal regarding the Discharge of Disqualified Maoist Army Personnel and Related Tasks." 16 December 2009.
"Somalia: Action Plan between the Transitional Federal Government of Somalia, Somali National Armed Forces and the United Nations regarding Children Associated with the Somali National Armed Forces." 03 July 2012.
"Somalia: Action Plan between the Transitional Federal Government of Somalia, Somali National Armed Forces and the United Nations to eliminate killing and maiming of children in contravention of international law." 6 August 2012.
"South Sudan: Action Plan between the Sudan People's Liberation Army (SPLA) and the United Nations Regarding Children Associated with the SPLA in Southern Sudan." 20 November 2009.
"Sri Lanka: Action Plan – Addressing the Needs and Care for the Children in the North East Affected by War." 22 April 2003.
"Sri Lanka: Action Plan between the Tamil Makkal Viduthalain Puligal (TMVP) and the Commissioner General of Rehabilitation, Government of Sri Lanka and the United Nations Children's Fund (UNICEF) regarding Children Associated with the TMVP." 1 December 2008.
"Sudan: Action Plan between the Sudan Liberation Movement/Army (SLM/A) and the United Nations Children's Fund regarding Children associated with the SLM/A." 11 June 2007.

"Sudan: Memorandum of Understanding between the Justice and Equality Movement (JEM) and the United Nations regarding Protection of Children in Darfur." 21 July 2010.

"Sudan: Sudan Liberation Movement / Abu Gasim: Action Plan (original in Arabic)." 15 August 2010.

"Sudan: Sudan Liberation Movement/Army SLA Free Will (North Darfur State): Action Plan to End Recruitment and Use of Child Soldiers." 14 June 2010.

"The Philippines: Action Plan between the Moro Islamic Liberation Front (MILF) and the United Nations in the Philippines regarding the Issue of Recruitment and Use of Child Soldiers in the Armed Conflict in Mindanao." 1 August 2009.

"Uganda: Action Plan between the Government of the Republic of Uganda and the Uganda Country Task Force on Monitoring and Reporting regarding Children Associated with Armed Forces in Uganda." 16 January 2009.

"Yemen: Action Plan between the Government of the Republic of Yemen and the United Nations regarding Children Associated with the Yemeni Government Forces." 14 May 2014.

CASE LAW AND COURT PROCEEDINGS

INTERNATIONAL CRIMINAL COURT

Prosecutor V. Ahmad Muhammad Harun ("Ahmad Harun") and Ali Muhammad Al Abd-Al-Rahman ("Au Kushayb"), Decision on the Prosecution Application under Article 58(7) of the Statute, International Criminal Court, ICC-02/05/-01/07 (27 April 2007).

Situation in Darfur, ICC-02/05, Prosecutor's Observations to Cassese's Observations on Issues Concerning the Protection of Victims and the Preservation of Evidence in the Proceedings on Darfur Pending Before the ICC (11 September 2006).

Submission of the Observations of the Special Representative of the Secretary General of the United Nations for Children and Armed Conflict pursuant to Rule 103 of the Rules of Procedure and Evidence, (ICC-01/04–01/06–1229 (2008)).

The Prosecutor v. Bosco Ntaganda, Warrant of Arrest, ICC-01/04–02/06–2-Anx-tENG (22 August 2006).

The Prosecutor v. Joseph Kony, Warrant of Arrest for Joseph Kony issued on 8 July 2005 as amended on 27 September 2005, ICC-02/04–01/05–53 (27 September 2005).

The Prosecutor v. Omar Hassan Ahmad Al Bashir, Warrant of Arrest for Omar Hassan Ahmad Al Bashir, ICC-02/05–01/09–1 (4 March 2009).

The Prosecutor v. Thomas Lubanga Dyilo, Closing Submission of the Defence, ICC-01/04/01/06–2773-Red-tENG (15 July 2011).

The Prosecutor v. Thomas Lubanga Dyilo, Decision Granting Leave to Make Representations in the Reparations Proceedings, ICC-01/04–01/06–2870 (20 April 2012).

The Prosecutor v. Thomas Lubanga Dyilo, ICC-01/04–01/06-T-342-ENG (01 April 2011).

The Prosecutor v. Thomas Lubanga Dyilo, ICC-01/04/-01/06-T-206-ENG (08 July 2009).

The Prosecutor v. Thomas Lubanga Dyilo, International Criminal Court, Case No: ICC-01/04–01/06, Trial Chamber 1, Decision establishing the principles and procedures to be applied to reparations, ICC-01/04–01/06–2904 (7 August 2012).

The Prosecutor v. Thomas Lubanga Dyilo, International Criminal Court, Case No: ICC-01/04–01/06, Transcription No:ICC-01/04–01/06-T-223-ENG (7 January 2010).

The Prosecutor v. Thomas Lubanga Dyilo, International Criminal Court, Case No: ICC-01/04–01/06, UNICEF Submission on the principles to be applied, and the procedure to be followed by the Chamber with regard to reparations, ICC-01/04–01/06–2878 (10 May 2012).

The Prosecutor v. Thomas Lubanga Dyilo, International Criminal Court, Case No: ICC-01/04–01/06, Trial Chamber 1, Judgement Pursuant to Article 74 of the Statute, ICC-01/04–01/06–2842 (14 March 2012).

The Prosecutor v. Thomas Lubanga Dyilo, International Criminal Court, Case No: ICC-01/04–01/06, Transcription No: ICC-01/04–01/06-T-38-EN (20 November 2006).

The Prosecutor v. Thomas Lubanga Dyilo, International Criminal Court, Case No: ICC-01/04–01/06, Transcription No: ICC-01/04–01/06-T-39-EN (21 November 2006).

The Prosecutor v. Thomas Lubanga Dyilo, International Criminal Court, Case No: ICC-01/04–01/06, Transcription No: ICC-01/04–01/06-T-41-EN (22 November 2006).

The Prosecutor v. Thomas Lubanga Dyilo, International Criminal Court, Case No: ICC-01/04–01/06, Transcription No: ICC-01/04–01/06-T-43-EN (23 November 2006).

The Prosecutor v. Thomas Lubanga Dyilo, International Criminal Court, Case No: ICC-01/04–01/06, Transcription No: ICC-01/04–01/06-T-44-EN (24 November 2006).

The Prosecutor v. Thomas Lubanga Dyilo, International Criminal Court, Case No: ICC-01/04–01/06, Transcription No: ICC-01/04–01/06-T-45-EN (27 November 2006).

The Prosecutor v. Thomas Lubanga Dyilo, International Criminal Court, Case No: ICC-01/04–01/06, Transcription No: ICC-01/04–01/06-T-47-EN (28 November 2006).

The Prosecutor v. Thomas Lubanga Dyilo, Judgement on the Appeals of the Prosecutor and the Defence against Trial Chamber I's Decision on Victims' Participation of 18 January 2008, ICC-01/04–01/06–1432 (11 July 2008).

The Prosecutor v. Thomas Lubanga Dyilo, Public Annex 1 to Corrigendum to "Decision on the applications by victims to participate in the proceedings", ICC-01/04–01/06–1556-Corr-Anx1 (13 January 2009).

The Prosecutor v. Thomas Lubanga Dyilo, Separate and Dissenting Opinion of Judge Odio Benito, ICC-01/04 01/06–2842 (14 March 2012).

The Prosecutor v. Thomas Lubanga Dyilo, Warrant of arrest, ICC-01/04–01/06–37 (10 February 2006).

The Prosecutor v. Thomas Lubanga Dyilo, Written Submission of the United Nations Special Representative of the Secretary-General on Children and Armed Conflict, Submitted in application of Rule 103 of the Rules of Procedure and Evidence, (18 March 2008).

The Prosecutor v. Thomas Lubanga Dyilo: Decision on the Confirmation of Charges, International Criminal Court, Case No. ICC-01/04–01/06 (29 January 2007).

The Prosecutor v. Thomas Lubanga Dyilo: Document Containing the Charges, Article 61(3)(a), International Criminal Court, Case No. ICC-01/04–01/06, Reference ICC-01/04–01/06–356-Anx2 (28 August 2006).

SPECIAL COURT FOR SIERRA LEONE

Prosecutor v. Morris Kallon (Case No. SCSL-2004-15-AR72(E)) and Brima Bazzy Kamara (Case No. SCSL-2004-16-AR72(E)), Special Court for Sierra Leone, Appeals Chamber, Decision to Challenge to Jurisdiction: Lomé Accord Amnesty (2004).

Prosecutor v. Samuel Hinga Norman, Special Court for Sierra Leone, Case No. SCSL-2004-14-AR72(E) (31 May 2004).

Prosecutor v. Samuel Hinga Norman: Fourth Defence Preliminary Motion Based on Lack of Jurisdiction (Child Recruitment), Amicus Curiae Brief of the United Nations Children's Fund, Special Court for Sierra Leone, Case No. SCSL-2003-08 (21 January 2004).

The Prosecutor v. Charles Taylor, Special Court for Sierra Leone, Case No. SCSL-03-PT, Prosecution's second amended indictment (2003).

OTHER INTERNATIONAL, HYBRID OR REGIONAL COURTS

Case of Soering v. the United Kingdom, Application no. 14038/88 (07 July 1989).

Prosecutor v. Akayesu, International Criminal Tribunal for Rwanda, Judgement No. ICTR-96-4-T (2 September 1998).

Prosecutor v. Dusko Tadić, Decision on the Defence Motion for Interlocutory Appeal on Jurisdiction, (2 October 1995).

The Case of X: a Child Prosecuted for Crimes against Humanity, Special Panels for Serious Crimes, Dili, Timor Leste Judicial System Monitoring Programme (2005).

The Trial of German Major War Criminals. Proceedings of the International Military Tribunal sitting at Nuremberg, Germany Part 22 (1 October 1946).

Veeber v. Estonia, 45771/99 (21 January 2003).

DOMESTIC COURTS

Magyar Kozlony No. 23/1992, Translated in Journal of Constitutional Law in Eastern and Central Europe 1 (1994): 136. (5 March 1992).

Omar Khadr, Petitioner v. United States of America, US Court of Appeals for the District of Columbia, Case No. 07-1405 (2008).

Penate v. Canada, (26 November 1993).

Poshteh v. Canada, (8 April 2005).

BOOKS

Ayissi, Anatole N., *Le défi de la sécurité régionale en Afrique après la guerre froide vers la diplomatie préventive et la sécurité collective*, Travaux de recherche / UNIDIR. New York, N.Y.: Nations Unies, (1994).

Barnett, Katy, and Anna Jefferys, *Full of promise: How the UN's Monitoring and Reporting Mechanism can better protect children*, Network Paper, Number 62(September 2008).

Bassiouni, M. Cherif, *Crimes Against Humanity: Historical Evolution and Cotemporary Application*. New York: Cambridge University Press, (2011).

Bayefsky, Anne F., and Joan Fitzpatrick, *Human Rights and Forced Displacement*: Martinus Nijhoff Publishers, (2000).

Beah, Ishmael, *A Long Way Gone: Memoirs of a Boy Soldier*. 1st ed. New York: Farrar Straus and Giroux, (2007).

Bell, Christine, *Peace Agreements and Human Rights*: Oxford University Press, USA, (2000).

Brett, Rachel, *Girl soldiers: Challenging the Assumptions*. Geneva: Quaker United Nations Office, (2002).

Brett, Rachel, and Margaret McCallin, *Children: The Invisible Soldiers*. Stockholm: Rädda Barnen, (1998).

Brett, Rachel, and Irma Specht, *Young Soldiers: Why they Choose to Fight*. Geneva: International Labour Organization, (2004).

Briggs, Jimmie, *Innocents Lost when Child Soldiers Go to War*. New York: Basic Books, (2005).

Brooks, Andrew, *The Disarmament, Demobilisation and Reintegration of Children Associated with Fighting Forces*. Dakar: UNICEF, (2005).

Cassese, Antonio, *International Criminal Law, Second Edition*: Oxford University Press, (2008).

Cassese, Antonio, Paola Gaeta, and John R.W.D. Jones, *The Rome Statute of the International Criminal Court: A Commentary*: Oxford University Press, (2002).

Child Protection Working Group, *Child Protection in Emergencies Coordinator's Handbook*, (2009).

—, *Minimum Standards for Child Protection in Humanitarian Action*, (2012).

Cipriani, Don, *Children's Rights and the Minimum Age of Criminal Responsibility*. Surrey: Ashgate Publishing, (2009).

Cohn, Ilene, Guy S. Goodwin-Gill, and Institut Henry-Dunant, *Child Soldiers: The Role of Children in Armed Conflict*: Oxford University Press, (1994).

Inter-Agency Standing Committee, *Mental Health and Psychosocial Support in Humanitarian Emergencies: What Should Humanitarian Health Actors Know?* Geneva: IASC Reference Group for Mental Health and Psychosocial Support in Emergency Settings, (2010).

de Greiff, Pablo, Duthie, Roger and International Centre for Transitional Justice (eds.), *Transitional Justice and Development: Making Connections*. Advancing Transitional Justice Series. New York: Social Science Research Council, (2009).

Detrick, Sharon, *A Commentary on the United Nations Convention on the Rights of the Child*: Martinus Nijhoff Publishers, (1999).

Detrick, Sharon, Jaap Doek, and Nigel Cantwell, *The United Nations Convention on the Rights of the Child: A Guide to the "Travaux Préparatoires"*. Dordrecht: Martinus Nijhoff Publishers, (1992).

Dörmann, Knut, *Elements of War Crimes under the Rome Statute of the International Criminal Court: Sources and Commentary*: Cambridge University Press, (2002).

Drumbl, Mark A., *Reimagining Child Soldiers in International Law and Policy*. New York: Oxford University Press, (2012).

Fleischman, Janet, and Lois Whitman, *Easy Prey: Child Soldiers in Liberia*: Human Rights Watch, (1994).

Gates, Scott, and Simon Reich, *Child soldiers in the age of fractured states*. Pittsburgh: University of Pittsburgh Press, (2010).

Happold, Matthew, *Child Soldiers in International Law*. Manchester: Manchester University Press, (2005).

Harrell, Peter E., *Rwanda's Gamble: Gacaca and a New Model of Transitional Justice*: iUniverse, (2003).

Herz, John H., *From Dictatorship to Democracy: Coping with the Legacies of Authoritarianism and Totalitarianism*. Westport: Greenwood Press, (1982).

Hodgkin, Rachel, and Peter Newell, *Implementation Handbook for the Convention on the Rights of the Child*. Geneva: UNICEF, (2008 (Third Edition)).

Honwana, Alcinda, *Child soldiers in Africa*. Philadelphia: University of Pennsylvania Press, (2006).

International Save the Children Alliance, *Where Peace Begins: Education's Role in Conflict Prevention and Peacebuilding*, (2008).

Keairns, Yvonne E., *The Voices of Girl Child Soldiers*. Geneva: Quaker United Nations Office, (2003).

Kritz, Neil J., *Transitional Justice*: United States Inst. of Peace.

Kuper, Jenny, *International Law concerning Child Civilians in Armed Conflict*: Oxford University Press, USA, (1997).

Lee, Roy S. (ed.), *The International Criminal Court: Elements of Crimes and Rules Of Procedure and Evidence*. Ardsley, NY: Transnational Publishers, (2001).

Lee Roy S (ed.)., *The International Criminal Court: The Making of the Rome Statute, Issues, Negotiations, Results*: Kluwer Law International, (1999).

Machel, Graça, *The Impact of War on Children: A Review of Progress Since the 1996 United Nations Report on the Impact of Armed Conflict on Children*: C. Hurst & Co. Publishers, (2001).

Magarrell, Lisa, *Reparations in Theory and Practice*, Reparations Justice Series. New York: International Center for Transitional Justice, (2007).

McConnan, Isobel, and Sarah Uppard, *Children, Not Soldiers*. London: Save the Children, (2001).

McRae, Robert G., and Dan Hubert, *Human Security and the New Diplomacy: Protecting People, Promoting Peace*: McGill-Queen's University Press, (2001).

Melzer, Nils, *Interpretive Guidance on the Notion of Direct Participation in Hostilities*. Geneva: International Committee of the Red Cross, (2009).

Mertus, Julie, *Women's Participation in the International Criminal Tribunal for the Former Yugoslavia (ICTY): Transitional Justice for Bosnia and Herzegovina*: Washington, DC: Women Waging Peace, (2004).

Meyer, Hubert, *The 12th SS Volume One: The History of the Hitler Youth Panzer Division*. Winnipeg: Stackpole Books, (2005).

Nicolaisen, Hans-Dietrich, *Die Flakhelfer: Luftwaffenhelfer und Marinehelfer im Zweiten Weltkrieg*. Berlin: Ullstein, (1981).

No Peace Without Justice, and UNICEF Innocenti Research Centre, *International Criminal Justice and Children*. Rome: NPWJ/UNICEF, (September 2002).

O'Donnell, Guillermo A., and Philippe C. Schmitter, *Transitions from Authoritarian Rule: Tentative Conclusions about Uncertain Democracies*: Johns Hopkins University Press, (1986).

Office of the United Nations High Commissioner for Human Rights, *Rule-of-Law Tools for Post-Conflict States: National Consultations on Transitional Justice* (2009).

O/SRSG-CAAC, UNICEF, and DPKO, *MRM Field Manual: Monitoring and Reporting Mechanism (MRM) on Grave Violations against Children in Situations of Armed Conflict*. New York: O/SRSG-CAAC, UNICEF, DPKO, (April 2010).

Otto Triffterer, ed., *Commentary on the Rome Statute of the International Criminal Court (Second Edition)*: C.H. Beck, Hart, Nomos, (2008).

Panizzo, Enny and Alcinda Honwana, *Final Evaluation of the Children & War Project: A Program of Save the Children Federation – USA*. Maputo: Save the Children, (1995).

Pictet, Jean S. (ed.), *Commentary: IV Geneva Convention Relative to the Protection of Civilian Persons in Time of War*. Geneva: International Committee of the Red Cross, (1958).

Pigeard, Alain, *L'armée de Napoléon: Organisation et vie quotidienne*. Paris: Tallandier, (2000).

Pilloud, Claude, Yves Sandoz, Christophe Swinarski, Bruno Zimmermann, International Committee of the Red Cross, and Jean Pictet, *Commentary on the Additional Protocols of 8 June 1977 to the Geneva Conventions of 12 August 1949: of 8 June 1977 to the Geneva Conventions of 12 August 1949*. Dordrecht: Martinus Nijhoff Publishers, (1987).

Rosen, David M., *Armies of the Young: Child Soldiers in War and Terrorism*. New Brunswick, N.J.: Rutgers University Press, (2005).

Rosen, David M, *Child Soldiers*: A Reference Handbook. Santa Barbara: ABC-CLIO, (2012).

Sanin, Kyra, and Anna Stirnemann, *Child Witnesses at the Special Court for Sierra Leone*. California: University of California, War Crimes Studies Center, (2006).

Save the Children, *Can the powerful protect? How the UN Security Council needs to shape up to protect children* (2006).

Schabas, William A., *An Introduction to the International Criminal Court, Third Edition*. Cambridge: Cambridge University Press, (2007).

Separated Children In Europe Programme, *Position Paper on Age Assessment in the Context of Separated Children in Europe*. Copenhagen: Save the Children, (2012).

Sharanjeet Parmar, Mindy Jane Roseman, Saudamini Siegrist, Theo Sowa (eds.), *Children and Transitional Justice*. Cambridge: Human Rights Program at Harvard Law School, (2010).

Taylor, Telford, *The Anatomy of the Nuremberg Trials – A Personal Memoir*. New York: Alfred A. Knopf, Inc., (1992).

Teitel, Ruti G., *Transitional Justice*. Oxford: Oxford University Press, (2000).

Tikka, Marko, *Terrorin Aika. Suomen Levottomat Vuodet 1917–1921*. Jyväskylä: Gummerus, (2006).

Triffterer, Otto, *Commentary on the Rome Statute of the International Criminal Court: Observers' Notes*. Oxford: Beck/Hart, (1999).

UNICEF, *The State of the World's Children 1996 (Children in War)*. New York: Oxford University Press, (1996).
—, *Innocenti Digest: Juvenile Justice*. Florence: UNICEF Innocenti, (1998).
—, *Adult Wars, Child Soldiers: Voices of Children Involved in Armed Conflict in the East Asia and the Pacific*: UNICEF Regional Office for East Asia and the Pacific, Bangkok, Thailand, (2002).
—, *Children and Truth Commissions*. Florence: UNICEF, (2010).
—, *Children are Everyone's Business: A practical workbook to help companies understand and address their impact on children's rights*. Geneva: UNICEF, (2012).
UNICEF, Coalition to Stop the Use of Child Soldiers and, *Guide to the Optional Protocol on the Involvement of Children in Armed Conflict* (December 2003).
UNICEF, Office of the Special Representative of the Secretary-General for Children and Armed Conflict and, *Machel Study 10-Year Strategic Review: Children and Conflict in a Changing World*. New York: OSRSG-CAAC and UNICEF, (2009).
United Nations, *IDDRS Module: Children and DDR* (2006).
—, *Integrated Disarmament, Demobilization and Reintegration Standards: Module 5.30 Children and DDR*. New York: United Nations, (2006).
—, *IDDRS Module: Transitional Justice and DDR* (2009).
—, *Integrated Disarmament, Demobilization and Reintegration Standards: Module 6.10 DDR and Security Sector Reform*. New York: United Nations, (2009).
—, *Integrated Disarmament, Demobilization and Reintegration Standards: Module 6.20 Transitional Justice and DDR*. New York: United Nations, (2009).
—, *A New Global Partnership: Eradicate Poverty and Transform Economies Through Sustainable Development*. New York: United Nations Publications, (2013).
—, *Legislative History of the Convention on the Rights of the Child, Volume 1 and 2*(New York and Geneva, 2007).
—, *Guidance Note of the Secretary-General: UN Approach to Justice for Children*. New York: United Nations, (September 2008).
United Nations Office on Drugs and Crime, *Handbook on Restorative Justice Programmes*. New York: United Nations, (2006).
Upton, Anthony F., *The Finnish Revolution 1917–1918*. Minneapolis: University of Minnesota Press, (1980).
Vandewiele, Tiny, *A Commentary on the United Nations Convention on the Rights of the Child: Optional Protocol on the Involvement of Children in Armed Conflicts*: Martinus Nijhoff Publishers, (2006).
Vinjamuri, Leslie, and Aaron P. Boesenecker, *Accountability and Peace Agreements, Mapping trends from 1980 to 2006*: Centre for Humanitarian Dialogue, (September 2007).
Watchlist on Children and Armed Conflict, *Getting It Done and Doing It Right: A Global Study on the United Nations-led Monitoring & Reporting Mechanisms on Children and Armed Conflict* (January 2008).
Watchlist on Children and Armed Conflict, The 1612 Monitoring and Reporting Mechanism: A Resource Pack for NGOs, Second Edition, (2015).
Watson, Geoffrey R., *The Oslo Accords: International Law and the Israeli-Palestinian Peace Agreements*: Oxford University Press, (2000).

Wessells, Michael G., *Child Soldiers: From Violence to Protection*. Cambridge: Harvard University Press, (2006).

BOOK SECTIONS

Aldrich, George H., "Comments on Ternerier's 'Combatants and Non-Combatants'", in Dekker, Iger F., and Harry H.G. Post, *The Gulf War of 1980–1988: The Iran-Iraq War in International Legal Perspective*. Dordrecht, Dordrecht: Martinus Nijhoff Publishers, 1992.

Aptel, Cecile. "International Criminal Justice and Child Protection." In *Children and Transitional Justice*, edited by Mindy Jane Roseman Sharanjeet Parmar, Saudamini Siegrist, Theo Sowa (eds.). Cambridge: Human Rights Program at Harvard Law School, 2010.Brady, Helen. "The System of Evidence in the Statute of the International Criminal Court." In *Essays on the Rome Statute of the International Criminal Court, Volume I*, edited by Flavia Lattanzi and Schabas, William A. Rome: Editrice il Sirente, 2004.

Cassese, Antonio. "The Rationale for International Criminal Justice." In *The Oxford Companion to International Criminal Justice*, edited by Antonio Cassese (editor-in-chief). Oxford: Oxford University Press, 2009.

Cryer, Robert. "Means of Gathering Evidence and Arresting Suspects in Situations of States' Failure to Cooperate." In *The Oxford Companion to International Criminal Justice*, edited by editor-in-chief Antonio Cassese. Oxford: Oxford University Press, 2009.

de Greiff, Pablo. "Establishing Links between DDR and Reparations." In *Disarming the past: Transitional justice and ex-combatants*, edited by Pablo de Greiff Ana Cutter Patel, and Lars Waldorf. New York: Social Science Research Council, 2009.

Happold, Matthew. "Child Recruitment as a Crime under the Rome Statute of the International Criminal Court." In *The Legal Regime of the International Criminal Court: Essays in Memory of Igor Blischenko*, edited by José Doria, Gasser, Hans-Peter and Bassiouni, M. Cherif. Leiden: Brill, 2009.

Mawson, Andrew. "Children, Impunity and Justice: some Dilemmas from Northern Uganda." In *Children in Extreme Situations: Proceedings from the 1998 Alistair Berkley Memorial Lecture*, edited by Lisa Carlson, Mackeson-Sandbach, Megan and Allen, Tim. London: London School of Economics and Political Science, 2000.

Nylund, Bo Viktor. "International Legal Protection for the Recovery and Reintegration of War-affected Children." In *Re-member: Rehabilitation, reintegration and reconciliation of war-affected children*, edited by Cindy Mels Ilse Derluyn, Stephan Parmentier and Wouter Vandenhole. Cambridge: Intersentia, 2012.

Pisani, Nicola. "The Mental Element in International Crime." In *Essays on the Rome Statute of the International Criminal Court, Volume II*, edited by Flavia Lattanzi and Schabas, William A. Ripa di Fagnano Alto: Editrice il Sirente Picoola Societa Cooperative ar.l., 2004.

Schotsmans, Martien. "No Return Home: The (non-)Reintegration of Youth Ex-combatants in Sierra Leone as a Challenge to the Contextualisation of DDR and Transitional Justice." In *Re-member: rehabilitation, reintegration and reconciliation of war-affected children*, edited by Cindy Mels Ilse Derluyn, Stephan Parmentier and Wouter Vandenhole. Cambridge: Intersentia, 2012.

Sereni, Andrea. "Individual Criminal Responsibility." In *Essays on the Rome Statute of the International Criminal Court, Volume II*, edited by Flavia Lattanzi and Schabas, William A. Ripa di Fagnano Alto: Editrice il Sirente Picoola Societa Cooperative ar.l., 2004.

Siegrist, Saudamini. "Child Rights and Transitional Justice." In *Children and Transitional Justice*, edited by Mindy Jane Roseman Sharanjeet Parmar, Saudamini Siegrist, Theo Sowa (eds.). Cambridge: Human Rights Program at Harvard Law School, 2010.

Smith, Alison. "Basic Assumptions of Transitional Justice and Children." In *Children and Transitional Justice*, edited by Mindy Jane Roseman Sharanjeet Parmar, Saudamini Siegrist, Theo Sowa (eds.). Cambridge: Human Rights Program at Harvard Law School, 2010.

Snyder, Ross. "Case Study: The Optional Protocol on the Involvement of Children in Armed Conflict." In *Human Security and the New Diplomacy: Protecting People, Promoting Peace*, 152–161: McGill-Queen's Press, 2001.

Sorger, Carmen, and Eric Hoskins. "Protecting the Most Vulnerable: War-Affected Children." In *Human Security and the New Diplomacy: Protecting People, Promoting Peace*, 134–151: McGill-Queen's Press, 2001.

Specht, Roger Duthie and Irma. "DDR, Transitional Justice, and the Reintegration of Former Child Combatants." In *Disarming the past: Transitional justice and ex-combatants*, edited by Pablo de Greiff Ana Cutter Patel, and Lars Waldorf. New York: Social Science Research Council, 2009.

Venturini, Gabriella. "War Crimes." In *Essays on the Rome Statute of the International Criminal Court, Volume I*, edited by Flavia Lattanzi and Schabas, William A. Ripa di Fagnano Alto: Editrice il Sirente Picoola Societa Cooperative ar.l., 2004.

Wessells, Michael G. "Psychosocial Well-being and the Integration of War-affected Children: Towards a Community Resilience Approach." In *Re-member: Rehabilitation, reintegration and reconciliation of war-affected children*, edited by Cindy Mels, Ilse Derluyn, Stephan Parmentier and Wouter Vandenhole. Cambridge: Intersentia, 2012.

Withers, Lucia. "Release and Reintegration of Child Soldiers: One Part of a Bigger Puzzle." In *Re-member: Rehabilitation, reintegration and reconciliation of war-affected children*, edited by Cindy Mels Ilse Derluyn, Stephan Parmentier and Wouter Vandenhole. Cambridge: Intersentia, 2012.

ARTICLES

Abbott, Amy Beth. "Child soldiers – The use of Children as Instruments of War." *Suffolk Transnational Law Review* 23, (1999): 499.

Amann, Diane Marie. "Calling Children to Account: The Proposal for a Juvenile Chamber in the Special Court for Sierra Leone." *Pepperdine Law Review* 29, (2001–2002): 167–186.

Ayissi, Anatole N. "Protecting Children in Armed Conflict: from Commitment to Compliance." *Disarmament Forum* no. 3 (2002): 5–16.

Bakker, Christine. "Prosecuting International Crimes against Children: The Legal Framework." *Innocenti Working Paper* IWP 2010–13, (June 2010).

Becker, Jo. "Child Soldiers-Changing a Culture of Violence." *Human Rights* 32: 17, (2005): 16–23.

Bell, Christine. "Dealing with the Past in Northern Ireland." *Fordham International Law Journal* 26, (2002): 1095–1147.

—. "Peace Agreements: Their Nature and Legal Status." *American Journal of International Law* 100, (2006): 373–412.

Bliss, Michael. "'Serious Reasons for Considering': Minimum Standards of Procedural Fairness in the Application of the Article 1F." *International Journal of Refugee Law* 12 (suppl 1), (2000): 92–132.

Boothby, Neil, Jennifer Crawford, and Jason Halperin. "Mozambique child soldier life outcome study: Lessons learned in rehabilitation and reintegration efforts." *Global Public Health* 1, no. 1 (2006): 87–107.

Borland, Rosilyne M. "The Gacaca Tribunals and Rwanda after Genocide: Effective Restorative Community Justice or Further Abuse of Human Rights?" *A Journal of International Affairs* 13, (2002): 19.

Braunstein, Elizabeth. "Are Gang Members, Like Other Child Soldiers, Entitled to Protection from Prosecution under International Law." *UC Davis Journal of Juvenile Law and Policy* 3, (1999): 75–92.

Breen, Claire. "The Role of NGOs in the Formulation of and Compliance with the Optional Protocol to the Convention on the Rights of the Child on Involvement of Children in Armed Conflict." *Human Rights Quarterly* 25, (2003): 453–481.

Cassese, Antonio. "On the Current Trends towards Criminal Prosecution and Punishment of Breaches of International Humanitarian Law." *European Journal of International Law* 9, (1998): 2–17.

—. "Special Court and International Law-The Decision Concerning the Leone Agreement Amnesty." *Journal of International Criminal Justice* 2, (2004): 1130.

Catani, Lucia. "Victims at the International Criminal Court: Some Lessons Learned from the Lubanga Case." *Journal of International Criminal Justice* 10, (2012): 905–922.

Clapham, Andrew. "Human Rights Obligations of Non-State Actors in Conflict Situations." *International Review of the Red Cross* 88, no. 863 (2007): 491–523.

Clark, Phil. "Hybridity, Holism and Traditional Justice: The Case of the Gacaca Courts in Post-Genocide Rwanda." *George Washington International Law Review* 39, no. 4 (2007): 765–838.

Cohn, Ilene. "Progress and Hurdles on the Road to Preventing the Use of Children as Soldiers and Ensuring their Rehabilitation and Reintegration." *Cornell International Law Journal* 37, (2004): 531.

Coomaraswamy, Radhika. "The Optional Protocol to the Convention on the Rights of the Child on the Involvement of Children in Armed Conflict Towards Universal Ratification." *The International Journal of Children's Rights* 18, no. 4 (2010): 535–549.

Corey, Allison, and Sandra F. Joireman. "Retributive Justice: The Gacaca Courts in Rwanda." *African Affairs* 103, no. 410 (2004): 73–89.

Corriero, Michael A. "The Involvement and Protection of Children in Truth and Justice-Seeking Processes: The Special Court for Sierra Leone." *New York Law School Journal of Human Rights* 18, (2001–2002): 337–360.

Crocker, David A. "Reckoning with Past Wrongs: A Normative Framework." *Ethics and International Affairs* 13: 1, (1999): 43–64.

—. "Truth Commissions, Transitional Justice, and Civil Society." *Truth v. Justice: The Morality of Truth Commissions* (2000): 99–121.

Cullen, Holly. "Does the ILO have a Distinctive Role in the International Legal Protection of Child Soldiers?" *Human Rights & International Legal Discourse* 5: No. 1, (2011): 63–81.

Duttwiller, Michael. "Liability for Omission in International Criminal Law." *International Criminal Law Review* 6, no. 1 (2006).

Fallah, Katherine. "Perpetrators and Victims: Prosecuting Children for the Commission of International Crimes." *African Journal of International and Comparative Law* 14, no. 1 (2006): 83–103.

Fonseka, Bhavani. "The Protection of Child Soldiers in International Law." *Asia-Pacific Journal on Human Rights and the Law* 2, (2001): 69–89.

Fox, Mary-Jane. "Child soldiers and international law: patchwork gains and conceptual debates." *Human Rights Review* 7, no. 1 (2005): 27–48.

Freeland, Steven. "Child Soldiers and International Crimes - How Should International Law Be Applied?" *New Zealand Journal of Public International Law* 3, (2005): 303–328.

Gaston, E.L. "Mercenarism 2.0-The Rise of the Modern Private Security Industry and Its Implications for International Humanitarian Law Enforcement." *Harvard International Law Journal* 49, no. 1 (2008): 221–248.

Gillard, Emanuela-Chiara. "Business and Humanitarian and Human Rights Obligations: The Position with Regard to International Humanitarian Law." *American Society of International Law Proceedings* 100, (2006): 129–140.

Graf, Roman. "The International Criminal Court and Child Soldiers." *Journal of International Criminal Justice* 10, (2012): 945–969.

Grossman, Nienke. "Rehabilitation or Revenge: Prosecuting Child Soldiers for Human Rights Violations." *Georgetown Journal of International Law* 38, (2006): 323–350.

Hamilton, Carolyn. "Child Protection in Complex Emergencies." *Protection of Children During Armed Political Conflict: A Multidisciplinary Perspective* (2006): 1–46.

Hansberry, Heidi L. "Too Much of a Good Thing in Lubanga and Haradinaj: The Danger of Expediency in International Criminal Trials." *Northwestern University Journal on International Human Rights* 9, (2010–2011): 357–401.

Happold, Matthew. "Excluding Children from Refugee Status: Child Soldiers and Article 1F of the Refugee Convention." *American University International Law Review* Volume 17, Issue 6, (2002): 1131–1176.

—. "International Humanitarian Law, War Criminality and Child Recruitment: The Special Court for Sierra Leone's Decision in Prosecutor v. Samuel Hinga Norman." *Leiden Journal of International Law* 18, no. 02 (2005): 283–297.

—. "Children Participating in Armed Conflict and International Criminal Law." *Human Rights & International Legal Discourse* 5: No.1, (2011): 82–100.

Helle, Daniel. "Optional Protocol on the Involvement of Children in Armed Conflicts to the Convention on the Rights of the Child." *International Review of the Red Cross* No. 839, (2000): 797–809.

Henckaerts, Jean-Marie. "Concurrent Application of International Human Rights Law and International Humanitarian Law: Victims in Search of a Forum." *Human Rights and International Legal Discourse* 1, (2007): 95–124.

—. "The ICRC Study on Customary International Humanitarian Law: Characteristics, Conclusions and Practical Relevance." *The Slovenian Law Revivew* 6, (2009): 225–273.

—. "Study on Customary International Humanitarian Law: A Contribution to the Understanding and Respect for the Rule of Law in Armed Conflict." *International Review of the Red Cross* 87: 857, (March 2005): 175–212.

Hodgson, Sophie. "Whose Action Plan? An Analysis of the UN Security Council Resolution 1612 Action Plan and Monitoring and Reporting Mechanisms in Nepal." *Journal of Human Rights Practice* 4, no. 2 (2012): 164–186.

Honwana, Alicada. "Negotiating Post-war Identities: Child Soldiers in Mozambique and Angola." *Codesria Bulletin* (1999): 4–13.

Iacono, Mark. "The Child Soldiers of Sierra Leone: Are they Accountable for Their Actions in War?" *Suffolk Transnational Law Review* 26, (2002–2003): 445–468.

Jesseman, Christine. "Protection and Participation Rights of the Child Soldier: An African and Global Perspective, The." *African Human Rights Law Journal* 1, (2001): 140–154.

Johnson, Larry D. "The Lubanga Case and Cooperation between the UN and the ICC." *Journal of International Criminal Justice* 10, (2012): 887–903.

Junod, Sylvie. "Additional Protocol II: history and scope." *American University Law Review* 33, (1983): 29.

Konge, Paola. "International Crimes and Child soldiers." *Southwestern Journal of International Law* 16: 41–265.

Kritz, Neil J. "Coming to Terms with Atrocities: A Review of Accountability Mechanisms for Mass Violations of Human Rights." *Law of Contemporary Problems* 59: no. 4, (1996): 127–152.

Landgren, Karin. "The Protective Environment: Development Support for Child Protection." *Human Rights Quarterly* 27, no. 1 (2005): 214–248.

Lara, Crystal E. "Child Soldier Testimony Used in Prosecuting War Crimes in the International Criminal Court: Preventing Further Victimization." *Southwestern Journal of International Law* 17, (2011): 309.

Leibig, Abigail. "Girl Child Soldiers in Northern Uganda: Do Current Legal Frameworks Offer Sufficient Protection?" *Northwestern University Journal on International Human Rights* 3, (2005): i.

Mann, Howard. "International Law and the Child Soldier." *International and comparative law quarterly* 36, no. 01 (2008): 32–57.

McIntyre, Angela, Emmanuel Kwesi Aning, and Nii Nortey Addo Prosper. "Politics, War and Youth Culture in Sierra Leone." *African Security Studies* 11.3, (2002): 6–15.

Meron, Ted. "The Martens Clause, Principles of Humanity, and Dictates of Public Conscience." *American Journal of International Law* 94, (2000): 78–89.

Mibenge, Chiseche. "Enforcing International Humanitarian Law at the National Level: The Gacaca Jurisdictions of Rwanda." *Yearbook of International Humanitarian Law* 7, (2007): 410–424.

Michels, An. "Psychosocial Support for Children: Protecting the Rights of the Child Victims and Witnesses in Transitional Justice Processes." *Innocenti Working Paper* 2010–14, (2009).

Morss, John R. "The Status of Child Offenders under International Criminal Justice: Lessons from Sierra Leone." *Deaking Law Review* 9, (2004): 213–226.

Musila, Godfrey M. "Challenges in Establishing the accountability of Child Soldiers for Human Rights Violations: Restorative Justice as an Option." *African Human Rights Law Journal* 5, (2005): 321–334.

Nagle, Luz Estella. "Child Soldiers and the Duty of Nations to Protect Children from Participation in Armed Conflict." Available at: http://works.bepress.com/luz_nagle/3 (2010).

Nobert, Megan. "Children at War: The Criminal Responsibility of Child Soldiers." *3 Pace International Law Review Online Companion* 1, (2011).

Novogrodsky, Noah B. "Litigating Child Recruitment Before the Special Court for Sierra Leone." *San Diego International Law Journal* 7, (2005–2006): 421–426.

Nylund, Bo Viktor. "International Law and the Child Victim of Armed Conflict-Is the First Call for Children." *International Journal of Children's Rights* 6, (1998): 23–53.

—. "From Standard-Setting to Implementation: The Security Council's Thematic Focus on Children and Armed Conflict." *Human Rights & International Legal Discourse* 5: No.1, (2011): 101–119.

Nylund, Bo Viktor, and Ida Margarita Hyllested. "Protecting Children Affected by Armed Conflict: Accountability for Monitoring, Reporting, and Response." *Journal of Human Rights Practice* 2, no. 1: 71–92.

Nylund, Bo Viktor, Jean-Claude Legrand, and Peter Holtsberg. "The Role of Art in Psychosocial Care and Protection for Displaced Children." *Forced Migration Review* 6, (1999): 16–19.

Paige, Arthur. "How Transitions Reshaped Human Rights: a Conceptual History of Transitional Justice." *Human Rights Quarterly* 31, no. 2 (2009): 321–367.

Pinero, Veronica Beatriz. "The Challenges of Reconstruction and Reconciliation Following an Armed Conflict: The Implementation for Child Soldiers as Perpetrators." *Eyes on the ICC* 1, (2004): 30–42.

Quéguiner, Jean-François. "Direct Participation in Hostilities Under International Humanitarian Law." *International Humanitarian Law Research Initiative, Working Paper* (2003).

Ratner, Steven R. "New Democracies, Old Atrocities: An Inquiry in International Law." *The Georgetown Law Journal* 87, (1999): 707–748.

Renteln, Alison Dundes. "Child Soldier: The Challenge of Enforcing International Standards, The." *Whittier Law Review* 21, (1999): 191.

Roberts, Anthea, and Sandesh Sivakumaran. "Lawmaking by Nonstate Actors: Engaging Armed Groups in the Creation of International Humanitarian Law." *Yale Journal of International Law* 37, no. 107–152 (2012).

Roberts, Rosalyn C. E. "The Lubanga Trial Chamber's Assessment of Evidence in Light of the Accused's Right to the Presumption of Innocence." *Journal of International Criminal Justice* 10, (2012): 923–943.

Robinson, JA. "The right of child victims of armed conflict to reintegration and recovery." *Potchefstroom Electronic Law Journal/Potchefstroomse Elektroniese Regsblad* 15, no. 1 (2012).

Romero, Joshua A. "The Special Court for Sierra Leone and the Juvenile Soldier Dilemma." *Northwestern University Journal on International Human Rights* 2, (2004): 2–19.

Rosen, David M. "The Dilemma of Child Soldiers." *Insights on Law and Society* 10, (2009): 6.

Rosen, David M. "Who Is a Child – The Legal Conundrum of Child Soldiers." *Connecticut Journal of International Law* 25, (2009): 81.

Schabas, William. "Reservations to the Convention on the Rights of the Child." *Human Rights Quarterly* 18, no. 2 (1996): 472–491.

Schachter, Oscar. "The Twilight Existence of Nonbinding International Agreements." *American Journal of International Law* 71, no. 1 (1977): 296–304.

Seneviratne, Lakmini. "Accountability of Child Soldiers: Blame Misplaced." *Sri Lanka Journal of International Law* 20, (2008): 29–48.

Sheppard, Ann. "Child Soldiers: Is the Optional Protocol Evidence of an Emerging "Straight-18" Consensus." *International Journal of Children's Rights* 8, (2000): 37–70.

SIlva, Jennifer R. "Child Soldiers: A Call to the International Community to Protect Children from War." *Suffolk Transnational Law Review* 31, (2007): 681.

Singer, Peter W. "Talk is Cheap: Getting Serious About Preventing Child Soldiers." *Cornell International Law Journal* 37, (2004): 561–586.

Surbeck, Jean-Jacques. "Dissemination of International Humanitarian Law." *The American University Law Review,* 33, (1983): 125–143.

Swiney, Gabriel. "Saving Lives: The Principle of Distinction and the Realities of Modern War." *The International Lawyer* 39, (2005): 733–758.

Teitel, Ruti G. "The Future of Human Rights Discourse." *Louis University Law Journal* 46, (2002): 449–463.

—. "Post-conflict Justice." *American Journal of International Law* 98, (2004): 872–879.

—. "Editorial Note-Transitional Justice Globalized." *International Journal of Transitional Justice* 2, no. 1 (2008): 1–4.

Todres, Jonathan. "Birth Registration: An Essential First Step Toward Ensuring the Rights of All Children." *Human Rights Brief* 10, no. 3, (2003): 32–35.

Van Zyl, Paul. "Dilemmas of Transitional Justice: The Case of South Africa's Truth and Reconciliation Commission." *Journal of International Affairs* 52, no. 2 (1999): 648–667.

Vigny, Jean-Daniel, and Cecilia Thompson. "Standards fondamentaux d'humanite: quel avenir?" *INTERNATIONAL REVIEW-RED CROSS* 82, (2000): 917–940.

Vité, Sylvain. "Protecting Children during Armed Conflict: international Humanitarian Law." *Human Rights & International Legal Discourse* 5: No.1, (2011): 14–39.

Ward, Sara A. "Criminalizing the Victim: Why the Legal Community Must Fight to Ensure that Child Soldier Victims are Not Prosecuted as War Criminals." *Georgetown Journal of Legal Ethics* 25, (2012): 821–857.

Webster, Timothy. "Babes with Arms: International Law and Child Soldiers." *George Washington International Law Review* 39, (2007): 227.

Wells, Sarah L. "Crimes Against Child Soldiers in Armed Conflict Situations: Applications and Limits of International Humanitarian Law." *Tulane Journal of International and Comparative Law* 12, (2004): 287–306.

Wessells, Michael. "Psychosocial Issues in Reintegrating Child Soldiers." *Cornell International Law Journal* 37, no. 524 (2004): 513–525.

Wiersing, Anja. "Lubanga and its Implications for Victims Seeking Reparations at the International Criminal Court " *Amsterdam Law Forum* 4: 39, (2012): 21–39.

Wirth, Steffen. "Co-perpetration in the Lubanga Trial Judgment." *Journal of International Criminal Justice* 10, (2012): 971–995.

Zack-Williams, Alfred B. "Child Soldiers in the Civil War in Sierra Leone." *Review of African Political Economy* 28, no. 87 (2001): 73–82.

Zia-Mansoor, Farkhanda. "The Dilemma of Child Soldiers: Who is Responsible?" *The King's College Law Journal* 16, (2005): 388–399.

REPORTS

Annual Report of the Special Representative of the Secretary-General for Children and Armed Conflict, Leila Zerrougui, UN Doc. A/HRC/28/54 (29 December 2014).

Aptel, Cecile and Virginie Ladisch, Through a New Lens: A Child-Sensitive Approach to Transitional Justice, (2011).

Brett, Rachel, Report on the Second Session of the Working Group to Draft an Optional Protocol on Involvement of Children in Armed Conflict, (1996).

Clara Ramirez-Barat, International Center for Transitional Justice, Engaging Children and Youth in Transitional Justice Processes: Guidance for Outreach Programs, (2012).

Coalition to Stop the Use of Child Soldiers, Child Soldier Global Report, (2008).

Committee of the Whole: Summary Record of the 35th Meeting, UN Doc. A/CONF.183/C.1/SR.35 (20 November 1998).

Council of the European Union, Declaration by the Presidency on Behalf of the European Union Concerning Listing of the LTTE as a Terrorist Organisation (9962/06), (31 May 2006).

European Council on Refugees and Exiles, Position on Exclusion from Refugee Status, (March 2004).

Global Reporting Initiative, KPMG, Unit for Corporate Governance in Africa, United Nations Environment Programme, Carrots and Sticks – Promoting Transparency and Sustainability: An update on trends in Voluntary and Mandatory Approaches to Sustainability Reporting, (2010).

International Committee of the Red Cross, Report of the Work of the Conference of Government Experts for the Study of the Conventions for the Protection of War Victims, Geneva, April 14–26, 1947, Series 1, no 5b (1947).

—, Final Record of the Diplomatic Conference of Geneva of 1949, Vol. II, Section A, (1949).
—, Final Record of the Diplomatic Conference of Geneva of 1949, Vol. III, (1949).
—, Report on the Work of the Preliminary Conference of National Red Cross Societies for the study on the Conventions and of various Problems relative to the Red Cross, Geneva, July 26 - August 3, 1946, (Geneva, 1947).
—, Draft Additional Protocols to the Geneva Conventions of August 12, 1949, (Geneva, October 1973).
—, Conference of Government Experts on the Reaffirmation and Development of International Humanitarian Law Applicable in Armed Conflicts, Geneva, 24 May - 12 June 1971: III Protection of Civilian Population Against Dangers of Hostilities, (January 1971).
—, Conference of Government Experts on the Reaffirmation and Development of International Humanitarian Law Applicable in Armed Conflicts, Geneva, 24 May - 12 June 1971: V Protection of Victims of Non-International Armed Conflicts, (January 1971).
—, Optional Protocol to the Convention on the Rights o the Child on Involvement of Children in Armed Conflicts: Position of the International Committee of the Red Cross, Fourth session of the working group (1998).
Independent Evaluation of Special Projects for Child Soldiers in the Democratic Republic of Congo, Final Report Presented to the World Bank's Multi-country Demobilization and Reintegration Program (5 February 2007).
Lee, Ah-Jung, Understanding and Addressing the Phenomenon of Child Soldiers, (2009).
Liebling, Helen, Henny Slegh, and Benoit Ruratotoye, Bearing Children through Rape in Eastern Congo: Community and State Responses, (17 April 2012).
Moneti, Gerry Mackie and Francesca, What are Social Norms? How are they Measured?, (2012).
Official Records of the Diplomatic Conference on the Reaffirmation and Development of International Humanitarian Law Applicable in Armed Conflicts, Geneva (1974-1977): Volume III, (Bern, 1978).
Official Records of the Diplomatic Conference on the Reaffirmation and Development of International Humanitarian Law Applicable in Armed Conflicts, Geneva (1974-1977): Volume IV, (Bern, 1978).
Official Records of the Diplomatic Conference on the Reaffirmation and Development of International Humanitarian Law Applicable in Armed Conflicts, Geneva (1974-1977): Volume VI, (Bern, 1978).
Official Records of the Diplomatic Conference on the Reaffirmation and Development of International Humanitarian Law Applicable in Armed Conflicts, Geneva (1974-1977): Volume VII, (Bern, 1978).
Official Records of the Diplomatic Conference on the Reaffirmation and Development of International Humanitarian Law Applicable in Armed Conflicts, Geneva (1974-1977): Volume VIII, (Bern, 1978).
Official Records of the Diplomatic Conference on the Reaffirmation and Development of International Humanitarian Law Applicable in Armed Conflicts, Geneva (1974-1977): Volume XII, (Bern, 1978).

Official Records of the Diplomatic Conference on the Reaffirmation and Development of International Humanitarian Law Applicable in Armed Conflicts, Geneva (1974–1977): Volume X, (Bern, 1978).

Official Records of the Diplomatic Conference on the Reaffirmation and Development of International Humanitarian Law Applicable in Armed Conflicts, Geneva (1974–1977): Volume XV, (Bern, 1978).

Preparatory Committee on the Establishment of an International Criminal Court, Proceedings of the Preparatory Committee during the Period 25 March – 12 April 1996, UN Doc. A/AC.249/CRP.3/Add.1 (8 April 1996).

Preparatory Committee on the Establishment of an International Criminal Court, Decisions Taken by the Preparatory Committee at Its Session Held from 11 to 21 February 1997, UN Doc. A/AC.249/1997/L.5 (12 March 1997).

Report of the Preparatory Committee on the Establishment of an International Criminal Court, (14 April 1998).

Report of the Secretary-General on Children and Armed Conflict, UN Doc. A/68/878-S/2014/339 (15 May 2014).

Report of the Secretary-General on Children and Armed Conflict, UN Doc. A/67/845-S/2013/245 (15 May 2013).

Report of the Secretary-General on Children and Armed Conflict, (26 April 2012).

Report of the Secretary-General on Children and Armed Conflict, (11 May 2011).

Report of the Secretary-General on Children and Armed Conflict, UN Doc. A/64/742–2/2010/181 (13 April 2010).

Report of the Secretary-General on Children and Armed Conflict, UN Document A/63/785-S/2009/158 (26 March 2009).

Report of the Secretary-General on Children and Armed Conflict, A/62/609-S/2007/757 (21 December 2007).

Report of the Secretary-General on Children and Armed Conflict, UN Doc. A/61/529-S/2006/826 (26 October 2006).

Report of the Secretary-General on Children and Armed Conflict, UN Doc. A/59/695-S/2005/72 (9 February 2005).

Report of the Secretary-General on Children and Armed Conflict, UN Doc. A/58/546-S/2003/1053 (10 November 2003).

Report of the Secretary-General on Children and Armed Conflict, UN Doc. S/2002/1299 (26 November 2002).

Report of the Secretary-General on Children and Armed Conflict, UN Doc. A/55/163-S/2000/712 (19 July 2000).

Report of the Secretary-General on Children and Armed Conflict in the Syrian Arab Republic. (27 January 2014).

Report of the Secretary-General on Children and Armed Conflict in Yemen, UN Doc. S/2013/383 (28 June 2013).

Report of the Secretary-General on Children and Armed Conflict in the Democratic Republic of the Congo, UN Doc. S/2014/453 (30 June 2014).

Report of the Special Representative of the Secretary-General for Children and Armed Conflict, UN Doc. A/69/212 (31 July 2014).

Report of the Secretary-General on the Establishment of a Special Court for Sierra Leone, UN Doc. S/2000/915 (4 October 2000).

Report of the Secretary-General on the Rule of Law and Transitional Justice in Conflict and Post-Conflict Societies, UN Doc. S/2011/634 (12 October 2011).
Report of the Secretary-General on the Rule of Law and Transitional Justice in Conflict and Post-Conflict Societies, UN Doc. S/2004/616 (23 August 2004).
Report of the Secretary-General on Uniting our Strengths: Enhancing United Nations Support for Rule of Law, UN Doc. A/61/636-S/2006/980 (14 December 2006).
Report of the Secretary-General: In Larger Freedom: Towards Development, Security and Human Rights for All, UN Doc. A/59/2005 (2005).
Report of the Secretary-General's Internal Review Panel on United Nations Action in Sri Lanka, United Nations (2012).
Report of the Seventeenth International Red Cross Conference, (Stockholm, 1948).
Report of the Working Group on the use of mercenaries as a means of violating human rigths and impeding the exercise of the rights of people to self-determination, A/HRC/21/43 (2 July 2012).
Republic of Liberia Truth and Reconciliation, Title II: Children, the Conflict and the TRC Children Agenda, (2009).
Rosa da Costa, UNHCR consultant, Legal and Protection Policy Research Series: Maintaining the Civilian and Humanitarian Character of Asylum, (June 2004).
Sablière, Jean-Marc de La, Security Council Engagement on the Protection of Children in Armed Conflict: Progress Achieved and the Way Forward, (2012).
The Save the Children Fund, Child Protection Systems in Emergencies – a Discussion Paper, (2010).
Truth and Reconciliation Commission Report for the Children of Sierra Leone: Child-Friendly Version, (2004).
UNICEF, Assessment of UNICEF Supported Programmes for Reintegration of Children Formerly Associated with Armed Groups and Forces in Sudan, (2008).
—, Thematic Report 2009: Child Protection from Violence, Exploitation and Abuse, (2010).
—, The Participation of Children and Young People in Emergencies, (October 2007).
UNICEF Sudan, Child Protection Situation Analysis, UNICEF Sudan (2008).
United Nations, Report of the Working Group on a Draft Optional Protocol to the Convention on the Rights of the Child on Involvement of Children in Armed Conflicts, E/CN.4/1995/96s (10 February 1995).
—, Report of the Working Group on a Draft Optional Protocol to the Convention on the Rights of the Child on Involvement of Children in Armed Conflicts on Its Third Session, UN Doc. E/CN.4/1997/96 (13 March 1997).
—, Report of the Independent International Commission of Inquiry on the Syrian Arab Republic, UN Doc. A/HRC/21/50 (16 August 2012).
—, Report of the Working Group on a Draft Optional Protocol to the Convention on the Rights of the Child on Involvement of Children in Armed Conflicts on Its Second Session, UN Doc. E/CN.4/1996/102 (21 March 1996).
—, Guiding Principles on Business and Human Rights: Implementing the United Nations "Protect, Respect and Remedy" Framework, UN Doc. A/HRC/17/31 (21 March 2011).
—, Report of the Working Group on a Draft Optional Protocol to the Convention on the Rights of the Child on Involvement of Children in Armed Conflicts on Its Fourth Session, UN Doc. E/CN.4/1998/102 (23 March 1998).

—, Report of the Working Group on a Draft Optional Protocol to the Convention on the Rights of the Child on Involvement of Children in Armed Conflicts on Its Fifth Session, UN Doc. E/CN.4/1999/73 (24 March 1999).
—, Impact of Armed Conflict on Children, UN Doc. A/51/306 (26 August 1996).
—, Report of the Working Group on a Draft Optional Protocol to the Convention on the Rights of the Child on Involvement of Children in Armed Conflicts on Its Sixth Session, UN Doc. E/CN.4/2000/74 (27 March 2000).
World Bank, The Economic Cause of Civil Conflict and their Implications for Policy, UN Doc. E/CN.4/2000/74 (2000).

NEWS ITEMS

BBC. "Under-18s Were Deployed to Iraq." 4 February 2007.
Chozick, Amy. "For Syria's Rebel Movement, Skype IS a Useful and Increasingly Dangerous Tool." *New York Times*, 30 November 2012.
Savege, Charlie. "U.S. Wary of Example Set by Tribunal Case." 27 August 2010.

www.ingramcontent.com/pod-product-compliance
Ingram Content Group UK Ltd.
Pitfield, Milton Keynes, MK11 3LW, UK
UKHW051912100926
8556IPUK00006B/860

9 781780 683942